Ministry *to the* Sick and Dying *in the* Late Medieval Church

MINISTRY
to the Sick and Dying in the Late
MEDIEVAL CHURCH

THOMAS M. IZBICKI

The Catholic University of America Press
Washington, D.C.

The paper used in this publication meets the minimum requirements of American National Standards for Information Science—Permanence of Paper for Printed Library materials, ANSI Z39.48–1992.

Cataloging-in-Publication Data is available from the Library of Congress
ISBN: 978-0-8132-3735-0 | eISBN: 978-0-8132-3736-7

Book design by Burt&Burt
Text set in Adobe Garamond Pro and Adobe Jenson Pro

INTRODUCTION

Christian ministry to the sick and dying has a long history. This study deals with the intersection of sin with bodily suffering in medieval thought and ritual. Physical healing received less attention from the clergy than did the salvation of souls, but both were accommodated in ministry. The focus of this book is on three sacraments—penance, the Eucharist, and anointing— provided in the medieval West to persons confined to sickbeds and possibly dying. A continuous ritual framework was created; but texts and practices varied from region to region, diocese to diocese, throughout the Middle Ages. This period is extended by continuity of practice until the reforms of the Council of Trent took root.[1] Occasional evidence of clerical conduct and interactions of priests with the laity can be discerned. However, this book is not a social history of clergy or laity, those ministering or those seeking healing by sacraments, medicine, magic, or pilgrimage to the shrines of holy healers.[2]

This book builds on the author's past work on the Eucharist, especially where it focused on communion of the sick or viaticum. To that is added treatment of sickbed penance, extreme unction, and prayers for the dying.[3] Attention will be given to how priests prepared to visit the sick, carrying the Eucharist and "oil of the sick" to them. A significant focus is on illness linked to sin and its forgiveness. Notably, the Lateran decree *Cum infirmitas* (1215) required physicians to call in confessors to comfort the sick

1 This allows use of sixteenth-century editions of manuals for parish priests showing no influence of Trent.

2 On pilgrimage to the shrines of healer saints, see Robert Bartlett, *Why Can the Dead Do Such Great Things? Saints and Worshippers from the Martyrs to the Reformation* (Princeton, NJ: Princeton University Press, 2013).

3 *The Eucharist in Medieval Canon Law* (Cambridge: Cambridge University Press, 2015), 178–220.

and heal their souls. Even those writers who did not specifically make this connection often treated sin as an illness and such rites as penance and extreme unction as medicine for the soul. Theologians and canon lawyers also considered the possibility that the anointing of the sick with holy oil, coupled with the appropriate prayers, might cause physical healing. Wherever possible, the actual administration of a rite is described. As penance had become private, and deathbed scenes are only occasionally recorded, such records of practice are valuable wherever found.

The project uses resources from throughout Europe, including canon law, theology, and ritual. Instructions for visits to the sick in manuals for priests have become available in the *Usuarium* database (cited below). A wide geographical view, from Portugal to Poland and Sweden to Italy, reveals significant continuities despite variations in details. Many scholarly works have been written about attitudes toward death, dying, commemoration, and beliefs about the afterlife in the Middle Ages. Likewise, there is a good deal of literature on the individual sacraments. Recently work has been done on disability and mental illness, including whether the disabled could receive grace through sacred rites. This study aims at connecting these literatures, focusing on priest and parishioner, placing their interactions in the context of the Lateran program for ministry to the faithful.

Many persons have contributed to this project. Librarians at the University of Pennsylvania, Rutgers University, Haverford College, Bryn Mawr College, and Princeton University have made manuscripts and printed texts available to the author. Margaret Schaus has been a consistent supporter of the research. Gerald Christianson, Vincent Evener, Donald F. Duclow, and Jovino Mirroy have provided useful information and hints for further research.

Online resources have been employed frequently in the age of COVID. One of the most useful was the *Usuarium* liturgical database (available at usuarium.elte.hu). Also of great value were the *Patrologia Latina Database*, *Early English Books Online*, the Hathi Trust Digital Library (available at hathitrust.org), the Medieval Canon Law Virtual Library (available at web.colby.edu/canonlaw/), and the digital resources of the Bayerische Staatsbibliothek (available at bsb-muenchen.de). Biblical texts are cited from the Latin Vulgate in the Bible Gateway (available at biblegateway.com). Any translations not documented in the footnotes are mine.

Thomas M. Izbicki, Rutgers University

LIST OF ABBREVIATIONS

DDSP	*D. Durandi a Sancto Porciano super sententias theologiae Petri Lombardi commentariorum libri quatuor*
De cons.	*De consecratione*, third part of the *Decretum Gratiani*
Friedberg	*Corpus Iuris Canonici, editio Lipsiensis secunda* (ed. Friedberg)
Glo. Ord.	Ordinary Gloss on the *Decretum Gratiani*
Mansi	*Sacrorum conciliorum nova, et amplissima collectio* (ed. Mansi)
MGH	Monumenta Germaniae Historica
PL	Patrologia Latina (ed. Migne)

1

MINISTRY TO THE SICK

edieval churchmen inevitably had to deal with sickness and mortality, including attendance at sickbed and deathbed. The priest was expected to focus on the health of the soul, but this could not be divorced entirely from care of the body. The body was believed to have become vulnerable to sickness and death through original sin. This opened the possibility that cures might be effected for the devout through the rejection of sins and vices. Death was inevitable, however long it might be delayed through religion and medicine.[1] In addition, bodily ailments could be treated as occasions for spiritual progress, the sick person regarding them as chastisements for sin.[2]

As Antoninus of Florence, among many others, wrote, there were three possibilities for the souls of the deceased. They might attain beatitude in Heaven. More commonly, they might be cleansed of their sins in the purifying flames of Purgatory. The worst possibility was eternal

1 Joseph Ziegler, "Fourteenth-Century Instructions for Bedside Pastoral Care," in *Medieval Christianity in Practice*, ed. Miri Rubin (Princeton, NJ: Princeton University Press, 2009), 103–8. Healing miracles were tied to the idea that illness was a penalty for sin relieved by reconciliation and penance; see Rob Meens, *Penance in Medieval Europe 600–1200* (Cambridge: Cambridge University Press, 2014), 34.

2 For exhortations of the sick to bear bodily suffering, see, e.g., Gregory I, *Pastoral Care*, ed. Henry Davis (Westminster, MD: Newman Press, 1950), 122–26.

torment in Hell.[3] To attain eternal life and avoid postmortem pains, confession was requisite, especially the last confession of a dying Christian. The dying believer was expected to leave this world not just confessed and anointed but comforted for the last journey by devout reception of the Eucharist, viaticum. Extreme unction might purge away remnants of past sins or remove venial sins. In addition, the priest might see physical cures effected by anointing. The teachings of the Fourth Lateran Council (1215) show how spiritual health was prioritized for pastoral care without giving up attention to the suffering body.

GENERAL TEACHINGS

In 1215, Pope Innocent III held the Fourth Lateran Council, which issued decrees covering many topics, some of a pastoral nature. Perhaps the most famous decree was *Omnis utriusque sexus* (c. 21), which required confession of sins by the faithful to their pastors at least once a year. They were to do penance and receive communion in Eastertide.[4] Immediately following *Omnis utriusque*, we have *Cum infirmitas* (c. 22), which claimed illness could be a result of sin. Stating that idea, the Council said: "We . . . order and strictly command physicians of the body, when they are called to the sick, to warn and persuade them first of all to call in physicians of the soul so that after their spiritual health has been seen to they may respond better to medicine for their bodies; for when the cause ceases so does the effect."

Cum infirmitas threatened physicians with censures for failing to follow the decree or for prescribing any measures harmful to the soul.[5] A factor in the making of this decree was the possibility that a person advised by a physician to send for a confessor might fall into despair for fear of death. As late as the sixteenth century, a sermon by Josse Clichtove treated

3 *Confessionale "Omnis mortalium cura,"* University of Pennsylvania Ms. Codex 281, fol. 1r–v.

4 *Decrees of the Ecumenical Councils*, ed. Norman P. Tanner, 2 vols. (London: Sheed and Ward, 1990), 1:245. Evidence for the enforcement of the canon is spotty; see Peter D. Clarke, "Enforcing Religious Conformity in Late Medieval England: Lateran IV Canon 21 and the Church Courts," in *Pastoral Care in Medieval England: Interdisciplinary Approaches*, ed. Clarke and Sarah James (London: Routledge, 2020), 143–57.

5 *Decrees* (ed. Tanner), 1:245–46. Norbert Brieskorn, "Heilen und Kontrollieren: Die Dekretale *Cum infirmitas* - ihre Entstehungs- und Wirkungsgeschichte," *Zeitschrift der Savigny-Stiftung für Rechtsgeschichte, Kanonistische Abteilung* 89 (2003): 363–414. This warning was reiterated, among others, in a statute of Richard le Grant, archbishop of Canterbury; see *Provinciale (seu Constitvtiones Angliae)* (Oxford: H. Hall, 1679; Farnborough: Gregg, 1968), 330, as well as *Praecepta antiqua* of Rouen, found in Giovan Domenico Mansi (ed.), *Sacrorum conciliorum nova, et amplissima collectio*, 53 vols. (Paris: Hubert Welter, 1901–27; Graz: Akamademische Druck- und Verlagsanstalt, 1961) [hereafter Mansi], 23:385; both loosely based on the Lateran canon.

this problem, blaming a wife for postponing a visit by a priest "because we fear the priest will upset him or make him sad." The wife called a physician instead, then waited until the husband was mute before sending for the priest to administer the last rites. This and the pious interjection of "Jesus!" by the bystanders might be postponed until it was too late for voluntary penance.[6]

Although some physicians seem to have considered confession a good start to their efforts, others are reported to have avoided urging this, again because the patient might despair.[7] Faced with this possibility, one set of questions for use by confessors included asking whether a physician gave medicine to a sick person who had not yet confessed (*Si medicinam infirmo apposuit antequam esset confessus*). The next question concerned extortion of money from the sick or letting them die neglected.[8]

The text of *Cum infirmitas*, giving priority to the care of souls, was widely distributed in the collected decrees of the Lateran Council. It also appeared in the collection of canons and decretals known as *Compilatio quarta* under the title *De penitentiis*.[9] Even wider distribution was attained when *Cum infirmitas* was included in the *Liber extra* or *Decretals of Gregory IX*, published in 1234, under the title *De poenitentiis et remissionibus*.[10] The wide diffusion of this canon suggests that the connection between sin and illness was made often to the clergy ministering at the diocesan and parish levels. Perhaps more important, the Lateran text can be used to open the question of how theologians and canonists balanced the needs of soul and body, prioritizing the one without neglecting the other. In the Christian scriptures a close connection was made between forgiveness and healing.

6 Larissa Taylor, *Soldiers of Christ: Preaching in Late Medieval and Reformation France* (New York: Oxford University Press, 1992), 125.

7 Joe Stadolnik, "Gower's Bedside Manner," *New Medieval Literatures* 17 (2017): 150–74, at 150–51.

8 Catherine Rider, "What to Ask in Confession: A List of Sins from Thirteenth-Century England," in *Pastoral Care in Medieval England* (ed. Clarke and James), 67–99, at 83 and 96.

9 *Constitutiones concilii quarti Lateranensis una cum commentariis glossatorum*, ed. Antonio García García (Vatican City; Biblioteca Apostolica Vaticana, 1981), 68–69; *Quinque compilationes antiquae nec non Collectio canonum Lipsiensis*, ed. Emil Friedberg (Leipzig: Tauschnitz, 1882; Graz: Akamademische Druck und Verlagsanstalt, 1956), 149 (IV 5.14.3). The rubrics to the manuscripts emphasize care of the soul, for example: "De medicis ut prius prouideant anime quam corpori." One says that a sick person should take communion before being treated; see *Constitutiones concilii quarti Lateranensis*, 149: "Ne quis physicus intromittat se de egroto nisi prius communicat egrotus."

10 *Corpus Iuris Canonici, editio Lipsiensis secunda*, ed. Emil Friedberg, 2 vols. (Leipzig: Tauschnitz, 1879; Graz: Akamademische Druck- und Verlagsanstalt, 1955) [hereafter Friedberg], 2:888 (X 5.38.13).

Sin and Illness in the Scriptures

There was a biblical background to *Cum infirmitas*.[11] The belief that illness, physical defect, or death could be caused by sin can be illustrated from many passages in the Bible. Thus, Paul says, notably, "For the wages of sin is death" (Rom 6:23). In the Hebrew scriptures, the psalms occasionally tied sin not just to sickness but to divine wrath aimed at the sinner (Pss 6, 31, 37). Other psalms said that God restores health or sustains the ailing (Pss 29, 40). One of the more famous biblical healings is that of King Hezekiah of Judah. The king had let an envoy from Babylon flatter his vanity, thus incurring divine punishment. Hezekiah prayed to God and recovered from his nearly mortal illness (2 Kgs 20; 2 Chr 32; Is 38).

The cures effected by Jesus are too many to list here. However, three Gospel texts tie Jesus' healing of a paralytic to proof that he could forgive the man's sins (Mt 9; Mk 2; Lk 5). John too shows Jesus healing a paralytic on the Sabbath and later telling him to stop sinning (Jn 5). That healing story points the way to the question, raised elsewhere in John's text, whether a sick man had sinned or whether his parents' offenses were punished with his affliction (Jn 9:2): "And his disciples asked him: Rabbi, who hath sinned, this man, or his parents, that he should be born blind?"[12] Jesus dismissed either possibility in favor of this explanation: "Neither hath this man sinned, nor his parents; but that the works of God should be made manifest in him" (Jn 9:3). The Epistle of James tied forgiveness of sins to healing (Jas 5:14–15): "Is any man sick among you? Let him bring in the priests of the Church, and let them pray over him, anointing him with oil in the name of the Lord. And the prayer of faith shall save the sick man: and the Lord shall raise him up: and if he be in sins, they shall be forgiven him."[13]

Medieval exegetes dealt with sin and illness when commenting on these texts, especially that of James. The Ordinary Gloss on the Bible said of the passage from John that the man's blindness was an illustration of

11 Jean-Claude Larchet, *The Theology of Illness*, trans. John and Michael Breck (Crestwood, NY: St. Vladimir's Seminary Press, 2002), 26–53. John of Freiburg said that a sick person should obey a physician but did not sin by disobeying; see Johannes de Friburgo, *Summa confessorum* (Augsburg: Zain, 1476) II, t. 1, q. 38.

12 *Biblia latina cum glossa ordinaria, Facsimile Reprint of the editio princeps of Adolph Rusch of Strassburg* [1480], ed. Karlfried Froehlich and Margaret T. Gibson, 4 vols. (Turnhout: Brepols, 1992), 4:247B: "Rabbi quis peccauit hic aut parentes eius vt cęcus nasceretur."

13 Ibid., 4:479A–B: "Infirmatur aliquis ex vobis. Inducat pręsbyteros ecclesię. vt orent super eum unguentes eum oleo in nomine domini: et oratio fidei saluabit infirmum et alleuat eum dominus. Si sit in peccatis sit remittentur ei."

the debility of the human mind on account of sin, beginning with the Fall of Adam.[14] The marginal gloss on James, however, provides a summary of the connection of sin to illness and death, including the possibility that penance might remove the cause of suffering. This remission, however, required confession by the sick person to a priest.[15] The interlinear gloss on James said that the anointing described in the text began as an effort to heal the body. However, the gloss said the person would be saved even if he or she died.[16] A marginal gloss altered this to saying the person would be saved spiritually and corporally, including the healing of the body, if it was expedient for the soul.[17] Later writers, as will be shown, consistently treated bodily healing as a secondary effect of the rite of anointing, which they connected to the sacrament of penance.

There was nothing new in the teaching of the gloss. The Carolingian liturgical writer Amalar of Metz said that "if sickness were not the result of sin, James would not have said, 'And if he be in sins, they shall be forgiven him.'"[18] A Carolingian council quoted James at length before saying that confession, medicine for illnesses afflicting both soul and body, was not to be slighted.[19] However, the gloss made these interpretations widely known.

Following after the Ordinary Gloss, these passages from John and James were addressed by Scholastic exegetes, especially the Dominican Hugh of St. Cher and the Franciscan Nicholas of Lyra. Hugh commented upon the text from John in some detail, saying that the disciples thought

14 Ibid., 4:247B: "Cęcum. Cęcus significat humanum genus in quo cęcitas naturalis quia peccante primo homine: vicium propter naturam inoleuit. vnde secundum mentem omnis homo cęcus natus est." The thirteenth-century Franciscan Nicholas of Aquavilla thought that this Gospel emphasized the fragility of life; see *Nicolai de Aquaevilla sermones moralissimi*, ed. Eva Odelman (Turnhout: Brepols, 2018), 28. Preaching on a different text, John Felton said that blindness of mind was worse than blindness of body; see John Felton, *Sermones dominicales*, University of Pennsylvania Ms. Codex 680, fol. 44r–v.

15 *Biblia sacra cum glossa ordinaria*, 4:479A–B: "Et si in pec. Multum propter peccata etiam corporis plectuntur morte. Si ergo infirmi in peccatis sunt. et hoc presbitero confessi perfecto corde reliquerint et emendare satigerint. Dimittuntur eis. Neque enim sine confessione emendationis queant peccata dimitti."

16 *Biblie iampridem renouate pars sexta* (Basel: Amerbach, 1502), fol. 216v, at v. Infirmatur, "ab infirmitate corporis"; v. Salvabit, "etiam si contingerit mori."

17 Ibid., at v. Salvabit: "Corporaliter et spiritualiter. Ideo subditur: . . . Ab infirmitate si expediat ei."

18 Amalar of Metz, *On the Liturgy*, ed. and trans. Eric Knibbs, 2 vols. (Cambridge, Mass.: Harvard University Press, 2014), 1:108–9. Amalar added a quotation from 1 Cor 28:30 blaming unworthy reception of communion for illness and death.

19 Monumenta Germaniae Historica [hereafter MGH], *Concilia* II, pt. 1, ed. Albert Werminghof (Hanover: Hain, 1906; Hanover: Hain, 1997), 283: "Non est itaque parvipendenda huiuscemodi medicina, quae anima corporisque medetur languoribus." The 825 Council of Paris warned against involving the sick in scandal through the misuse of images; see ibid., 499.

sin caused the man's blindness, for which it was a punishment.[20] Hugh, however, restated Jesus' reply that the affliction occurred to manifest God's power.[21] His exegesis said the Jews wrongly tied the man's blindness to sin, "but the Lord said that he had not sinned, nor his parents."[22] Nevertheless, Hugh went on to discuss at length the relationship of sin to bodily affliction, saying that pain is imposed in this life to purge the sin and corruption found even in the just.[23] Hugh repeated that the man was born blind to manifest God's glory.[24]

In Nicholas of Lyra's commentary, the moralization on John 9 said that the man's being born blind represented everyone's birth in original sin, deprived of the vision of God.[25] The man was born blind by divine permission to be given sight by Christ's miracle, also to represent the cleansing of original sin by divine power.[26] Nicholas treated the text from John in some detail when looking at the relationship of blindness to sin. He said that the man could not have been born blind by his own fault, as he could not have sinned before birth.[27] The sins of the parents also were not causal, although a weakness in the seed might be blamed.[28] This still left room for providence to have set the stage for Christ's miracle, worked by divine power "instrumentally" through his humanity.[29] This was part of Christ's work of teaching and working miracles to bring light to the world.[30] The opening of the man's eyes also represented baptism.[31] This passage and its interpretations left no room for sin as the cause of blind man's affliction.

20 *Biblia sacra cum postillis domini Hugonis cardinalis*, 7 vols. (Basel: Amerbach, 1498), vol. 6, fol. 345ra: "intellexerunt peccatum esse causam infirmitatis, propter hoc requirunt pro quo peccato iste suo an propinquorum."

21 Ibid.: "id est potentia dei ad operandum."

22 Ibid., fol. 345rb: "Sed dominus dicit quod non peccauit: neque parentes eius."

23 Ibid., fol. 345ra: "Dicendum quod omnis pęna in hac vita est ad purgationem quantum est de intentione percutientis: et intelligitur de purgatione a quocumque peccato vel corrputione quę est in quolibet iusto." Hugh added that it also was to damn those of perverse will.

24 Ibid., fol. 345rb: "vt Gloria dei patris in eo ostendatur."

25 *Biblie iampridem renouate pars quinta* (Basel: Amerbach, 1502), fol. 213vb: "Mystice cecus nascitur omnis habens peccatum originale: quia priuatus est dei visione."

26 Ibid., fol. 214rb: "sic enim permissus est nasci iste cecus vt illuminaretur Christi miraculo: et similiter emundatio peccati originalis est opus diuine virtutis."

27 Ibid., fol. 214ra: "quia ante natiuitatem peccare non potuit."

28 Ibid.: "propter indispositionem materie vel debilitatem virtutis que est in semine."

29 Ibid.: "hoc dixit quod miracula illa faciebat virtute diuina: et humanitas Christi oportebatur instrumentaliter."

30 Ibid.: "doctrina et miraculis illustrando."

31 Ibid., fol. 214rb: "per illuminationem fidei datam virtutem baptismi." The Ordinary Gloss (*Biblia sacra cum glossa ordinaria*, 4:247B) says: "Baptizatus a peccatis lumen recepit."

Hugh of St. Cher interpreted the passage from James about anointing, treating physical infirmity as provoking impatience. The prayers and anointing by the presbyters were to remedy this spiritual ailment. Hugh added there a reference to extreme unction.[32] Hugh said that sadness over suffering could be a sin, but we were not to regard the sin as our own. We were instead to bewail it and provide such a remedy as was possible.[33]

Nicholas of Lyra treated the Epistle of James minimally. One of his comments on the biblical passage "And if in sins" (*Et si in peccatis*, Jas 5:15), building on the Ordinary Gloss, said that many are punished with death on account of their sins, including sins of the body. This comment emphasized perfect confession of these sins, especially to a priest, and amendment of life, which was not possible without confession. However, Nicholas did not conclude with a promise of healing as the Gloss did.[34]

Sin and Illness in Canon Law

This was the biblical and post-biblical background of *Cum infirmitas*, with its instructions to the entire Church concerning sin and physical illness. The early summaries of the Lateran canon are brief, mostly underlining the instructions given in the canon. The *Casus Parisienses* said: "When a physician approaches a sick person, he should first lead him to confession."[35] The *Casus Fuldenses* added a warning against physicians who advised doing anything "contrary to the health of his soul, because the soul is more precious than the body."[36] The commentary of Vincentius Hispanus was more detailed, advising that "it is better to die than consent to evil." A physician who sinfully suggested sexual intercourse as a remedy

32 *Biblia sacra cum postillis domini Hugonis cardinalis*, vol. 7, fol. 322va: "Infirmatur . . . Hoc est secundum quod prouocat impatientiam, scilicet infirmitas. Contra quod dat remedium, orationem scilicet Presbyterorum & vnctionem olei. Vnde & agitur hic de extrema vnctione."

33 Ibid.: "Sed quia tristitia vt frequentiùs peccatum est, non debemus nostrum reputare; sed de ea dolere, & sicut possumus remedium apponere."

34 *Biblie iampridem renouate pars sexta*, fol. 216va: "Multi propter peccata etiam corporis plectuntur morte. Si ergo infirmi in peccatis sunt: et hoc presbytero confessi perfecto corde reliquerint sunt et emendare satigerint dimittuntur eis. Neque enim sine confessione emendationis queunt peccata dimitti. Vnde recte subditur: Confite."

35 *Constitutiones concilii quarti Lateranensis*, 469: "Cum medicus accedit ad infirmum, prius inducat eum ad confessionem."

36 Ibid., 486–87: "nec etiam ei consulat ad salutem corporis quod sit contra salutem anime sue, quia anima pretiosior est corpore."

for illness could be excommunicated.[37] Damasus listed biblical examples of illness inflicted on account of sin. However, even with the cause ceasing, *Cum infirmitas* was still applicable. Moreover, desperation could arise if the physician saw in the patient "signs of death" (*signa mortis*). Damasus's comment on the decree included a further reference to the belief that the soul is more precious than the body.[38]

The Ordinary Gloss of Bernard of Parma on the *Liber extra* treated *Cum infirmitas* briefly. The *casus* or summary of the text made two significant points. One affirmed the priority of the soul over the body, which explained why a physician was not to offer cures harmful to the soul.[39] The greater value of the soul was the reason a physician was to urge the patient to confess any sins before providing treatment. Sins, in turn, could be the cause of the illness, stating that "with the cause ceasing, the effect ceases."[40] Bernard admitted that a physician's urging a patient to take care of the health of his soul might push him or her into despair, further endangering the body.[41] The Gloss included a further argument, based on both Roman and canon law, that the more important thing, the soul, had priority over the less important one, the body. The greater threat of spiritual death thus had priority over the lesser one, bodily death.[42]

Some thirteenth-century canonists had little to say about *Cum infirmitas.* Geoffrey of Trani, in his *Summa super titulis decretalium*, and Pope Innocent IV, in his *Apparatus in quinque libros decretalium*, ignored the issues addressed in the Lateran canon. Henricus de Segusio (Hostiensis) had little to say on the subject in his compendious *Summa super titulis decretalium.* Writing about the urgency of confession, the canonist did warn against putting off penance when ill and in danger of death. The

37 Ibid., 316–17: "Quia Melius est mortem subire quam malo consentire . . . Quid si medicus ita dicat: 'Ego non consulo tibi, sed si coires cum domina, conferre posset?' Numquid medicus est excommunicatus? Ita."

38 Ibid., 429.

39 *Decretales D. Gregorii Papae IX svae integritati vna cvm glossis restitvtae* (Venice: Apud Iuntas, 1595), 1323B: "Quarto dicitur, quod cum anima sit multo preciosior corpore, nullus medicus suadeat aegroto, quod in periculum animae conuertatur."

40 Ibid., 1323B: "ideo prohibetur in hoc capitulo, ne medici infirmos in suam curam recipiant, nisi prius infirmi per medicum animę se curauerint emerdare; quia remota causa remouetur effectus . . . No. quod infirmitas corporis aliquando prouenit ex peccato. Item cessante causa cessat effectus."

41 Ibid.: "Secundo dicitur, quod hoc dedit causam huius constitutionis, quia quando infirmatur aliquis, & dicitur ei à medico, vt de salute animae disponat, cadit in desperatione, & facilius mortis periculum incurrit."

42 Ibid.: "Multo preciosior.] 12. q. 1. precipimus. 24. q. 3. Si habes. C. de sacrosan. eccl. l. sancimus. in fi. & ideo potius & prius est consulendum animae, quam corpori; quia vbi maius est periculum, cautius est prouidendum, 42. dist. quiescamus. & 7. q. 7. c. vl. vt ff. ad Carbo. l. 1. §. 2. Ber."

hour of death was not certain, and so confession should not be delayed. The sick person might not be willing to think of penance under those circumstances, or might be too afflicted to be able to think of that, as Augustine had observed.[43] Hostiensis added elsewhere that a sick person in danger of death could confess to a lay person, even a woman, in the absence of a priest (*deest sacerdos*).[44]

Hostiensis's commentary on the *Extra*, however, gave *Cum infirmitas* more attention. The commentary said the patient should not be made to fall into a worse illness when implementing the text's instructions.[45] Looking to the text's pastoral agenda, the canonist said that the spiritual was "greater and more worthy," and thus it was to take precedence over the corporeal.[46] This superiority included the importance of seeing to the spiritual welfare of the ailing.[47] Looking at the possibility of long disuse undermining the canon, Hostiensis said it could not be removed by contrary custom because of its importance.[48] The patient "should show himself a catholic and faithful."[49] The commentary admitted that the patient "should reasonably be freed from infirmity" (*debet ab infirmitate rationabiliter liberari*). However, it repeated the idea that illness could arise from sin.[50] Hostiensis thought *Cum infirmitas* important enough to be proclaimed often in churches.[51] He also stated elsewhere in his commentary that a priest who, by his own fault, let a sick person die without the sacraments was guilty of that person's soul.[52]

43 Henricus de Segusio, *Hostiensis summa aurea* (Venice: Iacobum Vitalem, 1574; Turin: Bottega d'Erasmo, 1963), 1762–63: "Primò, propter horae mortis incertitudinem . . . Sextò, propter finale periculosam conuersionem. Vix enim aut nunquam homo in aegritudine confiteri: quia nec de peccatis cogitare: sufficit enim dei militia sua ex infirmitate proueniens. Ideo cum ęgritudine opprimeris, vix aliud potest cogitare, quam sentis. & illinc rapitur intentio mentis, vbi est vis doloris. Aug."

44 Ibid., 1767.

45 Henricus de Segusio, *Commentaria et lectura in decretalibus* (Venice: Apud Iuntas, 1581; Frankfurt: Vico Verlag, 2009), vol. 5, at X 5.38.13, fol. 103va: "[*Ne deterius*] i. ne in deteriorem infirmitatem recidas corporalem."

46 Ibid.: "[*Spirituali*] quę tanquam maior, & dignior debet precedere corporalem."

47 Ibid.: "[*Spirituali*] istud vero non solum ob reuerentiam statuitur, sed vt prouideatur periculis infirmorum."

48 Ibid.: "[*Praecipimus*] cum pro salute animarum inductum sit hoc decretum, contra ipsum praescribi non potest, nec aliqua consuetudine tolli."

49 Ibid.: "[*Causam*] vt infirmus ostendit se catholicum et fidelem.

50 Ibid.: "[*Effectus*]. i. infirmitas proueniens ex peccato." Hostiensis said that the canon remained in effect even if the effects of illness ended.

51 Ibid.: "[*Incidunt*] ideoque & haec constitutio esset frequenter in eclesiis publicanda."

52 Ibid., vol. 1, fol. 129vb, at X 1.24.un.: "[*Moriantur.*] Quia si culpa sacerdotis hoc contingerit. Infirmi anima reus erit. xxvi. q. vi. si presbiter, & ca. sequen. & arg. supra. titu. i. ca. i. ante finem."

The "classical" period of canon law ended with the lay canonist Johannes Andreae, who taught in Bologna in the fourteenth century. His *Novella super decretalibus* was built on the Ordinary Gloss and writers like Hostiensis. The *Novella* on *Si infirmitas* began with a summary of the reasons for the text, that physicians should put spiritual welfare first, promoting confession of sins, and doing nothing endangering souls.[53] The lay canonist made specific mention of suffering like Job to increase merit or as a penance for vice.[54] To defend the priority of confession over medical treatment, Andreae repeated that the spiritual should precede the corporeal.[55] He repeated the idea that sin could cause illness.[56] Physicians were to know the precept that, with sin removed, illness might cease.[57] Looking to past commentaries, Andreae cited Vincentius Hispanus on the possibility that a physician might intimate to a patient that he could be healed by having sex, which was contrary to *Cum infirmitas*.[58]

Behind the *Extra* and its commentators lay a long tradition embodied best in the two recensions of Gratian's *Decretum* or *Concordia discordantium canonum*, compiled in the twelfth century,[59] together with its learned exegesis. The relevant texts in the *Decretum* are few but indicative, noting the sacramental role of bishops in consecration of altars and confection of chrism (D. 25, c. 1). Custom expanded the latter role to include blessing oil of the sick, made from soothing olive oil. Gratian distinguished the right to consecrate oils from the right to anoint with them (D. 68, a. c. 3). The *Decretum* quoted Pope Innocent I as saying that priests assumed the task of anointing thc sick bccause bishops were otherwise occupied.[60] Gratian also accepted the possibility that a bishop still might anoint the sick (D. 95, a. c. 3 and c. 3). The *Decretum* also quoted a passage of Gregory the Great's *Moralia* distinguishing the soothing effects of olive oil from the cleansing effects of wine (D. 45, c. 9).

53 *Ioannis Andreae in quintum decretalium nouella commentaria* (Venice: Franciscum Franciscum, 1581; Torino: Bottega d'Erasmo, 1963), fol. 128va: "Medici corporum ad infirmos vocati ante omnia debent illos ad confessionem inducer, nec debent pro salute corporum aliquod pernitiosum animae suadere."

54 Ibid.

55 Ibid.: "[Spirituali] quae quia maior est, pręcedre debet."

56 Ibid., fol. 128vb: "[Effectus] peccatum vocat causam, infirmitatem vocat effectum."

57 Ibid. "[Incursum] ex quo vero sciunt in omni infirmitate mortali & non mortali medicos hoc dicere ex praecepto, cessabit timor, & periculum."

58 Ibid.: "dicit Vin. quod medicus, qui dicit, non consulo, sed si accedes ad aliquam, sanaberis, hanc constitutionem transgreditur."

59 Anders Winroth, *The Making of Gratian's "Decretum"* (Cambridge: Cambridge University Press, 2000).

60 Gratian referred to anointing of the baptismal font and the baptized, documented by Augustine quoting Basil in d. 11, c. 5; see Friedberg 1:24–25.

The connection of sin to ill health in the Lateran decree and the larger canonistic tradition was a key factor in the making of medieval rites for the sick and, inevitably, those for the dying.[61] At the same time, spiritual welfare was addressed with similes drawn from physical well-being and illness, a rhetoric which compared soul to body, even while treating the former as immortal and more important than the latter, which was corruptible and not expected to rise before the Last Judgment.[62]

Physician of Souls

Behind this notion of bodily illness and spiritual health lay an identification of Christ as the medicine of original sin and physician of souls. Christ as *medicus animarum* appeared in an early work of Augustine, expounding the Sermon on the Mount. The text asked whether Christ wanted the faithful to tolerate any weaknesses with a patient soul, replying that a believer was to bear old age and illness until life passed. All wickedness had originated with weakness of the soul.[63] Augustine's teaching was reflected in the homilies of the Venerable Bede.[64] Rabanus Maurus too made use of Augustine's text when interpreting Matthew's Gospel.[65] Christ also was invoked as *medicus animarum* in a Mass for the sick found in the Gelasian sacramentary.[66] By the eleventh century, this concept was so firmly rooted that Peter Damian could expand upon it in medical terms in one of his letters.[67]

61 An Old Irish Penitential added that demons might cause sudden illness which could be cured by others' fasting; see *Medieval Handbooks of Penance: A Translation of the Principal "Libri poenitentiales" and Selections from Related Documents*, ed. John T. McNeill and Helena M. Gamer (New York: Columbia University Press, 1938), 159.

62 John of Freiburg used words about physical defects to represent moral failings of ordinands, e.g., treating blindness as indicating ignorance; see Johannes de Friburgo, *Summa confessorum* III, t. 18.

63 Augustinus, *De sermone Domini in Monte*, in Patrologia Latina, ed. J.-P. Migne (Paris, 1841–55) [hereafter PL], 34:1259: "a quibus multa saepe patiuntur, et si eorum salus id exigat, praebent se etiam ut plura patiantur, donec vel aetatis vel morbi infirmitas transeat. Quos ergo Dominus medicus animarum, curandis proximis instruebat, quid eos aliud docere posset, nisi ut eorum quorum saluti consulere vellent, imbecillitates aequo animo tolerarent? Omnis namque improbitas ex imbecillitate animi venit: quia nihil innocentius est eo qui in virtute perfectus est."

64 Beda, *Homiliae* (PL 94:353C and 514D–515A). See also Bede's exposition of Matthew's Gospel in PL 92:29D.

65 PL 107:826D.

66 *Missa pro aegrotis* in *Sacramentarium Gallicanum* (PL 72:552B). "Vere dignum et justum est, omnipotens Deus, te Dominum totius misericordiae in necessitatibus invocare, qui dominaris vitae et morti, qui es medicus animarum."

67 Petrus Damiani (PL 145:792A–B): "Illa satiatur et moritur; aegrotus autem, dum perdit sanguinem, recuperat sanitatem. Illa denique sua se morte satiat et exsultat; aegrotus autem, dum vulneratur, ad statum salutis erigitur. Quid igitur mirum, si Deus omnipotens, qui est medicus animarum, sic nos occulta sui moderaminis arte disponit, ut ex alienis vulneribus nobis medicamenta conficiat, quatenus dum nobis

Once the concept of Christ as physician of souls was firmly rooted in Western Christianity, it could be employed in wider contexts. Gregory the Great compared an adroit confessor to a skilled physician, a reference which helped mold a rhetoric of medicine and healing for the treatment of the sinful soul.[68] Jonas, a Carolingian bishop of Orléans, compared an incompetent physician of souls to an incompetent physician of bodies who made an ailment worse.[69] Writing centuries after Gregory and Jonas, the reformer Bonizo of Sutri used the same metaphor to treat the pastoral concerns of prelates.[70] Bernard of Clairvaux, the Cistercian abbot and mystic, compared treatment of ailing souls with treatment of wounds.[71] The Augustinian theologian Hugh of St. Victor combined the two types of physicians in the person of St. Luke, who was changed from a physician of bodies to a physician of souls.[72] Innocent III, in a sermon, contrasted St. Lawrence the archdeacon with Pharaoh, emphasizing how the former was a physician of souls, unlike the Egyptian tyrant of bodies.[73] Jean Gerson described the well-infirmed confessor as "a most learned doctor of spiritual

hostile vulnus infligitur, ex eo potissimum salutis antidotum procuretur. Tyrus plane genus serpentis est, ex cujus cruore theriaca fit, quae videlicet grassantem pestem in his qui venenantur exstinguit."

68 John Baldwin, *Masters, Princes and Merchants: The Social Views of Peter the Chanter and His Circle.* (Princeton, NJ: Princeton University Press, 1970), 1:53.

69 Jonas of Orléans, *De institutione laicali libri tres* (PL 106:140B): "Ut ergo artis medicinae nescius, dum curare nescit vulnus corporis, non illud minuit, sed magis plerumque incrementum ei addit: ita et imperitus medicus animarum, dum eorum languoribus mederi videri vult, quia his congrua medicamenta nescit adhibere, eosdem languores creditur incrementare." For a rare decree *Contra indoctos Medicos*, Trier (1310), see *Concilia Germaniae*, ed. Johann Friedrich Schannat and Joseph Hartzheim, 11 vols. (Cologne: Typo viduae Joan. Wilhelmi Krakamp et haeredum Christiani Simonis, 1759–90), 4:152–32.

70 William L. North, "Bonizo of Sutri, the *Dicta Bonizonis* and the Development of the Jurisprudence of Canon Law before Gratian," in *The Use of Canon Law in Ecclesiastical Adminstration, 1000–1245*, ed. Melodie H. Eichbauer and Danica Summerlin (Leiden: Brill, 2020), 159–84, at 178.

71 Bernardus Claraevallensis, *De gradibus humilitatis et superbiae* (PL 182:962C): "Sicut enim medicus, non solum unguento, sed igne utitur et ferro, quo omne quod in vulnere sanando superfluum excreverit, secet et urat, ne sanitatem, quae ex unguento procedit, impediat: sic medicus animarum Deus hujusmodi animae procurat tentationes, immittit tribulationes, quibus afflicta et humiliata, gaudium vertat in luctum, revelationem putet illusionem." In two sermons, Bernard returned to the idea that Christ was the physician of souls; see PL 183:39B and 288D.

72 Hugh of St. Victor, *Expositio in regulam beati Augustini* (PL 176:1354C): "*Salutat vos Lucas medicus charissimus* et Demas [Col 4:14]. Lucas iste primo fuit medicus corporum, deinde conversus ad Christum, factus est medicus animarum."

73 PL 217:570B: "Quia vero contraria juxta se posita clarius elucescunt, proponamus in medio Pharaonem, qui defecit in prosperis et adversis, ut ex comparatione duorum, illius vitium, istius virtutem extollamus. Ille namque fuit rex in terra Aegypti, iste archidiaconus in Ecclesia Christi. Ille tyrannus corporum; iste medicus animarum. Ille temporalium rector, iste spiritualium ministrator." Ivan Illich, *In the Vineyard of the Text: A Commentary on Hugh's "Didascalicon"* (Chicago: University of Chicago Press, 1993), 10–11, citing *De tribus diebus.*

illness," but he dismissed the confessor who hesitated to ask about certain sins as a "shy and inexperienced surgeon."[74]

This medical motif appeared in canon law, including in the canon *Omnis utriusque*, which said that a confessor should be discrete and cautious, like a physician of the body who pours wine and oil on wounds.[75] The Ordinary Gloss of Bernard of Parma on the *Gregorian Decretals* treated wine and oil as signifying the discipline and mercy to be employed in administering penance.[76] Bernard also argued that the confessor's inquiry into the circumstances of sins was not like the floundering of "an inexpert physician" (*non tamen sicut imperitus medicus*).[77] Raymond of Peñafort, in his *Summa confessorum*, quoting a mnemonic verse, compared interrogation of the penitent to "giving medicines to the soul" (*animae medicamenta dando*), knowing the problem in order to prescribe a remedy.[78]

Henricus de Segusio (Hostiensis) treated the medicinal theme more than once in his *Summa* on the *Gregorian Decretals*. Secular priests might be deceitful in providing God's medicine, the sacrament of penance.[79] When not being deceitful, they could administer medicine against shame (*pudor*), which prevented a good confession. The medicine was divinely instituted to help the believer avoid future punishment.[80] In such cases, according to Pope Leo I, penance was medicine for the wounded soul.[81] Hostiensis also was one of those who compared a discrete, prudent confessor to a skilled physician who poured wine or oil on wounds as appropriate.[82] The priest's interrogation of the penitent, which determined the appropriate penance to be enjoined, was described once more in terms of prescribing medicines for the sick.[83] Among the factors the confessor was to consider were human debility and infirmity.[84] Behind these statements

74 Jean Gerson, *Early Works*, trans. Brian Patrick McGuire (New York: Paulist Press, 1998), 367 and 374.

75 Friedberg 2:887 (X 5.38.12): "Sacerdos autem sit discretus et cautus, ut more periti medici superintendant vinum et oleum vulneribus sauciati."

76 *Decretales Gregorii papae IX*, 1323B.

77 Ibid.

78 Raimundus de Pennaforte, *Summa de poenitentia et matrimonio cum glossis Johannis de Friburgo* (Rome: Tallini, 1603; Farnborough: Gregg, 1967), 463B.

79 Hostiensis, *Summa aurea*, 1786: "pro beneficiis medicinę Dei dolosi sunt."

80 Ibid., 1798.

81 Ibid., 1800.

82 Ibid., 1805: "Sacerdos autem sit discretus & cautus, vt more periti medici, superfundat vinum & oleum vulneribus."

83 Ibid., 1811: "Quis, quid, ubi, per quos, quoties, cur, quomodo, quando, Quilibet hoc seruet animę medicamenta dando."

84 Ibid., 1836.

lay a supposition that the body, not just the soul, of a human being who was ailing spiritually had to be treated. The body, although weaker in some ways, inflicted pain and grief on the soul, and so it too needed treatment by the clergy.[85]

A theological example of this motif is found in a text by Thomas Aquinas. In a quodlibetal question, he presented an argument comparing a sick person who did not quickly consult a physician to a sinner who did not quickly consult a confessor. The Angelic Doctor, however, denied the parallel, saying nature might rally and save the patient; but the "illness of sin" (*morbus autem peccati*) required the remedy of penance. Thomas underlined the necessity of confessing before receiving communion at Eastertide, an obvious reference to *Omnis utriusque sexus*. Penance was not to be delayed out of contempt for the sacrament (*propter contemptum*); however, a delay might be acceptable, for example, to confess to a more prudent priest (*prudentiori*). Thomas also said confession was essential "if death was near him [the penitent]" (*si immineat ei mortis articulus*).[86]

Some theological texts treated confession itself in medical terms. For example, Robert Grossteste used two medical similies. He described confession as like the vomiting up of poison (*venenum*), and he wanted the penitent to be as quick to receive the sacrament of penance as a diseased limb should be swiftly shown to a physician.[87] Grosseteste wrote such things in the larger context of the integration of the soul and body, with the former able to care for the latter. The soul, he said, could both preserve and repair the body. Bodily pleasures, if unregulated, however, could lead to the dissolution of the soul's union with the body in death.[88]

A Theology of Pastoral Care

Concerns about the relationship of sin and illness were embedded in a larger theology of the sacraments. This theology was brought together in the *Sentences* of Peter Lombard, a twelfth-century compilation of theological excerpts, including patristic texts, arranged in four books. The fourth

85 Ibid., 1816: "Item vigilare debemus, quia custodes infirmorum. scilicet peccatorum sumus. infra eodem cum infirmitas. j. Cori.11. multi infirmi & imbecilles inter vos, multi dormiunt. duo infirmi sunt corpus & anima, contraria appetentes. Spiritus quidem promptus est, caro autem infirma, quia corpus quod corrumpitur, aggrauat animam."

86 *Sancti Thomae Aquinatis doctoris angelici ordinis Praedicatorum opera omnia* (Parma: Fiaccadori, 1859), 11:466A–B; *Quaestiones de quolibet* I, 6, a. 2.

87 F. A. C. Mantello and Joseph Goering, "Robert Grosseteste's *Quoniam cogitatio*: A Treatise on Confession," *Traditio* 67 (2012): 341–84, at 349, 369, 371, 373.

88 Richard C. Dales, "Robert Grosseteste on the Soul's Care for the Body," *Instrumenta Patristica et Mediaevalia* 27 (1995): 313–19.

book canonized the idea that there were seven sacraments: baptism, confirmation, the Eucharist, penance, extreme unction, holy orders, and matrimony. The first five of these were to be received by all the faithful, including anointing of the sick and dying. The two others were not received by all, with fewer receiving ordination than undertook marriage.[89]

In the fourth book of the *Sentences*, the Lombard also addressed pastoral care. This included the question regarding whether unction might bring bodily, as well as spiritual healing, by removing sins. Here he was building on the familiar passage from the Epistle of James. Someone who received this anointing with faith and devotion might be relieved in both body and soul, as long as a spiritual cure took precedence over physical one. It was not expedient that bodily health be acquired at any risk to the soul.[90] Writing before Peter Lombard, Hugh of St. Victor had called vice "your illness" (*morbus tuus*). He said the Spirit provided seven medicines against the seven primary vices. Those who did not resist their spiritual ailments would not be healed by these medications.[91] Alexander of Hales, among the earlier Scholastics, notably argued that sin might affect the body from within, and thus curing of the soul might also heal the body.[92]

Two of the most important commentators on the *Sentences*, the Franciscan Bonaventure and the Dominican Thomas Aquinas, touched on this issue in different ways, both when discussing extreme unction. Bonaventure argued that extreme unction deleted neither original sin nor mortal sins, but forgave venial sins.[93] This remedy removed obstacles to eternal glory. Bonaventure described this remedy as a cure of spiritual illness.[94] The Franciscan theologian admitted that the sacrament also might cure the body, as the soul's health affects that of the body. However, this was treated as a secondary effect of the sacrament. These cures happened only

89 The *Sentences* of Peter Lombard included (in the fourth book) all seven sacraments. A single distinction (d. 23) treated extreme unction; see *The Sentences*, trans. Giulio Silano (Toronto: PIMS, 2007–10), 4:136–38.

90 Ibid., 4:136.

91 *Hugonis de Sancto Victore de oratione dominica, de septem donis spiritus sancti*, ed. Francesco Siri (Turnhout: Brepols, 2017), 214–16.

92 Lesley Smith, "The End of a Single World: The Sacrament of Extreme Unction in Scholastic Thought," In *The End of the World in Medieval Thought and Spirituality*, ed. Eric Knibbs, Jessica A. Boon, and Erica Gelser (Basingstoke: Palgrave Macmillan, 2019), 281–313, at 308–9.

93 *Doctoris seraphici S. Bonaventurae opera omnia* (Quarrachi: Collegium S. Bonaventurae, 1889), 4:589; *In quattuor libros Sententiarum* IV, d. 23: "Et cum non sit contra originale nec contra mortale, reliquitur, quod sit contra peccatum *veniale*. Et hoc communis opinio tenet."

94 Ibid.: "et sic, cum anima possit trahere talia cremabilia, quae retrahunt a Gloria, instituit divina misericordia remedium, quo anima curare posset quantum ad remissionem *culpae*; et hoc est Sacramentum unctionis extremae."

per accidens.[95] A cause of these cures could be that the soul is "tranquilized, invigorated and made joyful," affecting the body.[96] This too happened because the soul's passions could have bodily effects.[97] However, bodily cures could not affect an illness of the soul.[98] Bonaventure said that the cures effected by the apostles when anointing the sick before the institution of this sacrament (Mk 6:13) were intended principally to heal the body, not the soul.[99]

In his commentary on the *Sentences,* Thomas Aquinas argued, citing Isaiah 27, that the sacraments cured the illness of sin.[100] He especially called extreme unction medicine for the soul and, therefore, a sacrament. This teaching he tied to the Epistle of James.[101] As is typical of the Scholastics, his teaching identified curing the "illness of sin" as the principal effect of the sacrament.[102] The supplement to the third part of the *Summa theologiae,* completed by a disciple after the Angelic Doctor's death, was derived from his previous writings. It says that extreme unction principally has a spiritual effect, curing the illness of sin (*ad sanandum infirmitatem peccati*).[103] Aquinas did warn that the patient's emotional reaction to anointing might bring on death. Therefore, he said the priest might forego administering the sacrament to a sick person.[104]

In the *Summa contra gentiles,* Thomas states that spiritual benefit could be derived from suffering affliction "humbly and patiently." His approach

95 Ibid., 4:589B: "Concedendae igitur sunt rationes probantes, istud Sacramentum valere ad corporales probantes, quod non valet *principaliter* contra illas, quoniam solum *per accidens* et *ex consequenti* valet."

96 Ibid.: "ideo non est mirum, si tranquillatur anima et vigoratur et laetificactur, si etiam hoc redundant ad corpus."

97 Ibid.: "Unde passiones animales multum redundat in carnalem, unde Sapiens dicit: *Spiritus tristis exsiccat ossa* [Ps 18:22]."

98 Ibid.: "quia corporalis medicina non sanat spiritualem morbum."

99 Ibid., 4:592B: "quia unctio illa principaliter fiebat ad sanitatem *corporalem,* non ad *curationem spiritualem principaliter.*"

100 Thomas Aquinas, *Super quarto libro sententiarum preclarum opus* (Venice: Herbort, 1481), fol. q4^{ra}, IV, d. 23: "Effectus autem intentus in administratione sacramentorum est curatio morbi peccati. Isaiae 27,9: Hic est omnis fruvctus, ut auferatur peccatum." Thomas added a reference to James as proof that this argument applied to extreme unction.

101 Ibid., fol. q3^{vb}: "extrema vnctio est quedam spiritualis medicina: quia valet ad remissionem peccatorum: vt habetur Jaco. v. ergo est sacramentum."

102 Ibid., fol. q4^{ra}: "effectus autem intentus in administratione autem sacramentorum est curatio morbi peccati . . . et ideo cum ad effectum pertingat extrema vnctio: vt ex verbis Jaco. patet." Thomas denied that the sacrament effected physical healing; see fol. q4^{va-b}: "ergo sanitas corporalis non est effectus huius sacramenti."

103 *Sancti Thomae Aquinitatis opera omnia*, vol. 12, *Tertia pars summae theologiae a quaestiones LX ad quaestionem XC* (Rome: Ex Typographia Polyglotta, 1906), *Supplementum*, 57B; q. 30, a. 1.

104 Ibid., 60A; q. 32, a. 2: "Sed si pensatur infrmitatis modus et status, non semper debet infirmitatibus hoc sacramentum dari."

to this issue involves linking the body to the soul, saying: "The body is the instrument of the soul." The afflictions of the soul might affect the body: "By dispensation of the divine judgment it happens sometimes that the disease of the soul, which is sin, spreads to the body; and this bodily ailment is sometimes profitable to the soul's heath, insofar as a man bears his bodily infirmity with humility and patience; because this is credited to him as punishment as it were in satisfaction for his sins."[105]

However, infirmity of the body might also impede spiritual welfare, being "an obstacle to virtue." Aquinas went on to argue that the spiritual remedy of extreme unction could heal the body, as well as the soul, because illness could derive from sin, being inflicted by divine judgment. Spiritual medicine could then be physical medicine as well, if physical healing was expedient for salvation.[106] Overall, Thomas addressed the connection of sin to sickness more directly than did Bonaventure, and his teaching cast light on how priests were likely to privilege saving souls over curing bodies when visiting a sickbed.[107]

The effect of anointing was mentioned by the Greek Dominican Manuel Calecas in his *De principiis fidei catholicae*. Calecas quoted the relevant passage from James to document the spiritual importance of the rite. Illness rarely could impede the doing of good and achieving spiritual health by doing it; however, it was for those rare occasions that the sacrament was administered with oil joined to prayers.[108]

Much of Scholastic theology regarding penance and illness was summarized in the *Speculum morale* of Vincent of Beauvais. Among the results he listed for penance was recovery of the lost souls, as well as delivery from evil and liberation from Hell. Vincent said that the Church Triumphant

105 *The "Summa contra gentiles" of Saint Thomas Aquinas, the Fourth Book* (London: Burns, Oates & Washbourne, 1923), 252–53; in *Sancti Thomae Aquinitatis opera omnia*, vol. 15, *Summa contra gentiles liber quartus* (Rome: Commisio Leonina, 1930), 233A: "Ex infirmitate igitur animae, quae est peccatum, interdum infirmitas derivatur ad corpus, hoc divino iudicio dispensante. Quae quidem corporis infirmitas interdum utilis est ad animae sanitatem: prout homo infirmitatem corporalem sustinet humiliter et patienter, et ei quasi in poenam satisfactoriam computatur."

106 Ibid.: "Est enim quandoque impedictiva spiritualis salutis, prout ex infirmitate corporali impediuntur virtutes. Conveniens autem fuit ut contra peccatum aliqua spiritualis medicina adhiberetur, secundum quod ex peccato derivatur infirmitas corporalis, per quam quidem spiritualem medicinam sanatur infirmitas corporalis aliquando, cum expedit ad salutem."

107 On the pastoral impact of Thomas's works, see Leonard E. Boyle, *Facing History: A Different Thomas Aquinas* (Louvain-La-Neuve: Federation Internationale des Instituts d'Etudes Medievales, 2000).

108 Manuel Calecas, *De fide deque principiis catholicae fidei* (in Patrologia Graeca, ed. J.-P. Migne [Paris, 1857–66], 152:606): "Haud raro tamen per eam aegritudinem impeditur homo ne bonum operetur, ac ne operando, spiritualem salutem consequatur; Idcirco extremae unctionis sacramentum (olei scilicet junctis precibus inunctio) datur."

rejoiced over the saved.[109] Penance was compared to Jacob's ladder, with angels carrying prayers and offerings upward while consolation descended, ending with the transport of the soul "to the kingdom" after death (*tandem in morte ad deducendum in regno*).[110] Toward contrition, the penitent was to consider the coming of death and the inevitability of divine judgment.[111] The just might die with trust and the perfect might die with joy, but most experienced fear. Sudden death was especially to be feared, as there was no time to prepare the soul.[112] The sinful had to fear death of body and soul, being afflicted by the devil in their passing.[113] Even those who were saved might endure the pains of Purgatory.[114]

INSTRUCTIONS FOR MINISTRY TO THE SICK

Rites for the sick, whether based on theology or canon law, had to be provided locally. This required provincial councils and diocesan synods to enact decrees guiding the clergy in their pastoral roles. Many of these regulations were based on general enactments, especially those issued by the Fourth Lateran Council. Canons not quoted directly from such statutes might paraphrase them with local bishops adjusting universal norms to local conditions.[115] In this context only two influential sets of statutes, those of Paris and Rouen, will suffice as examples. Others will be noted in context when relevant to a topic, such as the effect of sin on the body or that physicians should warn patients concerning salvation.[116] These statutes are most relevant when they discuss extreme unction, because it was the

109 Vincent of Beauvais, *Biblotheca mundi seu speculi Vincentii tomus tertius qui speculum morale inscribitur* (Douai: Belleri, 1624; Graz: Akademische Druck- und Verlagsanstalt, 1964), 1416–18. Vincent also treated death in *Speculum morale*, 462–63 and 467–70.

110 Vincent of Beauvais, *Speculum morale*, 1420.

111 Ibid., 1428: "Videt mortis exitum propinquantem . . . Debet inspicere diuinum & horrendum iudicium &c." On natural death and its anxieties, see 692–711; on judgment, see 757–809.

112 Ibid., 712–19.

113 Ibid., 725–29.

114 Ibid., 735–57.

115 Christopher R. Cheney, *English Synodalia of the Thirteenth Century* (Oxford: Oxford University Press, 1941), 34–89, and "Legislation of the Medieval English Church," in *The English Church and its Laws, 12th–14th Centuries* (London: Variorum, 1982), 1:193–417; Paul D. Pixton, *The German Episcopacy and the Implementation of the Decrees of the Fourth Lateran Council 1216–1245: Watchmen on the Tower* (Leiden: Brill, 1995), 184–219.

116 For a diocesan constitution from Fiesole tying the sacraments to the healing of both soul and body; see Richard C. Trexler, *Synodal Law in Florence and Fiesole, 1306–1518* (Vatican City: Biblioteca Apostolica Vaticana, 1971), 235: "cum dictorum sacramentorum effectus non solum anime, sed reverenter [recepta

sacrament most focused on the sick. The generalities were consistent, but the details varied widely.

The local statutes of Paris had a wide impact, probably through clerics who returned home after studying at the university.[117] The statutes of Odo of Sully, bishop of Paris (1197–1208), contain six precepts concerning extreme unction. The first treats how a priest was to carry oil of the sick and do anointing. There was to be no payment for the rite (simony), although the priest could accept offerings freely given.[118] The second required priests to teach anyone, rich or poor, fourteen years of age or older, about extreme unction so that they would be ready to receive the sacrament when necessary.[119] The next precept added that the people could be anointed "in any great infirmity when there is fear of death" (*in qualibet magna infirmitate unde metus est mortis*), and anyone who survived illness and anointing should resume normal life, including conjugal sex (*opus conjugale*).[120] Each priest was supposed to have a manual "in which is contained the order of the service of extreme unction" (*ubi continetur ordo servitii extremae unctionis*).[121]

In addition, the thirteenth-century statutes of Rouen grouped tests related to care of the sick, which often were scattered in other regional collections. This group begins with instructions to priests to teach the faithful about extreme unction (LXXIV). Rich and poor alike could receive that sacrament at the age of fourteen and above, and they could receive it as frequently as necessary. The priest was to have the oil for anointing ready and carry it reverently to the sick. The following statute (LXXV) restated the instructions of *Cum infirmitas* concerning the obligation of physicians to have patients confess their sins. Having addressed confession, the Rouen statutes dealt with communion of the sick (LXXVI). Priests were to have chalices for communion for the sick (viaticum). Priests, not deacons, were to carry the sacrament to the sick, carrying it in a pyx with a light and bell proceeding. General instructions were added about prayers at the sickbed.

---

fuerint, corpori] tribuant sanitatem." A decree of the 1310 Council of Trier was headed, *Ut Medici infirmos moneant de salute*; see *Concilia Germaniae* 4:156–57.

117 Odette Pontal, *Les statuts synodaux* (Turnhout: Brepols, 1975).

118 Mansi 22:680: "Cum reverentia deferatur oleum sanctum ad infirmos, & eos ungant sacerdotes cum magno honore & orationum celebritate quae ad hoc sunt ordinate, & nihil inde penitus exigatur, sive a pauper, sive a divitate: sed si quis gratis datum fuerit, gratis accipiant."

119 Ibid.: "Ad sacramentum extremae unctionis moneant populum sacerdotes, non tantum divites & senes, sed pauperes & juvenes omnes a tempore discretionis, maxime a quatuordecim annis & supra, & ad omnes communiter, ut se paratos exhibeant, cum necesse fuerit."

120 Ibid.

121 Ibid.

In addition, the faithful were to be taught to genuflect and pray when they saw the body of Christ being carried to the suffering. Next the statutes turned to absolution of the dying, the priest being able to absolve all the sins of those *in articulo mortis* (LXXVII). Further instructions for the communion of the sick were added (LXXVIII). The patient who could not easily receive the consecrated bread could be given one mixed with wine. The Rouen statutes were adopted not just in nearby Le Mans, but also in distant Würzburg.[122] The appearance of the Rouen statutes in Würzburg suggest that other statutes might be found, one modeled on another.

Pastoral Texts

Pastoral books were provided to responsible priests to guide their ministry. Many of these volumes were focused on confession and absolution, but even those could provide guidance in administering other sacraments.[123] More general works, like the popular *Manipulus curatorum* or the English texts *Occulus sacerdotis* and *Pupilla oculi*, sought to provide guidance for administering all seven sacraments.[124] These manuals often gave instructions for the visitation of the sick. For example, William of Pagula enjoined the priest to set a crucifix before the patient to be adored before moving on to anointing with oil of the sick, hearing confession, and giving viaticum. William said that, just as a capable physician was needed for a serious illness, so an able physician of souls was required, especially in a sudden illness or when death was imminent. This may have been a reflection of *Cum infirmitas*.[125] The practice of placing a crucifix before the sick person, mentioned in the *Pars dextera* of the *Oculus sacerdotis*, was mentioned again, using many of the same words, in the *Pars sinistra*. This is to be done to remind the sufferer of Christ's saving passion, a comfort in the face of death.[126]

122 Mansi 23:746–47; *Concilia Germaniae* 4:30–31.

123 Pierre Michaud-Quantin, *Sommes de casuistique et manuels de confession au Moyen Age (XII–XVI siècles)* (Louvain: Nauwelaerts, 1962); Thomas T. Tentler, *Sin and Confession on the Eve of the Reformation* (Princeton, NJ: Princeton University Press, 1977).

124 Guido of Monte Rochen, *Handbook for Curates: A Late Medieval Manual on Pastoral Ministry*, trans. Anne T. Thayer (Washington, DC: The Catholic University of America Press, 2011); Leonard E. Boyle, "The *Oculus Sacerdotis* and Some Other Works of William of Pagula," *Transactions of the Royal Historical Society* 5 (1955): 81–110.

125 William of Pagula, *Oculus sacerdotis*, University of Pennsylvania Ms. Codex 721, fol. 20rb: "Si enim morbis corporum medici periciores requiruntur siue exquiruntur, quanto magis morbis spiritualibus querendus est peritus medicus anime, quoniam uelox medicina subitaneis infirmitatibus uel in extremis positis est ualde necessaria." The *Sacramentale* of Guillelmus de Monte Lauduno too treated confession in medical terms as healing the illness of sin; see University of Pennsylvania Ms. Codex 72, fol. 46va–47ra.

126 *Oculus sacerdotis*, fol. 73rb. Compare this section of the *Oculus* with that at fol. 19va.

Likewise, an authoritative text, Archbishop John Peckham's text *Ignorantia sacerdotes*, required priests of the province of Canterbury to instruct the faithful in the basics of belief and practice. These duties, enumerated for the simple priest, appeared in the late fourteenth century in William Lyndwood's *Provinciale* with its gloss.[127]

Friars were prolific authors of pastoral texts. Thus, the Dominican theologian John of Freiburg dealt with *Cum infirmitas* and its canonistic commentaries in his *Summa confessorum*. He noted there that the text tied illness of the body to sin.[128] An extensive quotation from that canon followed; and so did references to the Ordinary Gloss on the *Extra*, as well as to the works of Pope Innocent IV and Hostiensis. All of these imposed penalties on transgressors of the Lateran statute. John, using such commentaries, emphasized the necessity of consciousness of mortal sin and confession.[129] John concluded, following canon law, that the soul was more precious than the body, and that ruled out any persuasion of the sick that they try medical remedies dangerous to salvation.[130]

The *Summa Pisanella* of Bartholomaeus de Sancto Concordio repeated established opinion on the meaning of *Cum infirmitas*. That text restated the decretal's teaching that physicians were to have their patients call in confessors to see to their spititual welfare. Only then, with the soul cared for, were physicans to treat the bodies of their patients. Physicians who disobeyed the decretal were threatened with spiritual censures.[131] The *Pisanella* repeated the threat of excommunication levelled against physicians who counseled the sick to undertake sinful remedies to save their lives.[132] In the fifteenth century, Antoninus of Florence cited *Cum infirmitas* to demonstrate that physicians were to lead their patients to confession.[133]

127 *Lyndwood's "Provinciale": The Text of the Canons Therein Contained, Reprinted from the Translation Made in 1534*, ed. J. V. Bullard and H. Chalmer Bell (London: Faith Press, 1929).

128 Johannes de Friburgo, *Summa confessoruum* III, t. 34, q. 69: "Nota statutum concilii generalis extra eo. Cum infirmitas. Quod tale est cum infirmitas corporalis nonnunquam proueniat ex peccato."

129 Ibid.: "Glo, Hostiensis. Ex quod dicit precipimus necessitate importat et transgressor peccat mortaliter."

130 Ibid.

131 Nicholas of Osimo, *Supplementum Summae Pisanellae* (Reutlingen: Greyff, 1482), v. Medicus: "Medicus vel cirugicus. Preceptum est medicus vt cum eos ad infirmos vocari contigerit Ipsos ante omnia moneant et inducant quod vocant medicos animarum vt postquam fuerit infirmo de spirituali salute prouisum. ad corporalis medicine remedium salubrius procedant. Si quis autem medicorum huiusmodi constitutionis transgressor extiterit tamdiu ab ingressu ecclesie arceatur scilicet per sententiam secundum glo."

132 Ibid.: "Item in eodem c. sub pena excommunicationis prohibetur medicis ne pro corporali salute aliquid suadeant quod in periculum anime conuertatur."

133 *Sancti Antonini archiepiscopi Florentini ordinis Praedicatorum summa theologica* (Verona: Seminarium Typographia, 1740; Graz: Akamademische Druck- und Verlagsanstalt, 1957), 3:445: "Et extra *De poeniten. & remis.* cap. *Quum infirmitas*, praecipitur medicis corporum, ut inducant infirmos ad confessionem faciendam."

The much later *Summa* of Sylvester Mazzolini (Prierias) said that a physician was obliged to adhere to the decree *Cum infirmitas*. Part of his duty was spiritual, moving the patient toward confession, especially when the physician was aware of the likelihood of death.[134] Violators of this statute sinned mortally. Nor could custom vitiate the Lateran decree.[135] Prierias did allow an exception to *Cum infirmitas* when the calling of a confessor, taken as a sign of impending death, might impede a cure.[136] Prierias was willing to presume, with the canonist Johannes Andreae, that this danger of ill effects out of fear was less likely when the physician judged death to be the likely outcome of an illness.[137] If the physician saw that death really was coming, he also was bound by the letter of *Cum infirmitas*.[138]

The fourteenth-century Franciscan Astesanus added to his treatment of penance for the sick a brief summary of the message of *Cum infirmitas*. He said that Pope Innocent III commanded physicians of bodies to tell the sick first that they should send for physicians of the soul and lead them to do so.[139] An added reference to the canonist Hostiensis described failure to do this as a mortal sin. Nor were physicians to prescribe sinful remedies. Excommunication could be imposed for not doing so, as "the soul is more precious than the body" (*cum anima sit multo preciosior quam corpore*).[140]

Sermons and the Ailing

Sermons were a means of educating the faithful concerning sin, the sacraments, and healing. For example, Bonaventure composed three Sunday sermons on these topics. A sermon for the fourth Sunday of Lent is especially relevant. Citing a text of John's Gospel (6:2), the friar said that infirmity of mind is worse than infirmity of body. The crowd that followed

134 Sylvester Prierias, *Summa Sylvestrina* (Lyon: Rouillé, 1520), fol. clvii[ra]: "Tertio queritur quomodo medicus se debeat habere in exhibendis medicinis spiritualibus cuiusmodi est motio ad confessionem: premonitio de futuro morte et huiusmodi . . . Primum tenetur medicus seruare decretum de pe. et re. cum infirmitas vbi statuitur: et districte precipitur medicis corporum: vt cum eos ad infirmos vocari contingat ipsos ante omnia moneant: et inducant vt medicos aduocent animarum scilicet confessores."

135 Ibid.

136 Ibid., fol. clvii[rb]: "ex quo patet quod si infirmitas indigeret tam celeri remedio corporali: quod expectatio confessoris obesset sanitati: eo casu non ligat ista constitutio."

137 Ibid.: "dicit Joan. an. quod ex quo infirmi sciant hoc medicos dicere in omni infirmitate mortali: et non mortali ex precepto cessauit timor et periculum."

138 Ibid., citing John of Naples in support of this opinion on death foreseen. Prierias sided with Johannes Andreae against Galen, who said the physician should encourage the dying patient; see fol. clviii[va].

139 Astesanus de Ast, *Summa de casibus conscientiae* (Nürnberg: Koberger, 1482), V, t. 14: "Ad hec nota statutum pape Inno. tercii. districte inquit precipimus medicis corporum vt cum eos ad infirmos vocari contigerit. ipsos ante omnia moneant et inducant vt medicos aduocent animarum."

140 Ibid.

Jesus into the desert because of his physical cures learned that, by following him, they might be freed from their spiritual infirmities as well.[141] This sermon drew on the idea that external infirmities were signs of interior ones. Christ, he said, cured external afflictions by first curing internal ones.[142] Bonaventure added that, just as physical ailments could arise from imbalance of humors, spiritual illnesses, including the tumor of pride, could arise from one of four affections: badly balanced hope, fear, inordinate joy, or excessive love. These failings could be counterbalanced by piety, charity, and voluntary poverty.[143] A sermon for the third Sunday after Pentecost treated the sacrament of penance as medicine for these spiritual ailments.[144] For the sixteenth Sunday after Pentecost, Bonaventure offered examples of physical ailments with their spiritual counterparts (like the tumor of pride) and the cures of these afflictions.[145]

Franciscus de Mayronis, an early fourteenth-century Franciscan, said in his sermons that "there is no misery without sin."[146] Following tradition, he compared the infirmity of the soul to infirmity of the body. Spiritual infirmity was worse than any other, because it could kill the soul.[147] Piety, which brought grace to cure the soul, was compared to physical exercise, which benefitted the body.[148] This included curing the many sinful desires arising from the weaknesses of the flesh.[149]

The fourteenth-century Dominican Petrus de Palude dealt with these issues in his Lenten preaching. In a sermon for Ash Wednesday, he treated fasting as a medicine against the sin of gluttony, which the preacher connected to Adam's eating forbidden fruit.[150] The same sermon referred to

141 *Sancti Bonaventurae sermones dominicales*, ed. J. G. Bougerol (Grottaferrata: Collegium S. Bonaventurae, 1977), 259: "Quoniam maior laesionis est infirmitas mentis quam corporis, ideo in hodierno evangelio exemplo multitudinis Christum sequentis per desertum propter signa sanitatis, quae videbant super infirmos fieri corporaliter, informantur omnes spiritualiter infirmi sequi Christum per desertum asperitatis et poenitentiae, ut ab eorum infirmitatibus liberentur."

142 Ibid., 261: "Et quia tunc temporis infirmitas exterior erat signum infirmitatis interioris, nam nullum curavit Dominus corporaliter, quam primo non curare spiritualiter."

143 Ibid., 261–66.

144 Ibid., 341–49.

145 Ibid., 426–32.

146 Franciscus de Mayronis, *Sermones ab adventu cum quadragesimali* (Venice: Ricius, 1491), fol. 132rb.

147 Ibid., fol. 132rb–va.

148 Ibid., fol. 132vb.

149 Ibid., fol. 133rb: "Ex languore corporis multa suggeruntur anime carnalia desideria." Franciscus added that these weaknesses were not incurable.

150 Petrus de Palude, *Sermones quadragesimales thesauri noui* (Strasbourg: Flach, 1494), fol. a 5[va]: "Sic ieiunium est medicina data contra morbum gule quo primus homo vetitum pomum commedit." Petrus added a reference to medicine pitting something contrary against the illness.

the Epistle of James when discussing anointing the sinner with the oil of penance for spiritual healing.[151] Petrus addressed the illness and repentance of King Hezekiah in a sermon delivered on the day after Ash Wednesday. This sermon connected the king's illness to his ingratitude for divine favor, saying it was inflicted by God on account of sin.[152] Petrus turned the king's prayer into an example of repentance, which brings forgiveness and restores health.[153] The sermon concluded with a discussion of superior (divine) and inferior (natural) causes. The friar argued that a person due to die on account of inferior causes might survive for superior ones, as Hezekiah survived his illness after repenting.[154]

Elsewhere, Petrus de Palude preached about a man that Jesus healed on the Sabbath (Jn 5). As Jesus told the man to "sin no more" (Jn 5:14), the friar said that the man ailed because of sin.[155] He was healed by submitting himself to the physician, Christ, who forgave his sins.[156] In another sermon on the same text, the friar compared mortal sin to illness.[157] Sin, in fact, impeded the judgment of the senses.[158] Penance was compared to a sick person entering the pool of Bethesda to be healed (Jn 5:2). In that pool, mortal sins were washed away.[159] This healing depended on Jesus, "the true physician of bodies and souls," and he was to be revered as such.[160] The faithful were reminded that their bodies would die, but their souls would face judgment hereafter.[161] The soul's health was a higher priority than that of the body, but the healing of the one might heal the other.

151 Ibid., fol. a 5vb–[a 6]^{ra}: "Et sic spiritualiter nunc sacerdotes debent vngere populum oleo penitentie."

152 Ibid., fol. [a 7]^{rb}: "Ex quo euidenter elicitor ad litteram quod sepe propter peccatum precipue ingratitudinis incurrunt homines infirmitates corporis."

153 Ibid., fol. [a 7]^{va}: "Pro ista egritudine vt curetur. idest. peccatum remittitur debet orare omnis homo." Petrus added that sinners should beseech the *celestis medicus* for forgiveness.

154 Ibid., fol. [a 8]$^{va–b}$.

155 Ibid., fol. c[1]^{vb}: "Manifeste patet quod propter peccatum suum languebat." Petrus also said (ibid.) that a person who was healed should not depart from a *bonum regimen* requested from the true physician, Christ.

156 Ibid., fol. c[2]^{va}, where the man is compared to any sick person submitting himself or herself to a physician.

157 Ibid., fol. c 2rb: "Nam peccatum mortale comparatur infirmitati."

158 Ibid., fol. c 3ra: "quia infirmitas iudicium sensitiuum permutat." Petrus expounded on the ill effects of sins on the senses.

159 Ibid.: "Ergo bene comparatur peccatum mortale infirmitati. Si igitur vis a tali spirituali infirmitati sanari. tunc debes ingredi piscinam. idest. penitentia in qua lauantur omnia peccata."

160 Ibid., fol. c 2vb: "Sic reuera saluator noster iesus christus qui est verus corporum et animarum medicus."

161 Ibid., fol. c 3ra: "Nam homo secutus cum corpus moritur tunc anima deo presentatibur. Cum ante faciem iudicium statuetur."

Preaching on the healing of Naaman the Syrian (Lk 4:27), Petrus de Palude said that Jesus was a physician according to the flesh (*secundum carnem*). Christ cures all inward, not just outward, infirmities.[162] Another sermon on the same text said that one sinner generated another spiritually, as one leper caused another's affliction bodily. This spiritual leprosy required a divine cure.[163] Treating chapter 4 of Luke's Gospel, which noted that many sick persons were brought to Christ, Petrus added that a miracle overcame nature in the healing of Simon's mother-in-law (4:38). By divine command, her health was restored at once.[164] Petrus also compared mortal sin to a fever in need of the true physician, Christ, moving attention yet again from physical to spiritual healing.[165] Overall, in a sermon concerned with healing on the Sabbath (Jn 7:23), Petrus concluded that it was a great thing to heal a person bodily but a greater one to heal one spiritually. The greatest thing was healing in both ways, as Christ did on that Sabbath.[166]

The famous Dominican preacher Vincent Ferrer, in a sermon for the octave of Corpus Christi, focused on the healing the soul by reception of communion. He added that the body too might be healed, if the soul was not harmed. If it could be harmed, a physical cure should not be desired instead of a spiritual one.[167] Nor should we forget that in this period the Black Death was believed to be a punishment that God inflicted for sins.[168]

A fifteenth-century Dominican, Leonardus de Utino, preached about the Apostle Thomas, including his "cures" in India. Although these were described in medical terms as purging, ameliorating, and preserving, Leonardus meant spiritual cures. Among these was placing the plaster of humility on "the cancer of pride" (*tumore superbie*).[169] The body endured wounds in sensitive places for the welfare of the soul. Because the senses

162 Ibid., fol. [i 7]^{vb}–[i 8]^{ra}.

163 Ibid., fol. [i 8]^{vb}: "Sicut enim leprosus generat leprosum corporaliter, sic peccator generat alium peccatorem spiritualiter."

164 Ibid., fol. l^{ra}: "tamen miraculum miraculum vicit naturam. Quia sanitas que domini datur imperio tota simul et integra redit."

165 Ibid., fol. l^{rb}: "Nota per febrem signatur peccatum mortale." Petrus related the seven deadly sins to different types of fever; ibid., fol. l$^{rb–vb}$.

166 Ibid., fol. n3^{ra}: "Magnum est sanare hominem corporaliter. Maius sanare spiritualiter. maximum sanare vtroque modo. taliter Christus sanauit."

167 Vincent Ferrer, *Sermones Sancti Vincentii ordinis predicatorum de temporiis estivalis* (Lyon, 1510?), fol. cviii^{vb}: "Item curat infirmitates corporis. Nam si infirmus communicat deuote et sanitas corporis non sit nociua anime: hoc sacramentum dabit sibi sanitatem: alias non debet appetere sanitatem."

168 *The Black Death*, ed. Rosemary Horrox (Manchester: Manchester University Press, 2013), 111–57. A French painting includes an angel showing a demon where to inflict plague; available at img.over-blog-kiwi.com/2/23/46/01/20200415/ob_6c2969_saint-sebastien-lanslevillard–1.jpg#width=1600&height=1191.

169 Leonardus de Utino, *Sermones aurei de sanctis* (Ulm: Johannes de Colonia, 1475), Sermo IX.

affect the soul, it was the soul which had to suffer harm, even in Purgatory.[170] His sermon on St. Stephen, however, gave stories of bodily healing.[171] One anonymous text argued that enduring suffering patiently at the time of death "is worthwhile to diminish the penalty [for sin]" (*valet ad diminutionem pene*).[172]

Works of Mercy

Among the things priests were to teach the faithful were the works of mercy. That this included visiting the sick was an idea as old as the Council of Aachen (816), which quoted the judgment scene in Matthew's Gospel (25:36), where the just are told: "[I was] sick, and you visited me" (*infirmus, et visitastis me*).[173] This text had a continuing history in teaching and preaching. For example, Peter the Chanter, a Paris theologian said one was "to visit the sick and imprisoned."[174] Peter's *Verbum abbreviatum* said that all the faithful were entitled to visits "of consolation or compassion."[175] The Cartagena manual for priests too listed *Uisitare infirmos* among the corporal works of mercy.[176] One manuscript included in its general confession a brief statement admitting failure to perform this work of mercy.[177]

The Dominican master general Humbert of Romans wrote a model sermon for the sick in hospitals, counseling them to treat illness as a brake upon human vices and a means of passing to glory. Humbert also wanted preachers to urge visiting the sick. He quoted both Ecclesiasticus 7:39 and Matthew 25:36 on the importance of doing this, the one text stating the need to visit and the other threatening eternal judgment for not doing so.[178] Antoninus of Florence gave a list of the works of mercy in his brief

170 Ibid., Sermo III.

171 Ibid., Sermo XI: "Nam quosdam sanauit in corpore sicut fratrem et sororem a concussione membrorum. & septuaginta infirmos a diuersis infirmitatibus liberauit." St. Matthias healed more than a hundred men who had received a poisoned brew; see Sermo XXIV.

172 University of Pennsylvania Ms. Codex 750, fol. 37v–38r.

173 *Concilia Germaniae* 1:512. This text also noted the foundation of "mansions" for the sick and elderly within cloistered residences of canons.

174 *Petri Cantoris Parisiensis verbvm abbreviatvm, textus alter*, ed. Monique Boutry (Turnhout: Brepols, 2012), 459.

175 Ibid.: "Visitatio consolationis uel compassionis a qua nemo potest excusare."

176 *Ordinarium manual de ministratione sacramentorum secundum consuetudinem ecclesię Carthaginensis* (Granada, 1544), fol. v[v]. Among the spiritual works of mercy mentioned is *Afflictos consolari*.

177 University of Pennsylvania Ms. Codex 750, fol. 25r: "Quarto Infirmum cum necesariis non visitaui." Jean Gerson's version of the Ps.-Anselm *Exhortatio infirmorum* and related texts appear at ibid.,fol. 29r–35r.

178 *Humberti sermones ad diuersos status cum epistola de tribus votis substantialibus* (Hagenau: [Gran], 1507–8), Tractatus I, Sermo XCII, Ad infirmos in Hospitalibus: "Thema Ecci. vii. Non te pigeat visitare

summary of Christian doctrine. In Italian, the injunction to visit the sick became *Uisitar linfirmi*.[179]

According to John Peckham's *Ignorantia sacerdotis*, one of the things the laity were to learn from priests through sermons was the "seven works of mercy." The archbishop noted that six, including "visit the sick and comfort prisoners," were derived from Matthew's Gospel. The seventh, "bury the dead," derived from the apocryphal Book of Tobit.[180] A sermon of James of the March, a fifteenth-century Franciscan observant, urged the faithful, along with giving alms, to remember the works of mercy. They were to visit the afflicted, because by that means they visited Christ. James quoted the judgment scene in Matthew as proof of this.[181] All Saints, Bristol has a window depicting the works of mercy;[182] this is just one example of windows and wall paintings that depicted these pious works.[183]

Visitatio infirmorum and Clerical Discipline

The faithful, taught to visit the sick, also were taught what to expect when ill themselves. Both ecclesiastical superiors and the laity expected parish priests to comfort the sick and dying.[184] This ministry included administration of the sacraments, offering the sufferer three of the canonical seven: penance, the Eucharist (viaticum), and anointing with the oil of the sick (*oleum infirmorum*). Viaticum and anointing, known as extreme unction, because it was offered only to the most dangerously ill, focused on those possibly "leaving this world."[185]

---

infirmum. Quia dicturus est quibusdam in die iudicij conquerendo: Infirmus fui et non visitasti me." The following sermon was addressed to lepers.

179 Antoninus of Florence, *Confessionale "Omnis mortalium cura" & Libretto della dottrina christiana* (Venice: Reynaldus de Novimagio, 1479), *Libretto*, v. Queste sono sete opera dela Misericordia corporale.

180 *Lyndwood's "Provinciale,"* 21 and 24.

181 Jacobus de Marchia, *Sermones dominicales*, ed. Renato Lioi (Ancona: Bibl. Francescana, 1978), 2:319–20: "Visito . . . Primo, visito; visitare infirmum et affectum, quia visitas Christum. Mt. 25, 43: *fui infirmuds et visitasti me* . . ."

182 Clive Burgess, *The Right Ordering of Souls: The Parish of All Saints Bristol on the Eve of the Reformation* (Woodbridge: Boydell, 2018), 333, 373, 380.

183 Depictions of these works might be gendered; see Katherine L. French, *The Good Women of the Parish: Gender and Religion after the Black Death* (Philadelphia: University of Pennsylvania Press, 2008), 198–99.

184 The priest was to add a deathbed scrutiny of the dying person's faith and morals to these comforts, defeating the devil's wily temptation of the dying to despair; see Miri Rubin, *Corpus Christi: The Eucharist in Late Medieval Culture* (Cambridge: Cambridge University Press, 1991), 315–17.

185 R. N. Swanson, *Religion and Devotion in Europe, c. 1215–c. 1515* (Cambridge: Cambridge University Press, 2012), 32, 61, 242. Greek writers criticized the Latins for restricting anointing to the dying; see Christiaan Kappes, "A New Narrative for the Reception of Seven Sacraments into Orthodoxy: Peter Lombard's *Sentences* in Nicholas Cabasilas and Symeon of Thessalonica and the Utilization of John Duns Scotus by the *Holy Synaxis*," *Nova et vetera (English Edition)* 15 (2017): 465–501.

That ministry was guided by manuals for priests containing texts for "visitation of the sick" (*visitatio infirmorum*) and extreme unction, as well as for baptism and matrimony.[186] Each diocese had its own manual; some of them were widely read. Few have received modern editions, as have one from York and one from Salisbury.[187] In addition, pontificals contained the texts that bishops used for confirmation and ordination; but they might contain instructions for ministry to the sick,[188] while the Mass and penance had their own books.[189] These manuals and pontificals might use the language of medical care when dealing with sin. The Salamanca text, for example, warned priests to behave like good physicians and not like bad ones, who make the patient's condition worse.[190]

Manuals were originally circulated in manuscript form, each copy with its unique features, even within the "use" of an individual diocese.[191] The instructions for *Visitatio infirmorum* contained in a manual often covered what the priest was to say on entering the house, how to hear the patient's confession, how to give communion, how to anoint, and a *Commendatio animae* to say when death was near. Parish priests were expected to have one or more copies toward use in daily ministry. Thus, the statutes of Autun declared that each parish priest needed a manual. The statutes of Melde said that the rite of extreme unction was to be included in the diocesan manual.[192] Bishops and archdeacons regarded manuals as among

186 Richard Pfaff, *The Liturgy in Medieval England: A History* (Cambridge: Cambridge University Press, 2009), 452–53. Within a Use, the actual texts and practices could differ significantly; see Matthew Cheung Salisbury, "Rethinking the Uses of Sarum and York," in *Understanding Medieval Liturgy: Essays in Interpretation*, ed. Helen Gittos and Sarah Hamilton (Farnham: Ashgate, 2016), 202–22.

187 *Manuale et processionale ad usum insignis ecclesiae Eboracensis* (Durham: Surtees Society, 1875). *Early English Books Online* dates the Gachet edition ca. 1530. For a manuscript of the York manual, see Matthew Cheung Salisbury, *The Use of York: Characteristics of the Medieval Liturgical Office in York* (York: Borthwick, 2008), 57.

188 Aimé Georges Martimort, *Les 'ordines', les ordinaires et les cérémoniaux* (Turnhout: Brepols, 1991).

189 Marcel Metzger, *Les sacramentaires* (Turnhout: Brepols, 1994); Joseph Goering, "The Internal Forum and the Literature of Penance and Confession," *Traditio* 59 (2004): 175–227.

190 *Manuale secundum consuetudinem alme ecclesie Salamanticense* (Madrid: In Edibus Joannis Junte, 1532), fol. xxxii[v]: "Ueluti medici corporum diuersa medicamenta: vel potiones facere contra diuersitatem infirmitatum. Ne forte per stultum medicum vulnera animarum putrescent et peiora fiant."

191 For example, a 1349 visitation of Wydecomb in the archdeaconry of Totnes included a report that the manual was *corrosum*; G. G. Colton, "A Visitation of the Archdeaconry of Totnes in 1342," *The English Historical Review* 26 (1911): 108–24, at 111. Istelegh had a manual which was *corrosum et male ligatum* (112); Bryxham lacked, among other things, a manual (114). Similarly, in 1301 Colyton in the diocese of Exeter had a manual which was declared worthless; see John Shinners and William Dohar (eds.), *Pastors and the Care of Souls in Medieval England* (Notre Dame, Ind.: University of Notre Dame Press, 1998), 301. Another parish had a manual bound with a worn-out psalter; see ibid., 305.

192 *Thesaurus novus anecdotorum: tomus quartus*, ed. Edmond Martène (Paris: Sumptibus Florentini Delaulne, Hilarii Foucault, Michaelis Clouzier, Joannis-Gaufridi Nyon, Stephani Ganeau, Nicolai Gosselin, 1717), 470 and 897.

the books a parish priest should have on hand and in good condition whenever a visitation was held. Visitors might list in their reports whether a manual was present or absent. The 1427 visitation of the archdeaconry of Madrid lists as many as three copies held by individual parishes, but this was not often the case.[193]

Discipline had to be imposed at the local level, including determining if priests ministered to the faithful as their manuals directed. This ministry was supervised at first by bishops. Charlemagne's *capitula*, early on, required bishops to go about in their sees, confirming, teaching, and inspecting. Bishops also were supposed to look to the welfare of the dying.[194] Theodulf of Orléans admonished priests twice about ministry to the sick in his capitularies. Once he threatened a priest guilty of "tardiness in visiting the sick" (*tarditas infirmos visitandi*) with purgatorial fire.[195] Theodulf also wanted priests warned to minister the appropriate sacraments to the sick, so that they would not die without penance, anointing, and viaticum, especially the latter.[196] Penance, however, was to come first. Theodulf also was an early proponent of trusting worthy witnesses at the sickbed, if the priest found the dying person mute, to give evidence that his or her desire for penance was strong enough for absolution.[197]

Bishops in following centuries could use texts by Regino of Prüm (d. 915) and Burchard of Worms (d. 1025) on these visitation trips or while judging cases at synods. These texts too sometimes used medical terms when discussing pastoral care.[198] Later bishops imposed punishments at their synods or while visiting parishes and monastic houses. A zealous bishop like Robert Grosseteste or Eudes Rigaud in the thirteenth century

193 Gregorio de Andrés, "Actas de la visiya al arcedianazgo de Madrid 1427," *Hispania sacra* 38 (1985): 153–245, at 164, 169, 171, 180, 184, 186–87, 190, 192, 195–96, 201–2, 208, 210, 214, 216, 218, 225, 227, 229–30, 232, 234, 238.

194 MGH *Capitula regum Francorum*, ed. Alfredus Boretius (Hanover: Hahn, 1883; Hanover: Hahn, 1984), 1:45; "Similiter de infirmis et poenitentibus, ut morientes sine sacrati olei unctione et reconciliatione et viatico non deficiant." The *capitula* proposed by the bishops ca. 802 required "mercifully" giving communion to the sick and following the instructions of the Fathers on anointing them; see ibid., 107.

195 PL 105:219D.

196 PL 105:220B: "Admonendi etiam sunt sacerdotes de unctione infirmorum et poenitentia et viatico, ne aliquis sine viatico moriatur."

197 PL 105:220B–D.

198 Regino of Prüm, *Libri duo de synodalibus causis et disciplinis ecclesiasticis*, ed. F. G. A. Wasserschleben (Leipzig: Engelmann, 1840; Graz: Akamademische Druck- und Verlagsanstalt, 1964); Greta Austin, *Shaping Church Law Around the Year 1000: The Decretum of Burchard of Worms* (Farnham: Ashgate, 2009); John Burden, "Reading Burchard's *Corrector*: Canon Law and Penance in the High Middle Ages," *Journal of Medieval History* 46 (2020): 77–97.

might conduct visitation tours of their sees.[199] However, this disciplinary role increasingly fell to archdeacons or their representatives. They too imposed punishments on clergy whose conduct fell short of disciplinary norms; and they might record problems with churches, manses, and cemeteries in poor condition. They might also report lapses in morals by priests and people.[200] However, visitation reports must be used with caution, because they often reflect problems better than they do diligent conduct of pastoral care. These reports also did not always distinguish between urban parishes with rich liturgical resources and poor rural parishes lacking basic liturgical implements.[201]

Failure to keep sacramental resources well was often reported. Thus, failure to lock the chrismatory, the container holding holy oils blessed by the bishop on Holy Thursday, was a frequent complaint. For example, Henri de Vézelay, archdeacon of Hiémois, found that the church at Fulbert-Felie failed to lock its chrismatory and font. At Bretteville-le-Rabet and Robehomme the chrismatory was found to be insufficient.[202] In 1301, the chrismatory at Colyton in the diocese of Exeter lacked a lock. Twenty-nine years later, visitors found that the ivory pyx for the Eucharist could not be locked, while the new chrismatory could be.[203] A visitation of churches dependent on St. Paul's Cathedral, London in 1297 noted the absence of locks for the oils.[204]

Another problem reported was failure to care properly for the Eucharist reserved to communicate the sick. Thus, a set of visitation questions found in the *Annales de Burton* included one about how the Eucharist was reserved.[205] Henri de Vézelay, on his visitation, found the priests of "Peti ville" and Anfréville negligent in care of the Eucharistic tabernacle.[206] In

199 Adam J. Davis, *The Holy Bureaucrat: Eudes Rigaud and Religious Reform in Thirteenth Century Burgundy* (Ithaca, NY: Cornell University Press, 2006), 65–103. Grosseteste's questions for visitations included one about the reservation of the Eucharist and its carrying to the sick; see *Pastors and the Care of Souls* (ed. Shinners and Dohar), 289.

200 Noël Coulet, *Les visites pastorales* (Turnhout: Brepols, 1977).

201 Jacob M. Blum, *Reformation of the Senses: The Paradox of Religious Belief and Practice in Germany* (Urbana: University of Illinois Press, 2019).

202 Léopold Delisle, "Visites pastorales de maître Henri de Vézelay, archdiacre d'Hiémois, en 1267 et 1268," *Bibliothèque de l'École des Chartes* 54 (1883): 457–67, at 463–65.

203 *Pastors and the Care of Souls* (ed. Shinners and Dohar), 301 and 303. Another church in the diocese had no pyx but had a locked chrismatory and a cup for sick communions; see 305.

204 *Visitations of Churches Belonging to Saint Paul's Cathedral in 1297 & in 1458*, ed. W. Sparrow Simpson (London: Camden Society, 1895; New York: Johnson Reprint, 1966), 5, 8, 11, 19, 22, 26, 29, 35, 39, 42, 45, 47, 49, 50, 52, 54, 58, 60, 63–64.

205 *Pastors and the Care of Souls* (ed. Shinners and Dohar), 289.

206 Delisle, "Visites pastorales," 466.

1342 the visitation of the archdeaconry of Totnes in the diocese of Exeter found defects in the Eucharistic pyx and the cup (*ciphus*) for giving consecrated wine to the sick at both North Bovey and Widdecombe. Likewise, the pyx was defective at Islington, as was the *ciphus* at Bovey-Tracy, Kingsteignton, and Abbot's Kerswell. The pyx at Cornworthy was criticized because it was made of copper, while, worse, that the one at Mary Tavy near Tavistock, was made only of wood. Even the bell for taking viaticum to the sick could be found insufficient, as at Lamerton.[207]

Examples of visitors approving the efforts of churches to care for the sacraments can be found in the reports of visitations in the archdeaconry of Josas near Paris. The Josas visitors in 1458 tended to examine the housing of the reserved Eucharist and holy oils, also the security and cleanliness of the baptismal font.[208] The visitors reported for the parish at Asnières, "they had kept properly the Body of Christ, the holy oils, and others things they had to visit" (*Corpus Christi, unctiones sacre et alia que sunt visitanda competenter se habebant*).[209] Similarly, reports that the sacraments were kept well, fittingly (*honeste*), or in a good state (*in bono statu*) were returned for Louveciennes, Bièvres, Gif, Briis-sous-Forges, Longpont, Chilly-Mazarin, Corbeil, Vitry, Villejuif, and others.[210] There were, of course, exceptions. Some churches within the archdeaconry lacked the Eucharist, the oils, or both. The oils might be present only in small quantities, or new supplies might not have been secured after they were consecrated by the bishop on Holy Thursday.[211]

Failures of the clergy also are noted on occasion. At Peterchurch in the diocese of Hereford (1397), the vicar was too sick to serve his parishioners. In Gakwy the priest knew no Welsh, while his parishioners knew no English.[212] The parishioners of Monmouth were unable to enter the priory for the vicar to administer viaticum and extreme unction. At Wolastonem, the priest went to a woman's deathbed vested but with an empty pyx. This led some persons to adore a pyx without a consecrated host, causing "a

207 G. G. Coulton, "A Visitation of the Archdeaconry of Totnes in 1342," *The English Historical Review* 26, no. 101 (January 1911), 108-24 at 110-15 and 119.

208 *Visites archidiaconales de Josas*, ed. Jean-Marie Alliot (Paris: Picard, 1902), xxii.

209 Ibid., 2.

210 Ibid., 4, 10, 12, 15–17.

211 See, e.g., *Visites archidiaconales de Josas*, 7–8 (Saint-Nom-la-Bretèche, Bois-d'Arcy), 8–9 (Buc), 14 (Dampierre).

212 A. T. Bannister, "Visitation Returns of the Diocese of Hereford in 1397, I," *The English Historical Review* 44 (1929): 279–89, at 281 and 289.

great scandal" (*ad magnum scandalum*).[213] At Leominster, the rector needed to find a cleric to carry the light and bell before him when taking communion to the sick.[214] The same was true at Eardesley, while Berdesley lacked a lantern to be carried before viaticum.[215] The parishioners were faulted when Wentenor lacked a vestment to be worn when baptizing or visiting the sick.[216] The pastor of Alderbury went to the sick without lamp or vestment.[217] Worse, Edward, the pastor of Clenbury, was denounced for letting a parishioner die without the sacraments.[218]

In the archdeaconry of Josas, some failings were blamed on the curate, as at Versailles and Longpont, the latter a place known to be impoverished. The chaplain was blamed for the lack of a lock on the tabernacle at Lisse.[219] Lack of clergy or even of parishioners might be blamed, as at Gometz-le-Chatel.[220] There are, however, indications that parishioners did not always report failures of priests to perform their sacramental duties.[221]

A priest might also fail in his duties through physical or mental disability, even dementia.[222] On the eve of the Reformation, the see of Lincoln had its share of priests who failed in their duties. Five priests of that diocese were reported to be too old to perform services. Less understandably, the vicar of Minster Lovell was reported to arrive only after a parishioner had died. The vicar of Asthall was reported to tend the sick in neighboring parishes, not just in his own, because those churches lacked ministers.[223]

Cases of conscience, including those involving ailing clergy, could be referred to the Roman curia. For example, in 1442 Richard Malton abandoned the Cistercian abbey of Garendon, married, and left his wife. He sought from the Apostolic Penitentiary absolution, readmission to the

213 Bannister, "Visitation Returns of the Diocese of Hereford in 1397, II," *The English Historical Review* 44 (1929): 444–53, at 445 and 449.

214 Bannister, "Visitation Returns of the Diocese of Hereford in 1397, III," *The English Historical Review* 45 (1930): 92–101, at 99.

215 Bannister, "Visitation Returns of the Diocese of Hereford in 1397, IV," *The English Historical Review* 45 (1930): 444–63, at 447 and 454; *Pastors and the Care of Souls* (ed. Shinners and Dohar), 299.

216 Bannister, "Visitation Returns of the Diocese of Hereford in 1397, IV," 457.

217 Ibid., 462.

218 Ibid., 458.

219 *Visites archidiaconales de Josas*, 25.

220 Ibid., 9. The visitors went easy on defects at Egly *praetextu paupertatis*; see 27.

221 Margaret Bowker, *The Secular Clergy in the Diocese of Lincoln 1495–1520* (Cambridge: Cambridge University Press, 1968), 113–15.

222 James R. King, "The Mysterious Case of the Mad Rector of Bletchingdon: The Treatment of Mentally Ill Clergy in Late Thirteenth-Century England," in *Madness in Medieval Law and Custom*, ed. Wendy J. Turner (Leiden: Brill, 2000), 57–80.

223 Bowker, *The Secular Clergy of the Diocese of Lincoln*, 113–14.

abbey, and promotion to all holy orders. His rationale for this change of heart was a grave illness contracted after the marriage, incurred because of his sins.[224]

SIMONY AND THE SICK

Ministering to the sick offered an occasion for greedy clergy to pressure them for monetary compensation. This was done despite long-standing prohibitions of extorting money from the faithful, sick or well, for pastoral care. Carolingian texts forbade exactions for any sacrament. For example, the Liège statutes of the early ninth century prohibited selling the things of God.[225] Later, Regino of Prüm included in his *De synodalibus causis* prohibitions of charging for baptism, chrismation, or communion.[226] Obtaining money for anointing the sick entered universal canon law when the Second Lateran Council (1139), following the condemnation of simony by the Gregorian Reform, forbade exacting money for, among other things, "chrism or holy oil" (*chrisma vel oleum sanctum*).[227] That text entered the *Decretum Gratiani* as *Si quis prebendas*.[228] Likewise, Alexander III's Third Lateran Council (1179) condemned exaction of money for burial, blessing marriages, and rites.[229] A version of the Third Lateran's canon was adopted by the Fourth Lateran Council (1215) in the decree *Ad apostolicam*.[230] Neither *Si quis* nor *Ad apostolicam* treated anointing with oil at length, but a letter of Alexander III denounced receipt of money for chrismation.[231]

Disciplinary canons of local councils condemned clergy who charged for anointing or failed to perform the rite, allowing parishioners to die

224 *Supplications from England and Wales in the Registers of the Apostolic Penitentiary 1410–1503*, ed. Peter D. Clarke and Patrick N. R. Zutshi (Woodbridge: Boydell, 2012–15), 2:118: "et tandem cum exponens ipse quadam gravi infirmitate teneretur, timens ne infirmitas illa ex iniquitate et peccato suo pervenisse [!], dictam mulierem dimisit."

225 MGH *Capitula regum Francorum*, 1:243: "quia nec vendere debent donum Dei."

226 Regino of Prüm, *De synodalibus causis*, xx.

227 *Conciliorum Oecumenicorum Generaliumque Decreta*, ed. Giuseppe Alberigo and Alberto Melloni (Turnhout: Brepols, 2007–17), II, pt. 1, 105, c. 2.

228 Friedberg 1:418 (C. 1, q. 3, c. 15 fin.).

229 Friedberg 2:751, c. *Cum in ecclesiae* (X 5.3.9). For the full Lateran canon, see *Conciliorum oecumenicorum generaliumque decreta* I, pt. 1, 132–33, c. 7. Similarly, see Pope Innocent III in Friedberg 2:759 and 766 (X 5.3.29 and 41).

230 Friedberg 2:766 (X 5.3.42).

231 Friedberg 2:754 (X 5.3.16). Similarly, see Pope Innocent III at 2:764 (X 5.3.36).

without spiritual comfort.[232] In the thirteenth century, concern about the administration of oil and chrism was expressed by Cardinal Ottobono in his legatine constitutions for England. Consequently, bishops and archdeacons were enjoined to inquire into simony in the care and administration of the holy oils.[233] The 1320 statutes of Nicosia forbade exactions for extreme unction but permitted free will offerings.[234] A 1318 statute from Olomuc in Moravia forbade exacting money for baptism, burial, and reconciliation of the sick.[235] In the mid-fifteenth century, Antoninus of Florence issued statutes for his diocese condemning as simony exaction of money for a sacrament.[236] A 1435 canon from Strasbourg forbade charging for "Baptismum, Eucharistiam, Unctionem extremam, Poenitentiam, ac alia Sacramenta."[237] Similarly, the 1447 Council of Eichstadt condemned extorting money from the faithful for administration of the sacraments.[238] The 1491 canon from Bamberg forbade charging for the sacraments but permitted priests to coerce the faithful to secure any offering which had become "a praiseworthy and devout custom" (*laudabilem et devotam consuetudinem*).[239] At least one English case shows a priest charging to communicate the sick.[240]

The possibility that ministry to the sick might be exploited for gain received serious attention in pastoral manuals. The Dominican theologian

232 Andrew Cuschieri, *Anointing of the Sick: A Theological and Canonical Study* (Lanham, Md.: University Press of America, 1993), 38–42. A capitulary of Charlemagne forbade letting the sick die without anointing, reconciliation, and viaticum; see *Medieval Handbooks of Penance*, 389.

233 Lyndwood, *Provinciale*, fol. 15v–16r of the *Constituitiones Othoboni*, accessed via *Early English Books Online*.

234 *The Synodicum Nicosiense and Other Documents of the Latin Church of Cyprus, 1196–1371*, ed. and trans. Christopher Schabel (Nicosia: Cyprus Research Centre, 2001), 230–31.

235 *Synody a statuta Olomoucké diecéze období středověku*, ed. Pavel Krafl (Prague: Historický ústav Akademie věd ČR, 2003), 132: "Nullus ex plebanis et clericis nostre dyocesis pro baptizandis infantibus, sepeliendis mortuis et reconciliandis infirmis munus aliquod exigat et requirat." Similarly see the 1413 and 1431 statutes in ibid., 191–92 and 207.

236 Richard C. Trexler, "The Episcopal Constitutions of Antoninus of Florence," *Quellen und Forschungen aus italienischen Archiven und Bibliotheken* 59 (1979): 244–72, at 269.

237 *Concilia Germaniae* 5:245–46.

238 Ibid., 5:370.

239 Ibid., 6:616: "Volumus ac districte praecipiendo prohibemus, ne Sacerdotes pro administrandis Sacramentis, vel pro sepultura fidelium, munera quantumcunque modica, a suis subditis exigent aut extorqueant. Ipsis autem Sacerdotibus non interdicimus, ut si subditi eorum post Sacramentorum administrationem, aut post funerum sepulturam, laudabilem & devotam consuetudinem, pro hujusmodi Sacramentorum administrationem a fidelibus introductam, nollent observare, ad officium nostrum, seu vicarii nostri implorando possint iidem subditi licite coactari, &, prout jus dictaverit, consueta ad persolvendum compelli." Christopher R. Cheney has commented on how custom fixed expected levels of offerings; see *From Becket to Langton: English Church Government 1170–1213* (Manchester: Manchester University Press, 1956), 161.

240 Clarke, "Enforcing Religious Conformity," 147.

John of Freiburg, updating the *Summa confessorum* of Raymond of Peña-fort, said offerings might be made "according to the devotion one had to the sacrament" (*secundum devotionem quam habuerit ad sacramentum*) or according to custom. However, there were corrupt reasons for making an offering, all of which were prohibited, just as exactions by ministers were illicit.[241] Looking at a related issue, Andreas Escobar, a minor penitentiary of the Roman curia in the fifteenth century, said that a bishop who failed to correct simony committed by his clergy could be suspended.[242]

The *Summa Pisanella* of Bartholomaeus de Sancto Concordio, a four-teenth-century Dominican, rearranged John of Freiburg's text into alpha-betical order by topic. His text was updated by the Franciscan Observant Nicholas of Osimo, who addressed a related issue, whether there might be "remote" causes for offerings to clergy performing rites for the dead or participating in the administration of extreme unction. His reply to this question permitted these "remote" causes for contributions, but not "direct" payment for the performance of spiritual offices. An example of a remote cause was benefaction to a colleagiate community, inspiring its members to participate in rites for the dying or the dead.[243]

Antoninus of Florence, in his *Confessionale "Defecerunt,"* listed the sacraments for which simoniacs charged. Among them were chrismation and extreme unction (*crismate [et] extrema unctione*). The archbishop said it was "like a price for that sacrament," a sign of when God gave grace.[244] He also said that it was not legitimate to refuse someone the sacraments for not paying a price. Nor did custom excuse charging for a sacrament, including *crismata et extrema vnctione.*[245] Antoninus also treated simony in his vernacular *Confessionale "Omnis mortalium cura."* There he permitted receiving alms for the sacraments but not asking for money "as a price of the sacraments" (*como precio deli sacramenti*). Antoninus said the same thing about exacting payment to say masses (*dire le messe*). In such cases

241 Johannes de Friburgo, *Summa confessorum* I, t. 1, qq. 10 and 29.

242 Andreas Escobar, *Lumen confessorum*, University of Pennsylvania Ms. Codex 1215, fol. 6va–b, 7vb–8ra.

243 Nicholas of Osimo, *Supplementum Summae Pisanellae,* v. Simonia I: "Vnde si quis dat pecuniam collegio alicui pro generanda deuotione et dilectione in ipso collegio vt ex illa deuotione exaudiatur in petitione quam petit quod fratres intersint exequijs mortui vel extreme vnctioni morientis et illi hoc faciunt ex dilectione et deuotione in eis taliter generate aut pro deuotionis ipsius dantis. Sic licet dare et accipere temporale pro spirituali secundum ly pro denotata causam motiuam remotam et non propinquam."

244 Antoninus of Florence, *Confessionale "Defecerunt"* (Speyer: Drach, 1487), fol. B ii[r]: "quasi precium huius sacramenti cuius signum est quando dat."

245 Ibid.

there was to be no pact between giver and receiver to pay for a rite.[246] The faithful, especially those who were ailing, expected to freely receive spiritual comfort. Priests also were supposed to be ready day or night to visit the sick, expecting no recompense for this necessary ministry.

246 Antoninus of Florence, *Confessionale "Omnis mortalium cura"* & *Libretto della dottrina christiana "Omnis mortalium cura," Libretto*, v. Simonia.

2

SICKBED CONFESSION

oman practice influenced the development of instructions for visiting the sick and dying, as will be noted below; but this did not create unity of practice. Each diocese had its own variations within a shared framework, and manuscript copies of a diocesan manual might have their own differences. Even in the later fifteenth century, when local manuals for priests became common in print, uniformity was not achieved in any one region. Each manual was likely to reveal those local variants even within a diocese.[1] Moreover, instructions were repeated in liturgical texts and synodal decrees in attempts to guide the clergy who themselves had no shared training. Nor would uniformity become more common until seminaries were founded under the influence of the Council of Trent.[2]

Although the liturgical order for visiting the sick began with the priest's arrival at the patient's home, preparation for this ministry preceded this arrival. The priest was expected to have at least one host reserved in the parish church for communion for the sick (viaticum). The reserved host was to be renewed weekly or fortnightly. Weekly renewal was required by many local authorities. For example, the Westminster council of 1200

1 Salisbury, "Rethinking the Uses of Sarum and York," 202–22.

2 Council of Trent, Session 23, c. 18, in *Conciliorum Oecumenicorum Generaliumque Decreta*, 3:120–23.

required renewal on each Sunday.[3] In addition, he was expected to have a stock of oils consecrated by the bishop on Holy Thursday to use in anointing. One council (ca. 1200) ordered that the vessels for chrism and other holy oils be cleaned once a year before the bishop's chrism Mass.[4] A provision of the Fourth Lateran Council (1215) required that both hosts and oils were to be kept under lock and key to avoid theft for magical practices.[5]

In addition, the priest and an attendant cleric were to have the appropriate vestments, plus a light and a bell to use when carrying communion to the sick. The light and bell were to warn the faithful that the consecrated bread, the body of Christ, was being carried among them. This, in turn, was to arouse the bystanders to reverence; and they could follow the priest, witnessing the administration of the sacraments and receiving the indulgences some bishops promised those who reverently participated in such processions. The laity, especially women, were warned against bad conduct while participating in this ritual. Moreover, some priests were permitted to vary this practice because of distance, bad weather, or dangers *en route*.[6]

THE PRIEST GOES TO THE SICKBED

Attending the sick required a priest to be present at the bedside, administering sacraments and reciting prayers. Due to the importance of saving souls, priests were told not to delay or omit these visits. They were to lead the sick to penance, hearing their confessions and granting absolution, especially to the dying. Sickness might be a divine scourge for sins, requiring the right attitude of penance in the ailing person. Priests, however, were instructed to make provision for the possibility of bodily healing, making penances light and able to be performed only if the patient recovered.

A text attributed to a council at Nantes contained some of these instructions for ministry:

> When a priest hears of someone who is sick among his people, he should go to him quickly. Having entered the chamber, he should sprinkle holy

3 Rubin, *Corpus Christi*, 44.

4 Mansi 22:736. Any damaged vessel and residue adhering to it were to be buried under the font or put down the *piscina*. The same council (ibid.) said that any spilled chrism or oil was to be scraped up and placed in either location.

5 Thomas M. Izbicki, "*Manus temeraria*: Custody of the Eucharist in Medieval Canon Law," in *Proceedings of the Thirteenth International Congress of Medieval Canon Law*, ed. Peter Erdö and S. A. Szuromi (Vatican City: Biblioteca Apostolica Vaticana, 2010), 535–52.

6 Thomas M. Izbicki, *The Eucharist in Medieval Canon Law* (Cambridge: Cambridge University Press, 2015), 178–220.

> water on him and throughout the chamber with the antiphon, "Thou shalt sprinkle me, [Lord]" [Ps 50:9] and the verse "Let God arise" [Ps 67:2]. Then he should say the prayer, "O God, Who gave your priests such grace above others" etc. Then let him sing seven psalms with prayers for the sick. After this, he should command all present to leave the chamber. Approaching the bed in which the sick person is lying, he should address him gently and mildly, so that he places all hope in God, so that he bears God's scourge patiently, so that he believes this provides purgation and reprimand, so that all his sins are confessed and emendation promised if the Lord grants life.

The remainder of the text deals with almsgiving in case a sick person survived, the blessing of that person, and leaving him or her to reflect on past sins.[7]

The text from Nantes indicated the predominant direction taken by instructions for the "visitation of the sick" (*visitatio infirmorum*) found in manuals and sometimes in pontificals. Each indicated that the priest had to travel to the sickbed and greet the household properly before proceeding to the rites reserved for the sick and dying, beginning with the sacrament of penance, which opened the way to other sacraments. After a proper greeting to the household, the priest could hear confession, followed, if not always directly, by administration of viaticum and extreme unction. The instructions for going to the house often, but not always, segue into the hearing of confession. Occasionally, the books separated these rites into individual *ordines* for communion of the sick and their anointing, both distinguished from the *Ordo commendationis animae* for the dying.[8]

This was not the only approach the clergy ever took in ministry to the sick. Theodulf of Orléans, in a capitulary from the Carolingian period, declared that a sick person who had confessed should, if possible, be dressed in white and carried to church. He or she was to be placed on

7 *Acta conciliorum et epistolae decretales, ac constitutiones summorum pontificum* (Paris: Ex Typographia Regia, 1714), 6:458B: "Cum sacerdos audierit aliquem infirmari in sua plebe, quam citius ad eum pergat, & ingressus cubiculum, aquam benedictam super eum & per omne cubiculum aspergat, cum antiphona, *Asperges me Domine*: & versu *Exsurgat Deus*. Deinde dicat orationem, *Deus qui sacerdotibus tuis tantum prae ceteris gratiam contulisti, etc*. Deinde cantet septem Psalmos, cum precibus pro infirmis. Post haec omnes jubeat extra cubiculum secedere; & appropinquans lecto, quo infirmus decumbit, cum blande leniterque alloquatur, ut omnem spem suam in Deo ponat, ut flagellum Dei patienter toleret, ut hoc ad purgationem & castigationem suam provenire credit, ut peccata sua confiteatur, ut emendationem promittat, si Dominus vitam concesserit." A short text follows, discussing how a patient who survived was to do penance according to the quality of past sins. This text appears in the *Decretum* of Burchard of Worms (PL 140:933C). Bishop Daniel of Nantes gave instructions for deathbed confessions and exhortation of the gravely ill; see *Thesaurus novus anecdotorum*, ed. Edmonde Martène and Ursin Durand (Paris: Apud Montalant, 1717), 4:957–59.

8 See, e.g., *Rituale Romanum* (Florence, ca. 1484), fol. [a 6]v–[a 8]r.

a cloth scattered with ashes.[9] Then three priests were to approach with a cross and holy water, sprinkle the person with water mixed with holy oil, and make signs of the cross on the body with ashes. Prayers and the penitential psalms were to be said. If the sick person could, he or she might stand with head bowed; but lying down was acceptable.[10] Anointing followed with more psalms accompanying it.[11]

However, a precedent was set for Continental churches by the *Rituale Romanum*. It began its instructions for ministry to the sick with the arrival of the priest at the home to give communion (*Ordo ad communicandum infirmum*). The priest was to greet the household, "Peace to this house" (*Pax huic domo*), receiving the reply, possibly from an accompanying cleric, "And to all those living in it" (*Et omnibus habitantibus in in eo*). He was then to sprinkle the sick person with holy water "in the form of a cross" (*in modum crucis*) and say the antiphon "Sprinkle me" (*Asperges me*) with the psalm "Have mercy on me, oh God" (*Miserere mei Deus*, Ps 40). A penitential rite with absolution was to be accompanied by the prayer, "Lord Jesus Christ, Who said to Your disciples, Whatever you bind on earth" (*Dominus iesus christus qui dixit discipulis suis quecunque ligaveris in terram*). Only then was he to approach the sick person with viaticum.[12]

The manual of the Roman-Neapolitan rite suggested that there might be a procession to the sick person's home. The priest would be preceded by three clerics, one with holy water, one with a cross, and one with candles. On arriving at the house, the priest was to greet the household and sprinkle the sick person with holy water. That person was to kiss the cross, following which he or she was supposed to say the *Confiteor*.[13]

Examples of local practices can be found in France. These variants become noticeable in instructions for the arrival of the priest at the sick

9 PL 105:220C: "Primitus autem infirmo poenitentia detur. Deinde, si permiserit infirmitas, abluto corpore, albis vestibus induatur, et in ecclesiam deportetur, et jaceat in cilicio superjecto cinere."

10 Ibid.: "Et, si potest, infirmus stet.genibus flexis et capite inclinato sive omni corpore prostratus."

11 The remainder of this account can be found in chapter 4.

12 *Rituale Romanum*, fol. [10]v–[11]v. An early instruction from Farfa said those receiving the priest into the house were to kneel; see G. J. C. Snoek, *Medieval Piety from Relics to the Eucharist: A Process of Mutual Interaction* (Leiden: Brill, 1995), 238.

13 *Manuale Romano-Neapolitanum* (Rome, ca. 1478), fol. xii[r]: "Imprimis precedat vnus qui portat aquam benedictam. Sequitur qui portat crucem. Tertio qui portat cereos. Deinde sacerdos cum corpore Christi dicendo plane ps. Miserere mei deus. Cum autem peruentum fuerit ad locum vbi iacet infirmum sacerdos intrans dicat. Pax huic domui. R' Et omnibus habitantibus in ea. deinde accedat ad egrotum ter in modum crucis aspergat cum aqua benedicta dicens. Asperges me domine ysopo et mundabor. cum ver, Miserere mei deus. Gloria patri et Sicut erat. Et repetitur antipho[n]. Asperges me. Deinde infirmus immediate adoret et oscultetur crucem et dicat. Confiteor deo omnipotenti et beate Marie semper virgini etc." The manual for Mâcon said the priest was to sprinkle both the sick person and the place with holy water before saying Ps 50; see the 1497 edition, fol. 66ra.

person's home. The Rouen *Visitatio infirmorum* began simply with the greeting of the priest, *Pax huic domo*, and the response, *Et omnibus habitantibus in ea*. The priest then sprinkled holy water, saying the antiphon *Aspeges me*.[14] The penitential psalms followed.[15] Likewise, the *Visitatio* from the manual for Coutances began with a greeting and included the penitential psalms.[16] The text for Angers began with the priest's greeting and the sprinkling of holy water (*asperges*). However, there followed the prayer, "Let him enter this house, Lord" (*Introeat domine domum hanc*). After that prayer, the manual provided for confession, "Let him reconcile the sick" (*Reconcilietur infirmis*), before the saying of the penitential psalms.[17] Note that some manuals, like that of Angers, gave instructions for administering penance to the sick early in the visit. Others mentioned confession in their instructions for communion of the sick or anointing, as will be noted below.

The visitation text in the manual for Paris began similarly to that of Rouen, with the same greeting and the sprinkling of holy water. However, it continued with Psalm 50, *Miserere*, in the Vulgate version, the verse "Show us, Lord" (*Ostende nobis domine*) and a prayer "Hear us, Lord holy Father" (*Exaudi nos domine sancte pater*). Only after that did the manual provide for the sick person's confession, if it had not already been heard.[18] (Another version of the Paris manual included texts in French concerning the confessions of the sick and remedies against temptation.)[19]

The Chartres pontifical added to the response *et omnibus habitantibus in ea*, a prayer beginning, "Bless, Lord, those fearful for the little ones" (*Benedic domine timentes de pusillis*).[20] That text allowed a transition from the blessing of the house and its inhabitants to a brief litany, invoking Sts. Piat, Caraunus, Quentin, and Remi. The litany was to be followed by prayers, including "Lord, Who Your servant Hezekiah" (*Deus qui famulo*

14 *Manuale secundum usum insignis ecclesiae Rothomagensis* (Paris, ca. 1500), fol. 30r. The version published by Guilemme du Val repeated this; see *Manuale sacerdotum continens ecclesie sacramenta et administrandi ea* (Paris, 1523), fol. xixr. A Paris *ordo* has the priest say the greeting three times with others (*alii*) replying; see *Pontificale Parisiense*, Paris Bibl. Nat. Lat. 961, fol. ccxxxiir.

15 *Manuale secundum usum ecclesiae Rothomagensis*, fol. 30r–34v.

16 *Manuale secundum usum ecclesie Constanciensis* (Rouen: Le Bourgeois, 1494), fol. 21r–24v.

17 *Manuale ad usum precelebris ecclesie Andegauensis* (Rouen: Le Roux, 1543), fol. xxxvi^{v}. This manual includes instructions for a visitation without anointing and without either anointing or viaticum; see fol. xlv^{r-v}.

18 *Manuale secundum usum ecclesiae Parisiensis* (Paris, ca. 1500), fol. [d5]rb: "Tunc si infirmus non fuerit confessus audiat eum in confessione." See also *Manuale ad usum Parisiensem* (n.p., 1504), fol. xxix^{v}.

19 *Manuale ad usum Parisiensem* (Paris, 1497), fol. [o7]^{va}–p ii^{rb}. Similarly, see *De remediis contra tentationes* in Jean Gerson, *Oeuvres complètes*, ed. Palémon Glorieux (Paris: Desclée, 1973), 9:518–24.

20 *Pontificale Carnotensis*, Paris MS BN Lat. 945, fol. 190r.

tuo Ezechię), referring to the cure of the biblical king. Only after that series of prayers was the priest to move to anointing.[21] The manual for Reims followed the sprinkling of holy water with the prayers: "Lord, bless this house" (*Benedic domine domum istam*) and "Hear us, holy Father" (*Exaudi nos domine sancte pater*). Then it permitted a transition to extreme unction if the sick person was of sound mind (*sanum intellectum*) and not near death (*et ultima hora non urgeat*), providing instructions for the transition in French.[22]

In England, the York manual said that the priest was to arrive at the sufferer's home wearing his stole. He was to say, upon crossing the threshold, "Peace to this house and to all those dwelling in it. Peace to those entering and leaving." The priest was then to sprinkle both the sick person and the house with holy water, saying a psalm, *Miserere mei, Deus* (Ps 51[50]) and a series of prayers. The penitential psalms and the litany of the saints with its concluding prayers were to follow. The first prayer after the Litany was based on the fifth chapter of the Epistle of James (Jas 5:13–15), which promised both the forgiveness of sins and potential healing.[23]

After these prayers were concluded, the priest was to hear the sick person's confession. He could absolve someone on the verge of death (*in articulo mortis*) even of sins reserved to the bishop or the pope. However, a person who recovered was to be enjoined to seek out the appropriate authority for absolution. In addition, the patient was urged to restore any ill-gotten gains as part of satisfaction for sins.[24] When preparing to hear the sick person's confession, the priest was to consult any privilege the Apostolic Penitentiary had granted authorizing full absolution and remission of all sins, even those reserved to higher authority. This permitted reconciliation with the Church of even the most soiled sinner.[25] The form

21 Ibid., fol. 190v–194r.

22 *Manuale seu agenda ad usu Remensem*, fol. 173r–v: "Mon am ou mamye. Les sains sacremens de legisle receuz deuotement profittent et aident au salut des ames grandement et au salut des corps ainsi comme plaist a notre seigneur. Et mesmement le sainct sacrament de la derniere vnction que ie vous vueil administer par le quell se dieu plaist la misericorde de notre seigneur vous sera propice."

23 *Manuale et processionale ad usum insignis ecclesiae Eboracensis*, 41–47.

24 Ibid., 47–48. For a late thirteenth-century Exeter statute permitting deathbed absolution, see *Councils & Synods, with Other Documents Relating to the English Church*, 2 vols., ed. Dorothy Whitelock et al. (Oxford: Clarendon Press, 1964 and 1981), pt. 2, 1076: "in articulo mortis a sacerdote simplici absolvantur." Similarly, the *Praecepta antiqua* of Rouen said this was true even if the pope had excommunicated the dying person; see Mansi 23:382–83.

25 *Manuale et processionale*, 48. On this privilege, see Kirsi Salonen and Ludwig Schmugge, *A Sip from the "Well of Grace": Medieval Texts from the Apostolic Penitentiary* (Washington, DC: The Catholic University of America Press, 2009), 64–68.

of absolution provided was different for a penitent with such a privilege than for one without one.[26]

The Sarum Use order for visitation of the sick began with the priest putting on gown and stole. Then, with his attendant ministers, he was to say the penitential psalms while on his way to the sick person's home. (This Use seems to presume that a cleric was dying, making more provisions for the presence of multiple clergy than does the York practice.) The priest was to show the patient a crucifix and then sprinkle him or her with holy water. There followed a series of prayers, one invoking Peter's healing of Tabitha in Acts 9:36–41.[27] The Sarum rite for the sick added an exhortation that the patient hold firm to the faith; and, if possible, the priest was to do an examination of his or her beliefs.[28] This examination was to precede hearing confession and absolving sins. The Sarum Use, like that of York, varied if the patient had a bull permitting absolution of all sins of someone *in articulo mortis.*[29]

In what is now Switzerland, the diocese of Lausanne provided two prayers, *Deus qui famulo tuo Ezechie* and "Consider, Lord, your servant"[30] (*Respice domine famulum*[*am*]), to say before the sprinkling of holy water. Another prayer, *Exaudi nos domine sancte pater*, preceded the blessing of the house (*Benedictio domus*). After the prayers, "Be present, Lord, for our supplications" (*Adesto domine supplicationibus nostris)* and "Bless, Lord God" (*Benedic domine deus*), the priest could hear the sick person's confession. The sick person was to say the *Confiteor* and the Apostles' Creed. If he or she could not speak, the priest could say these things instead before moving on to a series of prayers and absolution. Anointing followed this penitential rite.[31]

Manuals from outside Francophone regions differed only in details in these instructions for arrival. The manual for Chur said that the priest or an attendant was to carry a crucifix and holy water. In the case of a long or dangerous journey, the priest was to say the penitential psalms on the

26 *Manuale et processionale*, 48–49.

27 Ibid., 44*–45*.

28 Ibid., 45*–47*. The rite allowed for a shorter examination for a lay person or one "simply" learned.

29 Ibid., 48*.

30 This prayer allows for a male or female servant, depending on the gender of the ailing person.

31 *Manuale seu officiarium saceerdotum secundum usum ecclesie et diocesis Laudunensis* (Paris: Ad Signum Rose Rubre, 1538), fol. xx^v–xxii^v, at xxi^r: "Tunc qui infirmus est confiteatur sacerdoti si velit. saltem dicat Confiteor."

way.[32] The manual for Worms too wanted the penitential psalms said on the way to the sick person, whereas the Augsburg manual placed these psalms after the greeting.[33] The see of Brixen too had the visit start with the penitential psalms.[34] The Basel book placed the prayer "Omnipotent and merciful God" (*Omnipotens et misericors deus*) and the penitential psalms after the priest was in the house.[35] The manual for Passau inserted Psalm 40 [39], "Awaiting, I awaited" (*Exspectans exspectavi*), between the greeting and the penitential psalms.[36]

The instructions for Trier insert the prayer "Visit this habitation we ask, Lord" (*Visita quaesumus domine habitationem istam*) and setting down the tabernacle (or pyx) with the consecrated host between the greeting and the sprinkling of holy water. The administration of the Eucharist was to follow without any mention of confession.[37] The see of Cologne placed before the greeting and psalms three things that the priest needed to know: to whom to give the sacraments and to whom not; what to do about the excommunicated, cautioning them in front of witnesses lest they be deprived of viaticum (*ne viatico priuentur*); and how the priest was to dress for carrying viatcum and holy oils before going to the house with a light, cross, and holy water carried before him.[38]

On the frontiers of Western Christendom, there were greater differences. Thus, the see of Prague in Bohemia offered two rites for the sick. One consisted of a series of prayers, tailored to a man or woman, with the possibility of communion afterward. The other placed the penitential psalms before anointing.[39] The Olomuc instructions followed the greeting with the penitential psalms and then anointing, with no mention of

32 *Agenda sive exeqviale divinorum sacramentorvm pro ecclesiis parrochialibus dioecesis Curiensis* (Rosach: Straub, 1590), fol. y[v]: "debet portare crucifixum & aquam benedictum ad infirmum. Si mora est in periculo: Sacerdos oret septem Psalmos poenitentiales in via eundo ad infirmum."

33 *Agenda secundum ritum et ordinem ecclesie wormaciensis* (Speyer: Drach, ca. 1500), fol. b 4[r]–c 2[r]; *Obsequiale Augustense im Auftrag von Friedrich II, Graf von Zollern, Bischof von Augsburg* (Augsburg: Ratdolt, 1487), lxii. The practice at Eichstät resembled that at Augsburg; see *Obsequiale Eystetense* (Eichstät: Reyser, 1488), xii[r], but that at Naumberg resembled that at Worms; see *Agenda Numbergensis* (Naunburg: Saale, 1502), fol. [b 5][r].

34 *Obsequiale Brixiense* (Augsburg: Ratdolt, 1493), lv[v].

35 *Informatorium sacerdotum* (Basel: Wenssler, 1488), fol. [C 7] r–[D 8]r, adding: "Et si sit mulier que infirmatur dicas. Adiuua eam."

36 *Agenda seu benedictionale secundum vsum sancta ecclesie Patauiensis* (Passau: Hammen, 1498), fol. x[v]–xi[v].

37 *Agenda ecclesiae Trevirensis* (Trier: Rotaeus, 1574), fol. cxii[v]–cxiii[r].

38 *Agenda ecclesiastica Coloniensis* (Cologne: Apud Theodorum Baxer, 1562), fol. c 2[v].

39 *Obsequiale Pragense* (Nürnberg: Stuchs, ca. 1500), xix[v]–xiii[v]. The entry rite includes a prayer beginning *Benedic domine domum istam*; see ibid., fol. xix[v].

confession.[40] The diocesan manual of the see of Esztergom in Hungary reads similarly.[41]

In Scandinavia, the Danish region is represented by the manuals for Roskilde and Notmark. The Roskilde *Visitatio infirmorum* begins with the priest saying the penitential psalms on the way to the sick person's home. Then he was to wish peace to the household and say the prayer "Omnipotent eternal God, who to the priests" (*Omnipotens sempiterne deus qui sacerdotibus*). The priest was to sprinkle the sick person with holy water, followed by prayers and the hearing of his or her confession, using the absolution, "Omnipotent God, have mercy on you" (*Misereatur tui omnipotens deus*).[42] The manual added blessings to be used under varying circumstances.[43] The Notmark book had the priest start by blessing holy water, followed by saying the penitential psalms, a litany, and a prayer before hearing confession, followed by other prayers.[44] In Sweden, the manual for Uppsala has the priest say the penitential psalms on the way, giving the greeting when entering the house. Then he was to say the prayer "Omnipotent and merciful God" (*Omnipotens et misericors deus*), followed by the *asperges*, further prayers, confession, and absolution. The priest was also to secure a profession of faith from the sick person before administering communion.[45] The manual for Linköping provided a brief form, combining the greeting and the *asperges*, followed by two prayers and confession, "If it is necessary" (*si sit necessarie*). Only then was the priest to say the penitential psalms.[46]

On the Iberian peninsula, the manual for Calahorra details how the priest was to prepare to visit the sick, striking a bell once before he put on the appropriate vestments. He or his sacristan was to prepare the oils, as well as a small cross, a light, and holy water for the procession to the sick person. Once the priest arrived, he was to greet the household and say a prayer before proceeding to the penitential psalms and the order

40 *Agenda Olomucensis* (Nürnberg: Stuchs, 1498), fol. C III^{r}.

41 *Obsequiale seu baptismale secundum chorum almae ecclesiae Strigonensis* (Nürnberg: Stuchs, ca. 1500), fol. b 4^{r}–[b 7]^{v}.

42 *Manuale curatorum secundum usum ecclesie Roeskildensis*, ed. Joseph Freisen (Paderborn: Junfermann, 1898), 23–24. An absolution *Pro homicida* followed.

43 *Manuale curatorum secundum usum ecclesie Roeskildensis*, 25: "Iste benedictiones infirmorum possunt dici quandocunque placet. siue quando communicat. siue quando perungitur."

44 *The Manual from Notmark*, ed. Knut Ottosen (Copenhagen: Gad, 1970), 76–77.

45 *Manuale Upsalense* (Stockholm: Ghotan, ca. 1486), fol. 36^{v}–43^{r}.

46 *Manuale secundum titulum ecclesie Lincopensis* (Söderköping: In Edibus Olaui Vlrici, 1525), 62–71.

for penance. The order for penance included the *Confiteor* in Spanish (*Yo peccador me confesso*).[47]

At Urgell in the Pyrenees the church bell was to be rung and then a hand bell sounded at the door of the church, gathering the faithful to accompany the Eucharist. Other priests also might accompany the sacrament. Meanwhile, the pastor was to wash his hands and dress properly before entering the sacristy to take up the vessel holding the Eucharist. The procession was to be led by an attendant with a hand bell. The laity were to carry lights, and priests were to walk two by two. The pastor was to enter the house and offer a greeting before administering the sacraments. Returning to the church, he was to say psalms and confer indulgences on those who had accompanied him to the sickbed.[48]

The guidance provided to pastors for the hearing of sickbed confessions was not abstract. The focus was on saving souls by bringing the sick and dying to confession of their sins and reception of absolution. Otherwise they might be damned. The confessor might also bring the suffering to a realization that their pain might be made spiritually beneficial, including toward the avoidance of Purgatory. In all cases, priests were to move sinners toward a consciousness of divine mercy, which God would not deny even to the worst sinners.

47 *Manuale secundum consuetudinem Calagurritanensis et Calcianensis ecclesiarum* (Logroño: In Edibus Michaelis de Eguia, 1532), fol. lxi^{v}: "Cum igitur ad ungendum pulsetur unum signum campane: et interim sacerdos induat se superpelicio et stola: et minister seu sacrista preparat peluim ad hoc deputatam: et ampullam olei infirmorum: et crucem paruam et lumen et aquam benedictam: ad deferendum in domum infirmi. Et sacerdos in ingressu domus dicat. Pax huic domui et omnibus habentibus in ea." The prayer, penitential psalms, and instructions for confession appear at fol. lxi^{v}–lxiv^{v}.

48 *Ordinarium sacramentorum benedictionum et aliarum rerum a sacerdote animarum curam regent agendarum secundum sacrosancte Urgellensis ecclesie ritum* (Lyon: Cornelius de Septemgrangis, 1548), fol. cxii^{r}: "Primo sacerdos curatus faciat pulsare campanam: vt moris est: deinde usetur campanella per ianuas ecclesie: vt Christi fideles congregentur ad sociandum corpus christi. Interim curatus ablaut manus suas: et preparet se honeste ac reuerenter: indutus superpellitio mundissimo: stola et cappa breui: que vulgo dicitur mantela: et intrans sacrarium cum magna reuerentia et deuotione accipiat custodiam; seu vasculum sacrum: in quo reseruari solet corpus christi: an inquo plures forme consecrate debent esse: ne in reditu portetur custodia sine aliqua forma. Egrediens itaque curatus a sacrario dicat psalmus. Laudate dominum omnes gentes. Alij autem sacerdotes et laici sicut cum luminarijs deuote expectantes extra sacrarium. Deinde ordinetur processioaliter: vt portans campanellam precedat pulsando et aliquas pausas: semper coram corpore Christi. Postea vadant laici cum luminarijs: deinde sacerdotes bini et bini sequantur ordinatum: dicentes cum deuotione voce sonora. Canticum graduum. vel Officium beate marie . . . Et cum peruenerit portans custodiam ad domum infirmi dicat. Antiphonam. Pax huis domui." For the return, see fol. cxvv. For abbreviated versions of these instructions; see *Ordinarium sacramentorum valde copiosum ideo sacerdotibus maxime curatis utilissimum cum suis additamentis* (Barcelona: Posa, 1501), fol. r ii^{r}; *Ordinarium de administratione sacramentorum cum pluribus additionibus adeo necessarijs secundum ritum alme sedis maioricensis* (Valencia: Jeffre, 1516), fol. xlv^{v}.

PENANCE NOT TO BE WITHHELD

Early canon law stated that no Christian was to be denied final penance. Some of the texts saying this are found in the collection of Dionysius Exiguus. He quoted a letter of Pope Celestine I, based on scripture, especially Ezekiel 31:11: "I do not desire the death of the sinner, but that he should be converted and live." Celestine concluded that "at any time, penance is not to be denied to the one who asks [for it]."[49] The same collection included a letter of Pope Innocent I saying that penance and communion were not to be denied to those lapsed during a persecution. Innocent added that viaticum was to be given after the final penance to save the repentant from eternal death.[50] The seventh-century collection of Cresconius quoted the same texts of Innocent and Celestine.[51] The same texts appeared too in the ninth-century *De poenitentia* of Halitgar under the rubric: "That no one is to be denied final penance" (*Quod nulli sit ultima poenitentia deneganda).*[52]

The 769 capitulary of Charlemagne expanded this admonition to reconciliation, viaticum, and unction of the sick. No one was to leave this world without them.[53] The 829 Council of Paris said that confession should be made before the altar ordinarily; but sick persons could confess at home, even if they had to confess to bystanders for lack of a priest.[54] The *Pseudo-Isidorean Decretals* contained familiar texts concerning penance of the sick. Pope Innocent I's canon said penitents should wait until just before Easter for confession; but, whenever someone fell desperately ill, penance was to be permitted to avoid having someone leave this world without absolution and communion.[55] The *Penitential of Theodore* said that a priest who denied penance to dying persons was "answerable for

49 PL 67:275D: "quovis tempore non est deneganda poenitentia postulanti, cum illi se obliget judici, cui occulta omnia noverit revelari."

50 PL 67:247A: "Tribuetur ergo cum poenitentia extrema communio, ut homines hujusmodi vel in supremis suis, permittente Salvatore nostro, a perpetuo exitio vindicentur."

51 Klaus Zechiel-Eckes, *Die Concordia canonum des Cresconius: Studien und Edition* (Frankfurt: Peter Lang, 1992), 1:714–16.

52 PL 105:677B.

53 Mansi 17b:192: "Similiter de infirmis & poenitentibus, ut morientes sine sacrati olei unctione & reconciliatione & viatico non deficiant."

54 MGH *Concilia* II, pt. 2, ed. Albert Werminghof (Hanover: Hahn, 1906; Hanover: Hahn, 1997), 610. "Si autem infirmitas praepedieret, ut in ecclesia eadem fieri nequeat, in quamcumquelibet domo facienda est, nonnisi testibus similiter haud procul adstantibus fiat."

55 *Decretales Pseudo-Isidorianae et Capitula Angilramni*, ed. Paul Hinschius (Leipzig: Tauschnitz, 1863; Aalen: Scientia, 1963), 528: "Sane si quis in aegritudinem inciderit atque usque ad desperationem devenerit, ei est ante tempus paschae relaxandum, ne de seculo absque communione discedat."

their souls."[56] Regino of Prüm inserted texts concerning reconciliation and anointing of the sick into his *Concerning Synodal Cases* (*De synodalibus causis*).[57] The *Decretum* of Burchard of Worms contained Celestine's letter under the title, "That final conversion should be estimated according to [the penitent's] mind rather than what time it is" (*Quod ultima conversio mente potius aestimanda sit quam tempore).*[58]

The collections compiled by the Gregorian reformers gave scant attention to this matter. *The Collection in Seventy-Four Titles* contained few texts on penance of the sick. One, that of Pope Innocent I, reaffirmed that penitents should wait until the Thursday before Easter for release unless dangerously ill. Then penance could be administered to avoid a soul "departing from this world without communion."[59] A text attributed to Pope Leo I said that those who implored the clergy to grant them penance were not to be denied reconciliation; "neither can satisfaction be prohibited, because we can neither place a limit upon nor define a time for the mercy of God." Likewise, the sick were to be permitted communion. Witnesses were to be consulted if the sick person was unable to affirm the request for penance when the priest arrived.[60]

The collection of Anselm of Lucca deals briefly with the same topic. It quotes the Council of Elvira as saying that a person who asked for reconciliation of a grave offence was to be referred to the bishop unless too ill to wait. Then the priest or a deacon could offer not just penance but communion.[61] Anselm's collection ended with Pope Innocent I's text and a canon from the *Statuta ecclesiae antiqua*, attributed to a council of Carthage, saying a seriously ill person who received viaticum but survived was to receive laying on of the hands for full absolution.[62]

The *Decretum* of Ivo of Chartres attributes to Pope Celestine I the sentiment against denying penance to the sick, provided that the need for

56 *Medieval Handbooks of Penance*, 191–92.

57 Regino of Prüm, *De synodalibus causis et disciplinis ecclesiasticis*, ed. F. G. A. Wasserschleben (Leipzig: Engelmann, 1840; Graz: Akamademische Druck- und Verlagsanstalt, 1964), 107.

58 Burchardus Wormaciensis, *Decretum* (PL 140:938D). Time here means liturgical time.

59 *The Collection in Seventy-Four Titles: A Canon Law Manual of the Gregorian Reform*, trans. John Gilchrist (Toronto: PIMS, 1980), 212–13.

60 Ibid., 213–14.

61 Anselm of Lucca, *Collectio canonum una cum collectione minore*, ed. Friedrich Thaner (Innsbruck: Wagner, 1906–15; Aalen: Scientia, 1965), 514: "Apud presbyterum si quis gravi lapsu in ruinam mortis acciderit placuit agere poenitentiam non debere sed potius apud episcopum, cogente autem infirmitate, si necesse est, presbyterum prestare debere, et diaconum, se ei iusserit sacerdos."

62 Ibid., 516: "Poenitentes qui in infirmitate viaticum eucharistiae acceperunt non se credant absolutos sine manus imposition, si supervixerint." Innocent I, c. *In beati Jacobi epistola*, precedes ibid.

penance was urgent and the penitent was willing to reveal all hidden sins.[63] Ivo also included the canon from Nantes saying the dying were to be given penance according to the "quality" of their sins and reconciled at last.[64] Ultimately, the Celestine text was included in Gratian's *Decretum* as c. *Agnovimus* under the heading, "Penance is not to be denied to the dying" (*Poenitentia morientibus non est deneganda).*[65] However, Gratian limited this concession to the deathbed, when the bishop could not be consulted about grave sins.[66]

Gratian treated the availability of penance to the sick and dying in the *Tractatus de poenitentia*, included in the *Causae* of the *Decretum*. Distinction 7 of that tract begins with a statement that "penance extends to the last moment of life," buttressed with a quotation from Pope Leo I that we should not despair while "constituted in the body." The same opinion was supported by quotations from Augustine, who also warned against putting off penance. No one was to be denied the sacrament, although no one knows how they will fare after death. Both Cyprian and Augustine were displeased with those moved to penance by danger of death rather than contrition. Gratian treated this as one of the reasons why we should not postpone penance to the last moment.[67]

Commenting on the *Decretum*, Rufinus of Bologna dealt with differing texts about reconciliation of sinners and excommunicates in danger of death by distinguishing between public laying on of hands by bishops and private laying on of hands by priests.[68] Rufinus also said that penance was not to be imposed on those about to die (*morituris*), but they were to be told what they would have to do if they lived.[69] Rufinus said that the

63 PL 161:862D: "Cum ergo Dominus sit cordis inspector, quovis tempore non est deneganda poenitentia postulanti, cum ille se obliget judici, cui occulta omnia noverit revelari."

64 PL 161:863C: "Infirmus qui necessitate mortis urgente confitetur peccata sua, sub ea conditione a sacerdote reconcilietur, ut si ei Dominus vitam donaverit, sanitatemque reddiderit, secundum qualitatem delicti, et secundum canonum statuta, et poenitentialium probatorum poeniteat." Ivo added canons from Popes Leo I and Innocent I supporting this position; see 863C–864B.

65 Friedberg 1:1040 (C. 26, q. 6, c. 13).

66 Friedberg 1:1040 is followed by the dictum (C. 26, q. 6, p.c. 13): "Cui autem penitencia non denegatur, nec reconciliatio sibi deneganda est. Inconsulto ergo episcopo penitentem presbiter reconciliare non debet, nisi ultima necessitate cogat."

67 *Gratian's "Tractatus de penitentia": A New Latin Edition with English Translation*, ed. and trans. Atria A. Larson (Washington, DC: The Catholic University of America Press, 2016), 270–79. See also Larson, *Master of Penance: Gratian and the Development of Penitential Thought and Law in the Twelfth Century* (Washington, DC: The Catholic University of America Press, 2014), 250, which discusses deathbed penance with reference to C. 26, qq. 6–7.

68 Rufinus, *Summa decretorum*, ed. Heinrich Singer (Paderborn: Schöningh, 1902; Aalen: Scientia, 1963), 428; commenting on C. 26, q. 6. This issue is pursued further in chapter 3.

69 Rufinus, *Summa decretorum*, 428–29.

sacraments could be denied to someone who had not completed a solemn penance except when necessity required administration of those rites.[70] Stephen of Tournai repeated that opinion.[71]

The Ordinary Gloss on the *Decretum* states that a priest can reconcile penitents in the bishop's absence if necessary.[72] The Gloss also distinguishes between public and private reconciliation, as Rufinus had.[73] Dealing with the *De poenitentia*, Johannes Teutonicus doubted the utility of late penance, despite statements that no one is to be denied the sacrament.[74] The Gloss cites an opinion of Huguccio of Pisa on the need for evident signs of penitence.[75] Teutonicus quoted the opinion of Laurentius Hispanus that the truly penitent do not land in Purgatory.[76] This balanced the availability of deathbed penance with the possibility that the dying person might not experience pure penitence.

Theologians, like canonists, addressed the needs of the penitent in danger of death. The *Sentences* of Peter Lombard contain a discussion of confession to a lay person when in danger of death. The Lombard concluded that it was best to confess to a priest, who had the power to bind and loose. However, "if a priest is not available, confession is to be made to a neighbor or a friend."[77] Later, Peter added a discussion of whether anyone could repent at the end. He quoted Augustine concerning those who repent out of fear of dying. It was dangerous to delay penance to the end, in which case he or she was to experience purifying flame, a hint of the idea of Purgatory.[78] The Lombard quoted the *Penitential of Theodore* (actually Halitgar) and Pope Leo I on not imposing excessive penance on those in danger of death. The penance was to be fitting and moderate. Only if the sick person survived was the full penance to be performed.[79]

70 Ibid., 190: "quibus quidem omnia sunt deneganda sacramenta ante peractam penitentiam, nisi necessitas fecerit."

71 Stephen of Tournai, *Die Summa über das Decretum Gratiani*, ed. Johann Friedrich von Schulte (Giessen: Roth, 1891; Aalen: Scientia, 1965), 116.

72 Friedberg 1:1037 (C. 26, q. 6, c. 4). Ordinary Gloss on the *Decretum Gratiani* [hereafter Glo. Ord.] at ibid.: "Nam absente episcopo, sine mandato eius potest reconciliare si necessitas fuseit."

73 Glo. Ord. at C. 26, q. 6, c. 7.

74 Glo. Ord. at *De penitentia*, D. 7, a. c. 1.

75 Glo. Ord. at *De penitentia*, D. 7, c. 2, v. Non tu illa. Huguccio also permitted confession to a lay man by a dying person if no priest was available; see Cheney, *From Becket to Langton*, 156–57.

76 Glo. Ord. at *De penitentia*, D. 7, c. 3.

77 *The Sentences* (trans. Silano), 4:101–2. John of Freiburg said that such a confession could remove venial sins, but not mortal ones, which required absolution by a priest; see Johannes de Friburgo, *Summa confessorum* III, t. 34, q. 43.

78 *The Sentences* (trans. Silano), 4:120–22.

79 Ibid., 4:124–25.

The *Sentences* contained passages from Popes Leo I and Julius I on not denying anyone final penance. However, the next chapter reminded the reader that a bishop should reconcile penitents outside a case of necessity.[80] Someone hurrying to penance but dying before finding a priest was to be buried properly but with relatives and friends making offerings for his or her soul.[81]

A matter only occasionally discussed was confession and communion for those about to be executed. Canon law accepted capital punishment,[82] but the salvation of the souls of the condemned was at stake. As early as the ninth century, *capitula* of the Frankish kings said that those who were to be executed were not to be denied burial if they had made a good confession.[83] Much later, the Council of Vienne (1311–12) ordered that those condemned to death be granted penance if they requested it. Nor was any contrary custom binding. This text appeared in the *Clementines* as canon *Cum secundum*, saying that members of confraternities should try saving the souls of the condemned. Local bishops were expected to enforce the decree.[84] The Ordinary Gloss on the *Clementines* summarizes this canon and adds that the Eucharist too was not to be denied to a condemned person who was penitent.[85]

On the local level, in the thirteenth century Archbishop Boniface of Canterbury denounced those who denied prisoners a chance to confess their sins.[86] In 1397, Jean Gerson wrote a memorandum to the king of France threatening with Hell those who denied the sacraments to the condemned.[87] A 1446 council at Würzburg said that viaticum was not to be denied to the sick or the condemned.[88] Nicholas of Cusa's visitation instructions for the diocese of Brixen included asking if magistrates

80 Ibid., 4:125–26.

81 Ibid., 4:126.

82 Henri Gilles, "Peine de mort et droit canonique," *Cahiers de Fanjeux* 33 (1998): 393–416.

83 MGH *Capitula regum Francorum*, ed. Alfredus Boretius and Victor Krause (Hanover: Hahn, 1890; Hanover: Hahn, 1980), 2:182–83.

84 Friedberg 2:1190 (*Constitutions of Clement V* 5.9.1). Adriano Prosperi, "Consolation of Condemnation: The Debates on Withholding Sacraments from Prisoners," in *The Art of Executing Well: Rituals of Execution in Renaissance Italy*, ed. Nicholas Terpstra (Kirksville, Mo.: Truman State University Press, 2008), 98–117. For a citation by a jurist of the Clementine text, see Gigliola Rondinini Soldi, *Il Tractatus de principibus di Martino Garati da Lodi* (Milan: Cisalpino-La Golardica, 1968), 164.

85 Glo. Ord. at *Constitutions of Clement V* 5.9.1: "Damnatis ad mortem hoc petentibus poenitentia concedi debet, nec valet contraria consuetudo. Secundo locorum ordinarie ad hoc exequendum excitat: ubi, Locorum. hoc dicit. Io. And." The Gloss references the Eucharist at v. Pęnitentiae.

86 *Lyndwood's "Provinciale,"* 146.

87 Gerson, *Oeuvres completes*, 7:341–43.

88 *Concilia Germaniae* 5:355–56.

impeded access to the condemned for administration of penance and the Eucharist.[89] The 1534 synod of Plasencia reproved judges who prevented confession and housel of the condemned. These magistrates were threatened with excommunication *latae sententiae*.[90] Occasionally the Apostolic Penitentiary intervened, requiring authorities to give access to the condemned for sacramental ministry.[91] Martinus Garratus, a fifteenth-century Italian jurist, argued briefly that a prince should permit giving the sacraments to the condemned.[92]

The possibility of sacramental ministry to condemned heretics was more controversial. The inquisitor Nicholas Eymeric said that this should not be permitted. The canonist Felinus Sandeus, writing later, said that the condemned should be permitted confession and communion, but not extreme unction.[93] Executions without spiritual comfort seem to have occurred in some cases of heresy. The burning of relapsed heretics in Bologna in 1299 was resented, in part, because the inquisitors refused one of the condemned absolution and viaticum, which he had requested.[94]

The Carolingian Council of Mainz (847) asked why a person rightly condemned who was hanged after making a full confession and receiving viaticum should not receive Christian burial. Clearly the Council thought a burial service should be performed.[95] Much later, the Franciscan writer John of Erfurt also said that a condemned person who made a pure confession or wished to confess could receive Christian burial.[96]

89 Nicholas of Cusa, *Akten zur Reform des Bistums Brixen*, ed. Heinz Hürten (Heidelberg: Winter, 1960), 31.

90 *Synodicon Hispanum*, ed. Antonio García y García. 13 vols. (Madrid: Biblioteca de Autores Cristianos, 1981–2017), 5:471.

91 *Repertorium poenitentiariae Germanicum*, ed. Ludwig Schmugge et al. (Tübingen: Niemeyer, 1998–2016), 7:1877 (no. 1847) and 9:1605 (no. 1530).

92 Rondinini Soldi, *Il Tractatus de principibus*, 164 (no. 352).

93 Nicholas Eymeric, *Directorium inquisitorum*, ed. Francisco Peña (Rome: Stamperia del Popolo Romano, 1587), 647; Felinus Sandeus, *Commentaria in V libros decretalium* (Basel: Froben, 1567), 3:1098.

94 Janine Larmon Peterson, *Suspect Saints and Holy Heretics: Disputed Sanctity and Communal Identity in Late Medieval Italy* (Ithaca, NY: Cornell University Press, 2019), 202.

95 MGH *Concilia* II, Supplement 2, ed. Wilfried Hartmann (Hanover: Hahn, 1984), 174–75, at 174: "Quibus respondemus: Si omnibus de peccatis suis puram confessionem agentibus et digne penitentibus communio in fine secundum canonicum iussum danda est, cur non eis, qui pro peccatis suis poenam extremam persolvunt?"

96 Johannes de Erfordia, *Die Summa confessorum des Johannes von Erfurt*, ed. Norbert Brieskorn (Frankfurt: Lang, 1980), 2:871: "dampnati pro sceleribus suis, si pure confiteantur vel confiteri desiderant et tales possunt in cimiterio sepeliri et missa pro eis celebrari et oblatio offerri." John added that a judge's permission might be necessary to take the corpse off the gallows but not to bury it.

THE QUALITY AND QUANTITY OF PENANCE

The confessor was to press the sick person to make a full confession, but he was to avoid frightening the penitent into despair. This emphasis on mercy in ministry to the sick had a long history. Thus, the Frankish collection of canons known as the *Vetus Gallica* (ca. 600) gave guidance for ministering to the sick, saying that the priest should comfort them. Priests were to grant penance mercifully to anyone requesting it without "acceptance of person" (*absque persone acceptatione*). Even those negligent persons who repented later (*tardius*) were to be received by the clergy. This collection added an early example of taking the word of those surrounding a sick person, where the priest could not clearly discern the person's desire to repent insofar as he or she was too sick or agitated (*in frenisin*). A sick person might be absolved and receive viaticum, but anyone who survived a serious illness still needed imposition of hands in order to believe themselves absolved (*non se credant absolutus sine manus impositione*). The priest was supposed to refer difficult cases to the bishop except in his absence or "in a case of necessity" (*necessitate cogente*). Truly difficult cases were to be referred to Rome whenever possible. Those who died at sea without the administrations of a priest were to be remembered with prayers and offerings.[97] Earlier penitential writings had recommended that soldiers facing battle confess their sins.[98]

A ninth-century Frankish *capitulum* cites the *Penitential of Theodore* as proof that a quantity of penance (*quantitas penitentiae*) was not to be piled upon the sick. They were to be borne up instead by the prayers and alms of friends. Even if they were dying, a pure confession would relieve them of their sins. Someone who survived a dangerous illness was obliged, however, to perform whatever penance the confessor had imposed. Dying persons were to be sustained with holy oil and refreshed with viaticum in all cases.[99] The 847 Council of Mainz urged that the sick person make a

97 Hubert Mordek, *Kirchenrecht und Reform im Frankreich: Die Collectio vetus gallica, die älteste systematische Kanonssamlung des Fränkischen Gallen, Studien und Edition* (Berlin: de Gruyter, 1975), 507–613.

98 Rob Means, *Penance in Medieval Europe 600–1200* (Cambridge: Cambridge University Press, 2014), 105.

99 MGH *Capitula regum Francorum*, 2:182: "Ab infirmis in mortis periculo positis per presbiteros pura inquirenda est confessio peccatorum, non tamen est illis imponenda quantitas penitentiae, sed innotescenda, et cum amicorum orationibus et elimosinarum studiis pondus penitentiae sublevandum, ut, si forte migraverint, ne obligati excommunicatione alieni ex consortio venie fiant; a quo periculo si divinitus erepti convaluerint, penitentiae modum a suo confessore impositum diligenter observant. Et ideo secundum canonicam auctoritatem, ne illis ianua pietatis clausa videatur, orationibus et consolationibus

pure confession, repeating what the *capitularia* said about not imposing heavy penances and depending instead on the prayers and alms of others.[100] The early ninth-century statutes of Liège also provided for believing those gathered at the sickbed regarding the dying person's desire for confession if that person had become mute (*iam privatus fuerit officio loquendi*). The priest was instructed to proceed with the penitential rite in such a case.[101]

Gratian's *Decretum* cites Theodore as evidence that heavy penances were not to be heaped on persons in danger of death. They were to be supported by the prayers and alms of friends, even if they were dying. Dying persons also were to be sustained with holy oil and viaticum. Someone who survived a dangerous illness was obligated to perform whatever penance the priest had imposed. All of this required the confessor to use some judgment in the administration of this healing sacrament.[102] The canonist Hostiensis incorporated into his general thoughts about the pastoral labors of confessors that they should regard the infirmity or debility of a dangerously-ill penitent.[103]

Thomas of Chobham, in his manual for confessors, thought that the priest should determine whether a patient rendered mute was penitent. He concluded that any past wish for final penance sufficed for absolution.[104] Raymond of Peñafort cited Theodore in his *Summa* as evidence that a dying person needed a pure confession but not a heavy penance. Dying persons were to be supported by others' prayers and alms to ease the penalties for sin.[105] Raymond cited "Pope Julius" as saying that a priest who let parishioners die without penance "will be guilty of their souls" (*reus erit animarum*).[106] He added that this was not true when the priest could not

ecclesiasticis sacra cum unctione olei animati secundum statuta sanctorum patrum communion viatici reficiantur." This text does not appear as Theodore's in *Medieval Handbooks of Penance*.

100 MGH *Concilia* II, Supplement 2, 173–74. The same canon recorded the need for viaticum and anointing.

101 MGH *Capitula regum Francorum*, 1:244.

102 Friedberg 1:1041 (C. 26, q. 7, c. 1): "sacra unctione olei inuncti, secundum statuta sanctorum Patrum conmunione uiatici reficiantur."

103 Hostiensis, *Summa aurea*, 1836.

104 *Thomae de Chobham Summa confessorum*, ed. F. Broomfield (Louvain: Nauwelaerts, 1968), 136.

105 Raimundus de Pennaforte, *Summa de poenitentia*, 486B: "tenenda est forma super hoc a Theodoro definita: videlibet, ab infirmis in periculo mortis positis pura est confessio peccatorum inquirenda; non tamen illis imponenda est quantitas paenitentiae, sed innotescenda, & cum amicorum orationibus, & eleemosynarum studijs pondus paenitentiae subleuandum." Raymond continued that a surviving person had to complete the penance.

106 Ibid.

be present. In his absence, contrition sufficed for salvation.[107] If the priest was asked to go to the sickbed but found the patient mute, mindless, or agitated, he could still absolve the person and put communion into his or her mouth, if it could be done safely. The priest was allowed to accept the testimony of those gathered by the sickbed that the person wanted to confess.[108] William of Rennes, in his gloss on Raymond's *Summa*, added that viaticum was not to be denied to the dying.[109]

John of Freiburg, updating Raymond's text, considered true penance at the end of life to be difficult but possible. Many things might impede this, but they could not absolutely prevent it.[110] John's *Summa* maintained the doctrine of canon law that any priest could absolve a dying person of all sins.[111] John said that "the gate of mercy" (*ianua pietatis*) was not to be closed to the dying. They were to be given all consolations, including viaticum and anointing.[112] John said, following theological opinion, that the priest should concentrate on internal penance, which was possible for the sick, not on exterior penance, which might not be possible. However, if the sick person recovered, an external penance should be performed.[113]

John of Freiburg also offered a practical reason for accepting any sign of penance from a dying person, even one mad or mute. Otherwise that person might be taken for one who died impenitent and thus unworthy of Christian burial.[114] He also followed Raymond of Peñafort, saying that the priest, going to the sickbed but finding the patient mute, mindless, or agitated, still should absolve and put communion into his or her mouth, if it could be done safely. The known intent of the sick person or the witness

107 Ibid.: "si non potuit habere cui confiteretur ipse moriens, & non stetit per eum, & habuit contritionem, salus erit."

108 Raimundus de Pennaforte, *Summa de poenitentia*, 486B–487A: "Item si infirmus petijt sacerdotem, & iterum, dum veniret, obmutuit, vel factus est amens, vel phreneticus, sacerdos veniens, siue ad nutum infirmi, siue ad testimonium illorum, qui audierunt ipsum paenitentiam petentem, vel sacerdotem, debet ei quicquid potest humanitatis impendere, absoluendo, reconciliando, &, si potest fieri sine periculo, Eucharistiam ori eius infundendo." William of Rennes too accepted the evidence of bystanders; see 487A, at *Qui recedunt*.

109 Raimundus de Pennaforte, *Summa de poenitentia*, 487A, at *Si quis de corpore*.

110 Johannes de Friburgo, *Summa confessorum* III, t. 34, q. 159: "Hoc tamen quamuis sit possibile tamen est valde difficile . . . Sed quoniam multa sunt que impediunt et languentem retrahunt periculosissimum est interitu vicinum ad mortem protrahere penitentie remedium. Sed magnum est cui deus tunc inspirit si quis est veram penitentiam assecutus de pe. di. v. I."

111 Ibid., q. 160: "Nam in articulo mortis omnibus sacerdotibus in omnes homines et de omnibus peccatis et sententiis permittitur absolutio a iure vide eo. ti. q. xxix. Quid si subditis. ver. Septimo."

112 Ibid., q. 161.

113 Ibid., qq. 161–62.

114 Ibid., I, t. 16, q. 3: "Item prohibentur omnes qui in peccato mortali decedent." John added a prohibition of burying suicides in consecrated ground.

of bystanders sufficed as evidence of penance, allowing absolution and reconciliation.[115] Signs of penance also might be indicated by the sick person raising hands or beating the breast without words.[116] Natural death did not remove the punishment for sins which was to be expurgated in Purgatory; but a good death, even one suffered justly, might alleviate those pains. It might even remove them under certain circumstances, if the dying person showed patience and was contrite.[117]

The *Summa Pisanella* of Bartholomaeus de Sancto Concordio reorganized John of Freiburg's *Summa* into an alphabetical compendium. Bartholomaeus addressed the question regarding whether one could repent at the end of life. He answered that Christians had free will and could repent. Their last opportunity was at the end of life.[118] Nicholas of Osimo, a fifteenth-century Franciscan, added to the *Pisanella* that it was rare for someone to repent from charity at the last moment.[119] However, both Bartholomaeus and Nicholas believed that "any priest can absolve" (*quilibet sacerdos potest absoluere*) a person in danger of death.[120] The *Summa Pisanella* underlined the possibility that unexpiated sins required punishment in Purgatory. Natural death was the punishment of original sin, but other sins committed by the faithful in life needed expiation.[121] Patiently bearing final affliction might diminish these pains. There might even be liberation of the dying from such punishment, because of patience and contrition.[122] Nicholas added mention of the contribution friends might

115 Ibid., III, t. 34, q. 161: "Item si infirmus petijt sacerdotem et iterum dum venire obmutuit vel factus est amens vel frententicus sacerdos veniens ad eum sive ad nutum infirmi siue ad testium illorum audierunt ipsam penitentiam petentem vel sacerdotem debet ei quicquid potest humanitatis impendere absoluendo et reconciliando et si potest sine periculo eucharistiam ori eius infundendo." This was repeated by Antoninus of Florence; see *Sancti Antonini archiepiscopi Florentini ordinis Praedicatorum summa theologica* (Graz: Akamademische Druck- und Verlagsanstalt, 1957), 1740 (3:450).

116 Johannes de Friburgo, *Summa confessorum* III, t. 34, q. 161.

117 Ibid., q. 162: "sed per mortem illatam bene potest purgari vnde si aliquis mortem illatam libenter sustineat etiam si pro criminibus sit illata valet ad diminutionem pene et ad liberationem etiam a tota pena secundum quanitatem culpe et patientie et contritionis etc." John also considered the utility of indulgences for those in Purgatory; see ibid., q. 191.

118 Nicholas of Osimo, *Supplementum Summae Pisanellae*, v. Penitentia i: "Tempus penitentie est vsque ad vltimum articulum vite."

119 Ibid., "A . . . rarum est quod ex caritate quis in extremis positis peniteat. B."

120 Ibid.

121 Ibid., v. Penitentia ii: "Mors naturalis est pena consequens originale peccatum."

122 Ibid.: "Vnde si aliquis mortem illatam pacienter sustineat. Etiam si pro alijs criminibus sit illata. Valet ad diminutionem pene. et ad liberationem etiam a pota pena secundum quantitatem culpe et pacientie et contritionis."

make to such a person's salvation through "prayers and the pursuit of alms" (*orationibus et elimosinarum studijs*).[123]

The Franciscan Astesanus de Ast noted the times at which individuals should confess. The second on his list was when that person was in imminent peril of death.[124] A priest was obligated to hear the confessions of those who were gravely ill or in danger of death.[125] Astesanus considered whether a person in need of confessing might have recourse to a lay person if no priest was available. The most he would concede, as a lay person could not absolve, was that a person might be worthy of mercy for wishing the presence of a priest.[126] Not even in a case of necessity might confession be made to a heretic or schismatic, who lacked the power of the keys and could not absolve.[127] Looking at the confessions of those in danger of dying, Astesanus said not to impose penances which would have been given to a healthy person, but the dying person should be informed what the "quantity and quality" of that penance would have been. Astesanus added a formula of absolution conveying that information, including a provision that a person who recovered still had to perform the penance.[128] No penance was to be imposed which could not ever be performed.[129] If the person died, the prayers and alms of friends were supposed to aid the soul. Astesanus added that the person was to be anointed and refreshed with viaticum before death.[130]

William of Pagula described love of God and love of neighbor as the two wings "by means of which the dying person could "rise to the heavens" (*quibus euoletur ad celos*).[131] William said that a sick person might recover and be obliged to do a full penance. However, a dying Christian was faced

123 Ibid., v. Penitentia i.

124 Astesanus de Ast, *Summa de casibus conscientiae* V, t. 11: "Secundus est ratione periculi. vt quando est in mortali. et imminente periculo mortis."

125 Ibid., t. 14: "quando sunt in infirmitate graui constitute: vel imminent eis aliquod periculum mortis."

126 Ibid., t. 13: "vt si desit presbiter confieatur homo proximo: et si ille potestatem absoluendi non habeat sit tamen dignus misericordia ex desiderio sacerdotis . . . hoc est argumentum quod laycus non potest absoluere in necessitate."

127 Ibid., t. 14: "Respondeo quod non. quia nullus habet claues ecclesie nisi sit catholicus."

128 Ibid.: "Infirmo tamen non est penitentia iniungenda. sed innotescenda quantitas et qualitas penitentie. Dicendo sic Si sanus esses talem penitentiam agere deberes. sed quia infirmus es non iniungo tibi eam. Sed si decesseris tantum pro anima tua facias pro hac pena dari: et si conualueris eam age."

129 Ibid.: "Nullus autem ad id obligari debet: quod facere non potest."

130 Ibid.: "oleo ante mortem vngendus. et sacro viatico reficendus."

131 William of Pagula, *Oculus sacerdotis*, fol. 19ra–b.

with time spent in Purgatory, especially if unable to do even a simple penance. This made moving the patient to penitence the more urgent.[132]

Andreas Escobar said the confessor should be cautious with the sick. Instead of imposing a penance, he was to "show" the penance to the patient. Andreas dictated a form of words for doing this, which says that a certain penance was to be performed if the person recovered.[133]

Some of these opinions entered into diocesan manuals. Thus, the manual for Minden told priests not to impose a penance on the dying unless it was one quickly done and which the person wished to do. The purpose was consolation, not fright.[134] The same text urged caution in dealing with ecclesiastical censures, restoring the fallen to church unity (*restituendo eum unitati sancta matris ecclesie*).[135] The same text wanted the excommunicated cautioned before witnesses to promise amendment of life and to express willingness to do penance if he or she survived.[136]

HOW TO HEAR THE CONFESSIONS OF THE SICK

Certain surviving texts suggest that the priest was to make a single visit to the sick person, hearing confession, administering communion, and anointing. For example, the 1435 Council of Strasbourg dictated that the same priest was to administer both viaticum and unction.[137] The 1447 Council of Eichstadt declared that any instruction about carrying viaticum included the holy oils.[138] However, a late thirteenth-century council at

132 Ibid., fol. 42rb–va: "Notandum est eciam quod si sacerdos audierit confessionem alicuius infirmi constituti in periculo mortis non debet sibi inungere aliquam penitentiam. Sed audita confessione illus debet sibi dicere. Tantam penitentiam deberes facere si uiueres. Sed quia nunc vadis ad forum. s. ad purgatorium non inungo tibi aliquam penitentiam. Quia dominus a te recipiet / quantam emendacionem voluerit. et quam diu voluerit. Et si superuixeris fili mi redibis ad me et iniungam tibi penitentiam." William added elsewhere advice to the sick person about ascending to the temple with a soul fittingly arrayed (*ornatus*); see ibid., fol. 20rb. The Scottish statutes of 1225 took a different tack, wanting the priest, if the patient desired to make a will, to urge remembering the needs of the diocesan cathedral; see Mansi 22:1143.

133 Andreas Escobar, *Lumen confessorum*, fol. 9rb: "Et si confitens uit infirmus tunc sit cautus confessor quod non det sibi penitentiam sed ostendat eam sibi xxvi. q. i. per totum et ii. q. vii. In Summa sic dicendo Si esses sanus talem penitentiam debes habere pro peccatis tuis sed quia est infirmus non iniungo tibi eam sed quando conualeris postea agis eam."

134 *Agenda Mindenensis dioecesis* (Leipzig: Lotter, 1522), fol. xvi[r]: "Notandum: quod infirmo de cuius morte timetur nulla penitentia est imponenda: nisi talis fuerit penitentia quam statim posset et uelit implore. Sed innotescenda est sibi per modum consolationis: et non horroris."

135 Ibid., fol. xvi[v].

136 Ibid., fol. xvi[r–v]. The text also obligated the person's goods in case of his or her decease.

137 *Concilia Germaniae* 5:236.

138 Ibid., 5:367.

Münster wanted the priest, if possible, to visit the person first without the Eucharist to hear his or her confession. Only then was he to return to the church, vest properly, and return with viaticum.[139] The dioceses of Cambrai and Liège, a few years later, also recommended a two-step process, a visit for confession and one for communion.[140] A statute of Eichstat (1447) suggested that the priest should be carrying viaticum or oil of the sick on returning to a bedridden person (*decumbentem*).[141] The manual for Astorga in Spain said that the priest was to visit the sick person and determine if he or she had confessed. If not, the sick person was to be exhorted to do so.[142] As will be noted in the later chapters, some manuals also embedded mention of confession in instructions for communion of the sick or extreme unction.

William of Pagula gave thought to sickbed confessions. The priest, according to William, was especially to exhort a dying person to prepare for the last journey.[143] Most of this exhortation came from a Pseudo-Augustine text and was concerned with penance. A true confession was supposed to be brought forth by such a discourse.[144] The sick person also was exhorted to confess fully but accurately, without admitting sins never committed.[145]

In greater detail, the *Summa* of Antoninus of Florence provided a discussion of *De poenitentibus in extremis*. The archbishop said anyone should always be ready to confess, but especially when ill. He described illness as "the messenger of death."[146] In some cases, the penitent could not perform

139 Ibid., 3:647–48: "Item praecipimus, ut cum aliquis infirmus communicare voluerit, quod Sacerdos, si commode fieri potest, prius visitet sine corpore Domini, & diligenter confessionem infirmi audiat, & postea redeat ad Ecclesiam allaturus corpus Domini, & communicaturus infirmum. Sacerdos autem eat, dicendo septem Psalmos, & si via fuerit longior, legat Lytaniam & alias orationes. Incedat Sacerdos ad communicandum infirmum cum campanula, si infirmus est extra villam, ubi est Ecclesia parochialis: si vero infirmus est in villa, ubi Parochia sita est. Sacerdos incedat ad infirmum cum campana, & lucerna praecedente."

140 *Les statuts synodaux Français du XIIIe siècle*, ed. Odette Pontal and Joseph Avril (Paris, 1971–2001), 4:41–42; Mansi 24:898; *Concilia Germaniae* 3:691.

141 *Concilia Germaniae* 5:367: "cum autem Sacerdos Eucharistiam, vel Oleum infirmorum ad decumbentem deportaverit." A detailed description of the priest's vestments, as well as the light and bell, follows

142 *Manuale secundum consuetudinem Astoricensis ecclesie* (Leon, 1526): "ante omnia visited illum sciatque eum bene atque legitime confessum: et ita non est exhortet ad penitentiam et confessionem."

143 William of Pagula, *Oculus sacerdotis*, fol. 18vb: "Fili amantissime, 'uiam uniuerse carnis ingredi festinas, quo uisurus es parentes tuous patriarchas, propheta Apostolos martires et sanctos. Et ne ad tanti itineris deficias in uia, subsidium grande uiaticum est tibi necessarium.'"

144 See Pseudo-Augustine, *De visitatione infirmorum*, c. 6 (PL 40:1151).

145 William of Pagula, *Oculus sacerdotis*, fol. 19vb–20rb.

146 Antoninus of Florence, *Summa theologica*, 3:449: "praecipue tamen infirmus magis se disponere debet, quia infirmitas est nuntius mortis."

an exterior penance, and so none should be imposed. Instead, the priest was to concentrate on interior penance.[147] The priest was to focus on conveying God's mercy, not arousing horror by concentrating on the threat of postmortem punishment.[148] Antoninus provided a formula for telling the patient what the penance would have been "if you were healthy" (*si esses sanus*).[149]

Manuals for diocesan priests only occasionally offered basic instructions for hearing the confessions of the sick. Thus, the manual for Naples, derived from the Roman Use, moved directly from the arrival of the priest to penance. Under the rubric, "The priest, having heard confession, should say this prayer to absolve" (*Facta confessione sacerdos absoluere dicat hanc orationem*), the focus was not on confession but absolution. It also prescribed a prayer of absolution: "Lord Jesus Christ, who said to the apostles, Whatever you bind on earth" (*Dominus ihesus Christus qui dixit apostolis, Quecunque ligaueris super terram*).[150] The manual for the see of Brataslava had the priest ask the sick person whether he or she desired penance, to which he or she was to reply, *Desidero*. The priest was to hear the patient's sins, giving a warning, after granting absolution, that survival meant making another confession and accepting penance.[151]

On the Iberian peninsula, instructions to priests in the fifteenth and sixteenth centuries offer varying evidence regarding the practice of penance at the sickbed. The manual for Toledo omitted any preliminaries and began with the sacrament of penance.[152] Much more detailed instructions can be found in the Salamanca manual. That text required the priest to go quickly (*cito*) to the sick person, greet the household, and then order everyone to leave the sick room. Then he was to urge the sick person

147 Ibid.: "quum in tali statu infirmus non possit facere poenitentiam exteriorem, sed interiorem; ideo exterior poenitentia tunc non est ei imponenda, quia non posset facere, sed innotescenda, ut per hoc provocetur ad interiorem poenitentiam." Antoninus seems not to have had Jean Gerson's emphasis on contrition; see D. Catherine Brown, *Pastor and Laity in the Theology of Jean Gerson* (Cambridge: Cambridge University Press, 1987).

148 Antoninus, *Summa theologica*, 3:449.

149 Ibid.

150 *Manuale Romano-Neapolitanum*, fol. xiii^{r-v}: "Deinde sacerdos tradens infirmo eucharistiam dicat: Accipite frater vel soror viaticum corpus domini nostri iesu christi te custodiat ab hoste maligno et perducat te ad vitam eternam. Amen." The instructions for washing fingers with wine and water follow the post-communion prayer: "Domine sancte pater omnipotens eterne deus te fideliter deprecamur."

151 *Liber agendarum rubrice dioecesis Wratislaviensis emendatus* (Breslau: J. P., 1510), fol. x^{r}: "Finita confessione absoluat eum ponendo sibi pro penitentia si conualescat ut redeat et iterato confiteatur: et penitentia accipiat."

152 *Manuale seu baptisterium ad vsum alme ecclesie Toletane* (Toledo, 1484), fol. e [1]^{r}: "primeramente lo deue oyr de penitencia." The manual added a requirement that the priest help the sick person make a will.

mildly (*blande*) to trust God and accept the divine scourge which purged and chastised sinners.[153] The sickbed interview could include teaching the patient to affirm the faith. Once the person was confirmed in faith, he or she was to be blessed.[154] Then the priest was to make the sign of the cross, followed by hearing a general confession (*Et dicat confessionem generalem cum eo*).[155] The confessor was to reconcile the penitent, warning that recovery of health would require doing penance, conforming to the penitential canons and obeying the commandments of the Church (*quod obediet mandatis ecclesie*).[156] The manual permitted encouraging the penitent not to be ashamed of confessing sins: "Brother, do not blush to confess your sins" (*Frater noli erubescere peccata tua confiteri*).[157]

In such a dangerous situation, with the penitent *in extremis*, the priest was able to absolve any crime or sin "according to the Church's form."[158] No penance was to be imposed unless the sick person recovered, but this formula was to be employed in giving absolution: "If you were well, you should do such a penance for this and that thing; but, because you are sick, I do not enjoin it on you" (*Si sanus esses: talem penitentiam agere deberes pro tali et tali re. sed quia infirmus es eam tibi non iniungo*).[159] The sick person was to be urged to trust in divine mercy. In case of survival, the sick person was to be penitent and give alms.[160] After absolution, viaticum and extreme unction were to be administered. The bystanders were to be urged to help

153 *Manuale secundum consuetudinem alme ecclesie Salamanticense* (Madrid, 1532), fol. xxxi^{v}–xxxii^{r}: "Est post aliquod sermones: modico interuallo facto: sacerdos omnes iubeat extra cubiculum exire. Et proprius accedens ad lectum in quo infirmus decumbit: eum blande leniterque alloquatur: vt omnem spem suam in deo ponat: vt flagellum dei patienter ferat: vt hoc ad purgationem et castigationem suam prouenire concedat: vt peccata sua confiteatur."

154 Ibid., fol. xxxii^{r}.

155 Ibid. The priest could ask about the seven vices; see fol. xxxii^{v}.

156 Ibid., fol. xxxii^{r}.

157 Ibid., fol. xxxii^{r-v}.

158 Ibid., fol. xxxiii^{r}: "quod dum infirmus agit in extremis: de quocunque crimine vel peccato per presbyterum suum iuxta formam ecclesie debet et potest absolui."

159 Ibid.

160 *Manuale secundum consuetudinem alme ecclesie Salamanticensis* (Salamanca, 1532): "Cum sacerdos audierit aliquem infirmari in sua plebe: vel vocatus fuerit ad infirmum: non moram faciat: sed cito ad eum pergat. Et ingressus domum dicat. Pax huic domui etc., vt coram videbis. Et post aliquos sermones: modico interuallo facto: sacerdos omnes iubeat extra cubiculum exire. Et proprius accedens ad lectum in quo infirmus decumbit: eum blande leniterque alloquatur: vt omnem spem suam in deo ponat: vt flagellum dei patienter ferat: vt hoc ad purgationem et castigationem suam prouenire concedat: vt peccata sua confiteatur: vt emendationem promittat: vt si deus vitam ei concesserit: penitentiam pro culpis commissis spondeat: et substantiam suam dum adhuc sensus et ratio viget disponat: vt peccata sua elemosinis redimat: his qui in se peccauerunt indulgeat: Et vt a dei misericordia numquam desperet doceat."

the dying person with prayers and alms (*amicorum orationibus et elemosinis*).[161] The manual for Cuenca gave similar instructions.[162]

The Urgell manual had the priest address the sick person in the vernacular, saying God had inflicted physical ailments; but that he, on God's behalf, brought spiritual medicine.[163] The priest could ask the patient if he or she desired to confess something.[164] The book offered instructions for a general confession and a vernacular version of the *Confiteor*. After an injunction to the sick person to think on the passion of Christ came absolution and the showing of a crucifix. Next came a detailed profession of faith in the form of interrogatories with affirmative replies. Only afterward was the sick person to receive viaticum.[165]

PRACTICAL PROBLEMS

The clergy had to deal with practical problems arising from the confessions of the sick. This might include the absence of a priest or the priest being faced with sins usually reserved to higher authority.[166] Thus, Lyndwood's *Provinciale* included a text by Archbishop Edmund, which said that deacons could not "give penance" to the dying unless no priest was present.[167] The 1287 statutes of Exeter said that penitents guilty of offenses which were absolved only by a bishop should be sent to him. However, a simple priest could absolve such a person who was *in articulo mortis*.[168] A 1446 council of Würzburg cited a decree of Pope Boniface VIII permitting absolution of the gravest offenses of dying persons when obstacles prevented their receiving release by higher authority.[169] Likewise, the statutes

161 *Manuale Salamanticensis*, fol. xxxiii^{v}.

162 *Manipulus siue manuale vel potius practica ministrandi sacramenta sanctae matris ecclesie Conchensis* (Cuenca: Christophori Gallici, 1528), fol. l ii^{v}.

163 *Ordinarium sacramentorum benedictionum et aliarum rerum*, fol. cxii^{v}: "Lo senyor de tot lo mondo quius havisitat per militia corporal arave a visitat vos per medicina spiritual."

164 Ibid.: "Recordan vos de alguna cosa que vullau dire in confessio."

165 Ibid., fol. cxii^{v}–cxiv^{v}.

166 Some guides for confessors included lists of censures reserved to bishops; e.g., Antoninus of Florence, *Confessionale "Defecerunt,"* University of Pennsylvania Ms. Codex 68, fol. 390v–396v. Some other censures were reserved to the pope; see fol. 387r–390v.

167 *Lyndwood's "Provinciale,"* 147.

168 *Councils & Synods* II, pt. 2, 1075–76: "Similiter in casibus in quibus mittendi sunt ad episcopum penitentes, in articulo mortis a sacerdote simplici absoluantur."

169 *Concilia Germaniae* 5:348.

of Sisteron said that a priest could absolve a dying person of all censures and sins.[170]

Another problem was priests from outside a parish ministering to the sick. A 1461 statute of Brno said this required a license from the local bishop, his vicar, or the parish priest, except in a case of necessity, which "knows no law"; then a sick person could not be denied penance or baptism.[171] The 1413 statutes of Olomuc ignored the exception for necessity when trying to prevent Franciscans and Dominicans hearing confessions without proper licensing by a bishop. The Olomuc decree based this prohibition on the Lateran canon *Omnes utriusque sexus*, which required annual confession to one's "proper priest."[172]

William of Pagula dealt with issues which might arise from the presence of an "alien" priest at the sickbed. Matters were simplest if the confessor was one's proper priest. However, an "alien" priest, perhaps a friar or a domestic chaplain, if he were the only confessor available, was to urge seeing one's own priest for penance and absolution in case of recovery from illness.[173] In addition, either the penitent or those nearest to him or her might substitute prayers and alms for the assigned penance.[174] William ended this discussion with advice that the sick person be given the Eucharist if he or she could receive it safely.[175]

Nicholas of Osimo, expanding the *Summa Pisanella*, addressed this issue. Looking at cases in which an individual might not be able to confess to his or her "proper" priest, the friar made room for bishops authorizing some other priest to serve. However, Nicholas said that an "alien" priest not authorized by the bishop could still hear confessions in a case of

170 *Statuts synodaux* 2:220. Jean Gerson expressed a similar opinion; see his *Oeuvres Compeletes*, 9:649: "excipitur mortis articulus."

171 *Synody a statuta Olomoucké* (ed. Krafl), 221: "nec eciam parrochianum alterius parrochie sine petita licencia nostra et obtenta aut nostri officialis aut sui propria sacerdotes, qui super eum obtinuit, curam animarum ecclesiasticis sacramentis audeat procurare, nisi necessitas ingruet, que legem non habet, tunc sacramenta penitencie et baptismi non sunt deneganda."

172 Ibid., 182–83. On the efforts of Popes Boniface VIII and Clement V to resolve disputes between friars and seculars, see Thomas M. Izbicki, "The Problem of Canonical Portion in the Later Middle Ages: The Application of *Super cathedram*," in *Proceedings of the Seventh International Congress of Medieval Canon Law, Cambridge, 23–27 July 1984*, ed. Peter Linehan (Vatican City: Biblioteca Apostolica Vaticana, 1988), 459–73.

173 William of Pagula, *Oculus sacerdotis*, fol. 42va. For issues involving the hearing of confessions, see Decima L. Douie, *The Conflict between the Seculars and the Mendicants at the University of Paris in the Thirteenth Century* (London: Blackfriars, 1964).

174 William of Pagula, *Oculus sacerdotis*, fol. 42va. William drew on the Hostiensis for this answer; see *Summa aurea*, 1830–31.

175 *Oculus sacerdotis*, fol. 42va: "Et si potest fieri sine periculo eukaristiam ori eius infundet."

necessity, when someone was in danger of death.[176] Nicholas added that a messenger or letter could be sent to the bishop requesting a license (*licentiam postulare*) to absolve.[177] When a priest was lacking, Nicholas permitted confession to a lay person, not of necessity or a precept but—according to the *Pisanella*—as a matter of counsel. Only priests had received the power to bind and loose.[178]

An additional issue was the possibility that a sick person might have found confession to the parish priest very difficult or even impossible. In such a case, a privilege from the Apostolic Penitentiary might be acquired, permitting complete confession to the patient's chosen priest when he or she was *in articulo mortis*.[179] Likewise, the Penitentiary occasionally gave indulgences which were applied to the recipient on his or her deathbed, in contemplation of the purgatorial pains to be endured.[180] Antoninus of Florence reminded priests to apply any such indulgence to a dying person.[181]

The manual of the diocese of Calahorra gave instructions for applying an indulgence following confession and absolution. The form to be used also covered absolution of excommunication or interdict inflicted on anyone, as well as irregularity or suspension incurred by clergy.[182] The Cartagena manual too provided a formula for applying an indulgence during sickbed rites.[183] It also provided a brief absolution to use when there was fear that a sick person might die before a full absolution could be offered. That text also allowed a bystander to speak for anyone who had lost the power of speech.[184]

176 Nicholas of Osimo, *Supplementum Summae Pisanellae*, v. Confessio iii: "in casibus in quibus potest confiteri alteri quam proprio sacerdoti non possunt audire confessiones illi sacerdotes quibus non est data potestas ab episcopo." Except "articulo necessitatis . . . A. Ibi dicitur de necessitate periculi mortis."

177 Ibid.

178 Ibid.: "A. Et ratio potest esse. quia solis sacerdotibus concessa est potestas ligandi atque soluendi. de pe. di. i. verbum dei. B. Et licet laico confiterri non de precepto est tamen de consilio." The *Pisanella* tried to confine confession to a lay person to venial sins.

179 *Documents on the Papal Plenary Indulgences 1300–1517 Preached in the Regnum Teutonicum*, ed. Stuart Jenks (Leiden: Brill, 2018), 17–18 and 30–31.

180 See Salonen and Schmugge, *A Sip from the "Well of Grace,"* and *Supplications from England and Wales* (ed. Clark and Zutshi), 2:163n78.

181 Antoninus of Florence, *Confessionale "Defecerunt,"* fol. xcvi^{va}–xcvii^{va}, *De infirmis*.

182 *Manuale secundum consuetudinem Calagurritanensis* et Calceatensis ecclesiarum, fol. lviii^{v}–lx^{v}; *Ordinarium manuale de ministratione sacramentorum secundum consuetudinem ecclesię Carthaginensis* (Granada, 1545), fol. lxxxi^{r}.

183 *Ordinarium manuale de ministratione sacramentorum secundum consuetudinem ecclesię Carthaginensis*, fol. lxxx^{v}–lxxxi^{r} and ci$^{r–v}$.

184 Ibid., fol. lxxxi^{r}: "Sequitur breuis modus absoluendi infirmum quando timetur de morte / antequam absoluatur. Primo dicat infirmus: vel alius pro eo si amiserit loquelam. Yo peccador me confesso . . . Quo facto dicat sacerdoa. Misereatur tui omnipotens deus."

An important challenge which might arise during visit a sickbed was finding the parishioner delirious or *in extremis*. A question about the definition of *in extremis* was referred to Pope Gregory IX in 1234 by the Franciscan minister and Dominican prior assigned to the Christian enclave in Muslim Tunis. Could friars, who were permitted to absolve "in case of necessity," absolve someone afflicted with a fever or infection? The pope's reply, relayed by Raymond of Peñafort, said that this could be done when death was "feared or can be feared."[185]

Astesanus de Ast faced the problem of a priest finding the sick person mute, mindless, or frantic. He privileged that person's request for the sacrament or the evidence of those who heard the request for penance and the presence of a priest. That allowed for absolution and reconciliation of the sick person, followed, if possible, by pouring the Eucharist into his or her mouth.[186] The person who died showing signs of contrition (*cum certis signis contritionis*) before the priest arrived was to be treated as having been absolved.[187]

Like others before him, Antoninus said that a priest who was asked to hear a sick person's confession and, when he arrived at the sickbed, found the person mute, agitated, or mindless, should act mercifully, believing those who had heard the request for penance. He was to offer absolution and, if possible, the Eucharist. If that person survived, he or she was to be warned by the witnesses to do a fitting penance.[188] For any persons who had died showing sure signs of penance before a priest came, postmortem absolution "by the Church" was recognized on account of evident

185 John Tolan, "Ramon de Penyafort's *Responses to Questions concerning Relations between Christians and Saracens*," in *Convivencia and Medieval Spain: Essays in Honor of Thomas F. Glick*, ed. Mark T. Abate (Cham: Palgrave Macmillan, 2019), 159–92, at 163, 181, 191: "Respondemus: ubi timetur uel timeri potest periculum mortis."

186 Astesanus de Ast, *Summa de casibus conscientiae* V, t. 14: "Quid si eger petat presbiterum et interim dum venit obmutescat. vel fiat amens vel freneticus. Respondeo. presbiter veniens vel ad nutum infirmi, vel ad testimonium eorum: qui audierunt ipsum petere penitentiam. vel presbiterum: debet ei quicquid potest humanitatis impendere. absoluendo. reconciliando. Et si fieri potest sine periculo ori eius eucharistiam infundendo." Astesanus added that the patient who survived was warned by those witnesses to follow the statutes for penances.

187 Ibid.

188 Antoninus of Florence, *Summa theologica*, 3:450: "Et nota, quod si infirmo petenti sacerdotem, interim eum venire, obmutuit, vel effectus phreneticus vel amens, sacerdos adveniens sive ad nutum infirmi sive ad testimonium illorum, qui audierunt eum poenitentiam petentem, vel sacerdotem, debet ei impendere quicquid potest humanitatis absolvendo, reconciliando: &, si sine periculo fieri potest, ei eucharistiam praebendo: & si supervixerit, admoneatur a praedictis testibus suae petitioni satisfactum, & subdatur statutis poenitentiae legibus."

contrition.[189] Antoninus concluded this discussion saying anyone could repent at the very end but that anyone who died without "perfecting" (*perfecit*) the necessary penance would endure it in Purgatory (*in purgatorio sustinebit*).[190]

The widely circulated *Manipulus curatorum* said that the confession of an ailing sinner was to be heard before giving communion. The priest could absolve a dying excommunicate. If the person was found incapable of speech, any sign of repentance could be accepted toward absolution.[191]

Many of the issues of granting penance and absolution to the sick came together in the *Confessionale "Defecerunt"* by Antoninus of Florence, in which he provided a chapter "Concerning the Sick" (*De infirmis*).[192] The archbishop allowed for the possibility that any priest might act without special permission "when there is danger in delay" (*cum periculum est in mora*). Nor was the priest to depend entirely on medical advice. Antoninus noted that danger of death was not always evident, and "frequently men happen to die from that illness" (*frequenter contingit homines mori ex illa infirmitate*) while physicians doubted the danger. In his *Confessionale "Defecerunt"* he provided a formula for absolving *in articulo mortis* which applied any papal indulgence to a dying person. These grants must have provided some comfort to sensitive souls *in extremis*.[193]

A person who had lived well and received the sacraments could be absolved, with heirs or kin making provision for his or her soul. Someone who had led a bad life could be absolved if he or she had shown signs of penance. If not mute or mad, such a person needed to make a pure confession, covering the main points and being contrite in the face of death. A person not *in extremis* should be led to make a general confession covering his or her entire life. If an excommunicated person survived such an illness, absolution was to be sought from the appropriate authority, probably the bishop. A public usurer was not to be permitted absolution without restitution of ill-gotten gains. After absolution had been given, the Eucharist

189 Ibid.: "& si tales decedant contriti, vel cum certis signis contritionis, ut dictum est, & post mortem absolvuntur ab ecclesia, idest absolutos fuisse in contritione obstenduntur." Antoninus added Pope Julius's warning that a priest who let persons die without penance was "guilty of their souls" (*reus erit animrarum*).

190 Ibid., 3:450–51.

191 Guido of Monte Rochen, *Handbook for Curates*, 85–86.

192 Antoninus, *Summa confessionalis*, fol. xcvi^{va}–xcvii^{va}.

193 Antoninus of Florence, *Confessionale "Defecerunt,"* fol. xcvii^{va-b}: "Forma absolutionis in articulo mortis. Miseratur tui etc. Auctoritate domini nostri iesu Christi et beatorum apostolorum Pe. et pau, et domini nostri pape. N. et sanctione romane ecclesie. in hac parte tibi concessa specialiter et mihi commisa. concedo et do tibi plenariam indulgentiam et remissionem omnium peccatorum tuorum de quibus ore confessus es."

might be given by one's own priest, if he was available. Otherwise, a secular priest, but not a member of a religious order, might provide the sacrament.

No penance was to be enjoined upon a person who could not perform it. However, the penitent could be warned to perform it if his or her life was spared by God. The penance, however, could be imposed on friends or family. The executors of the deceased's estate could make offerings for pious causes and offer restitution. Antoninus added that those in peril on the sea, in war, when ill or in danger of violent death might confess to someone other than his own parish priest.[194] In fact, crusading armies were accompanied by priests, usually friars, who could absolve those facing death in battle.[195]

The important thing expected of clergy, secular or religious, was the salvation of the dying person's soul. Most often this meant comforting those confined to their deathbeds. The dying person was to be exhorted to both penitence and trust in divine mercy. The merits of Christ's passion and the salvation of the good thief on the cross (Lk 23:39–40) were offered as evidence that God desired anyone's salvation. Each of those persons was expected to receive devoutly the last sacraments, penance, viaticum, and extreme unction, in order to make a good death and enter the afterlife, even if facing cleansing in Purgatory.

194 Ibid., fol. 7r.

195 David S. Bacharach, "The Friars Go to War: Mendicant Crusade Chaplains, 1216-c. 1300," *Catholic Historical Review* 90 (2004): 617–33.

3

SICKBED COMMUNION

ORIGINS OF VIATICUM

After confession, sick persons were to be refreshed with the Eucharist. This communion was called viaticum, sustenance on the way to the next world. Usually it was given as a consecrated host, which, according to the doctrine of concomitance, contained the entire risen Christ. However, if a sick person was unable to swallow or digest consecrated bread, blessed wine, mixed with a little water, might be administered instead.

There is evidence of the Eucharist in late antiquity being reserved at home and consumed for protection against evils. That practice gave way to reservation in the sacristy or the church itself, with communion carried to those too sick to come to Mass. In addition, only a priest was to touch the consecrated elements.[1] These elements were for both the sick and for personal devotion.[2] Consecrated hosts might even be buried with the dead.[3]

1 Snoek, *Medieval Piety*, 44–45 and 382.

2 Ibid., 32–33, 205, 208. The text in the *Admonitio synodalis* on reservation was repeated by the 867 Council of Reims and later writings; see 216, 222, 227.

3 David Grumet, *Material Eucharist* (Oxford: Oxford University Press, 1916), 193–205.

Later developments placed the Eucharist in clerical hands for communion of the bedridden sick.

Communion of the sick has a long history in canon law and pastoral practice. An early example is the title on penance in the *Collectio vetus gallica* (ca. 600), which includes texts concerning communion of the mortally ill. Two of these texts state that such a person was not to be denied communion; however, anyone reconciled to the Church on his or her sickbed, if surviving long enough, was still to perform penance.[4]

The need to have the Eucharist on hand for viaticum was recorded in Carolingian regulations. The *Capitula ecclesiastica* required priests to always have communion ready to take to the sick, who might die without the sacraments.[5] Likewise, an eighth-century council said that the road to eternity, whether it led to death or life, was long without communion, viaticum.[6] The early ninth-century statutes of Liège also instructed priests not to let parishioners die without viaticum.[7] A decree attributed to the Council of Worms required reservation of the Eucharist, so that no parishioner died without communion.[8] A canon attributed to the Council of Orléans but found in the *Cummean Penitential* imposed forty days of penance on anyone who allowed a mouse or other animal to consume the consecrated bread.[9] The Orléans text also appeared in the *Penitential of Theodore* and in Halitgar's writings.[10] The *Roman Penitential* contains the same text without attribution.[11] It was widely diffused in the *Decretum* of Burchard of Worms, and likewise contained in the *Decretum* of Ivo of Chartres.[12] The text also appears in the *Panormia*, once attributed to Ivo.[13] The Frankish penitential of Halitgar imposed punishments for failing to

4 Mordek, *Kirchenrecht und Reform im Frankreich*, 600–601.

5 MGH *Capitula regum Francorum*, 1:179: "Ut presbyter semper eucharistiam habeat paratum, ut, quando quis infirmaverit aut parvulus infirmus fuerit, statim eum communicet, ne sine communione moriatur." See also MGH *Capitula regum Francorum, nova series* 1: *Die Kapitulariensammlung des Ansegis*, ed. Gerhard Schmitz (Hanover: Hahn, 1996), 513–14.

6 MGH *Concilia* II, pt. 1, 52: "ut longum est iter, ubi ad aeternam miramus sive ad mortem sive ad vitam absque viatico faciamus."

7 MGH *Capitula regum Francorum*, 1:243: "Ut omnis presbyter curam et sollicitudinem agat, ne aliquis in infirmitate positus ad extremum veniens sine viatico de hoc saeculo exeat ad quos accedere potuerit: quod si exinde negligens fuerit, periculum sui honoris subiaceat."

8 This text appears in Charlemagne's *capitularia*; see PL 87:326A.

9 PL 87:996A; *Medieval Handbooks of Penance*, 114.

10 PL 99:951B and PL 105:701C.

11 PL 105:724A.

12 PL 140:762B and PL 161:173B.

13 *Panormia Project*, "[Penitentia male servantis sacrificium] Ex concilio Aurelianensi, cap. vi," pt. 1, 97 (no. 156); available at www.wtamu.edu/~bbrasington/panormia.html.

guard the host from mice, dropping or losing it, spilling consecrated wine or losing chrism, as well as vomiting the host.[14] This chain of texts was intended to guarantee the availability of viaticum to the dangerously ill.

By the twelfth century, the French liturgist Johannes Beleth specified use of bread in communion of the laity, because wine too easily was spilled or turned sour, and because bread represented the new dispensation replacing the old.[15] This matched a move toward communion of the laity in bread alone.[16] As late as 1491, a council at Bamburg worried about spilling consecrated wine on floor, altar, or altar linens. It also imposed penance on any priest who spilled the chalice.[17] During these centuries, the practice of giving the laity communion with bread only was reinforced as theologians concluded that the whole Christ was present under either species (concomitance). In the same period, communion by intinction, dipping the bread in the wine, largely ceased.[18]

Communion under both species, bread and wine, was so far from daily practice by the thirteenth century that John of Freiburg dismissed it in a few sentences in his *Summa confessorum*. The efficacy of the sacrament was equal under both forms; but, because of the symbolism, ministers consumed both consecrated elements. The Greeks could worthily give the laity consecrated wine; but not the Latins, who did better—John said—by giving only one species to the laity.[19]

Dealing with the Hussite demand that communion be given under both species, the Council of Constance rejected this as unnecessary.[20] When the question was raised at the Council of Basel in its debates with the Hussites, the Bohemians demanded the chalice for the laity, which they were grudgingly granted in the Compacts of Iglau.[21] Dominican theo-

14 *Medieval Handbooks of Penance*, 308–9.

15 Johannes Beleth, *Summa de ecclesiasticis officiis*, ed. Heribert Douteil (Turnhout: Brepols, 1976), 182–83. Beleth said that a chalice used to reserve consecrated wine should not be washed; see ibid., 183–84.

16 Rubin, *Corpus Christi*, 48. Communion from the cup was replaced in some locations with a sip of unconsecrated wine to make swallowing the host easier.

17 *Concilia Germaniae* 5:615–16.

18 Snoek, *Medieval Piety*, 39–40.

19 Johannes de Friburgo, *Summa confessorum* III, t. 24, q. 110: "Efficacio vere equalis est sub vtraque forma sed non significancia. Ideo omnibus traditur sub vtraque specie in qua potest tradi cum reuerencia et cautela maiori: a maioribus vero tamen id est presbiteris et ministris sumitur sub vtraque specie. Et licet greci bene faciant sumendo sub vtraque specie tamen latini melius faciunt ratione predicta."

20 *Conciliorum oecumenicorum generaliumque decreta* I, pt. 1, 562–63.

21 Anton Frind, *Kirchengeschichte Böhmens in der Hussitenzeit* (Prague: Tempsky, 1872), 3:354–58; E. F. Jacob, "The Bohemians at the Council of Basel, 1433," in *Prague Essays Presented by a Group of British Historians to the Caroline University of Prague on the Occasion of its Six-Hundredth Anniversary*, ed. R. W. Seton-Watson (Oxford: Clarendon Press, 1949), 81–123.

logians John of Ragusa and Juan de Torquemada, debating the Hussites about communion during their visit to Basel, argued for the practices of the Latin Church.[22] So did another Dominican, Heinrich Kalteisen, who said that consecrated wine might be spilled on the ground, on men's beards or women's dresses.[23] Kalteisen recounted how a Hussite priest, rushing to a sick person, spilled the chalice, scattering the wine with his feet.[24] Nicholas of Cusa addressed this issue in his *De usu communionis ad Bohemos.* His argument for communion with a host alone turned partly on concomitance; but he also claimed that the Church could alter rites for practical reasons, including the danger of lay communicants spilling consecrated wine.[25]

In practice, a council of Reims prohibited anyone but a cleric carrying communion to the sick.[26] The decree was based on reports that some priests, not sensitive to "the divine mysteries," were letting this happen.[27] Halitgar said priests were not to give the blood of Christ to women to take home; it was to be retained in a church for use as needed.[28] Regino of Prüm copied the Reims text as the canon "It came to our attention" (*Pervenit ad notitiam nostrum*).[29] Burchard of Worms took up the prohibition of women carrying the sacraments, using the condescending word "little women" (*mulierculae*).[30] Ivo of Chartres included the prohibition in his *Decretum* but using the more neutral term *mulieres.*[31] The Reims text also appeared in the *Panormia.*[32]

22 Thomas M. Izbicki, "Dominican Ecclesiology, the Council of Basel and the Hussites," forthcoming in *Memorie Domenicane.*

23 Thomas Prügl, "Die Verhandlungen des Basler Konzils mit den Böhmen und die Prager Kompaktaten als Friedensvertrag," *Annuarium Historiae Conciliorum* 48 (2016–17): 249–308, at 291: "nunc super terram, nunc in barbis virorum, nunc in pepla mulierum."

24 Ibid., 294: "Pariformiter quidem sacerdos concuciens, dum in Bohemia portaret calicem ad infirmum, contingit, quod cecidit et sanguinem Domini effudit, qui statim pedibus illum conculcavit et sic dispersit." See also 307.

25 Nicholas of Cusa, *Writings on Church and Reform*, trans. Thomas M. Izbicki (Cambridge, MA: Harvard University Press, 2008), 2–85.

26 The 874 *capitula* of Reims said someone could not be a canon and a parish priest, administering to both sick and well; see Mansi 15:493–94.

27 Friedberg 1:1323 (*De consecratione*, third part of the *Decretum* [hereafter *De cons.*], D. 2, c. 29): "Pervenit ad notitiam nostrum, quod quidem presbiteri in tantum paruipendant diuina misteria, ut laico aut feminae sacrum corpus Domini tradant ad deferendum infirmis."

28 MGH *Capitula regum Francorum*, 1:243.

29 Regino of Prüm, *Libri duo de synodalibus causis*, xx.

30 PL 140:758B: "*De presbyteris qui corpus Dominicum ad deferendum infirmis mulierculis tradunt.*"

31 PL 161:169B–C: "*De presbyteris qui corpus Dominicum ad deferendum infirmis, mulieribus tradunt. Ex concilio Remensi, cap.* 2."

32 *Panormia Project*, pt. 1, 95–106 (no. 153): "[Quod laici vel femine non debeant ferre corpus dominicum ad aliquem communicandum] Ex concilio Remensi, cap. ii."

In the tenth century, Regino of Prüm required priests to have a fitting pyx or other vessel for the reserved hosts, quoting a text from the Carolingian Council of Worms.[33] That canon reappeared in the *Decretum* of Burchard of Worms under the rubric *"That the priest should have the Eucharist ready" (Ut presbyter Eucharistiam in promptu habeat).*[34] The same text appeared in the *Decretum* of Ivo of Chartres, as well as in the *Panormia.*[35] Ivo also included in his *Decretum* a text attributed to the Council of Nicaea saying that penitents were not to be denied viaticum.[36]

Viaticum in Canon Law

Much of this material was included in the *Decretum* of Gratian.[37] Treatment of Eucharistic issues was concentrated in the third part of the collection, the tract *On the Consecration of a Church* (*De consecratione ecclesiae*) in Distinction 2.[38] Some older canons were included. Thus it contained the decree from Worms, requiring that the communion be kept ready for "whenever someone will be sick" (*quando quis infirmatus fuerit*).[39] Texts of Jerome and Hilary were quoted to show that the whole Christ was present in any portion of the sacrament.[40] In disciplinary matters, Gratian quoted the canon of Orléans on the penance done for failing in custody of the sacraments and Cyprian on not entrusting holy things to actors or mages.[41] Reasons for sacramental practice appear in *Cum omne*, a text, attributed to Pope Julius I, saying that one should follow the doctrine of the apostles and ecclesiastical custom.[42] This involved doing as Christ had done, and not doing what he had omitted. Christ had given the apostles bread

33 Regino of Prüm, *Libri duo de synodalibus causis*, xx. Regino also included a text forbidding women to enter the sanctuary; see ibid., 200. Peter Browe, "Die Eucharistie als Zaubermittel im Mittelalter," *Archiv für Kulturgeschichte* 20 (1930): 134–54, at 135n1. "Pyx" was used in the later Middle Ages to mean a receptacle for reserved hosts, the vessel used for taking communion to the sick, or both. The 1287 council at Liège specifically applied the term to both; see Mansi 24:897. The 1224 Council of Winchester, however, distinguished a pyx for communicating the sick from the vessel used to reserved hosts in a church; see *Councils & Synods* II, pt. 1, 126.

34 PL 140:754C–D.

35 PL 161:165C, *Panormia Project*, 90: "Ut presbiter semper eucharistiam habeat paratam, ut quando quis infirmatus fuerit aut parvulus infirmus fuerit, statim cum communicet, ne sine communione moriatur"; available at documentacatholicaomnia.eu/03d/1040-1116,_Ivo_Carnotensis,_*Panormia*,_LT.pdf.

36 PL 16:864C.

37 Winroth, *The Making of Gratian's "Decretum."*

38 John C. Wei, *Gratian the Theologian* (Washington, DC: The Catholic University of America Press, 2016), 229–31, 248–49, 277–89, says that D. 2 is badly structured.

39 Friedberg 1:1251–52 (*Presbyter*; *De cons.*, D. 2, c. 93).

40 Friedberg 1:1345–46 (*Singuli* and *Ubi pars*; *De cons.*, D. 2, cc. 77–78).

41 Friedberg 1:1352 (*Qui bene* and *Pro dilectione*; *De cons.*, D. 2, cc. 94–95).

42 *De cons.*, D. 2, c. 7.

and wine, water in the wine representing the people with whom he was united. However, the bread was not to be dipped in the wine, intincted, because Christ had done this with the dipped bread he gave to Judas (Jn 13:26–27).[43]

Discussion of intinction by commentators on the *Decretum*, the Decretists, began with Rufinus. His theology of the priesthood emphasized the priest's acting on behalf of Christ, the mediator between God and humanity, with the people transmitting prayers, vows, and offerings through him.[44] His gloss on *Ubi pars* reflected the idea of concomitance, the whole savior present under both species, although bread symbolized his body and wine his blood.[45] This identification allowed Rufinus to propose that the host alone could be given to the laity, as the whole Christ was present in it.[46] The consecrated wine usually was reserved to the celebrant of the Mass.[47] Rufinus concluded that intinction was frowned upon because Jesus gave a dipped morsel to Judas.[48] However, he permitted intinction for communion of the sick. The priest was to say to any communicant: "The body and blood of Christ accomplish for you," etc.[49]

Attached to the *Summa* of Stephen of Tournai on the *Decretum* is a commentary on "Moses built a tabernacle" (*De consecratione*, *Fecit Moyses tabernaculum*) the author of which knew the Scholastic language of Paris. Like Rufinus, the author limited communion by intinction to those debilitated by sickness (*debilitas aegrotantis*). The priest, representing Christ, was the only one who drank consecrated wine.[50] Likewise, Simon of Bisignano permitted intinction only for communion of the sick, as a sick person

43 Friedberg 1:1316. The text referred to the morsel, but it omitted mentioning Judas in favor of the morsel not being involved in the institution of the Eucharist.

44 *De cons.*, D. 2, c. 51. See Rufinus, *Summa decretorum*, 548: "et vocatur missa quasi transmissa vel quasi transmissio, eo quod populus fidelis per ministerium sacerdotis, qui mediatoris vice fungitur inter Deum et homines, preces et vota et oblationes Deo transmittat."

45 Rufinus, *Summa decretorum*, 557: "Ubi pars est corporis, id est illius specie, in qua latet corpus, est totum essentialiter ipsum corpus Christi" (*De cons.*, D. 2, c. 78).

46 *In sacramentorum*; *De cons.*, D. 2, c. 1.

47 Rufinus, *Summa decretorum*, 551.

48 Ibid.: "Intinctam vero eucharistiam sumere vel tradere omnino prohibter, quia, cum Dominus intinctam bucellam Iude dedit, eum esse proditorem." Rufinus lists discarded Eucharistic practices at 553.

49 Ibid., 553: "Sed aliud est quod pro necessitate geritur infirmorum, aliud quod generaliter fit in communione aliorum . . . que sacra oblatio intincta debet esse sanguine Christi, ut veraciter possit presbiter infirmo dicere: 'Corpus et sanguinis Christi purificiat tibi' etc." Rufinus was addressing an argument for intinction drawn from the *Decretum* of Burchard. See Izbicki, *The Eucharist in Medieval Canon Law*, 216–17.

50 *Fecit Moyses Tabernaculum* in Stephen of Tournai, *Die Summa*, 269–70. Peter Landau, "Die Dekretsumme *Fecit Moyses tabernaculum* – ein weiteres Werk der Kölner Kanonistik," *Zeitschrift der Savigny-Stiftung für Rechtsgeschichte, Kanonistische Abteilung* 127 (2010): 602–8.

might not be able to swallow a dry host.[51] Simon also argued against communion of the laity with wine alone, because it was easily corrupted or spilled. The laity could receive consecrated bread because body and blood were present under one species.[52]

The Ordinary Gloss on the *Decretum* required caution in administering consecrated wine, even in a case of necessity (*causa necessitatis*).[53] Communion by intinction should not be done ordinarily "on account of caution" (*propter cautelam*), meaning the possibility of spilling the chalice.[54] The Gloss cautioned against intinction for sick communion, because penance was imposed on anyone who vomited the Eucharist.[55] The Gloss was more permissive than had been Huguccio of Pisa, who said that intinction had been abrogated.[56]

Quinque verba, a fourteenth-century vademecum for priests, brought up the danger of spilling the wine when communicating the laity, and the author worried about a sick person vomiting a host.[57] Nonetheless, communicating the sick was expected of parish priests. In France, the statutes of Arras required priests to be ready to minister to the sick who requested communion. Only persons under interdict or excommunication could not request it.[58] Even ecclesiastical censures might not prevent last communion. The *Decretum* included a text of Pope Martin I saying dying persons who wanted viaticum should have permission from the bishop to receive it.[59] However, a council of Orléans (c. 7) said that deathbed reconciliation was to be permitted without laying on of hands by the bishop, unless the person survived, but with communion allowed.[60] The deathbed was

51 *De cons.*, D. 2, c. 7. *Summa in Decretum Simonis Brisinianensis*, ed. Petrus V. Aimone Braida (Vatican City: Biblioteca Apostolica Vaticana, 2014), 516: "Excipitur tamen in infirmis quibus intincta poterit dari eucharistia, quam per se propter substantie ariditatem deglutiare non poterat."

52 *Summa in Decretum Simonis Brisinianensis*, 518.

53 *Scriptura* and *Presbyter*; *De cons.*, D. 2, cc. 2 and 93; Glo. Ord. at *De cons.*, D. 4, cc. 2 and 93.

54 Glo. Ord. at *De cons.*, D. 2, c. 93.

55 Glo. Ord. at C. 26, q. 6, c. 8: "Et infundatur. Sed qualiter recipiat eucharistiam, qui ita infirmatur. Si enim intincta in pane datur ei, hoc prohibitur. de consec. dist. ii. cum omne. nec alio modo videtur danda: quia punitur infirmus, qui euomit eucharistiam: vt de consec. dist. ii. ca. si quis per ebrietatem."

56 Huguccio, *Summa decretorum*, Admont Ms. 7, fol. 423rb–va, "prohibetur intinctam dari." Izbicki, *The Eucharist in Medieval Canon Law*, 216.

57 *Pastors and the Care of Souls* (ed. Shinners and Dohar), 137.

58 *Statuts synodaux* 4:192: "Quacumque hora infirmus communionem petierit, nisi ab hoc quidem interdictus vel excommunicatus fuerit, sacerdos sit paratus accedere."

59 Friedberg 1:1037 (C. 26, q. 6, c. 6): "Qui ergo in exitu mortis sunt, si desiderant accipere sacramentum, cum consideratione et probatione episcopi accipere debent."

60 Friedberg 1:1037–38 (C. 26, q. 6, c. 7): "Qui recedunt de corpore penitencia accepta, placuit sine reconciliatoria manus impositione eis communicare, quod mortientis sufficit reconciliationem secundum deffinitionem Patrum, qui huiusmodi communionem, uiaticum congrue, nominauerunt. Quod si

supposed to be the site of a last contention over the soul; and Satan was believed to dread the bringing of a host, because it drove him away.[61]

Local canons condemned priests who failed the dying. The third statutes of Worcester threatened priests with censures for failing to provide the dying with confession, communion, and extreme unction. Such failure proved the priest to be useless to the faithful.[62] Thomas of Chobham, in his manual for confessors, said that priests had to remain sober to be ready to go to a sickbed. Otherwise, a parishioner might die without absolution and communion.[63] A parish controlled by a Premonstratensian monastery in Lancashire petitioned to have more priests assigned to it, because parishioners were too many for one priest to minister to all sick persons.[64]

RESERVATION OF THE SACRAMENT

Many early canons required reservation of the consecrated Eucharist for viaticum. Reservation of the Eucharist was treated especially in two texts in the *Decretum*. The canon from Worms reappeared as *Presbyter*, requiring reservation of the Eucharist, so that no one died without communion.[65] The Orléans canon came back as *Qui bene* (c. 94), imposing penance on anyone so negligent that a mouse or other animal consumed the host.[66] Moreover, *Pervenit* (c. 29), attributed to a Council of Reims, prohibited anyone but a cleric carrying communion to the sick.[67]

superuixerint, stent in ordine penitentiam, ut ostensis necessariis penitencie fructibus legitimam communionem cum reconciliatoria manus impositione recipiunt. §. Clericis quoque desiderantibus penitencia non est deneganda."

61 Snoek, *Medieval Piety*, 374–75.

62 *Councils & Synods* II, pt. 1, 305: "Sacerdos autem qui se pigrum exhibit in visitandis infirmis, ex quo quandoque forsitam accidit quod egrotus absque confessione vel dominici corporis et sanguinis perceptione decedat, expers unctionis extreme, perniciosum se non solum inutilem subditis exhibit et tantam eius incuriam per nos noverit condigna pro viribus animadversione plectandam."

63 *Pastors and the Care of Souls* (ed. Shinners and Dohar), 8.

64 Geoffrey Barraclough, *Papal Provisions: Aspects of Church History Constitutional, Legal and Administrative in the Later Middle Ages* (Oxford: Blackwell, 1935), 52–53.

65 Friedberg 1:1351–52 (*De cons.*, D. 2, c. 93): "Presbiter eucharistiam semper habeat paratum, ut, quando quis infirmatus fuerit, statim eum communicet, ne sine communione moriatur."

66 Friedberg 1:1352 (*De cons.*, D. 2, c. 94). The Ordinary Gloss on this text expressed the opinion that a host did not cease to be consecrated if a mouse or spider was found on it.

67 Friedberg 1:1323–24 (*De cons.*, D. 2, c. 29): "Peruenit ad notitiam nostram, quod quidam presbiteri in tantum paruipendant diuina misteria, ut laico aut feminae sacrum corpus Domini tradant ad deferendum infirmis."

The Ordinary Gloss on the *Decretum* said little about some of these canons. Johannes Teutonicus, original compiler of the Gloss, said something about *Qui bene*. Writing about the possibility that the host might cease to be Christ's body if a mouse simply remained atop it, Johannes concluded that it does not cease to be the sacrament.[68] On *Pervenit* the Gloss said carrying communion was denied to women. However, it could be carried by a deacon or even a layman in a case of necessity.[69]

Increased reverence for the consecrated bread led to the creation of special housing for reserved hosts, some of it modeled on reliquaries, and the burning of lights before that housing. The terminology for this housing did not become fixed, although "tabernacle" became common. The repository for reserved hosts might also be called a ciborium.[70] The word "pyx" was used; but it could mean the housing of the Eucharist in church, the vessel used taking communion to the sick, or both.[71] In England the pyx tended to be a vessel hanging over the altar, pulled down with a hook when viaticum was needed.[72] The portable pyx usually was made of metal, but poor parishes might use wood or leather; and the portable pyx might be wrapped in silk.[73] Although some Italian churches housed reserved hosts and chrism in the sacristy, most churches placed a receptacle on, near, or above the main altar.[74] The practice of keeping a

68 Glo. Ord. at *De cons.*, D. 2, c. 94: "Sed numquid desinit esse sacramentum, si mansit super illlud corpus mus vel aranea. Non credo quod desinit esse sacramentum."

69 Glo. Ord. at *De cons.*, D. 2, c. 29: "Ex quibus. Scilicet feminis . . . Per semetipsum. vel per diaconum, si necesse est: vt xciij. distin. pręsente. vel per laicum catholicus. xxiiij. q. j. coepit."

70 *Museum Schnütgen*, 261. A distinction between a ciborium and a monstrance for displaying the host can be difficult to make; see 245.

71 On two parishes that in a 1458 visitation had a pyx for viaticum nested inside a pyx for reservation, see *Visitations of Churches Belonging to St. Paul's Cathedral* (ed. Simpson), 83 and 91. The Eucharist often was kept with the relics, but a carried pyx was to be closed and covered with cloth; see Snoek, *Medieval Piety*, 222–24, 233, 289.

72 Snoek, *Medieval Piety*, 227–307; Elizabeth Saxon, *The Eucharist in Medieval France: Iconography and Theology* (Woodbridge: Boyell, 2006), 32 and 243. The 1287 council at Liège applied the term to both types of vessel; see Mansi 24:897. The 1224 Council of Winchester, however, distinguished a pyx for communicating the sick and the vessel used for reserved hosts in a church; see *Councils & Synods* II, pt. 1, 126. On the hook, see Rubin, *Corpus Christi*, 47.

73 *Visitations of Churches Belonging to St. Paul's Cathedral*, 5, 8, 14, 22. For a cruciform vessel for administering viaticum, see *Museum Schnütgen: A Survey of the Collection*, ed. Moritz Woelk and Manuela Beer (Munich: Hirmer, 2018), 317. For an ivory pyx, see ibid., 129.

74 Archdale King, *Eucharistic Reservation in the Western Church* (London: Mowbray, 1965), 71–95. Chrism and oils might be kept in a separate locked chrismatory; see *Visitations of Churches Belonging to St. Paul's Cathedral*, xxxii–xxxiii.

light in front of the reserved Eucharist became common, although local councils did not always mention it.[75]

By the thirteenth century a concern emerged for the security of the reserved host and other holy things. One decree of the Fourth Lateran Council, *Statuimus*, demanded keeping the Eucharist and holy oils under lock and key:

> We decree that the chrism and the Eucharist are to be kept locked away in a safe place in all churches, so that no audacious hand can reach them to do anything horrible or impious. If he who is responsible for their safe-keeping leaves them around carelessly, let him be suspended from office for three months; if anything unspeakable happens on account of his carelessness, let him be subject to graver punishment.

The Council was vague about what an "audacious hand" might do, clarification of which would be attempted by canonists. However, it reinforced older canons concerning reservation of the sacraments for the sick.[76]

Statuimus, like the other Lateran decrees, made its way into medieval canon law. It was included in *Compilatio quarta* under the title "Concerning baptism and its effect" (*De baptismo et eius effectu*).[77] Raymond of Peñafort included the canon in the *Liber extra* as the first chapter of the title *De custodia eucharistiae, chrismatis et aliorum sacramentorum.*[78] The other chapter under this title, *Relinqui*, canon 19 of the same council, required that churches not store furniture, and also that liturgical vessels and cloths be kept "neat and clean."[79] Both of these texts were intended to make churches fit places for worship, not facsimiles of lay households.

There were complaints from bishops and local councils justifying such legislation, including long-established concerns about hosts decaying or being consumed by mice.[80] The reference to an "audacious hand" in *Statuimus*, however, was not tied to polemics against heretics violating the

75 The Worcester statutes required that a light burn before the repository of the reserved sacrament; see Mansi 23:528–29. So did the 1453 Council of Eichstadt; see *Concilia Germaniae* 5:435.

76 *Decrees* (ed. Tanner), 1:244; *Constitutiones concilii quarti Lateranensis una cum commentariis glossatorum* (ed. García), 67. Rubrics in manuscript copies mention keeping the sacraments *sub clave* or *sub clavibus*.

77 Concerning custody of the Eucharist, chrism, and other sacraments: *Quinque compilationes antiquae* (ed. Friedberg), 144 (IV 3.16.2).

78 Friedberg 2:649 (X 3.44.1).

79 *Decrees* (ed. Tanner), 1:244; Friedberg 2:649–50 (X 3.44.2). For regulations concerning altar cloths, see Thomas M. Izbicki, "*Linteamenta altaria*: The Care of Altar Linens in the Medieval Church," *Medieval Clothing and Textiles* 12 (2016): 41–60.

80 Rubin, *Corpus Christi*, 43–45.

sacrament.[81] Claims that Jews suborned Christians to steal consecrated hosts to torture in imitation of Christ's passion were not prevalent until after the Council.[82] A rare declaration that either Jews or Christians might use hosts for nefarious purposes is found in the Coventry statutes of Alexander of Stavensby (1224–38).[83] This text suggested that either group might attempt magic with the Eucharist and oils. Such superstitious practices were not recorded in earlier penitentials; but by the twelfth century complaints appeared that chrism, hosts, or other holy things were stolen for magical uses.[84] Richard Wyche, bishop of Chichester, said that Eucharist, oil, and chrism were to be locked up *propter sortilegia*.[85] Similar fears were expressed about misuse of baptismal water.[86]

The Reserved Sacraments in Canon Law

Medieval canonists varied in their interest in the Lateran decree. Few were interested at first in explaining its rationale. The apparatus of Johannes Teutonicus referred to *Pervenit* in the *Decretum*, which forbade women entering the sanctuary or a lay person taking communion to the sick.[87] He was most concerned with the culpability of a negligent priest.[88] Vincentius Hispanus cited *Pervenit* as relevant to custody of the Eucharist. He also cited a decree of Pope Alexander III, *Plene*, about a struggle over a host displaying the flesh of Christ.[89] Damasus too cited *Pervenit*, making

81 Reports of Eucharistic wonders before Lateran IV usually involved devout persons who wanted to see Christ in the sacrament; see Gary Macy, *The Theologies of the Eucharist in the Early Scholastic Period: A Study of the Salvific Function of the Sacrament according to the Theologians, c. 1080–c. 1220* (Oxford: Clarendon Press, 1984), 86–93. For polemicists' Eucharistic concerns, see Jessalynn Bird, "The Construction of Orthodoxy and the (De)construction of Heretical Attacks on the Eucharist in *pastoralia* from Peter the Chanter's Circle in Paris," in *Texts and the Repression of Medieval Heresy*, ed. Caterina Bruschi and Peter Biller (York: York Medieval Press, 2003), 45–61.

82 Earlier tales of supposed atrocities by Jews were focused on other matters; see Miri Rubin, *Gentile Tales: The Narrative Assault on Late Medieval Jews* (Philadelphia: University of Pennsylvania Press, 1999).

83 *Councils & Synods*, 2, pt. 1, 210: "Quia ergo solent quidam propter obprobria Christi ut increduli, quidam qui propter nimium contemptum descendunt in profundum abyssi, quidam autem propter veneficia, ut mali christiani et iudei, aliqua turpia circa eucharistiam et chrisma et oleum sanctum ausu temerario, immo nimis ausi, presumere, praecipimus ut sub optima clausura clavium reponantur in diversis vasis prout decet honestas."

84 Valerie I. Flint, *The Rise of Magic in Early Medieval Europe* (Princeton, NJ: Princeton University Press, 1991), 214, 285, 298; Izbicki, "*Manus temeraria*."

85 *Councils & Synods* II, pt. 1, 453.

86 Some English statutes required locking the baptismal font *propter sortilegia*; see Cheney, *English Synodalia*, 82.

87 Friedberg 1:1323–24 (*De cons.*, D. 2, c. 29).

88 *Constitutiones Concilii quarti Lateranensis*, 208.

89 *Quinque compilationes antiquae* (ed. Friedberg), 38 (I 3.26.30).

a connection between the Lateran decree and magic. He also referred to a decretal of Pope Clement III imposing penance on a woman who kept a host she received in her teeth to magically reawaken her husband's passion with a kiss.[90] Both Vincentius and Damasus said the sacristan was responsible for keeping host and chrism safe.[91]

The Decretalists, canonists of the thirteenth and early fourteenth centuries, commented on the *Liber extra*. The *casus* by Bernardus Parmensis, the compiler of the Ordinary Gloss, summarized *Statuimus*, noting that, if anything nefarious (*nefandum*) happened to reserved hosts or chrism, the one entrusted with their care was to be punished as if guilty of the offense.[92] The Gloss repeated the old concern about lay folk taking communion to the sick. Only a deacon could play that role in the absence of a priest. The Gloss did say that a negligent custodian was to be held responsible for whatever followed from his negligence.[93]

An early discussion of custody can be found in the "Summa on the titles of the Decretals" (*Summa super titulis decretalium*) by Geoffrey of Trani. He discussed keeping the Eucharist in a place both clean and safe, conserved "honorably and devoutly."[94] Geoffrey denied that a woman or a layman could take communion to the sick. In line with established opinion, he said that only a deacon could substitute for a priest. He also noted that chrism was to be kept secure together with the Eucharist.[95] Pope Innocent IV composed an apparatus on the Gregorian Decretals as a private doctor.[96] He was uninterested in *Statuimus*, only mentioning texts in the *Decretum* concerning measures taken if the consecrated elements fell to the ground or if someone vomited after receiving communion.[97]

Much more significant discussions of this matter were penned by Henricus de Segusio, Hostiensis. Henricus had studied canon law at the same time as Pope Innocent IV and served as a cardinal. He was capable of

90 *Constitutiones Concilii quarti Lateranensis*, 428. Damasus cited II 5.17.2; see *Quinque compilationes antiquae* (ed. Friedberg), 102.

91 *Constitutiones Concilii quarti Lateranensis*, 314 and 428.

92 Glo. Ord. at X 3.44.1, Casus.

93 Glo. Ord. at X 3.44.1.

94 *Summa perutilis et valde necessaria do. Goffredi de Trano super titulis decretalium* (Lyon: Morin, 1519; Aalen: Scientia, 1968), fol. 165vb.

95 *Summa Goffredi*, fol. 165vb. Godfrey quoted c. *Pervenit*, denying any role to the laity in taking communion to the sick.

96 Alberto Melloni, *Innocenzo IV: la concezione e l'esperienza della cristianità come regimen unius personae* (Genoa: Marietti, 1990).

97 Innocentius IV, *Commentaria apparatus in V libros decretalium* (Frankfurt: Sigismundus Feyrabend, 1570; Frankfurt: Minerva, 1968), fol. 457ra.

disagreeing with Innocent's opinions and of having interests that differed when commenting the same text.[98] Hostiensis composed both a *Summa super titulis decretalium* and a commentary on the *Gregorian Decretals*. His *Summa*, based on Geoffrey's, was earlier, its first version completed ca. 1253. The commentary was completed, in its last version, just before Hostiensis's death in 1271.[99]

In his *Summa*, Hostiensis connected custody of the Eucharist and chrism with the canon law governing celebration of Mass and baptism. He summarized *Statuimus* and then commented: "This he said was enacted on account of those who commit sorceries thereupon."[100] Hostiensis went on to discuss the proper persons and processes for carrying communion to the sick.[101] His discussion of the *De custodia* concluded with a review of the penalties inflicted on negligent guardians of the Eucharist and chrism, plus the penances imposed on those who vomited up communion because of drunkenness.[102] In the final version of his *Commentary*, Hostiensis addressed these things again, expressing his concern about magical practices attempted using sacred things. At the word *manus*, the cardinal commented in a personal vein: "Sorcery, those who commit thereupon many horrible and nefarious things, as follows; and we have heard many things about this in confessions and which we experience daily, about which it is safer to keep silence . . ."[103] Hostiensis added that a negligent custodian was to be punished even if nothing nefarious happened. Negligence was a grave sin deserving severe correction.[104] The commentary on *Statuimus* ended with a discussion of dropped hosts and vomited communion.[105]

Hostiensis's opinion in the *Commentary* was restated by Johannes Andreae in his fourteenth-century *Novella commentaria* on the *Decretals*. Thus, he says, at v. *Manus*: "Sorcery, which is done with these things, about

98 Kenneth Pennington, *The Prince and the Law, 1200–1600: Sovereignty and Rights in the Western Legal Tradition* (Berkeley: University of California Press, 1993), 48–51.

99 Kenneth Pennington, "Henricus de Segusio (Hostiensis)," in Pennington, *Popes, Canonists and Texts, 1150–1550* (Aldershot: Variorum, 1993), xvi and 1–12.

100 Hostiensis, *Summa aurea*, 1198: "Hoc autem statutum est propter illos qui inde sortilegia committant."

101 Ibid.

102 Ibid., 1199.

103 *Henrici de Segusio cardinalis Hostiensis in tertium decretalium librum commentaria* (Venice: Apud Iuntas, 1581; Frankfurt: Vico Verlag, 2009), fol. 172ra: "[*Manus*]. Sortilegium, qui inde multa horribilia & nepharia committunt, ut sequitur, & in confessionib[us]. Multa circa hoc audiuimus, & quotidie experimur, quae tutius e[st] tacere."

104 Ibid., [*Suspendatur*] and [*Et si per negligentiam*].

105 Ibid., [*Ultioni*]. See also Hostiensis, *Summa aurea*, 1840–41, enjoining penances for spilling the chalice or letting mice eat reserved hosts.

which it is more discrete to be silent."[106] Andreae agreed with Hostiensis that negligence was to be punished even if nothing nefarious resulted. (Being a layman, he had nothing to say about confession of magical practices.)[107] Andreae concluded his discussion of the *Statuimus* by discussing the law governing hosts dropped or eaten by mice.[108] Nothing new was added to the canon law of reservation later in the Middle Ages.

Local Enactments

Local enactments concerning the Eucharist abound, but fewer addressed custody of oils as well. A letter attributed to Pope Leo III and included in the *Liber extra* entrusted to rural archpriests (and rural deans in the north) the task of ensuring that the Eucharist was reserved for the care of the sick.[109] Another text of Leo permitted archpriests to grant penance and anointing to the sick in the absence of the bishop.[110] Likewise, the 1284 Council of Nîmes warned against letting the sick die without communion.[111]

Notably, Odo of Sully, bishop of Paris, issued synodal legislation in 1175 on topics related to the Eucharist, including reverencing altars, especially one on which the Eucharist was reserved and Mass celebrated. A priest or a deacon was to carry communion to the sick with the laity genuflecting whenever they saw the sacrament being carried.[112] Odo decreed that "the most holy body of the Lord should be kept locked with a key on the most beautiful part of the altar, with greatest diligence and respect."[113]

One notes a greater concern for decorum than security. An undated English council of the same period restated Bishop Odo's enactments on custody of the Eucharist, reverence for the altar, and taking communion to the sick. It also required that the reserved sacrament be kept in a clean pyx (*in munda pyxide conservetur*) and be renewed weekly.[114] This last provision

106 *Ioannis Andreae in tertium decretalium librum novella commentaria* (Venice: Apud Franciscum Franciscum, 1581; Turin: Bottega d'Erasmo, 1963), fol. 229va: "[*Ne posit*] ratio [*Manus*] sortilegiarum, quae operantur ex his, quod discretius tacere. 41 dist. [*rectius*: 43 dist.] sit rector. Hostien."

107 Ibid., [*Suspendatur*].

108 Ibid., [*Contingerit*].

109 Friedberg 2:154 (X 1.24.3). Pope Innocent III equated archpriests and rural deans; see ibid., 2:151 (X 1.23.7).

110 Friedberg 2:154 (X 1.24.2).

111 Mansi 24:525.

112 Mansi 22:677–78. For Odo's influence in England, see Cheney, *English Synodalia*, 83 and 88.

113 Mansi 22:678: "7. In pulcriore parte altaris cum summa diligentia & honestate sub clave sacrosanctum corpus Domini custodiatur"; see Peter Browe, *Die Verehrung der Eucharistie im Mittelalter* (Munich: Húber, 1933; Rome: Herder, 1967), 18.

114 Mansi 22:725 and 731–32; *Councils & Synods* II, pt. 1, 184.

of Odo's decrees was repeated almost verbatim by Richard Poore, bishop of Salisbury, in his influential statutes of 1217. So was the provision about using a clean pyx. Many English statutes of the early thirteenth century made some use of Poore's enactments.[115]

Likewise, a set of statutes frequently described as prepared by Archbishop Langton for his Oxford council included a statute *De sacramento altaris*, providing, in language drawn almost verbatim from Odo of Sully, that altars should be reverenced, especially those on which the Lord's body was reserved and Mass celebrated.[116] These canons also repeated the current phrasing about a "clean pyx," adding that it should be of "ivory or some other material fitting and worthy of so great a sacrament."[117] Odo's language about the worthy placing of the reserved Eucharist was repeated in a statute of Fulk Basset (1245–59) for the diocese of London.[118]

A similar concern can be found in a 1255 canon from Valencia, issued after the *Decretals* had been published. The Eucharist was to be kept, it said, "in the middle part of the altar" under lock and key, if at all possible.[119] Synodal statutes from Girona in 1274 combined placing reserved hosts, oil, and chrism on a consecrated altar with security. The Lateran decree's warning against an "audacious hand" was added in the council's own words.[120] The 1279 Council of Buda also required placing the reserved Eucharist on an altar under lock and key.[121] The 1280 Council of Cologne used the same words about reservation on an altar.[122] Similar statements were made by other bishops. The statutes of William

115 Mansi 22:1118–19; *Councils & Synods* II, pt. 1, 78–79. Poore warned against consuming unconsecrated hosts in the mistaken belief that they had been consecrated. Cheney, *English Synodalia*, 51–62, noted that Poore was at Lateran IV and knew its decrees first-hand. The provisions about a "clean pyx" and replenishment of the reserved species were repeated at a Scottish council of 1225 (Mansi 22:1239) and the statutes attributed to a 1230 council of Edmund, archbishop of Canterbury (Mansi 23:373); see Cheney, *English Synodalia*, 65–67. Similar provisions are found in the 1235 *Praecepta antiqua* of the archdiocese of Rouen; see Mansi 2:374.

116 Mansi 22:1175; Cheney, *English Synodalia*, 62–65.

117 Mansi 22:1175: "Eucharistia in munda pixide argentea, aut eburnean, aut alia tanto sacramento digna & idonea conseruetur." The same phrasing is found in the "synodal statutes for an English diocese" (ca. 1225); see *Councils & Synods* II, pt. 1, 142. Langton also required a "clean pyx" in his statutes for the diocese of Canterbury; see ibid., 27.

118 *Councils & Synods* II, pt. 1, 639–40.

119 Mansi 23:1890: "& in media parte altaris cum summa diligentia & honestate sub claue, si fieri potest, Corpus Christi custodiatur."

120 Mansi 23:936–37: "Chrisma, oleum & eucharistia caute seruentur, clauibus adhibitis, necnon & altare consecratum diligent seruetur custodia, ne ad aliquod praedictorum manus temeraria se extendat pro aliquibus nefariis exercendis." See also see *Councils & Synods* II, pt. 1, 115.

121 Mansi 24:316.

122 Mansi 24:352.

de Blois for the diocese of Worcester (1229) specified two pyxes, one of silver, ivory, or *de opera Lemovitico* (Limoges work) for communicating the sick, and another for reserving the host "under faithful custody of a key according to the intention of the council" (*sub fideli custodia clavi . . . secundum tenorem Concilii*).[123] The statutes attributed to Edmund, archbishop of Canterbury (d. 1240), specify a pyx of silver or tin (*stanneum*).[124] Similarly, a 1280 Council of Cologne required a pyx made of "gold, silver, ivory, or at least well-polished copper" (*aurea, argenta, eburnean, uel ad minus cuprea bene eminata*).[125] A 1287 synod at Exeter specified silver or ivory.[126] The 1287 synod of Liège specified pyxes made of gold, silver, or at least copper.[127]

Alongside the Paris statutes, *Statuimus* continued influencing local canon law. It was among the texts read aloud at English synods where priests with minimal education might be taught.[128] Moreover, we find echoes of *Statuimus* in a statute of Stephen Langton's 1222 Council of Oxford. It assigned archdeacons the duty of seeing that oil and chrism are kept locked up "according to the form of the general council." The Eucharist too was entrusted to a "faithful custodian."[129]

The 1240 Council of Worchester too addressed custody of the Eucharist, oil, and chrism in language from the Lateran canon, requiring them to be held within "a sufficient enclosure" (*sub competente clausura*). Concern also was expressed that mice or damp might make hosts vile to taste or sight. If archdeacons found sacred things "blasphemed" by sacrilegious persons, parish priests were threatened with punishment for negligence.[130]

123 *Councils & Synods* II, pt. 1, 171.

124 *Visitations of Churches Belonging to St. Paul's Cathedral*, xxxviii–xxxix.

125 Mansi 24:351. A 1287 council of the see of Liège provided for a pyx of "ivory, or silver, or at least well-polished copper"; see 24:897.

126 Mansi 24:789.

127 Mansi 23:897.

128 Cheney, *English Synodalia*, 31–33 and 45–48; Cheney, "Some Aspects of Diocesan Legislation during the Thirteenth Century," in Cheney, *Medieval Texts and Studies* (Oxford: Clarendon Press, 1973), 185–202. Cheney noted that statutes with copious addenda might have confused unlearned priests.

129 Mansi 22:1159: "XXIV: Quod oleum & Eucharistia custodiantur sub sera, & similiter chrisma. Prouideant utique archidiaconi, quod diligenter, juxta formam concilii generalis, Eucharistia, chrisma, & oleum sanctum, salua sub clauibus recondantur, fideli custodiae deputata." A 1280 synod of the diocese of Saintonge made separate provision for putting holy oils in fitting vessels; see ibid., 24:378. Archdeacons were key players in enforcing ecclesiastical discipline at the local level; see Cheney, *English Synodalia*, 22.

130 Mansi 23:528: ". . . secundum statuta Concilii generalis, Eucharistia simul cum oleo & chrismate, sub competente clausura seruetur: ne, quod absit, contingat in ipsis per sacrileges nomen Domini blasphemari. Quod si neglectum fuerit, ad archidiaconi uel uisitantis arbitrium, rectoris uel uicarii residentis negligentia puniatur." The same council decreed that lamps should burn day and night before the receptacle in which the Eucharist was reserved; see 23:528–29. See also *Councils & Synods* II, pt. 1, 299–300. The language

Ralph Walpole, bishop of Ely (d. 1302), required a locked pyx and chrismatory, so priests of the diocese "will be able to lay their hands on them easily, and to fulfill their duties without danger."[131]

On the Continent, a 1246 council at Fritzlar decreed, in language drawn from the Lateran Council, that the baptismal font, chrism, and Eucharist be kept "under faithful custody" (*sub Fideli custodia*) lest an "audacious hand" be extended to them.[132] A statute of Le Mans one year later restated *Statuimus*.[133] So too did a synod of Passau in 1284.[134] A provincial council of Tours (1253) reorganized the Lateran text with the Eucharist kept "under faithful custody." The font, as well as the containers of oil and chrism, were to be securely locked. Archdeacons, archpriests, and rural deans were charged with enforcing that regulation.[135] A synod at Nîmes in 1284 said a priest was not to be found negligent or careless in treating the sacraments, including by not keeping the Eucharist in a clean, locked place, honorably located.[136]

A few synods and councils enacted regulations phrased slightly differently. Thus, the 1281 Lambeth council required each parish to have a "decent and fitting" tabernacle, able to be locked; but it was to fit the size and resources of a church.[137] The 1287 council at Liège permitted reservation in a fitting place *sub altari* or in a small chest (*armariolo*), either under lock and key.[138] John Peckham, archbishop of Canterbury, required

about damp and mice appears in Robert Grosseteste, *Constitutions*: "Observent etiam sacerdotes cum omni diligentia ne sacra Eucharistia per vitium aut diutinam conservationem contraheret humiditatem seu mucorem, unde reddatur vel turpis aspectu vel gustui abominabilis" (*Councils & Synods* II, pt. 1, 265–78). See James Ginther, "Robert Grosseteste's Theology of Pastoral Care," in *A Companion to Pastoral Care in the Late Middle Ages*, ed. Robert J. Stansbury (Leiden: Brill, 2010), 95–122. The Worcester statutes probably used Grosseteste as a source; see Cheney, *English Synodalia*, 90–96. The same language was used in the statutes of Ely; see *Councils & Synods* II, pt. 1, 518.

131 Rubin, *Corpus Christi*, 43–44.

132 Mansi 23:725. The phrase "ne posit ad illa temeraria manus extendi" is a direct quotation from c. *Statuimus*.

133 Mansi 23:725. A reference to a Lateran canon against displaying relics for venal purposes followed without a rubric separating the texts.

134 Mansi 24:504, with the added words, "secundum constitutionem Lateranensis Concilii."

135 Mansi 23:809.

136 Mansi 24:534. "discrete praecipimus, quatenus a sacerdotibus Eucharistia in loco singulari mundo, & clavi firmato, simper honorifice collocate, devote ac fideliter conservetur."

137 Mansi 24:406: "& in qualibet ecclesia parochiali fiat tabernaculum cum clausura, decens & honestum, secundum magnitudinem & ecclesiae facultates." See also *Councils & Synods* II, pt. 2, 894.

138 Mansi 24:899: "XLII. Corpus domini in honesto loco sub altari vel in armariolo sub clave sollicite custodiatur. Similiter chrisma & oleum in alio loco."

keeping reserved hosts in a pyx so that they could be extracted without being harmed.[139]

In 1310, Antonio d'Orso Biliotti, bishop of Florence, adapted the Lateran decree, combining use of a clean pyx with secure reservation on or near an altar. No one was to be furnished with the body of Christ, chrism, or oil except within a sacramental rite. Violators of that rule merited excommunication. Nor was anyone to touch them without the priest's knowledge lest they be used for sacrilegious purposes. Biliotti also reflected concern that the reserved Eucharist and holy oils might be used in magical practices.[140]

Enacting regulations about reservation continued in the fifteenth century. A 1440 statute from Freising quoted *Statuimus* in its instructions about protecting reserved sacraments. The text added to established penalties for negligence payment of a pound of wax to the church.[141] A 1435 statute from Strasbourg extended this regulation to care of altar cloths and ecclesiastical ornaments.[142] The 1447 Council of Eichstadt included abuse of the Eucharist or holy oils among the *casus episcopales*, sins absolved by the bishop except in cases of utter necessity.[143] Another Eichstadt statute warned that the priest, and not a secular person, should have the keys to the sacraments.[144] A canon from Schwerin said that clergy were not to open locked repositories because the laity wished it.[145] A synod in Mecklenburg (1492) issued a similar command.[146] The Bamberg statutes of 1491 included abuse of sacred things among the *casus episcopales*.[147]

139 *Visitations of Churches Belonging to St. Paul's Cathedral*, xxx.

140 Trexler, *Synodal Law*, 267–68.

141 *Concilia Germaniae* 5:276: "Item praecipiendo mandamus, ut secundum Constitutionem *Lateranensis Concilii*, Eucharistia, Chrisma, & Oleum Sanctum sub fideli custodia, & reverentia debita, clavibus adhibitis, conserventur: ne possit ad illa temeraria manus extendi ad aliqua horribilia, & nefanda exercenda. Si vero is, ad quem spectat custodia, ea incaute reliquerit, ultra juris communis poenas, in librae cerae eidem Ecclesiae solvenda, & applicanda puniatur." This statute was repeated in 1480 with additional instructions about keeping liturgical cloths clean to avoid horrifying the faithful; see ibid., 6:520–21.

142 *Concilia Germaniae* 5:239. See also a Würzburg statute of 1446 in 5:341.

143 Ibid., 5:369.

144 Ibid., 5:367: "clavibus apud Sacerdotes, & non in manibus compagnatorum, & aliarum secularium personarum semper retentis."

145 Ibid., 5:646: "Item praecipimus, statuimus, & ordinamus, volumusque, & mandamus, ne venerabile Sacramentum Eucharistie in capsulis, seu locis seratis publicis, ad nutum Parochianorum aperiendis, habeatur. Sed in Ciboriis Ecclesiarum (locoque decenti & apto) locates sub congrua clausura, per Plebanum, & non custodem, in ruralibus Ecclesiis reverenter honorificeque cum omni cura recondatur."

146 Ibid.: "ne venerabile Sacramentum Eucharistie in capsulis, seu locis seratis publicis, ad nutum Parochianorum aperiendis, habeatur."

147 Ibid., 5:631: "Item abutiens quomodo Sacramentis Ecclesiae, ut puta Hostia, Crismate vel alia re sacra. Casus Episcopales."

Further afield, a 1413 statute of Wenceslaus, commendatory bishop of Olomuc, expressed concern that chrism might fall into the hands of irreverent lay people who might sell it or work magic. Enforcement of this statute was entrusted to rural deans.[148] The 1461 diocesan statutes from Brno in Moravia required that only the parish priest have keys to the repository of hosts, chrism, and oils.[149] Even a Hussite council in Prague (1421) issued statutes concerning reservation of the Eucharist, baptismal water, and oils.[150]

Enforcement of Local Enactments

How well reservation matched the Lateran Council's norms or those of synods is difficult to determine. Reservation was not at first a subject of intensive enforcement. Even Juliana of Mont Cornillon, visiting the recluse Eve, sensed the absence of the reserved Eucharist in the church of St. Martin, but was unsure whether that was the local custom.[151] However, from the thirteenth century onward, archdeacons were charged with responsibility to see that the Eucharist was reserved for communion of the sick. Negligent priests were threatened with punishment for failing in performance of that duty.[152] The Council of Le Mans extended this supervisory responsibility to archpriests and rural deans.[153]

As archdeacons were to enforce regulations about vessels, vestments, and books, local councils and synods told parish priests and church wardens that they were to present all liturgical objects for inspection (*visitatio rerum*).[154] Part of the equipment required in a parish was that used for the communion of the sick. This equipment included items that could be used for more than one purpose. Thus, the 1287 Council of Exeter ordered parishes to have a bell to ring at the elevation of the host and during viaticum processions.[155]

148 *Synody a statute Olomoucké* (ed. Krafl), 179.

149 Ibid., 222.

150 *Concilia Germaniae* 5:199–201.

151 *The Life of Juliana of Mont-Cornillon*, trans. Barbara Newman (Toronto: Peregrina, 2002), 55. See also Barbara R. Walters, "The Feast and its Founder," in *The Feast of Corpus Christi*, ed. Walters, Vincent Corrigan, and Peter T. Ricketts (University Park: Pennsylvania State University Press, 2006), 3–54, at 18.

152 Mansi 23.528; *Councils & Synods* II, pt. 1, 299. See also the first Salisbury statutes in pt. 1, 148. Walter de Cantelupe also required that a lamp burn before the reserved host, see pt. 1, 300

153 Mansi 23:753.

154 For example, see the statutes attributed to Robert Winchelsey, archbishop of Canterbury, in *Councils & Synods* II, pt. 1, 1386–87. *Visitatio rerum* was supposed to accompany inquiry into the conduct of clergy and laity, *visitatio hominum*; see Coulet, *Les visites pastorals*, 30–31.

155 Mansi 23:801; *Councils & Synods* II, pt. 2, 1006.

The pyxes available in parishes for communion of the sick could differ widely. In England, for example, visitations of parishes dependent on St. Paul's Cathedral showed a variety of materials employed in their making, possibly because of differing economic conditions of these churches.[156] The 1297 visitation of churches belonging to St. Paul's found repositories for the Eucharist varying in material from wood to enamel, where a proper receptacle was present. Four of the sixteen churches were found to be deficient in the quality of the housing or its lack of a lock.[157] During the 1458 visitation, a pyx for carrying communion was found nested inside one for reservation.[158] As late as the reign of Henry VIII, there were concerns in the diocese of Lincoln about the lack of a pyx or its being in poor condition.[159] When a strict Reformation was implemented under Edward VI, the inventories of Albury, Chiswick, and St. Pancras still included pyxes, though two reported that theirs were made of latten, a copper alloy.[160]

Some visitation instructions focused on larger issues. The archdeacons of the diocese of Lincoln were told in 1233 to inquire whether the Eucharist was housed fittingly, as well as whether it was borne properly to the sick.[161] In 1281, John Peckham, archbishop of Canterbury, commanded bishops and archdeacons to take care that the consecrated species not be found corrupted.[162] John Waltham, bishop of Salisbury (1388–95), inquired during visitations how parishes kept "pyx, font, and, chrismatory" secured.[163] The 1301 visitation of Clyton in the diocese of Exeter noted that the parish had a pyx of ivory "securely" hanging but not locked; nor was the "lead chrismatory" locked.[164]

When visitors found defects in care of the sacraments, the clergy might be threatened with penalties. Thus, the statutes of York (ca. 1241–45)

156 *Visitations of Churches belonging to St. Paul's Cathedral*, xxxi–xxxii.

157 Ibid., xxx–xxxi and 8.

158 Ibid., 83 and 91.

159 *Visitations in the Diocese of Lincoln 1517–1531*, ed. A. Hamilton Thompson (Woodbridge: Boydell, 2008), 1:13, 22, 24, 138. One parish lacked a pyx and kept reserved hosts wrapped in a cloth; see 16.

160 *Visitations of Churches Belonging to St. Paul's Cathedral*, 115–16 and 119. These parishes may have hidden or sold some vessels in advance of confiscation by the crown; see Eamon Duffy, *The Stripping of the Altars: Traditional Religion in England 1400–1580* (New Haven, CT: Yale University Press, 1992), 482–86.

161 Mansi 23:327. Ross William Collins, "The Parish Priest and His Flock as Depicted by the Councils of the Twelfth and Thirteenth Centuries," *The Journal of Religion* 10 (1930): 313–32.

162 Rubin, *Corpus Christi*, 44. A bishop of Bordeaux warned about hosts found eaten by worms; see 44–45.

163 King, *Eucharistic Reservation*, 69. Salisbury visitations from 1220 twice mentioned the type of pyx used at a church; see Browe, *Verehrung der Eucharistie im Mittelalter*, 18n119.

164 *Pastors and the Care of Souls* (ed. Shinners and Dohar), 301. Visitations of the diocese of Hereford also noted the removal of the lock from one baptismal font and the lack of one on another; see 293 and 295.

mandated a three-month suspension for careless custody of the Eucharist.[165] The bishop might also use the threat of a visitation to coerce priests into following liturgical norms.[166] A priest might also be asked by his confessor whether he had let the reserved sacrament become corrupt or infested with worms, as well as about neglecting custody of chrism.[167] The early fifteenth-century visitations by the dean of Salisbury pointed out failures of churches to lock pyx, font, or chrismatory. In those cases, church wardens, rather than the clergy, were threatened with censures if they did not remedy these defects.[168] Providing fit housing for reserved sacrament and oils was an obligation of church wardens in other parts of England. Complete conformity of practice, however, never was achieved.[169]

The prospect of a visitation must have sent parishes scrambling to present a good appearance. To prevent deception, the third Winchester statutes forbade parishes borrowing vestments and ornaments from nearby churches.[170] Likewise, a synod of Exeter (1287) complained that parishes borrowed ornaments, including a pyx for viaticum.[171] One reason a parish might need to borrow ornaments was theft. Pyxes, especially those made of silver or gold, were among the objects often stolen.[172] Church wardens' accounts can show what items were purchased. The wardens of Morebath in Devon, for example, bought a new "purse" for carrying communion to the sick in the period before the Reformation.[173]

Housing of the reserved Eucharist remained an issue on the Continent. The visitation records of Eudes Rigaud, archbishop of Rouen, for 1249 show him requiring the monastery at St. Ouen see to the proper care

165 *Councils & Synods* II, pt. 1, 491. See also the statutes of Chichester of 1289 in pt. 2, 1087. Visitors to the churches under the jurisdiction of St. Paul's London in 1297 found, however, that seven of sixteen parishes lacked copies of the appropriate statutes; see Cheney, *English Synodalia*, 143.

166 Fulk Basset's statutes for London in *Councils & Synods* II, pt. 1, 649.

167 Hostiensis, *Summa aurea*, 1786–87: "non custodiunt chrisma, vel eucharistiam, sicut debent." Catherine Rider, "What to Ask in Confession," 81–82 and 94.

168 *The Register of John Chandler Dean of Salisbury 1404–1417*, ed. T. C. B. Timmins (Devizes: Wiltshire Records Society, 1984), 18, 22, 27, 113, 116–17.

169 Rubin, *Corpus Christi*, 45–47.

170 *Councils & Synods* II, pt. 1, 710. See also the first Canterbury statutes (1213–14) in pt. 1, 28–29.

171 Mansi 24:801; *Councils & Synods* II, pt. 2, 1006. The same synod also required that clergy, not the laity, have custody of church ornaments. It apportioned blame to the priest if something was stolen from the chancel, but to the laity if the theft occurred in the nave of the church.

172 A parish might resort to the crown's courts for a remedy when liturgical objects were stolen; see Robert C. Palmer, *Selling the Church: The English Parish in Law, Commerce and Religion, 1350–1550* (Chapel Hill: University of North Carolina Press, 2002), 69–70.

173 Eamon Duffy, *The Voices of Morebath: Reformation and Rebellion in an English Village* (New Haven, CT: Yale University Press, 2001), 66.

of the sacraments reserved in its church.[174] A fifteenth-century visitation in the diocese of Geneva reported finding hosts "scattered uselessly in the pyx among the dust and worms and without a corporal."[175] In the mid-fifteenth century, Cardinal Niccolò Albergati ordered a visitation for the cathedral of Bologna, which was to include inspecting the reserved Eucharist, oils, and relics.[176] Antoninus of Florence began visitations by checking whether the Eucharist was well kept. In one case, he ordered a church to create a tabernacle together with "some devout picture" (*cum quadam pictura deuota*).[177] His *Confessionale "Defecerunt"* asked priests whether they kept the reserved Eucharist so badly that it was eaten by mice or even lost.[178]

The 1455 instructions of Nicholas of Cusa for visitations in the diocese of Brixen expanded the list of items to be kept under lock and key to relics.[179] Cusanus wanted to know if the Eucharist, chrism, and baptismal water were kept decently.[180] He also issued a statute requiring priests to keep the keys of the reserved Eucharist and oils, except when they were kept in chapels far from the parish church. Only then could the keys be committed to other reliable persons.[181] The rites that priests of Brixen were expected to know included consecrating the Eucharist and administering extreme unction.[182]

Records of archdeacons' visitations for France include those of Henri de Vézelay, archdeacon of Hiémois in the diocese of Bayeux. They give us a glimpse of ecclesiastical discipline in thirteenth-century Normandy. Thus, in 1267 Henri required the parish of Folie to buy a lead chalice for viaticum.[183] The next year he told the parish of Bavent to acquire a lantern for

174 *The Register of Eudes of Rouen*, trans. Jeremiah F. O'Sullivan (New York: Columbia University Press, 1964), 62–63; Davis, *The Holy Bureaucrat*, 8, 81, 84, 88–89, 101–2, 138 (esp. 88).

175 Rubin, *Corpus Christi*, 44.

176 Riccardo Parmegiani, *Il vescovo e capitulo: Il cardinale Niccolò Albergati e I canonici di S. Pietro di Bologna (1417)* (Bologna: Bononia University Press, 2009), 117.

177 Stefano Orlandi, *S. Antonino (arcivescovo di Firenze, dottore della Chiesa): Studi bibliografici* (Florence: Edizioni il Rosario, 1959), 1:147–48.

178 University of Pennsylvania Ms. Codex 18, fol. 134r: "Si non diligenter preseruauit eucharistiam sub sera propter quod aliquid perditur. uel a muribus deuoratur." He also was concerned about magical uses of baptismal water and holy oil; see fol. 27v.

179 *Akten zur Reform des Bistums Brixen* (ed. Hürten), 26: "Item an eucharistie sacramentum reliquieque sanctorum, sacra vnctio, baptismus et vasa sacrata sub clave et debitis custodia teneantur et qualiter."

180 Ibid., 28.

181 Ibid., 35: "Item sacerdotes habeant claves ad sacramentum eucharistie et oleum sacrum, nisi propter distantiam capellarum opporteat committi edituis fide dignis, qui tandem sub magna custodia teneant easdem claves."

182 *Akten zur Reform des Bistums Brixen*, 26.

183 Delisle, "Visites pastorales," 463–64.

viaticum processions.[184] One of the issues to be addressed in the 1408 visitations of Reims was whether worms were found in the reserved sacrament.[185]

The visitations of the archdeaconry of Josas in the 1460s and 1470s often documented which churches handled the reserved Eucharist fittingly, as well as which had defects requiring remedies. Some parishes were told to build a tabernacle, repair one, install a lock, and be careful not to leave the keys lying around. A church might lack a pyx for carrying viaticum, or keep reserved hosts wrapped in a cloth. Worms or mice were found in tabernacles, and priests were told to refresh the reserved Eucharist more often.[186]

It is harder to document misuse of chrism or hosts. Church courts mention hearing cases of sorcery, but the records are few in number.[187] Some cases may have been handled in the internal forum of penance. Thus, William of Rennes, glossing the *Summa* of Raymond of Peñafort, asked whether clerics who worked magic with the sacraments, especially the Eucharist, chrism, blessed oil, or baptismal water, incurred canonical irregularity. He noted differing opinions but recommended getting the cleric a dispensation.[188]

John of Freiburg thought misuse of sacraments and sacred things a sacrilege. He made a point of saying how dreadful a sin was any evil act contrary to the Eucharist.[189] John of Erfurt, a fourteenth-century Franciscan, wanted clergy negligent in custody of holy things subjected to canonical censures.[190] Andreas Escobar said that loss of a host or part of one earned a cleric thirty days of penance.[191] Antoninus of Florence wanted

184 Ibid., 466.

185 Mansi 26:1070.

186 *Visites archidiaconales de Josas*, 4, 13, 17–18, 23, 25, 27, 38, 41, 47–49, 65, 72–73, 76, 79, 96, 100, 108, 126, 151, 155, 183, 196, 238, 267–68, 277, 280, 322, 356, 359, 378, 382. One priest gave part of a broken host to a sick woman but reserved the remainder; see 131.

187 See, e.g., *Lower Ecclesiastical Jurisdiction in Late-Medieval England: The Courts of the Dean and Chapter of Lincoln, 1336–1349, and the Deanery of Wisbech, 1458–1484*, ed. L. R. Poos (Oxford: British Academy, 2001), 26, 64, 106, 352–53, 463, 553.

188 *Summa Sancti Raymundi de Peniafort de poenitentia, et matrimonio* (Rome: Tallini, 1603; Farnborough: Gregg, 1967), 105–6: "aut qui de sacrame[n]tis Ecclesiae, Eucharistia scilicet, vel Chrismate, vel oleo benedicto, aut aqua fontium facit sortilegium, vel baptizat imaginem. Unde in hoc consulendu[m] est talibus, q[uod] petant dispensationem."

189 Johannes de Friburgo, *Summa confessorum* I, t. 13, q. 3: "Item grauissimum peccatum est sacrilegium contra sacramentum eucharistie. Quia hoc continet ipsum Christum."

190 Johannes de Erfordia, *Die Summa confessorum*, 2:119.

191 Andreas Escobar, *Lumen confessorum*, fol. 7vb, citing *De cons.*, D. 2, c. *Qui bene.*

confessors to ask about magical acts with sacred things. He was, however, suspicious of the belief that witches could fly.[192]

There is some evidence that hosts were reported to have been misused. A fifteenth-century necromancer's manual recommended using consecrated bread in rituals.[193] Tales of stolen hosts abound in the literature of witchcraft and accusations against Jews. Christians, particularly servants, were suspected of obtaining hosts for abuse by Jews. Usually, these thefts were supposedly done while receiving communion without swallowing the host, rather than by breaking into a tabernacle or pyx to steal one.[194] The fear of misuse of the Eucharist was sufficiently grave that the inquisitor Bernard Gui provided a formula of abjuration for those who did magic using the body of Christ.[195] Bernardino of Siena, a century later, warned priests against performing magical rites with sacred items. He also told priests to lock up the Eucharist and chrism to prevent old women from taking them to use in magic.[196]

In Rome during the reign of Pope Nicholas V, the Apostolic Penitentiary absolved a priest from Salzburg who took "the sacrament," chrism, and holy water from another church in order to conduct a secret baptism.[197] Such an offense was rare compared with the numerous requests for the Penitentiary to remedy illegitimacy, but it points to reasons why the canon law of reservation was a concern of pastors and prelates.

CARRYING VIATICUM TO THE SICK

A long-established question in ecclesiastical circles was who might carry to the bedridden viaticum, food for life's last journey.[198] Carrying viaticum

192 Antoninus, *Confessionale "Defecerunt"* (Cologne: Zel, 1470), *De decem praeceptis, De aqua* & *De terra*. Thomas M. Izbicki, "Antoninus of Florence and the Dominican Witch Theorists," *Memorie Domenicane* 42 (2012): 347–62. See also Izbicki, "Defending a Conservative View on Witches: Juan de Torquemada on c. *Episcopi* [C. 26 q. 5 c. 12]," in *Law as Profession and Practice: Essays in Honor of James A. Brundage*, ed. Kenneth Pennington and Melodie Harris Eichbauer (Farnham: Ashgate, 2011), 27–41.

193 Richard Kieckhefer, *Forbidden Rites: A Necromancer's Manual of the Fifteenth Century* (University Park: Pennsylvania State University Press, 1998), 137, 226, 331, 338.

194 Walter Stephens, *Demon Lovers: Witchcraft, Sex and the Crisis of Belief* (Chicago: University of Chicago Press, 2002), 221–23; Rubin, *Gentile Tales*, 33, 52, 61, 73, 75.

195 Rubin, *Corpus Christi*, 341.

196 Franco Mormando, *The Preacher's Demons: Bernardino of Siena and the Social Underworld of Early Renaissance Italy* (Chicago: University of Chicago Press, 1999), 96.

197 *Verzeichnis der in den Supplikenregistern der Pönitentiarie Nikolaus' V. vorkommenden Personen, Kirchen und Orte des Deutschen Reiches, 1447–1455*, ed. Ludwig Schmugge et al. (Tübingen: Niemeyer, 1999), 10 (no. 68).

198 Guido of Monte Rochen, *Handbook for Curates*, 51.

to the sick probably was informal at first, but by the tenth century formal processions were being conducted.[199] In fact, reservation of the Eucharist cannot be divorced from the carrying of viaticum. When the Decretalists discussed *Statuimus*, some focused on the proper person to take viaticum to the dangerously ill, building on older texts. Although the issue had been settled in practice many years before,[200] the Ordinary Gloss on the *Gregorian Decretals* denied that lay persons could carry communion. In the absence of a priest, only a deacon could (with permission) perform this pastoral function.[201] Similarly, Geoffrey of Trani's *Summa super titulis decretalium* specified that no lay man or any woman could carry viaticum.[202] Hostiensis stated a similar opinion in his *Summa* and in his *Commentary*, both saying little more about carrying viaticum in procession.[203]

One papal decretal did affect viaticum processions by requiring veneration of the host being carried to a sick person. Pope Honorius III, in his decretal *Sane*, required priests to teach the faithful to reverence the carried Eucharist as they would the elevated host at Mass. This text appeared in *Compilatio quinta*.[204] Then it entered the *Gregorian Decretals* in the title "On the Celebration of Masses, the Sacrament of the Eucharist and Divine Offices" (*De celebratione missarum et sacramento eucharistiae et divinis officiis*).[205] Honorius threatened those prelates who failed to enforce *Sane* with his wrath and that of God.[206]

Some canonists gave attention to those provisions of *Sane*. Hostiensis explained that the priest should wear a suitable garment with a stole. The priest was to take more than one host, so that he would not be without one when returning to the church. The faithful might otherwise be deceived into venerating a mere creature, lacking the sacrament, if he returned with an empty pyx. However, if he had to expend all his hosts communicating sick persons, the priest was to prevent the faithful falling into idolatry. Hostiensis told him to have the lamp extinguished and the bell silenced to keep the faithful from thinking he still carried the sacrament.[207]

199 Snoek, *Medieval Piety*, 251.

200 Ibid., 44–45.

201 Glo. Ord. at X 3.44.1.

202 *Summa Goffredi*, fol. 165vb, citing *Pervenit*.

203 Hostiensis, *Summa aurea*, 1198, also citing *Pervenit*. Hostiensis, *In tertium librum decretaium commentaria* II, fol. 166rb.

204 *Quinque compilationes antiquae* (ed. Friedberg), 178 (V 3.24.1).

205 Friedberg 2:642 (X 3.41.10).

206 Ibid.

207 Hostiensis, *Decretalium commentaria* II, fol. 166rb.

Johannes Andreae restated Hostiensis's discussion of the way a priest should dress to carry viaticum.[208] He also gave instructions for how a priest was to carry the host in its pyx, holding it reverently on his breast, not beneath his outer garment or under his chin. Johannes also repeated what Hostiensis had said about carrying more than one host or, when returning without one, extinguishing the lamp and silencing the bell.[209]

The canonists agreed that the faithful were to be taught to venerate the carried host just like one that was elevated at Mass. Hostiensis instructed parish priests to tell their parishioners to send him their children for instruction in the rudiments of the faith and to learn such reverent conduct.[210] Johannes Andreae said the faithful were to be instructed to bow reverently to the carried sacrament, telling them to reverence it.[211]

The Script for Viaticum Processions

These generalities aside, arrangements for delivery of communion to the sick were left to local councils and synods. These assemblies almost always presupposed the priest's role as the bearer of viaticum.[212] Their decrees laid down rules for priests going to ailing parishioners. Councils also gave guidance, through the parish priest, to those who might see a consecrated host being carried in procession. The script for these viaticum processions had become fixed in practice by the end of the twelfth century.

One of the most influential enactments about viaticum processions was that of Odo of Sully, bishop of Paris. In his instructions concerning the sacrament of the altar, Odo commanded that the Eucharist be carried with reverence and maturity "enclosed in an ivory pyx" with a lamp borne before. The priest and his attendant were to chant the penitential psalms and a litany both going out and returning.[213] The bishop also wanted the laity taught to kneel "as if to their Lord and Creator," praying with their

208 Johannes Andreae, *In tertium decretalium librum novella commentaria* (Venice, 1581; Turin, 1966), fol. 223vb, v. *Decenter.*

209 Ibid., fol. 223vb [*Referat*].

210 Hostiensis, *Decretalium comentaria* II, fol. 166ra, [*Doceat*] & [*Idem faciens*].

211 Johannes Andreae, *In tertium decretalium librum novella commentaria*, fol. 223vb [*Decenti*].

212 A legatine council at Westminster (1138) allowed, in the absence of a priest or even a deacon, carrying of communion by whomever (*per quemlibet*) in a case of necessity (*necessitate instante*); see *Councils & Synods* I, pt. 2, 774–75.

213 Mansi 22:677–78; *Statuts synodaux* 1:58–61. The 1279 Council of Münster specified saying the penitential psalms and other prayers; see Mansi 24:315. The 1281 synod of Liège said to start with the penitential psalms but add other psalms, the litany, and prayers if the way was long; see Mansi 23:897–98. Likewise, see the 1410 *Liber synodalis* of Salamanca in *Synodicon Hispanum* 4:131.

hands clasped, when viaticum passed.[214] Even when the host was enclosed and veiled, the faithful were expected to believe that they were in the presence of the divinity.

In 1238, Robert Grosseteste, bishop of Lincoln, instructed his clergy to teach the faithful to bow their heads at the elevated host or viaticum. Also, reserved hosts were to be kept in a clean, sealed receptacle, allowing the priest, properly robed, to carry them to the sick, whole and decently veiled. A "light" was to be carried before, and a bell was to call attention of the laity to the procession, with the faithful adoring Christ carried among them.[215] (The canonist Antonius de Butrio gave the lamp a symbolic meaning, the "splendor of eternal light" [*candor lucis eternae*].)[216]

The 1287 statutes of Liège required carrying the host reverently atop a chalice marked with a cross and wrapped in a cloth with silk tassels.[217] The province of Reims required the priest to be decently dressed, an injunction coupled with requirements that all vestments and ornaments be kept clean.[218] The 1481 synod at Tournai required both of these things, quoting the Reims statutes. Negligence was to be reported to the bishop's curia for canonical punishment.[219]

Such instructions were widely diffused in England.[220] Thus, an unidentified council reused Odo's text on the carrying of viaticum.[221] Odo's instructions to the laity also made it, with minor changes, into statutes prepared on behalf of Stephen Langton, archbishop of Canterbury, for the 1222 Council of Oxford. The faithful were to be instructed to reverence the host "like their creator and redeemer," praying humbly. Langton, like Grosseteste after him, tied adoration of the carried host to the reverence given at the elevation of the host and the chalice during Mass.[222]

214 Mansi 22:678.

215 Letter 52*; *The Letters of Robert Grosseteste Bishop of Lincoln*, ed. Frank A. C. Mantello and Joseph Goering (Toronto: University of Toronto Press, 2010), 182–93. Grosseteste's instructions were reordered here for clarity. See also *Councils & Synods* II, pt. 1, 268. Ginther, "Robert Grosseteste's Theology of Pastoral Care," in *A Companion to Pastoral Care* (ed. Stansbury), 95–122.

216 Antonius de Butrio, *Super tertio libro decretalium* (Venice: Apud Iuntas, 1578; Turin: Bottega d'Erasmo, 1967), fol. 194ra–b.

217 *Concilia Germaniae* 3:692: "Referatur [Deferatur] autem Corpus Domini venerabiliter & sublimiter, posito decenter cooperculo, super calice, quod sit cum cruce supposita, & panno fimbriis sericis adornato."

218 *Les actes de la province ecclésiastique de Reims*, ed. Thomas Marie Gousset (Reims: Jacquet, 1843), 2:751.

219 *Concilia Germaniae* 5:526–27: "Curiae nostrae referant canonice puniendos."

220 Cheney, *English Synodalia*, 83 and 88.

221 Mansi 22:731–32. Rubin, *Corpus Christi*, 80.

222 Mansi 22:1175–76. Langton also discussed the possibility that a deacon might carry viaticum if a priest was not available; see 22:1175.

Such instructions were not limited to England and France. A Scottish council of 1225 ordered a priest to use a clean purse (*bursa*) when carrying the Eucharist. A lamp was to precede, and a bell was to be rung to arouse the devotion of the faithful. An exception was permitted if the sick person lived far from the church.[223] In Eastern Europe, the diocese of Olumuc required a priest, cleanly and fittingly robed, to carry the Eucharist with a small banner (*cum vexillo parvo*) and a light, or a light and a bell, going before. The faithful were to kneel when the saw the procession pass.[224] In Spain, the 1320 synod of Santiago de Compostella reported that it was acting because priests failed to administer the sacrament to the sick. It required the priest to go dressed properly with a cross, bell, and candle (inside the city) or a lantern (outside) going before. Priests who failed to do this were to be fined, with the money going to the fabric of the cathedral.[225] Bishop Odo's instructions were replicated down to the recommended use of an ivory pyx in the 1240 synodal decrees from Lisbon.[226] The Mecklenburg statutes of 1492 required the priest to carry the pyx reverently before his breast (*ante pectus*).[227]

In Catalonia, the *Ordinarium* for Barcelona offered instructions for communion. It began with instructions of how the priest was to take up the repository of the reserved sacrament and say psalms on the way to a sick person's home.[228] Much of the text was given in Catalan, including the greeting when the priest reached the sickbed.[229] An opportunity for confession and absolution was to be offered, followed by giving the sick person a crucifix to venerate (*Ador te senyor deu meu iesu crist*).[230] The rite for viaticum, given in Catalan, began with asking the sick person about receiving the sacrament. One could receive it or adore the host instead. Then the

223 Mansi 22:1240. The preceding canon required use of a clean pyx for reservation of the Eucharist and the replacement of the reserved sacrament once a week; see 22:1239.

224 Krafl, *Synody a statuta Olomoucké diecéze*, 132: "Item quod plebani et clerici infirmos visitant et Ipsos reconcilient et post ipsorum confessionem et iniunctam penitenciam ipsos oleo sancto ungant et propria manu communicant equidem et corpus Domini ad infirmos Ipsos cum vexillo parvo, lumine et nola antecedente deferant reverenter" (162, 178, 220). Some of these canons connect reverencing viaticum with adoration of the elevated host at Mass.

225 *Synodicon Hispanum* 1:298. The same thing was said briefly by the 1281 Council of Braga; see ibid., 2:22–23.

226 Ibid., 2:288.

227 *Concilia Germaniae* 5:646.

228 *Ordinarium sacramentorum Barcinonense* (Barcelona: Posa, 1501; Barcelona: Institut d'Estudis Catalans, 1991), fol. r ii^{r}: "accepta custodia vel alio in quo sit repositum corpus christi tendat: et per viam dicat aliquos psamos secundum consuetudinem loci."

229 Ibid.: "Senyer o madona lo sant spirit sia ab vos."

230 Ibid., fol. r ii^{v}–[r 3]^{r}.

priest was to wash his fingers (*ablutis digitis*) before handling the host.[231] He was to say the formula, "The body of our Lord Jesus Christ keep you, sinner, and lead you to eternal life. Amen" (*Corpus domini nostri ieus cristi custodiat te peccatorem, et perducat te in uitam eternam Amen*).[232] The priest could return to the church saying the Athanasian Creed. Upon reaching the church he could grant indulgences to those who accompanied him.[233]

The Majorca *Ordinarium* provided instruction for communicating the sick, one set for the laity and another for a priest. The former was mainly in the vernacular rather than Latin, including an examination of the patient's belief.[234] The Cartagena *Ordinarium* provided more detailed instructions. The priest was to begin by ringing the great bell (*campana*) and then a small bell (*campanella*) at the doors of the church, gathering the faithful to accompany him. Then he was to wash his hands and dress properly for ministry. Thus outfitted, he was to enter the sacristy and take the pyx (*custodiam*) or some other sacred vessel with many consecrated hosts (*plures forme consecratę*). A procession was formed with a cleric leading, sounding a bell before the body of Christ. The laity were to come next, and then any other priests, two by two. The priests were to say the *Magnificat* (*Canticum graduum*) and the office of the Virgin on the way.[235] The curate carrying the sacrament was to walk near the end with the older priests.[236]

The island of Cyprus had both Latin and Greek populations. Differences over sacramental matters were among the problems between them. A provincial council at Nicosia tried to defuse these tensions by advocating coexistence, saying they were to live "in concord, like true worshipers." Furthermore, "a different custom in the Church of God is no hinderance to the unity of the faith."[237] The provincial instructions said Greeks were

231 Ibid., fol. s i^{r-v}: "Si dicat sic: tradit illi. Si dicit non: adoret illud."

232 Ibid., fol. s ii^{v}.

233 Ibid., fol. [s 3]$^{r-v}$.

234 *Ordinarium de administratione sacramentorum cum pluribus additionibus adeo necessariis secundum ritum alme sedis maioriensis*, fol. xlv^{v}–l^{v}. Instructions for sick communion during an interdict followed at fol. l^{v}.

235 *Ordinarium manuale de ministratione sacramentorum secundum consuetudinem ecclesię Carthaginensis* (Granada, 1545), fol. lxxx^{r-v}, at lxxx^{v}: "Alii autem sacerdotes: et laici stent cum luminarijs / et palio deuote expectantes extra sacrarium. Deinde ordinetur sic processionaliter: vt portans campanellam pręcedat pulsando semper coram corpore christi. Postea vadant laici: deinde sacerdotes bini et bini sequantur ordinati / dicentes cum deuotione / voçe Sonora. Canticum graduum et Officium beate marię."

236 *Ordinarium secundum consuetudinem ecclesię Carthaginensis*, fol. lxxx^{v}–lxxxi^{r}. The text added mention of taking holy water to the sickbed. Those who saw the sacrament being carried were expected to bow their heads and genuflect (*inclinent capita sua: et flectent genua sua*).

237 *The Synodicum Nicosiense* (ed. Schabel), 118–19. Schabel, "Martyrs and Heretics, Intolerance of Intolerance: The Execution of Thirteen Monks in Cyprus in 1231," in Schabel, *Greeks, Latins, and the Church in Early Frankish Cyprus* (Farnham: Ashgate, 2010), 1–31.

to be taught by their priests to kneel when the Eucharist was carried to the sick (probably by a Latin priest), saying "Hail the world's salvation, clean flesh, holy flesh, immaculate flesh, true God, true man."[238] Priests also were to determine to which rite a sick person belonged before giving communion.[239] The Greeks, according to Pope Innocent IV, were to renew the reserved Eucharist every fifteen days to be on hand for viaticum.[240] The constitutions of Nicosia added instructions regarding how a Latin priest was to dress for carrying viaticum, preceded by a cleric carrying a light.[241] The fourteenth-century constitutions of Archbishop Philip added that priests were not to administer the sacraments to members of a different ecclesial community "except in a case of evident necessity" (*nisi in casu necessitatis evidentis*).[242]

Problems of Distance and Danger

Problems of distance to be traversed and potential dangers on the way were not ignored by Latin churches. Thus, a provincial council held by Edmund, archbishop of Canterbury in 1230 required a parish to have a vessel of silver or tin for carrying communion to the sick. The council provided, however, that a light or lamp might be left out of the priest's procession to a sick person far away, possibly because it might go out during a long walk.[243] The 1247 Council of Le Mans also permitted omitting the light if the weather was unfavorable.[244] A Würzburg statute of 1446 forbade priests from wearing clogs when carrying communion on muddy roads.[245] Taking a slightly different tack, the synodal statutes of Winchester (ca.

238 *Synodicum Nicosiense*, 124–27, at 126: "Quapropter districte praecipiant tam clericis quam laicis ut, cum ad infirmos Eucharistia portatur, praesentes flectant genua et eidem reverenter inclinent, dicentes haec verba quae eos doceri volumus: 'Ave salus mundi, caro munda, caro sancta, caro immaculara verus Deus, verus homo.'"

239 Ibid., 128–31.

240 Ibid., 124–27, at 126. For Innocent's letter to the legate Eudes of Châteauroux, see 308.

241 Ibid., 98–101.

242 Ibid., 268–71.

243 Mansi 23:373. The 1279 Council of Münster specified use of lamp and bell if the sick person was nearby, but only a bell if he or she was farther away; see 24:315. The legatine council at York (1195) made allowances for "intemperate air" and the difficulty of the way; see *Councils & Synods* I, pt. 2, 1048.

244 Mansi 23:746–47. See also the Worcester statutes in 23:528–29 and 615.

245 *Concilia Germania*, 6:341: "Insuper nullus de cetero Sacerdotes in deportatione saluberrimi Corporis Domini nostri Sacramenti, quantumcunque aura mala, via lubrica, vel lutuosa existat, in calopediis ire presumat." Other statements on "clogs" were issued by a 1483 synod at Constance and the 1491 assembly at Bamburg; see 6:560.

1224) specified a ritual for carrying the Eucharist in towns with a candle and holy water carried before the host.[246]

A 1307 synod of Lisbon took cognizance of a potential problem not often mentioned, the carrying of viaticum on horseback to remote locations. The decree described the practice as possibly scandalous and dangerous to the priest. It was permitted only when the cross and other things necessary for communion also were carried on horseback.[247] A 1281 statute of Liège urged those present on horseback to dismount and venerate Christ in a carried host.[248]

On rare occasion some thought was given to potential dangers to priests going to the sick. Thus, Honoré Bonet presented an argument that a priest carrying communion could lawfully defend himself if attacked on the way, even if he could not reach the parishioner in time to "housel" him or her. Bonet noted too that many holy men, including John the Baptist, Peter, and Paul, had died without viaticum. Thus the salvation of a dying parishioner would not be endangered if the priest took measures to save his own life on the way.[249] A 1216 synod of Segovia told priests that, if attacked while carrying the Eucharist, they were to defend it as they would the Church.[250]

Occasional efforts were made to see that a priest engaged a deacon or lesser cleric to assist in his duties, including by walking before him with bell and light when he carried viaticum. However, some priests failed to hire such helpers. Thus, at a visitation of Eardisley in the diocese of Hereford in 1397, a priest was ordered to hire a cleric to help.[251] Another parish in the same diocese, Leominster, had a rector who failed for three years to engage a cleric to assist him.[252] The statutes of All Saints, Bristol expected the cleric to be "lovingly attendant" on the priest.[253] If no deacon or cleric was available, a respectable lay person might be permitted to carry the light and ring the bell.[254]

246 *Councils & Synods* II, pt. 1, 126.

247 *Synodicon Hispanum* 2:313–14.

248 *Staturs synodaux* 1:186–87.

249 Honoré Bonet, *The Tree of Battles*, trans. G. W. Copland (Liverpool: Liverpool University Press, 1949), 171–73.

250 *Synodicon Hispanum* 6:305.

251 *Pastors and the Care of Souls* (ed. Shinners and Dohar), 299.

252 Ibid., 298.

253 Burgess, *Right Ordering of Souls*, 348.

254 Rubin, *Corpus Christi*, 78.

These enactments required enforcement according to the instructions given by bishops to their archdeacons for visitations. As Hostiensis said at *Perniciosus*, archdeacons were to correct scandals.[255] Among other things, they were to inquire whether each parish had the means for properly conducting viaticum processions. Behind them was belief in the real presence of Christ in the Eucharist being carried to the sick. A sixteenth century version of Lyndwood's *Provinciale*, translating a statute of John Peckham, described these processions as bearing "the king of Glory hidden in bread," requiring reverence and decorum.[256]

The Spiritual Benefits of Attending Viaticum Processions

Councils and synods ordered that the laity be taught to reverence the Eucharist whenever they saw it was carried to the sick. Several decrees offered a rationale similar to that found in the statutes of Odo of Sully. Thus, the 1240 Council of Worchester claimed that adoration of the elevated host would arouse torpid souls and inflame them with charity. The council also thought that catching sight of the host being carried, even enclosed in a pyx, was spiritually beneficial. The laity was to kneel devoutly even on muddy ground (*luto non obstante*).[257] In the same year, the synod of Lisbon said the laity were to be admonished frequently to kneel "as if to their Lord and creator" (*tanquam Domino et creatori suo*) and join their hands in prayer.[258] The 1281 statutes of Liège were more accommodating about when the laity had to kneel, urging them to do so if they could conveniently (*commode*). It was more demanding of those who were on horseback, who were urged to descend, honoring Christ, who came down from Heaven for their salvation.[259] The statutes of Angers wanted children, not just adults, taught to genuflect and pray when they saw their Lord and creator carried to the sick.[260] A Strasbourg decree of 1435 urges carrying

255 Hostiensis, *In tertium decretalium commentaria*, fol. 166vb (X 3.41.13).

256 *Lyndwood's "Provinciale,"* 104.

257 Mansi 22:528; *Councils & Synods* II, pt. 1, 299–300.

258 *Synodicon Hispanum* 2:288.

259 Mansi 23:789.

260 *Statuts synodaux* 1:186–87.

the Eucharist to women near childbirth.[261] This was quoted, in turn, from legatine constitutions issued in Würzburg in 1287.[262]

The spiritual benefits of seeing viaticum procession were augmented with recommendations that the faithful follow along behind. Such devotion was encouraged by granting indulgences, a growing part of late medieval piety, to participants.[263] In the fourteenth century, the 1349 statutes of Olomuc granted ten days of indulgence for accompanying the priest going to a sick person and returning home but fifteen for returning with him to the entry way of the church (*ad ecclesie atrium*).[264] A 1447 synod of Eichstat granted ten days for accompanying the priest in daytime but twenty for nighttime, whether carrying one's one light or following that of another.[265] The 1483 synod at Constance too promised ten days for processing by day but twenty by night.[266] The 1491 Council of Bamburg offered forty days of indulgence. It also punished priests who carried viaticum in another way (*aliter*) than as instructed or even secretly (*occulte*).[267] A council at Bratislava (1446) promised a hundred-day indulgence to those who followed a viaticum procession.[268] Some synods required saying certain prayers and being "truly penitent and confessed" (*vere penitentibus et confessis*) to receive an indulgence of as few as ten days.[269] The manual of Regensburg allowed

261 *Concilia Germaniae* 5:236: "Sanctissimum Corpus Christi, cujus dignae venerationi fragilitas humana non sufficit, cum ad infirmos, vel ad mulieres vicinas partui, vel ad alia de causa extra Corpus Ecclesiae deportatur, veneratione mandamus solita venerari."

262 Ibid., 3:727: "*De portatione Corporis Christi*. Sanctissimum Corpus Christi, cujus dignae venerationi fragilitas humana non sufficit, cum ad infirmos, vel ad mulieres vicinas partui, extra corpus Ecclesia deportatur, veneratione solita mandamus venerari: videlicet, ut Clericus indutus superpellicio cum stola circa collum portet; nisi locis distantia, & temporis qualitas secus exposcat."

263 Mansi 23:24, 378, 406, 505. Rubin, *Corpus Christi*, 78–80. See also R. N. Swanson, *Indulgences in Late Medieval England: Passports to Paradise?* (Cambridge: Cambridge University Press, 2007). On the Continent, confraternities became involved in viaticum processions; see Rubin, *Corpus Christi*, 236.

264 Krafl, *Synody a statute Olomoucké diecéze*, 162.

265 *Concilia Germaniae* 6:367: "omnibus etiam vere poenitentibus & confessis, qui se Sacerdoti, Eucharistiam, vel Oleum infirmorum taliter deficienti eundo vel redeundo associaverint, si hoc in die fecerint, decem: Si vero de nocte cum lumine proprio vel alieno viginti dies, de injunctis sibi poenitentiis preter indulgemus ab aliis concessis auctoritate nostra ordinaria misericorditer in Domino relaxamus."

266 Ibid., 6:560.

267 Ibid., 6:614. Pope Urban VI had already commanded preachers to offer a hundred days of indulgence; see 6:615.

268 Ibid., 3:727 and 5:292. The 1416 statute of the same diocese offered this indulgence for accompanying a priest who was returning from a sickbed; see 5:159–60.

269 Ibid., 5:159–60 (Bratislava, 1416), 236 (Strasbourg, 1435), 338 (Würzburg, 1446). This last cited a decree of Pope Urban VI granting the indulgence.

the priest to announce indulgences for those who accompanied him to minister to the sick.[270]

A council of Münster, however, was not even-handed in offering this opportunity, threatening women with censures for disrupting a procession.[271] The provincial Council of Trier of 1227 invited the laity to follow the procession but warned against making noise.[272] More stringently, the 1281 synod of Liège threatened anyone who disrupted a procession with excommunication.[273]

Wrong messages given the faithful were discussed. Thus, the Valencia constitutions of 1255 specified that bells were to be rung and a lamp lighted only if the priest was still carrying a host when returning to the church. Otherwise the faithful might venerate a mere creature no longer carrying the body of Christ.[274] Similarly, the 1281 synod of Liège also said that the lamp could be lighted and the bell rung before a priest returning to his church only if he still carried a consecrated host. Otherwise the laity might adore in vain.[275] (This rationale was similar to a warning of the 1287 Council of Liège that elevating an unconsecrated host might lead to the adoration of a material object.)[276] The 1491 canon of Bamberg warned the priest to carry any unused hosts back to the church, not leaving them in some "indecent" place.[277]

The *Pupilla oculi*, an English manual for priests, recited the usual instructions for carrying the Eucharist, including use of the bell to arouse devotion in the faithful. The author also warned against using the bell when returning to the parish church without a host, lest the laity be led to idolatry.[278] A visitation in 1397 in the diocese of Hereford reported that the vicar of Pluytone Forresta went to a dying woman, Alice Clerke, properly

270 *Obsequiale Ratisponense* (Nürnberg: Stuchs, 1491), fol. xxviii^{v}: "Et postquam ad ecclesiam redierit pronunciat indulgentias sequentibus corpus christi. Cum portatur ad infirmum concessas."

271 Mansi 24:315. Similarly, the 1280 synod of Cologne warned women away; see 24:351.

272 Mansi 23:77.

273 Mansi 23:898.

274 Mansi 23:889.

275 Mansi 23:898.

276 Mansi 23:1191.

277 *Concilia Germaniae* 5:615: "In nulloque indecenti loco illud ponat, sed ad Ecclesiam de infirmo studeat reportare."

278 *Pupilla oculi*, Cambridge, Corpus Christi College Manuscript 255, fol. 32r, found in the *Parker Library on the Web*; available at parkerweb.stanford.edu/parker/. This warning is absent from the *Oculus sacerdotis* of William of Pagula; see *Pastors and the Care of Souls* (ed. Shinners and Dohar), 146. William required the priest to punish those who do not venerate the Eucharist on these occasions.

vested with light and bell but with an empty pyx, causing great scandal to the people.[279]

Viaticum processions remained important past the Middle Ages, because the sick and dying needed "housel." Thus, the 1543–44 synodal statutes of Orense in Spain repeated the requirement that communion be carried to the sick with a lamp preceding.[280] The 1528 synod of Tuy offered more detailed instructions, including use of a chalice and paten where a pyx (*el reliquario*) was lacking. The synod required that holy water, bell, and lantern be carried with the host. The enactment also required veneration by bystanders on horse or foot and promised indulgences to those who followed the priest.[281] A 1510 synod of Segovia ordered any cleric or sacristan, if suitably dressed and not prevented from doing so, to accompany the priest.[282] The 1403 synod of Lisbon and the 1500 synod of Guarda allowed a priest to set up a temporary altar by the bed to celebrate Mass for a dying person.[283] The see of Coimbra in Portugal also permitted the priest to go to a sick person after celebrating a Mass *pro infirmo*.[284]

COMMUNION OF THE SICK AND DYING

A rationale for viaticum was offered by the Council of Worcester in 1240.[285] Its tone is military in part, saying that viaticum provides strength to sustain a sick person for war (*ad bellum*), the battle with sin and death. More theologically, the sacrament could sustain the soul because it was the pledge of redemption, the body and blood of Christ sustaining the faithful. The host was to be kept free from damp so that it would not have a foul taste or a disgraceful appearance when administered.

279 Bannister, "Visitation Returns of the Diocese of Hereford in 1397," *The English Historical Review* 44 (1929): 279–89, 444–53; 45 (1930): 92–101, 444–63, at 450: "Item quod Philippus, nuper Vicarius, venit cum lumine et campana, superpellici vestitus, ut est moris, as visitandum quadam Aliciam Clerke, in mortis articulo constitutam, cum pixide vacuo, sine corpore Christi, ad magnum scandalum, faciendo populum adorare sacramentum, ubi non erat."

280 *Synodicon Hispanum* 1:227. Orense forbade monks, women, and other "secular persons" to carry holy oil and chrism under pain of excommunication; see 1:197.

281 Ibid., 1:495–96. Similarly see the 1553 synod of Astorga; 3:136–37.

282 Ibid., 6:510.

283 Ibid., 2:232 [Guarda] and 333–34 [Lisbon]. The same synod offered indulgences to those who followed a viaticum procession; see 2:231–32.

284 *Manuale secundum consuetudinem almae Coimbricensis ecclesiae* (Lisbon: Gazini, 1518), fol. xii[ra–b]: "Celebrata missa pro infirmo veniat sacerdos cum clericis et ipse indutus alba stola et cappa. et cruce cum aqua benedicta et oleo sancto."

285 *Councils & Synods* II, pt. 1, 299.

William of Auxerre said that a dying person was not to be refused viaticum, adding that unconsecrated hosts could not be substituted, as this would constitute a dissimulation and a lie.[286] That would be contrary to the sickbed interrogation: "Do you believe this is the body of Christ?"[287] The priest might use an unconsecrated host without that query, but he was subject to punishment for his negligence in not bringing one which was consecrated.[288] John of Freiburg said that unconsecrated hosts were not to be given in place of consecrated ones, treating the false as true.[289] John also threatened priests with punishment for elevating unconsecrated hosts, leading the faithful to idolatry.[290] Antoninus of Florence said that communion was not to be denied to the dying in a time of interdict. He extended this permission to healthy persons condemned to death.[291] The statutes of Norwich, among others, warned that the faithful, when sick, should not be allowed to die without confession, viaticum, or last anointing.[292]

It is hard to ascertain how many clergy failed in the duty of taking communion to the sick. A few cases can be noted. In 1397, the vicar of Eardisley in the diocese of Hereford was reported to have allowed parishioners to die without confession, viaticum, or anointing.[293] The vicar of Minster Lovell in the diocese of Lincoln was reputed to arrive only after a sick parishioner had died.[294] In 1458, the vicar of Pelham Arsa, one of the churches subject to St. Paul's Cathedral, was reported to have failed to visit the sick when he was in his most prosperous days.[295] This concern

286 *Magistri Guillelmi Altissodoriensis summa aurea*, ed. Jean Ribaillier (Paris: CNRS, 1985), 175: "Unde ibi simulatio et mendacium non debet habere locum. Sed debet ei dicere: Crede, et manducasti."

287 Ibid., 175: "quia in hoc casu non oportet querere hoc: Credis hoc esse corpus Christi?"

288 Ibid., 176–77.

289 Johannes de Friburgo, *Summa confessorum* III, t. 24, q. 79: "quia in sacramentum veritatis non debet esse aliqua fictio." John added, following Augustine, that this led to idolatry.

290 Johannes de Erfordia, *Die Summa confessorum*, 2:123. John also condemned priests who celebrated while in mortal sin; see 2:130.

291 Antoninus de Florentia, *Tractatus de censuris ecclesiasticis*, University of Pennsylvania Ms. Codex 72, fol. 126va: "Item permittitur eucharistia dari decedentibus de pe. et re. quod in te [X 5.38.11]. Sanis etiam damnatis ad mortem dari potest tempore interdicti quia censetur tunc in articulo mortis." Antoninus cites (fol. 126vb) the opinion of Johannes Calderinus that carrying viaticum to the sick at a time of interdict still merited a full procession with light and bell preceding the priest. Antoninus argued, however, that a pregnant woman could not be brought communion in such a time unless she was in danger of death.

292 Synodal Constitutions, Norwich, Cambridge, Corpus Christi College Ms. 255, fol. 209v–211v, at fol. 210r: "ne eorum negligentia quod absit moriatur infirmus sine confessione aut dominici corporis communione aut unctione extrema."

293 *Pastors and the Care of Souls* (ed. Shinners and Dohar), 299. This is an example of the "spiritual murder" feared when a pastor failed in his cure of souls; see Rubin, *Corpus Christi*, 81–82.

294 Bowker, *The Secular Clergy in the Diocese of Lincoln*, 113.

295 *Visitations of Churches Belonging to St. Paul's Cathedral*, 106.

was real enough in the minds of prelates for visitation questions, formulated in 1253, to include an inquiry whether clerical negligence caused lay persons to die "intestate or without the sacraments."[296] A 1440 synod of Segovia ordered any priest who allowed a parishioner to die without the sacraments deposed from his benefice.[297]

Theologians and canonists rarely seem to have discussed what to do if a sick person was present at Mass. Thomas Aquinas did say the priest was to reserve the third part of the host he broke at the altar to give to that person. That was aside from saving consecrated hosts for viaticum.[298]

Instructions for Priests

Manuals for priests gave instructions for giving communion at the sickbed, which must have happened more often than communicating the sick in church. Thus, the *Rituale Romanum* provided an order for communion within a *visitatio infirmorum*. The text bears repeating, beginning after absolution:

> Afterward, the priest should raise the Lord's body from the chalice; and the sick person, adoring, should say, "Lord, I am not worthy that you should enter under my roof. Say but the word and my soul shall be healed" [Mt 8:8]. Then the priest should give the Eucharist to the sick person, saying, "Accept, brother, viaticum of the body of our Lord Jesus Christ, who should guard you against the malignant foe, and may He lead you to eternal life."[299]

There follow instructions for the priest washing his fingers over the chalice.[300] The communion rite ends with a prayer and Psalm 50, *Miserere*.[301] The manual for Naples, based on Roman usage, provided a formula for giving

296 *Pastors and the Care of Souls* (ed. Shinners and Dohar), 289.

297 *Synodicon Hispanum* 6:413.

298 *Sancti Thome de Aquino Ordinis Predicatorum super quarto libro sententiarum preclarum opus* (Venice: Jenson, 1481), fol. 51rb: "Si autem infirmus communicandus tunc occurrat hostiam consecratam sibi diuidat. Nam et olim propter hoc seruabatur usque in fine misse pars tertia. Potest esse de pluribus hostis consecratis reseruare quot sibi visum fuerit. Nec tenetur omne consecratum sumere: dum tamen sub vtraque specie sumat."

299 *Rituale Romanum* (Florence: Per Antonium Francisci, ca. 1484), fol. [12]r: "Postea sacerdos eleuet corpus domini de calice: et infirmus adorans dicat. Domine non sum dignus ut intres sub tectum meum: sed tantum dic verbo et sanabitur anima mea. Deinde sacerdos tradat infirmo eucharistiam dicens. Accipe frater uiaticum corporis domini nostri yhesu christi qui te custodiat ab hoste maligno: et perducat ad uitam eternam."

300 Ibid.

301 Ibid., fol. [12]r–v.

communion, followed by the priest's washing his fingers, a post-communion prayer, and anointing the sick.[302]

In France, the Angers manual provided for giving communion to the sick, following extreme unction. Immediately before communion the minister was to show the sick person a crucifix, asking if he or she believed. Lay persons were expected to respond in French, "I believe and adore" (*Je le croye et adore*). An ailing priest was to respond in Latin.[303] Then the priest was to sprinkle the sick person with holy water before displaying the consecrated host and delivering an exhortation. Lay persons were to be exhorted in French, but clergy in Latin. Communion was to be given accompanied by these words, "The body of our Lord Jesus Christ save and strengthen your soul to eternal life. Amen" (*Corpus domini nostri Jesu christi saluet et confirmet animam tuam in uitam eternam. Amen*). There followed a brief prayer and an instruction for giving viaticum to a woman.[304] The last text in this sequence was an interrogation of the dying attributed to St. Anselm.[305]

The Chartres manual gave specific instructions for communicating the sick, *Modus administrandi sacramentum eucharistie infirmis*. These instructions began with reservation of many hosts, treated with great reverence.[306] If taking communion to a sick person, the priest was to say, upon entering the house, the prayer, "Visit, we ask, Lord, this habitation" (*Uisita quesumus domine habitationem istam*).[307] The sick person was to be warned to confess before receiving the host. Any signs of penance could be accepted from a person unable to speak. Then the priest was to take a host in his hands "honorably" and, while showing it to the sick person, deliver an exhortation in French. Once the patient had begged pardon from God, those present and even those absent, the priest was to give communion, saying, "The body of our lord Jesus Christ keep your soul and your body to eternal life" *(Corpus domini nostri iesu christi custodiat animam tuam et*

302 *Manuale Romano-Neapolitanum*, fol. xiii$^{r–v}$: "Deinde sacerdos tradens infirmo eucharistiam dicat: Accipite frater vel soror viaticum corpus domini nostri iesu christi te custodiat ab hoste maligno et perducat te ad vitam eternam. Amen." The instructions for washing fingers with wine and water follow. The subsequent post-communion prayer starts: "Lord, holy father, eternal God, we faithfully entreat you" (*Domine sancte pater omnipotens eterne deus. te fideliter deprecamur*).

303 *Manuale ad usum precelebris ecclesie Andegauensis*, fol. xliii^{v}.

304 Ibid., fol. xliii^{v}–xliiii^{v}.

305 Ibid., fol. xliiii^{v}.

306 *Manuale sacerdotum secundum usum diocesis Carnotensis* (Paris: Yolande Bonhomme, 1544), fol. xxxiiii^{rb}: "In primis currunt presbyteri diligenter reseruare pro infirmis plures hostias . . . et cum maxima reuerentia salutaris hostia semper est tractanda."

307 Ibid., fol. xxxiiii$^{rb–va}$.

corpus tuum in uitam eternam).[308] The priest was to wash his fingers and say at least one prayer. Next, he was to make the sign of the cross on the sick person's head, praying against "sudden and unprovided death" (*subitanea et inprouisa morte*). The priest was to conclude with prayers in French.[309] After determining whether the person had made a will, the priest was to return to the church, kneel devoutly, and then face the people, saying a prayer in French and offering a blessing. Then was he to restore the Eucharist to its place (*reponit corpus christi in loco suo*).[310]

The diocese of Reims had similar instructions for communion of the sick, issued by Renaud de Chartres (ca. 1415). At the sick person's home, the priest was to say the prayer *Uisita quesumus domine habitationem istam* and warn the patient to confess before receiving viaticum. The manual offered forms in French for administering the sacrament, including an exhortation in French to say before the host was administered "honorably."[311] The sick person was to beg pardon from all before receiving the host. The words for giving the sacrament were: "The body of our lord Jesus Christ keep you to eternal life."[312] After communion, the priest was to wash the fingers he used in giving communion and recite the prologue to John's Gospel. Then he was to hold a cross before the patient, sprinkle holy water, and pray in French before leaving.[313] If the sick person could not receive communion, the need to ask pardon remained. Then the priest was to hold a host before the sufferer, asking whether he or she would gladly receive if it were it possible. That person was to reply "Yes."[314] After that, the priest was to return the host to its receptacle (*locatello*), wash his fingers, and say John's prologue.[315] In either case, the priest was to return the remaining hosts to their repository in the church, pray, and bless any persons present.[316]

In England, the York manual added instructions for communion of the sick after those for anointing but permitted earlier communion.[317] The

308 Ibid., fol. xxxiiii^{va-b}, at xxxiiii^{vb}.

309 Ibid., fol. xxxiiii^{vb}–xxxv^{rb}.

310 Ibid., fol. xxxv^{va-b}.

311 *Manuale seu agenda ad usum Remensem* (n.p., ca. 1500), [151]–[56].

312 Ibid., [155]: "Corpus domini nostri iesu christi conseruat te in uitam eternam."

313 Ibid., [156]–[58].

314 Ibid., [158]: "Et presbyter tenens hostiam dicit. N. Se vous peussies recevoir ce tressaint sacrament tres uolentiers vous les recussiez. Respondeat Oyl."

315 Ibid., [158]–[59].

316 Ibid., [159].

317 *Manuale et processionale ad usum insignis ecclesiae Eboracensis*, 51.

instructions for communion began with an inquiry by the priest regarding whether the patient believed that the consecrated elements were Christ's body and blood. Then he was, under ideal circumstances, to give that person a consecrated host while saying: "The body of our Lord Jesus Christ keep your body and soul to eternal life. Amen." The York Use did not allow giving the consecrated host to a believer who might vomit it, nor to someone drunk or mad, likewise not to children below the age of reason, who would not understand the sacrament.[318] This rite concluded with prayers and blessings.[319] The Sarum Use said that the priest was to inquire if the parishioner recalled any other sins and recognized the body and blood of Christ in the Eucharist before offering communion.[320]

On the borders of France, the see of Tournai had an order for communion of the sick. The manual said that the Eucharist was food in cases of temptation, infirmity, and adversity.[321] The priest was to remind a sick person that the sacrament was a sign of Christ's love for the faithful, which he displayed at the Last Supper.[322] The patient also was to remember that death was not the end, but transition to a better life.[323] If he administered communion, the priest was to remind the sick person that not everyone died fed with the Eucharist and to be grateful for receiving it.[324] In giving communion, the priest was to judge whether the sick person might vomit. If this was so, the host was to be shown but not given to be kissed (*Non detur autem infirmo Sacramentum osculandum*).[325] After that, he was to put the host back into the pyx (*in pyxide*) and return to the church. There he was to tell the faithful "to pray for the sick" (*ad orandum pro infirmo*).[326]

The process for communion for the sick differed little in Germanic countries. The order from Basel began with the vesting of the priest and his proceeding to the sickbed. The rite allowed for blessing the sick person

318 Ibid., 51–52.

319 Ibid., 52–54. Some of the prayers were supposed to be said by a bishop if present.

320 Ibid., 50*–52*.

321 *Manuale pastorum ad uniformem administrationem sacramentorum aliorum officiorum ecclesiasticum per civitatem et dioecesim Tornacensem* (Louvain: Masius, 1591?), 39: "Dum ergo premunt tentationes, vrgent infirmitates & aduersitates, ad hunc cibum recursum habere debemus."

322 Ibid., 37: "Admoneatur infirmis, meminerit summae istius charitatis Saluatoris nostri erga nos, quam in huius Sacramenti institutione, in nouissima coena maximè ostendit."

323 Ibid., 38–39: "non est mors, sed transitus ad vitam meliorem."

324 Ibid., 40: "Post administrationem Eucharistiam, moneatur infirmus, vt gratias Deo agat, qui eum hoc salutari viatico reficere dignatus est, quam gratiam omnibus non facit, cum multi improvisa & subita morte moriantur."

325 Ibid., 42.

326 Ibid., 42–43.

with holy water and hearing his or her confession after others left the room (*et recedant alij ut solus confessus*). Then the priest was to wash his fingers, take a host from the pyx (*ex inclusorio*) and give communion. Afterward he was to wash his fingers in wine and say prayers, leaving with the words *Pax tecum* (Peace be with you).[327]

The Augsburg manual permitted doing a separate procession with viaticum after a previous confession. If there was no previous confession, the priest was to greet the household and exhort the sick person to have patience before hearing his or her confession and granting absolution. The *Confiteor* was to follow, possibly in the vernacular for the edification of bystanders.[328] The priest was to get the sick person to ask for viaticum and then give it with washed fingers, saying: "The body of our lord Jesus Christ keep you to eternal life. Amen."[329] The priest was to say more prayers and depart after once more urging patience and perseverance, even in case of recovery.[330]

A Danish manual had communion follow an interrogation of the sick person concerning the Catholic faith. The patient was to ask pardon from God, those present, and those absent before the priest gave communion, saying: "The body of our lord Jesus Christ keep your soul and your body to eternal life." Afterward the priest was to say a prayer before proceeding to extreme unction.[331]

On the Iberian peninsula, the Toledo manual included instructions in Spanish for communication of the sick. The rite was to begin with confession, absolution, and will-making (*conseje le que faga su testamento*). An altar could be improvised by the sickbed for a Mass, with communion following.[332] The Palencia manual provided instructions in Spanish and Latin for communion of the sick. A domestic Mass for a sick person also

327 *Informatorium sacerdotum* (Basel: Wenssler, 1488), fol. f ii^{r}–f iii^{v}.

328 *Obsequiale Augustense* (Augsburg: Zainer?, 1471), fol. lxix^{r-v}: "Tunc dicat ei. Confiteor. Et vtile videtur materna lingua fieri· propter astantes laicos."

329 Ibid., fol. lxx^{r}: "Et si petat: communicet eum sacerdos lotis prius digitis suis dicendo Corpus domini nostri ihesu christi: proficiat tibi in vitam eternam. amen."

330 Ibid., fol. lxx^{r-v}.

331 *Manuale curatorum secundum usum ecclesie Roeskildensis*, 24–25.

332 *Manuale seu baptisterium secundum vsum ecclesie Toletane* (Seville: Pegnitzer, 1494), fol. e [1]ib–e [7]ib. The Cuenca manual includes a Mass for the sick, its readings stemming from the Epistle of James and the account of the healing of the centurion's servant in Matthew's Gospel; see *Manipulus siue manuale vel potius practica ministrandi sacramenta sanctae matris ecclesie Conchensis* (Cuenca: Christophori Gallici, 1528), fol. xciv^{v}–xcvi^{r}. Portable altars, which survive beginning in the eleventh century, may also have been used at the sickbed; see *Museum Schnütgen*, 50.

was permitted.[333] In addition, the Toledo book provided instructions for the renewal of the reserved Eucharist. At Mass, a priest was to consecrate three hosts, one to consume and two to reserve.[334]

The Astorga manual wanted the priest to deliver exhortations in Spanish. If there was a display of reluctance, he was to persuade the sick person to confess before receiving viaticum. Otherwise, he or she might eat a judgment with the host.[335] A bell was rung even during an interdict, while the priest prepared chalice and paten with a host, wine, and water. Once the priest had viaticum ready, he was to carry it to the sick person. The patient was to be given a crucifix to kiss. Then the priest was to interrogate him or her about belief and any further sins to confess. When the sick person was ready, the priest was to provide communion via a host on a paten or a chalice held to the mouth. The sick person was to receive reverently or, if unable to receive, communicate spiritually (*spiritualiter*).[336]

The Salamanca manual required that a home be prepared for the administration of viaticum, including creating "a small altar" (*un altarico pequeño*) near the sickbed.[337] The text included directions for a vested priest, going to the house, sprinkling holy water, praying, and giving communion from a paten.[338] These instructions included getting the sick person to profess belief that the host contained the real presence of Christ and that he or she wished to live and die in the faith.[339] The sick person was to say humbly, "Lord, I am not worthy that You should enter under my roof" (*Domine non sum dignus vt interes sub tectum meum*) when receiving the host.[340]

Vomiting the Host

Concern for communicants having unfortunate reactions to receiving the sacrament appeared early on. A priest had to consider the possibility that,

333 *Manuale secundum vsum sanctę Ecclesię Psallantinę* (Medina del Campo: Canto Fratres, 1554), fol. xxxiiii^{v}–xli^{r}. One of these instructions focused on communicating an ailing priest.

334 Ibid., fol. xlir–xlii^{r}.

335 *Manuale secundum consuetudinem Astoricensis* (León: s. n., 1526), fol. lix^{r}: "et si ita non est exhortet ad penitentiam et confessionem: ne iudicium sibi manducet."

336 Ibid., fol. lix^{r}–lxi^{r}.

337 *Manuale secundum consuetudinem alme ecclesie Salamanticense* (Salamanca: Junta, 1532), fol. xxxiii^{v}–xxxiiii^{r}.

338 Ibid., fol. xxxiii^{r}–xxxix^{r}. The book provides texts for giving communion to an ailing priest.

339 Ibid., fol. xxxix^{r}: "Credis quod habeo in manibus est verum corpus domini nostri iesu christi. credo . . . Uis viuere et mori in hac fide catholica. volo."

340 Ibid., fol. xxxix^{v}.

when he arrived at the sickbed, the patient might not be able to communicate or might vomit the host. The *Penitential of Cummean* introduced a requirement that anyone who vomited the host was to fast for forty days.[341] The *Bigotian Penitential* imposed forty days on gluttons who vomited the host but only twenty on the infirm.[342] The *Preface of Gildas* prescribed "special" fasts of seven days for gluttony but four for sickness.[343] The *Penitential of Theodore* excused the sick from penance for vomiting the host.[344] The *Penitential of Columban* imposed seven days for vomiting the host but required a year for a priest who lost it.[345]

On the Continent, the *Judgment of Clement* ordered seven days on bread and water for eating before communicating, except for children, who were to be beaten for doing so.[346] It also imposed a year on bread and water for a priest who lost the host.[347] The *Penitential of Silos* imposed a range of penances on those who vomited the host, especially from drunkenness.[348] Regino of Prüm too imposed penances for vomiting the Eucharist.[349]

The Decretists raised this question on occasion when dealing with the tract *De consecratione*. A text attributed to Bede concerned with vomiting the host had been added to the *Decretum* as *Si quis*, prescribing penances for vomiting the host because of drunkenness or gluttony, but it went easier on the sick.[350] Rufinus addressed this question in his apparatus on the *De consecratione*. His commentary too went light on those who vomited the Eucharist because of sickness, requiring only seven days of penance.[351]

Vomiting the host also was a worry for Thomas of Chobham in his book on penance. He wanted the priest to judge if the person could swallow a host, but he rejected the possibility of giving an unconsecrated host instead. Thomas told a story, used earlier by Maurice, bishop of Paris, about a dying person offered unconsecrated hosts who detected the

341 *Medieval Handbooks of Penance*, 102.

342 Ibid., 154.

343 Ibid., 176.

344 Ibid., 184.

345 Ibid., 250. Leaving the vomited host lying there required 120 days on bread and water; see ibid., 253.

346 Ibid., 272.

347 Ibid., 275.

348 Ibid., 286.

349 Regino of Prüm, *Libri duo de synodalibus causis*, 151.

350 Friedberg 1:1323 (*De cons.*, D. 2, c. 28): "Si quis per ebrietatem uel uoracitatem eucharistiam conuenerit, XL. diebus peniteat; clerici, uel monachi, seu diaconi, presbiteri LXX. diebus peniteat; episcopi XC. Si pro infirmitatis causa euomerit, VII. diebus peniteant."

351 Rufinus, *Summa decretorum*, 552: "Si autem hac occasione eucharistiam quis evomuerit, pro varietate personarum acriter puniendus est; si pro infirmitate, septem diebus peniteat."

difference and refused them.[352] Ida of Nivelles is said to have received communion on behalf of a sick woman unable to swallow even a bit of a host, but there are no known examples of priests sanctioning such a practice.[353]

Penances for vomiting the host reappeared later in the Middle Ages. John of Erfurt said those vomiting from gluttony or drunkenness might sin mortally for deliberate excess or venially from unintentional effects.[354] In the *Lumen confessorum*, Andreas Escobar expressed concern for incautious handling and reception of the Eucharist. He said lay people who vomited the host on account of gluttony or drunkenness deserved forty days of penance. Prelates and religious deserved seventy days, and bishops ninety. However, a sick person only was to do seven days of penance, unless an "arbitrary" penance was imposed.[355]

Some clergy considered alternatives should the patient be likely to vomit solid food or consecrated bread.[356] The host might be placed on the person's breast or shown for adoration, and a blessing might be given as viaticum.[357] A text attributed to a council of Carthage, found in the *Decretum*, said that, when a sick person had been reconciled by laying on of hands, the Eucharist might be "poured into his mouth" (*infundatur ori eius eucharistiam*).[358] Raymond of Peñafort also accepted pouring consecrated wine into a sick person's mouth, if it could be done "without peril."[359] Hostiensis specified using a host dissolved in unconsecrated wine.[360] At the diocesan level, a French statute of 1247 permitted this usage with the sick.[361]

The Cartagena manual required saying psalms and prayers before administering communion to those who were infirm. It gave different texts to use when communicating sick priests, deacons, subdeacons, those

352 Thomas of Chobham, *Summa confessorum*, ed. F. Bloomfield (Louvain: Analecta Mediaevalia Namurcensia, 1968), 136–37.

353 *Send Me God: The Lives of Ida the Compassionate of Nivelles, Nun of La Ramés, Arnulf, Law Brother of Villers, and Abundus, Monk of Villers*, trans. Martinus Cawley (Turnhout: Brepols, 2003), 61. Sarah Ritchey, "Affective Medicine: Later Medieval Healing Communities and the Feminization of Health Care Practices in the Thirteenth-Century Low Countries," *The Journal of Medieval Religious Cultures* 40 (2014): 113–43, at 123.

354 Johannes de Erfordia, *Die Summa confessorum*, 2:121–22.

355 Andreas Escobar, *Lumen confessorum*, fol. 7va–b, at 7va: "Et si causa infirmitatis illud factum fuerit vii diebus preniteat vel detur penitentia arbitraria de con. di. v. c. Si quis. xxxiiii q. ii. Qui bene."

356 The Amsterdam host relic originated as vomited viaticum, which was cast into the fire but remained intact; see Snoek, *Medieval Piety*, 333.

357 Ibid., 294–95.

358 Friedberg 1:1038 (C. 26, q. 6, c. 8).

359 *Summa Sancti Raymundi*, 467: "Eucharistiam ori eius infundendo."

360 Mansi 22:731–32; Rubin, *Corpus Christi*, 80.

361 Mansi 23:746–47.

condemned to death, and the laity. It also gave instructions for giving communion during an interdict.[362] An unusual account of communion with consecrated wine is hagiographic. Bona of Pisa is said to have appeared together with Christ to a dying girl, urging that she and those around her receive communion with wine (*vino communionem*).[363]

Writing about communion of the sick in the *Pupilla oculi*, John de Burough said not to give viaticum to those who might vomit it or show disrespect, placing decorum above the physical act of receiving communion.[364] John also suggested breaking up the host when the patient was unable to receive it whole. Even a small particle contained Christ and sufficed for viaticum.[365] John also permitted giving communion to a sick person who has not fasted, but not to those who had dined.[366]

Priests also might err in judging the communicant's condition, leading to vomiting of the host. A canon of the diocese of Liège said that any identifiable fragments were to be picked up and consumed with wine. The rest of the vomit was to be burned, the ashes being place at some sacred place like the altar.[367] Thomas of Chobham made the same point.[368]

The possibility of those who ate or drank too much vomiting the host, or sick persons doing so, reappeared in later synodal texts. The 1491 Bamberg statutes commanded consuming or burning the vomited material, the ashes being buried by the altar.[369] Looking at the possibility of a mouse or spider falling into the chalice after the wine was consecrated, the diocese of Bamberg also required that it be captured, washed, and burned, the ashes being buried in the sanctuary of the church.[370]

362 *Ordinarium manuale de ministratione sacramentorum secundum consuetudinem ecclesię Carthaginensis*, fol. lxxxvi^v^–lxvvvii[i]^r^.

363 Mary Harvey Dono, *The Lay Saint: Charity and Charismatic Authority in Medieval Italy, 1150–1350* (Ithaca, NY: Cornell University Press, 2019), 141.

364 *Pupilla oculi*, fol. 107ra. See also fol. 28ra, where John also warned against unnecessary spitting after receiving the host. John also gave instructions on cleaning and burning any Eucharistic fragments found in vomit.

365 Ibid., fol. 28va–b: "Item etiam sacerdos videat infirmum ita debilem quod integram hostiam sumere et transglutire non poterit licite potest hostiam sacram frangere et unam partem valde modicam et dare ei et sufficient quia sub qualibet hostie particula quantumcunque modica retinetur veram speciem."

366 Ibid., fol. 27rb–va: "Non est danda eucharistia pransis sed Ieunis nisi causa infirmitatis uel necessitatis articulus hoc deposcat de con. di. 2^a^ liquido."

367 Mansi 24:898.

368 *Thomae de Chobham Summa confessorum*, 136–37.

369 *Concilia Germaniae* 5:616. "Item si quis per ebrietatem, voracitatem, vel infirmitatem, Eucharistiam evomuerit, debet vomitus ille sumi diligenter, & cremari, & cineres juxta Altare recondi."

370 Ibid., 5:615.

At Urgell, communion of the sick was to be conferred "with great moderation" and a ritual formula.[371] Looking at a different problem, the priest was told to give a sick person a little water to help in swallowing, so that none of the host would remain in the mouth.[372] The priest could take communion himself if the sick person was not disposed to communicate or could not receive. In any case, the priest was to finish with prayer and a blessing.[373]

Another approach permitted spiritual communion by devout sight of a consecrated host. This form of communion (*spiritualiter accipiat*) could replace physical reception. The statutes of Cambrai and Liège said this could be done when the sick person might vomit the sacrament.[374] John of Erfurt said the person's faith should suffice, especially if a host was shown and seen devoutly. Such a person received with the heart, not with the mouth (*credit et manducavit corde sed non ore*).[375] John asked whether communion was permitted to those born mentally afflicted. Although some said this was acceptable, if there was no danger of irreverence in receiving, he said they were incapable of recognizing the sacrament and thus of receiving sacramentally.[376] A person who became mad *ex infirmitate* could receive during a lucid interval; so could someone who had expressed a wish for communion before losing sanity.[377]

The Eucharistic Fast

Another matter theologians and canonists had to consider was the effect of the Eucharistic fast on the sick. The 1491 statutes of Bamberg state that parish priests are to exhort the sick to receive communion "opportunely" (*tempestive*) and with fasting, unless danger of death required doing

371 *Ordinarium sacramentorum secundum sacrosancte Urgellensis ecclesie ritum*, fol. cxv^{v}: "Hic conferat ei sacerdos cum magna moderatione corpus christi: et dicat: Corpus domini nostri Iesu christi custodiat te peccatorem: et perducat te in vitam eternam. Amen."

372 Ibid., fol. cxv^{v}: "Et detur infirmo parum aque vt facilius transglutiat: et nihil de dicto corpore christi in ore remaneat." The manual also gives a form for communicating a sick priest or deacon; see fol. cxvi^{v}–cxix^{r}.

373 Ibid., fol. cxv^{v}–cxvi^{v}.

374 *Statuts synodaux* 4:41–42; Mansi 4:898. Izbicki, *The Eucharist in Medieval Canon Law*, 101–25.

375 Johannes de Erfordia, *Die Summa confessorum*, 3:121.

376 Ibid., 3:872: "furiosus a nativitate potest baptizare et eucharistiam percipere, praesumitur sine periculo derisionis sumpturus secundum quosdam, quod tamen non credo, quia talis non reciperet eucharistiam, ut sacramentum, sed ut panem, et ideo non sumeret sacramentaliter." John also states (2:143) that children and those lacking reason lacked the teeth of faith to spiritually chew the sacrament.

377 Ibid., 3:872–73.

otherwise.[378] John of Freiburg argued that the sick, debilitated, or elderly could be spared fasting under certain circumstances, as the priest might judge to be appropriate. This, he said, was better than following a fixed rule.[379] John also thought that a physician could use excessive food or drink to cause a sick person to vomit for medical purposes. He rejected, however, causing a sick person to become drunk.[380]

A related question was whether medicine or food eaten for medicinal purposes broke the fast.[381] Simon of Bisignano, in his commentary on the *Decretum*, described the Eucharistic fast as being done "on account of reverence," except when a sick person was in danger of death.[382] Durandus de Sancto Porciano, in his commentary on the *Sentences*, discussed this question, distinguishing between things unacceptable per se and those that were prohibited. Taking medicine or even eating food before communion was forbidden unless the recipient of the Eucharist was in danger of death. Durandus's opinion was grounded on the *Decretum*, and the permission extended not just to medications but to necessary nourishment.[383] He extended this permission to eluctuaries, medicines mixed with honey, because medications did not violate the fast.[384] Apart from necessity, however, eating or taking medicines before communion was

378 *Concilia Germaniae* 5:615: "Item quivis Rector Ecclesiae hortetur plebem suam, ut infirmi tempestive, & jejunii Sacramenta percipiant, nisi periculum mortis aliter exposcat, si immineret."

379 Johannes de Friburgo, *Summa confessorum* I, t. 12, q. 25: "Qvid de infirmis & debilibus. Respondetur. Excusantur. Et dicit hic Glossa. Pro quanta autem infirmitate vel delibitate solui possit ieiunium ab infirmis & debilibus arbitrio boni viri immutandum est quam per aliquam doctrinam generalem. Innocentius in glosa huius tituli ait idem. dicimus in senibus sicut in infirmis et debilibus."

380 Ibid., III, t. 4, q. 3: "Dicendum quod in hoc casu non est peccatum: quia licet talis cibus vel potus sano esset superfluus: non tamen infirmo. Sed tamen propter hanc causam non debet potus dari vsque ad ebrietatem quia tunc non excusaretur a peccato."

381 The question was not new. The Penitential of Silos allowed the "infirm and feeble" to eat before receiving the sacrament; see *Medieval Handbooks of Penance*, 287.

382 *Summa in Decretum Simonis Brisinianensis*, 512: "Propter reuerentiam autem huius sacrament non nisi a ieiunis debet sumi, nisi mortis urgente periculo."

383 Durandus de Sancto Porciano, *Super sententias theologicas Petri Lombardi commentariorum libri quatuor* (Paris: Apud Carolam Guillard, 1550), hereafter DDSP fol. 268va, d. 8, q. 4: "Vtrum corpus Christi possit licitè sumi post medicinam, vel post cibum sumptum per modum medicinae . . . QVANTVM ad primum dicendum quòd sumere corpus Christi post talia prius sumpta non est malum secundum se. Cuius ratio est, quia quod est illicitum secundum se nullo modo potest esse licitum, sed sumere corpus Christi post huiusmodi potest esse in casa licitum, sicut cum imminet alicui periculum mortis vt habetur de consecratione distinctione secunda capitulo praesbyter infirmum staim communicet ne sine communione moriatur, ergo sumere hoc sacramentum post cibum non est secundum se illicitum." See Friedberg 1:1351–52 (*De cons.*, D. 2, c. 93).

384 DDSP, fol. 268va, d. 8, q. 4: "medicinae & electuaria non soluunt iueiunium ecclesiae, ergo post electuarium & medicinas potest sumi licitè sacramentum eucharistiae."

prohibited. Neither prevarication nor fraud excused those who ate or medicated unnecessarily before receiving communion.[385]

Most of these Eucharistic practices continued down to the Reformation. Even that upheaval did not cause complete displacement of traditional rites for the sick and dying. However, the Reformers eventually establish their own rites for the sick. The English Reformation took the old rites seriously enough to forbid the use of lights or bells in taking viaticum to the sick. Eventually even processions were suppressed in favor of a reformed rite for the ailing faithful.[386] Sickbed communion continued in some form; but, as we shall see, anointing of the sick was unacceptable to many Protestant divines, at least as a sacrament.

385 Ibid., fol. 268vb: "Dicendum est ergo aliter quòd extra casum necessitatis illicitum est sumere hoc sacramentum post medicinam vel quemcumque cibum. Quod patet sic. Aliquis enim efficitur transgressor praecepti dupliciter. Vno modo faciente contra tenorem praecepti & iste dicitur praeuaricator. Alio modo faciendo contra intentione praecipientis, & iste dicitur fraudator, & vtroque modo est esse transgressor praecepti ecclesiae qui sumit eucharistiam post medicinam vel quemcumque cibum quantumcunque modicum quod patet primo sic. Hoc enim sacramentum à ieiunis tantum debet sumi & non solum à ieiuniantibus."

386 Duffy, *Stripping of the Altars*, 466–67, 472, 474. These transformations will be reviewed in this book's epilogue.

4

ANOINTING OF THE SICK

THE THEOLOGY OF ANOINTING

By the later Middle Ages, anointing was often the third sacrament administered to the sick. It also offered the possibility of physical healing accompanying spiritual betterment. Unction had been a part of Christianity since biblical times. Anointing by the apostles to cure the sick was mentioned in Mark's Gospel (6:13): "And they cast out many devils, and anointed with oil many that were sick, and healed them."[1] A more detailed biblical text is found in the Epistle of James (5:13–15). Both biblical passages fit into a larger Judeo-Christian context of anointing with oil for healing and consecration. This tradition is represented by the *Rationale* of the elder Guillelmus Durantis, which concerned itself with external anointing of the body and internal anointing of the soul.[2]

1 Cuschieri, *Anointing of the Sick*, 61–62. The Latin Vulgate reads: "et daemonia multa eiciebant, et ungebant oleo multos aegros, et sanabant." The Council of Trent cited this text as proof that Christ established the sacrament; see Charles W. Gusmer, *And You Visited Me: Sacramental Ministry to the Sick and Dying* (New York: Pueblo, 1989), 6–7.

2 *The "Rationale divinorum officiorum" of William Durant of Mende: A New Translation of the Prologue and Book One*, trans. Timothy M. Thibodeau (New York: Columbia University Press, 2007), 89–90.

Anointing the Sick in the Scriptures

Exegesis of sacred texts affected how ministry was conducted. The Ordinary Gloss on Mark 6:13 tied that text to visitation of the sick, citing the Epistle of James. The Gloss cited both Mark and James to prove that anointing with oil consecrated by a bishop began with the apostles.[3] The interlinear gloss on James mentioned anointing with consecrated oil (*consecrato vel quando iniungitur*) and invoking the Lord's name (*nomine domini inuocetur*). Release from sin applied even to a patient who died (*etiam si contigerit mori*).[4] A marginal gloss on James, treating the words "If anyone among you is sick" (*Infirmatur quis in vobis*; Jas 5:14), said that the passage referred to extreme unction and penance, both made available to the dying.[5] It treated anointing as applying only to those in danger of leaving this world.[6] The Gloss also said Christ instituted this sacrament, but James made it public.[7]

The Dominican theologian Hugh of St. Cher, writing in the thirteenth century, interpreted the reference in Mark's Gospel to anointing as treating the origin of extreme unction.[8] Hugh said that James was giving guidance for the sacrament, which was given only to those who requested it.[9] Priests were to administer the rite. However, Hugh said that the importance of prayer permitted choosing a better priest, whose prayers were likely to be heard.[10] This was different, he said, from the effectiveness of holy orders or the Eucharist, which depended not on the worthiness of the priest but on whether he followed the *ordo* of the Church.[11] Perhaps Hugh meant healing here. Later in the same commentary, he tied the rite to penance, which was administered by priests. Anointing pertained only to the sick in danger of

3 *Biblia latina cum glossa ordinaria*, 4:104A: "Et ungebant. B. Jacob. Dicit. Infirmatur quis in vobis: indu. p. ec. et o. super. e. vn. e. o. etc. Unde patet ab apostolis hunc morem esse traditum vt eregumini et alii egroti vngantor oleo a pontifice consecrato."

4 Ibid., 4:479B.

5 *Biblie iampridem renouate pars sexta*, fol. 216vb, v. Infirmitatur: "Primum facit in duplici sacramento. scilicet vnctionis extreme et penitentie."

6 Ibid.: "Infirmitate de qua tamen est exeuntium de hac vita."

7 Ibid., fol. 216vb, v. Inducat presbyteros: "Licet istud sacramentum fuerit a Christo institutum: tamen per beatum Iacobum fuit publicatum."

8 *Biblia sacra cum postillis domini Hugonis cardinalis*, 6:99ra: "ET VNGEBANT OLEO MULTOS EGROS ET SANABANTUR. Ex hoc et ex illo Jaco. vlti. c. Infirmatur quis in vobis etc. traxit originem extrema vnctio."

9 *Hugonis de Sancto Charo tomvs septimus in epistolas omnes D. Pauli, Actus Apostolorum, epistolas septem canonicas, Apocalypsin B. Ioannis* (Lyon: Huguetan, 1669), fol. 322va: "hoc Sacramentum non datur nisi his qui petunt verbo, vel signo manifesto."

10 Ibid.: "sed quia in hoc Sacramento exigitur oratio, quae melior est in vno quam in alio, & maiorem habet efficaciam, propter hoc debet eligi melior."

11 Ibid., 322va–b.

death.[12] Because the apostles had instituted extreme unction, bishops, their successors, consecrated the oil. However, they assigned anointing to priests "because [the bishop] cannot be present to all the sick in their infirmity" (*quia omnibus infirmis in sua necessitate praesens esse non posset*).[13]

The sacrament of extreme unction did not always provide healing of bodies, because the patient was unworthy or because it was not expedient.[14] However, Hugh said that the rite could be repeated as needed, as it did not imprint a character on the soul (*non confertur character*) like baptism, confirmation, and ordination did.[15] Hugh interpreted the words of James about the prayer of faith saving a sick person as asking God for "health of both soul and body" (*à Domino sanitatem animae et corporis impetrabit*).[16] He cited the Ordinary Gloss as saying that many died "on account of sins" (*propter peccata*), combining health of body and soul.[17] The fourteenth-century Franciscan Nicholas of Lyra wrote little about anointing, but he said that Christ instituted the sacrament when he sent the apostles to anoint and heal the sick (Mk 6:13).[18]

The Origins of the Practice of Anointing

James became the crucial authority for administration of extreme unction by priests. Reminders exist, however, of a past involvement of the laity in anointing the sick with oil.[19] Early Christians kept holy oils at home, using them manually or even orally to treat ailments. By the third century, consecrated oil was used in anointing by clergy, lay persons, and even the sick themselves. There is evidence of lay anointing from Italy, Gaul, and Spain. A letter of Pope Innocent I, referring to the Epistle of James, mentioned anointing by the laity using chrism blessed by a bishop.[20]

12 Ibid., 322vb: "hoc sacramentum institutum est ad supplementum Poenitentiae; propter quod non datur nisi infirmis, & in eo statu in quo desperatur de eorum salute. Ad aliud, quia sacramentum poenitentiae non datur nisi à solis Sacerdotibus, ideò nec istud, cum sit complementum poenitentiae, datur nisi à solis Sacerdotibus." Hugh adds at ibid. that priests pray for alleviation of illness when a sick person cannot pray (*cùm ipse infirmus non possit*).

13 Ibid.

14 Ibid.: "quia indignus est, qui petit, vel pro quo petitur, vel meliùs, quia non semper expedit."

15 Ibid.

16 Ibid., fol. 323ra.

17 Ibid.

18 *Biblie iampridem renouate pars quinta*, fol. 100vb: "ET VNGEBANT MUL. etc. Ex hoc loco patet quod vnctio extrema que est infirmorum fuit instituta a christo."

19 The canonists eventually reserved ministry to the sick to parish priests and (with their permission) deacons; see Izbicki, *The Eucharist in Medieval Canon Law*, 202.

20 Michael G. Lawler, *Symbol Sacrament: A Contemporary Sacramental Theology* (Omaha, NE: Creighton University Press, 1995), 162–63; Gusmer, *And You Visited Me*, 23. On blessings of oil, see Antoine Chavasse, Études sur l'onctione des infirmes dans l'église du III*e au XIe siècle* (PhD diss., Lyon, 1942), 1:29–89.

A blessing of oil is found in the third-century writings of Hippolytus of Rome.[21] The Gregorian Sacramentary of the fourth or fifth century also included a prayer for blessing oil, asking that "those who anoint themselves with it . . . or apply it to themselves" receive "a bodily remedy that robs the body of all pain, all weakness, all sickness."[22] Liturgical texts in Spain and Gaul invoked the Holy Spirit for both physical cures and forgiveness of sins.[23] The *Sacramentary of Hadrian* included prayers for the sick, one used in church and one at home. This was a step toward an order for visitation of the sick.[24] Halitgar's ninth-century penitential included a prayer for recovery based on the sickbed prayer of King Hezekiah of Judah (Is 38). None of these necessarily required clerical intervention.[25]

There was, however, increasing sentiment, noted by the Venerable Bede, for anointing by clergy using oil consecrated by a bishop. In Merovingian times, Caesarius of Arles employed the James text to compose a clerical rite of anointing tied to penance.[26] In the eighth century, Boniface, the Anglo-Saxon missionary to the Germans, set Holy Thursday for priests receiving chrism from their bishops.[27] Boniface also forbade the clergy from turning over chrism to the laity, as only priests were to touch it.[28]

Carolingian reformers and councils treated anointing as a penitential rite with priests as its ministers. Recipients had to be in danger of death and need removal of spiritual stains by forgiveness of sins. An additional factor in this development was fear that ailing persons might use consecrated oil for magical healing.[29] The laity eventually were removed entirely

21 Aimé Georges Mortimort, "Prayer for the Sick and Sacramental Anointing," in *The Church at Prayer*, vol. 1: *Principles of the Liturgy*, ed. Irénée Henri Dalmais et al. (Collegeville, MN.: Liturgical Press, 1998), 117–37, at 118–19.

22 Ibid., 121.

23 Ibid., 121–22.

24 Ibid., 127–28.

25 *Medieval Handbooks of Penance*, 302.

26 Gusmer, *And You Visited Me*, 15–18. Bede was the last to mention self-anointing; see Philippe Rouillard, "The Anointing of the Sick in the West," in *Handbook for Liturgical Studies*, ed. Anscar J. Chupungco (Collegeville, MN: Liturgical Press, 1997), 4:171–90, at 173.

27 *Concilia Germaniae* 1:49: "Et in coena Domini semper novum chrisma accipiat ab Episcopo." Another statute states that only bishops were to consecrate chrism; see 2:311A.

28 Ibid., 1:73: "Ut Presbyteri sub sigillo custodiant Chrisma, & nulli sub praetextu medicinae, vel cujuslibet rei donare praesumant. Genus enim Sacramenti est, non ab aliis, nisi à Sacerdotibus contingi debet: quod si fecerint, honore priventur."

29 MGH *Concilia* I, pt. 1, ed. Albert Werminghof (Hanover: Hahn, 1906; Hanover: Hahn, 1997), 283: "Secundum beati Iacobi apostoli documentum, cui etiam decreta patrum consonant, infirmi oleo, quod ab episcopis benedictur, a presbyteris ungui debent." See also MGH *Concilia* III, ed. Wilfried Hartmann (Hanover: Hahn, 1984), 223–24, which connects forgiveness of sins to possible physical healing. Cuschieri, *Anointing of the Sick*, 17–29 and 161–66; Lawler, *Symbol Sacrament*, 163–64; Gusmer, *And You Visited Me*, 20–21; Frederick Paxton, *Christianizing Death: The Creation of a Ritual Process in Early Medieval*

from anointing the sick.[30] Thus, an 804 *capitulum* of Charlemagne forbade clerics on pain of degradation to turn over chrism to the laity for any necessity.[31] The *Capitula ecclesiastica* said a priest was to take two ampullas to the Holy Thursday Mass to receive blessed chrism and olive oil. The text treated the oil as used for anointing both catechumens and the sick. It included a quotation from James on praying for and anointing the sick.[32]

The 868 Council of Worms forbade anyone but the bishop consecrating chrism.[33] The Carolingian liturgist Amalar of Metz wrote at length about the consecration of holy oils on Holy Thursday.[34] He treated defense of the oils as a role of the doorkeeper of a church.[35] The ninth-century statutes of Liège required that the clergy keep oil and chrism "with all protection, reverence, and religion." Nor was the priest to be intoxicated or neglectful when the need to minister arose.[36] By the eleventh century a synod of Arras quoted Isidore of Seville about using olive oil "for relief of sick persons" (*qua lassi atque infirmi*).[37] Eventually, blessing oil at the bishop's chrism Mass on Holy Thursday was done according to Roman practice.[38] The canon law collection of Deusdedit, compiled during the Gregorian Reform, included an excerpt from a Roman pontifical attributing that practice to Pope Sylvester I.[39]

Europe (Ithaca, NY: Cornell University Press, 1996), 50–51. On the fear of magic done using sacred things, see Rouillard, "The Anointing of the Sick in the West," 172; Izbicki, "*Manus temeraria*."

30 Gusmer, *And You Visited Me*, 25–26.

31 Mansi 17b:418: "Ut nullus Presbyter, nec Diaconus, nec Clericus, chrisma alicui dare praesumat pro aliqua necessitate. Qui hoc fecerit, degradetur."

32 MGH *Capitula regum Francorum*, 1:179: "Ut presbyter in coena Domini duas ampullas secum deferat, unam ad chrismam, alteram ad oleum ad cathecuminos inungendum vel infirmos iuxta sententiam apostolicam; ut, quando quis infirmatur, inducat presbyteros ecclesiae, et orent super eum, ungentes eum oleo in nomine Domini." See also MGH *Capitula regum Francorum, nova series* 1, 1:513–14.

33 Mansi 15:869: "Chrisma conficere nullus praeter episcopum praesumat: nam illi soli dignitias concessa est."

34 Amalar of Metz, *On the Liturgy*, 1:102–27 and 222–27.

35 Ibid., 1:406–7.

36 MGH *Capitula regum Francorum*, 1:244: "Ut presbyter non sine crismate et oleo sacrato ad baptizandum alicubi proficiscatur neque sine sacro sacrificio, ut, ubicumque ei contigerit, suum ministerium circa infirmos implere possit, et ipsum oleum et crisma atque sacrificium *cum omni custodia et reverentia atque religione custodiat*, ne per ebrietatem aur per aliquod neglectum suum inhonoratum fiat sacrum illum suprascriptum."

37 *Gerardi Cameracensis acta synodi Atrebatensis*, ed. Steven Vanderputten and Diane J. Reilly (Turnhout: Brepols, 2014), 41; citing Jn 9:2 and Jas 5:14–15, at 42.

38 Martimort, "Prayer for the Sick and Sacramental Anointing," 129. See, e.g., the 836 Council of Aachen; MGH *Concilia* II, pt. 2, 710. The councils of Meaux (845) and Paris (846) forbade consecrating chrism on any other day; see ibid., 2:710, and Supplement 2, ed. Wilfried Hartmann (Hanover: Hahn, 1984), 107.

39 *Die Kanonessamlung des Kardinals Deusdedit*, ed. Victor Wolf von Glanvell (Paderborn: Schöningh, 1905; Aalen: Scientia, 1967), 1:227.

Prayers for sanctifying oil of the sick (*oleum infirmorum*), distinguishing it from chrism and oil of catechumens, appeared.[40] Chrism was to be made of olive oil mixed with balsam, while the others were made of olive oil alone.[41] In Magdeburg, a cleric in the chapel of Sancta Maria Rotunda was to present oil of the sick at the altar before the canon of the chrism Mass, when priests were saying the words of blessing together with the bishop.[42]

A rite for anointing the ailing body, especially the senses, was in use at least in Carolingian times. Thus, Theodulf of Orléans described anointings of bodies in a capitulary for his diocese:

> After the litany, a prayer having been said, [the priest] begins anointing with certain others singing fitting psalms and antiphons; and he makes on [the sick person] twelve signs of the cross. The first is a large cross between the shoulder blades up to the neck and across between the shoulder blades with a prayer. Then on the neck up to the nape. Third, on the head on the forehead and across from ear to ear. Then the fourth and fifth on the eyes, that is on the eyelids. The sixth is on the sense of smell, that is the nose or the nostrils. The seventh is on the sense of taste, that is, on the lips. The eighth and ninth crosses are on the sense of hearing, that is on the outsides of the ears. The tenth is on the throat. The eleventh is on the breast. The twelfth and thirteenth on the sense of touch, that is on the outside of each hand. The remaining two are on the feet. We make a total of fifteen crosses with holy oil on the sick person to signify the mystery of the Trinity and the five senses.[43]

40 A *dictum* in d. 95 of the *Decretum* of Gratian identified "sanctified oil" for the sick, quoting Pope Innocent I to show that a bishop could anoint the sufferer; see Friedberg 1:332. Wei, *Gratian the Theologian*, 272–73.

41 See *Pontificale Rothomagense*, Paris Bib. Nat. nouv. acq. lat. 306, fol. 61v: "Incipit consecratio olei infirmorum . . ." followed by an exorcism and a benediction. See also *Liber pontificalis Chr. Archieiscopi Eboracensis*, ed. William George Henderson (Edinburgh: Surtees Society, 1875), 201–6 and 252–65. That pontifical had a blessing for an ampule or ampules; see ibid., 305.

42 *Caremonialia ex ordinario ecclesie Magdeburgensis sub compendio extracta* (Leipzig: Brandis, ca. 1487), fol. 26r–27r.

43 Theodulf of Orléans, *Capitularia* (PL 105:220D–221B): "Post litaniam dicta oratione incipiat unctionem canentibus caeteris psalmos et antiphonam congruentes, et faciat de oleo super eum duodecim signa crucis, hoc est: primum inter scapulas magnam crucem usque ad collum et ex transverso usque super scapulas cum oratione, deinde in collo usque ad cervicem; tertiam super caput usque ad frontem in transverso ab aure usque ad aurem; deinde quartam et quintam in visu, hoc est, in superciliis oculorum; sextam in olfactu, id est, in naso sive in naribus; septimam in gustu, hoc est, in labiis; octavam et nonam crucem in auditu, id est, in auribus deforis; decimam in gutture, undecimam in pectore, duodecimam et decimam tertiam in tactu, id est, in unaquaque manu deforis, reliquas duas in pedibus. Hoc autem numero quindenario facimus cruces de oleo sancto super hominem infirmum propter Trinitatis mysterium et quinque sensum significationem" (author's translation).

Theodulf noted differences in the number of crosses made with oil, including signing the hands of priests and the bodies of the newly baptized. He also explained that the Greeks imitated the apostles in the act of anointing.[44]

In 1124, Otto of Bamburg preached a sermon calling anointing of the sick the third sacrament, useful even to "the dead." It was a means by which the Holy Spirit remitted sins. The rite also was useful against spiritual wickedness and malignant spirits afflicting the dying. The sacrament armed the soul against their threats. Every Christian was to be taught to value that reliable remedy for the soul.[45]

Monasteries developed liturgies for the sick and dying. Eventually, a Cluniac rite for visiting the sick spread through Christendom via Rome and the Franciscans. It coupled anointing with penance, viaticum, and prayers for the dying.[46] Peter the Venerable, a twelfth-century abbot of Cluny, argued that anointing of the sick could be repeated. He based this on the Epistle of James, arguing that both spiritual and physical health could lapse. If an illness could recur, so could sin, each needing treatment. Thus, anointing of the sick could be repeated, unlike anointing in baptism, confirmation, and holy orders, each of which imposed a character on the soul.[47]

By the twelfth century, anointing of the sick was known as extreme unction or last anointing because it was limited to the gravely ill. The clergy feared that the ailing faithful might avoid asking for it out of fear of death.[48] Theologians and bishops were aware that God could anoint invisibly; but they knew that humans, "on account of animality," needed external anointing.[49] Having embraced this, they addressed questions

44 Theodulf of Orléans, *Capitularia* (PL 105:221B–D). Theodulf attributed this formula to the Greeks: "*Ungo te in nomine Patris, et Filii, et Spiritus sancti, ut oratio fidei salvet te, et alleviet te Dominus, et si in peccatis sis, remittantur tibi.*"

45 *Concilia Germaniae* 3:303A: "Tertium sacramentum est *unctio infirmorum*, quod ideo mortuis necessarium est, quia in illa unctione per virtutem Spiritus Sancti remissio datur peccatorum, & ipse, qui moriturus est, contra spirituales nequitias, id est, contra malignos spiritus in exitu vitae animabus insidiantes eadem Spiritus Sancti virtute pugnaturus armature. Hoc omni Christiano in agone mortis ardentissime desiderandum & devotissime percipiendum est, utpote remedium animae certissimum."

46 Rouillard, "The Anointing of the Sick in the West," 176–77; Martimort, "Prayer for the Sick and Sacramental Anointing," 128 and 132.

47 *The Letters of Peter the Venerable*, ed. Giles Constable (Cambridge, MA: Harvard University Press, 1967), 1:353–60, at 355: "Ac sequitur: *Et oratio fidei saluabit infirmum, et alleuiabit eum dominus. Et si in peccatis sit* dimittentur *ei*. Cum igitur certum sit causa unctionis hanc esse ut oratio fidei salvet infirmum, ut alleuet eum dominus, ut si in peccatis sit, dimittentur ei, cur non iterabitur unctio, praecedente unctionis causa? Nam si eger post semel redditam sanitatem, numquam deinceps in morbum incideret, si numquam deinceps unctionem iam dictam iterari fas esset."

48 Daniel Bornstein, "Administering the Sacraments," in *The Routledge History of Medieval Christianity 1050–1500*, ed. R. N. Swanson (London: Routledge, 2015), 133–46, at 135; Smith, "The End of a Single World," 283–84.

49 *Gerardi Cameracensis acta synodi Atrebatensis*, 42: "Potest Deus per se oleum spiritualem tribuere sine corporali, sed propter animales aguntur inuisibilia ut inuisibilihugha facilius capiantur."

about doctrine and practice, including the origin, purpose, and effects of the sacrament, its relationship to penance, the appropriate minister, material, and words, whether the rite could be repeated and, if the sufferer survived, whether normal life could be resumed. A notable factor in this development is Bede's insistence that anointing should follow penance, a teaching adopted by Rabanus Maurus and Paschasius Radbertus in Carolingian times.[50]

THE SCHOLASTIC THEOLOGY OF ANOINTING

As Scholastic theology of the sacraments took shape, the purpose of anointing had to be clarified. Theologians and canonists emphasized the connection of sin to illness, including the need for the suffering to confess. Even after absolution, there might be a need to care for the souls of those who might soon die, making anointing more a spiritual than a physical practice.[51] Nonetheless, theologians like Peter Abelard and Alan of Lille treated anointing of the sick. Hugh of St. Victor discussed the purpose of the rite as being "for the remission of sins and for the alleviation of sickness." He said it was possible to have the former without the latter. Hugh also said the rite cleansed the soul for eternal glory. Anointing could be repeated because illness could recur, just as sins could be repeated. This strengthened the belief that unction was tied to penance without abandoning hope for bodily cures.[52] The connection to penance also helps to explain the practice of anointing the five senses, the feet, and the loins, the physical means of sin.[53]

Robert Pullen may be the author of a text concerning ceremonies appearing with the works of Hugh of St. Victor. "Pullen" said that extreme unction was founded by the apostles.[54] The text treated anointing as the

50 Smith, "End of a Single World," 284.

51 Gonzalo Florez, *Penitencia y unción de los enfermos* (Madrid: Ediciones Universidad de Navarra, 1993), 317–23; José Luis Larrabe, *La iglesia y el sacramento de la unción de los enfermos* (Salamanca: Ediciones Sigueme, 1974), 14–19 and 25–30.

52 Hugo de S. Victore, *De sacramentis* (PL 176:117–618B, at 577B–580B); *Hugh of St. Victor on the Sacraments of the Christian Faith (De sacramentis)*, trans. Roy J. Deferrari (Cambridge, MA: Medieval Academy of America, 1951), 430–32; Cuschieri, *Anointing of the Sick*, 43–44, 48–49, 63–64, 72, 167–70; Bernhard Poschmann, *Penance and the Anointing of the Sick* (New York: Herder and Herder, 1964), 234–36 and 249–57; Gusmer, *And You Visited Me*, 28–30; Smith, "End of a Single World," 284–86.

53 Cuschieri, *Anointing of the Sick*, 102–4 and 106.

54 Robertus Pullen, *De caeremoniis, sacramentis, officiis et observationibus ecclesiasticis* (PL 177:396B): "Unctio infirmorum ab apostolis est instituta. Unde Jacobus: *Infirmiatur quis in vobis? Inducant presbyteros Ecclesiae et ungant eum oleo sacro, et alleviabit Dominus infirmum; et si in peccatis fuerit, dimittentur ei* (Jac. V)."

sacrament but remission of sins as the effect. The author concluded that the sacrament could be repeated but not with the same annual supply of oil.[55]

Peter Lombard's *Sentences* listed the sacraments in order as: baptism, confirmation, Eucharist, penance, extreme unction, holy orders, matrimony. He also distinguished anointing bishops and kings from anointing neophytes, and both from anointing the sick. Basing himself on James, Peter said that unction brought remission of sins to the sick and, sometimes, bodily healing.[56] Spiritual healing was internal, and the olive oil used represented a pure conscience. The oil was to be blessed by a bishop, and anointing was to be repeated when necessary.[57]

Early teachers at Paris varied in their interpretations of the *Sentences*. Master Simon regarded the sacrament of extreme unction as for those leaving this world, but he affirmed repeating the rite at least once if the sick person survived.[58] Radulphus Ardens too said this was the sacrament of those exiting life.[59] However, Gilbert of Poitiers regarded anointing of the sick as a sacramental, similar to holy water. Jesus did not "model" this rite in his ministry; nor did it confer automatic healing. This critique failed to move the Paris masters, who would keep to the Lombard's list of seven sacraments.[60]

Peter the Chanter followed the Lombard's list. He treated extreme unction as the last received of all the sacraments (*conclusio et finis omnium sacramentorum*).[61] The sick person was to call for a priest when "peril of death is imminent" (*immineat periculum mortis*).[62] The Chanter treated Mark's text as showing that priests had to anoint the sick and mentally afflicted.[63] Even those who were *non compos mentis* could receive the sacrament.[64] Oil of the sick was to be blessed by a bishop on Holy Thursday,

55 Ibid., PL 177:396B–C. See also Hugh's *Sentences* (PL 176:153B–154C).

56 *The Sentences* (trans. Silano), 4:136; Cuschieri, *Anointing of the Sick*, 1–11, 91–92. Oil of the sick was more readily distinguished from chrism, which included balsam, than from oil of catechumens; see ibid., 94–96.

57 Silano, *The Sentences*, 4:136–38; Smith, "End of a Single World," 285–91.

58 Marcia L. Colish, *Faith, Fiction & Force in Medieval Baptismal Debates* (Washington, DC: The Catholic University of America Press, 2014), 50–51.

59 Bornstein, "Administering the Sacraments," 133.

60 Smith, "End of a Single World," 287.

61 Peter the Chanter, *Summa de sacramentis et animae consiliis*, ed. Jean-Albert Dugauquier (Louvain: Nauwelaerts, 1954), 116 and 120–21; Baldwin, *Masters, Princes and Merchants*, 2:241–45.

62 Peter the Chanter, *Summa de sacramentis*, 115: "In precepto [Jacobi] quippe illo non determinatur. Videtur quod debeat statim uocare."

63 Ibid., 118: "Sicut autem habetur ex auctoritate supradicta de Marco evangelista, apostoli iniungebant energuminos, freneticos, arrepticios qui petere non poterat, nec uolebant, et tales curabantur."

64 Ibid., 117–18.

except when a supply was exhausted.[65] Peter said that anointing was to be done by one priest, not several, nor by a lay person. Even a healer saint like Geneviève of Paris needed oil blessed by a bishop. As it was not a sacrament of necessity, like baptism, extreme unction could be omitted if not possible under certain circumstances. Old oil usually was discarded, but it had not lost its spiritual potency.[66]

Peter asked whether anointing could be repeated, and permitted this for a person who remained ill for more than a year. He also suggested that the words of the sacrament, which referred to sinning through the senses (*per visum, per auditum*, etc.), did not preclude sinless children from being anointed.[67] Later theologians usually concluded that extreme unction could be repeated because it imprinted no character on the soul. However, they denied extreme unction to children and the mad outside limited circumstances.

The Scholastics differed on the results of receiving the sacrament. William of Auxerre said it could alleviate physical infirmity, but that was not its essence (*res*). The rite signified remission of sin, resulting in spiritual improvement but physical healing only when it was useful to the soul.[68] William also discussed the practice of anointing the senses, saying that death entered through the "windows of the senses." The rite signified the remission of these sins.[69] William said that extreme unction, imprinting no character on the soul, was repeatable.[70] Olive oil was the material of extreme unction, as water was of baptism and chrism of confirmation.[71]

The Franciscans and Dominicans, treating the Lombard's collection, agreed on many, but not all, issues. The biggest difference concerned the spiritual effects of the sacrament. The Franciscans usually regarded it as removing venial sins, but the Dominicans often said it removed "remnants of sin" (*reliquiae peccati*). Nonetheless, physical healing remained a desired, if secondary, effect of the rite.[72]

65 Ibid., 123–26.

66 Ibid., 114–15, 118, 122–23. Thomas M. Izbicki, "Saint Geneviève and the Anointing of the Sick," *Catholic Historical Review* 104 (2018): 393–414.

67 Peter the Chanter, *Summa de sacramentis*, 119–20; Smith, "End of a Single World," 291–98.

68 *Magistri Guillelmi Altissodoriensis summa aurea* (ed. Ribaillier), 364.

69 Ibid., 363: "Sed probatur quod ipsa unctio passio est sacramentum, quia unctio oculorum est signum sacre rei, quia significat remissionem peccati quod contractum est per oculos. Mors entrat per fenestras sensuum; ergo sacramentum vel sacramentale. Non sacramentale, quia non deservit alicui sacramento; ergo est sacramentum, et non est aliud quam extrema unctio; ergo ipsa unctio passio est essentia huius sacramenti."

70 Ibid., 362–64.

71 Ibid., 361.

72 Cuschieri, *Anointing of the Sick*, 67–68; Larrabe, *La iglesia y el sacramento de la unción de los enfermos*, 54–72. The Augustinian Thomas of Strasbourg said that the sacrament shortened the soul's time in

The Dominican Theology of Anointing

One of the most important thirteenth-century Dominicans teaching at Paris was Albertus Magnus. He wrote extensively on the *Sentences*, including on the topic of extreme unction. He treated it as a sacrament founded by Christ, especially in Mark's Gospel.[73] Albertus identified the sacrament as a cure for a special illness of sin with no other remedy, "the remains of spiritual infirmity."[74] He defined the sacrament thus: "Extreme unction is a sacrament done by anointing with consecrated oil, conferring a remedy on the sick against the remains of sin, and, if expedient, conferring alleviation of infirmity of the body."[75] Anointing helped those going forth from the world (*exeuntium*) through the trials and temptations of death. The dying were not leaving the Church, but might join the Church Suffering in Purgatory or even the Church Triumphant.[76] Thus, extreme unction was only for those dangerously ill.[77]

The material of the sacrament was olive oil "sanctified for use with the sick" (*ad vsum infirmorum sanctificatum*).[78] A bishop blessed the oil but delegated anointing to priests, because he might be unable to go to the sick. This availability of priests to the sick pleased God.[79] In *De sacramentis*, Albertus treated this delegation from bishop to priest as showing the

Purgatory; see *Thomae ab Argentina commentaria in IIII. Libros sententiarum* (Venice: Ex Oficina Stellae, 1564; Ridgewood, NJ: Gregg, 1965), fol. 137rb.

73 Albertus Magnus, *Scriptum diui Alberti Magni super quartum sententiarum* (Basel: Jacobus de Pfortzen, 1506), fol. [aaa vii]^{rb}, v. An extra vnctio sit sacramentum: "Respondeo quod absque omni dubio est sacramentum extrema vnctio quod a domino et apostolis habetur ortum sue institutionis." For a reference to Mk 6, see ibid., fol. bbb^{vb}. See also *Alberti Magni de sacramentis*, ed. Albertus Ohlmeyer (Opera omnia 26; Münster: Aschendorf, 1958), 133.

74 Ibid., fol. [aaa vii]^{rb}, v. An extrema vnctio sit sacramentum: "Dicendum ergo ad primum quod illud sacramentum est ordinatum contra morbum specialem peccati contra quem nullum aliud specialiter ordinatur et si secundario aliud possit cooperari. Est autem ille morbus reliquie infirmitatis spiritualis ex originali et actuali remanentis."

75 Ibid., fol. [aaa vii]^{va}, v. An vnctio extrema sit bene definita: "extrema vnctio est sacramentum vnctione per oleum sanctificatum facta conferens infirmis remedium contra peccati reliquias et si expediat alleuiationem conferens corporis infirmitati."

76 Ibid., fol. bbb^{rb}, v. An sacramentum extreme vnctionis bene ordinatur inter alia sacramenta: "istud sacramentum est personarum exeuntium et non ecclesie exeuntis."

77 Ibid., fol. bbb^{vb}–bbb ii^{ra}, v. An solum infirmi sint particibiles sacramenti; ibid., fol. bbb ii^{ra-b}, v. An in omni egritudine aliquis sit prerceptibilis huius sacramenti.

78 Ibid., fol. [aaa vii]^{vb}–[aaa viii]^{rb}, v. An oleum consecratum ab episcopo sit materia sacramenti extreme vnctionis. See also *Alberti Magni de sacramentis*, 130.

79 Albertus Magnus, *Scriptum quartum super quartum sententiarum*, fol. bbb^{va}, v. An oporteat eum esse episcopum qui consecrat oleum quod est materia extreme vnctionis: "Et ad primum dicendum quod exercitium sacramenti conceditur sacerdoti propter periculum infirmorum: sepe enim contingit in sacramentis diuinis. Et hoc ideo fit: quia ecclesia secundum consilium dei instructa omnibus modis infirmis consulit in vtilitate sacramentorum: et ideo tales vult habere ministros quales de facili possunt haberi ab his qui sint infirmi in sacramento isto placuit deo quod essent simplices sacerdotes qui in omnibus locis de propinquo haberi possent."

perfection of the sacrament.[80] The form of extreme unction could be found in the indicative in old liturgical books, but James used the deprecative, begging divine aid for the sick.[81]

Albertus believed those members should be anointed which are "the first occasion of sin," the senses.[82] He said that certain powers in the body made up the efficient cause of sins. From them arose bad dispositions interacting with the remains of sin, and so the senses were treated with consecrated oil.[83] Albertus admitted that there were various usages in anointing the body, concluding: "Nevertheless, I think that it suffices to anoint the places of the five senses. I give this explanation, because all our will or appetite is formed by reason and species arising from fantasy or reasoning. All that is in fantasy or reason originates from the senses."[84] The senses were the "font of our appetites" (*fons appetitum nostrorum*), and so anointing these sufficed.[85] The places of lost or defective senses were to be anointed because of the potential for a sinful desire despite the inability to complete the act.[86] These anointings made up a single sacrament. Even if a priest died while anointing, another priest did not need to repeat what he had done.[87]

Albertus regarded young children, once cleansed from original sin, as not needing the sacrament, even if dangerously ill. Only at the age of reason could they understand the sacrament and receive it piously. Moreover, only then could they commit sins requiring sacramental medication.[88]

80 *Alberti Magni de sacramentis*, 130–34, at 131: "oportet significari hunc descensum in perfetione sacramenti, ita scilicet quod vel praeparatur materia a superiore vel praeparatur et exhibeatur."

81 Albertus Magnus, *Scriptum quartum super quartum sententiarum*, fol. bbb[ra], v. Que sit forma huius sacramenti: "Et cum hic effectus totus committatur diuine dispositioni: patet quod competentissime exprimitur per deprecatiuum." See also *Alberti Magni de sacramentis*, 131.

82 *Alberti Magni de sacramentis*, 133: "Dicimus, quod illa membra debent iniungi in quibus prima est occasio peccati."

83 Albertus Magnus, *Scriptum quartum super quartum sententiarum*, fol. bbb iii[rb], v. An infirmus percipiens hoc sacramentum in aliquo loco determinato sit iniungendus: "per illas operatur circa delectationes et communicationes cum hominibus: et ideo contrahunt malas dispositiones."

84 Ibid., v. In quibus partibus corporis infirmus sit iniungendus: "puto tamen quod sufficit vngere loca quinque sensuum: huius autem hanc assigno rationem: quia omnis nostra voluntas vel appetitus informatur de ratione et specie veluti ex fantasia vel ratione: omne autem quod est in fantasia vel ratione oritur ex sensu."

85 Albertus Magnus, *Scriptum quartum super quartum sententiarum*, fol. bbb iii[rb], v. In quibus partibus corporis infirmus sit iniungendus.

86 Ibid.: "quia licet membro careant non tamen potential qua completur actus peccati intra licet non extra." See also *Alberti Magni de sacramentis*, 133.

87 Albertus Magnus, *Scriptum quartum super quartum sententiarum*, fol. bbb iii[va–b], v. An extrema vnctio sit vnum vel plura sacramenta; fol. bbb iii[vb], v. An sacerdos iniungens iniungendo moriatur et aliud sacerdos inungens debeat incipere a nouo.

88 Ibid., fol. bbb ii[ra], v. In qua etate infirmus particibilis est sacramenti extreme unctionis.

Albertus also considered whether the mentally afflicted might be anointed, concluding that they could not recognize the sacrament, even showing irreverence to it.[89] Extreme unction, however, might be administered to one having a lucid interval.[90]

As extreme unction did not imprint a character on the soul, it could be repeated.[91] If the cause recurred, the sacrament dealing with it could be administered again.[92] Anyone showing signs of imminent mortality could be anointed, even if death did not occur.[93] Albertus added in *De sacramentis* that, because no character was imprinted, anointing could be repeated in the same year.[94] Also, if an illness endured for more than a year, extreme unction could be repeated.[95] Albertus conceded that his opinion was not to be followed if one of the holy fathers or the pope determined otherwise. The Church's inspiration trumped anyone's private reasoning in uncertain matters.[96]

Thomas Aquinas argued in his commentary on the fourth book of the *Sentences* that all the sacraments were spiritual medicine, curing the illness of sins.[97] Extreme unction itself was the medicine for sins.[98] The sacrament removed sins, and it belonged to the New Law because it conferred grace.[99] Thomas also interpreted James as saying the sacrament removed

89 Ibid., v. Quare furiosi et amentes et alij similibus infirmitatibus laborantes prohibentur a perceptione huius sacramenti: "Responsio dicendum quod talibus non est danda extrema vnctio quia non recognoscunt / et possit esse periculum irreuerentia sumptionis: quia possunt proiijcere vel immudicijs alijs irreuerenter se habere in sacramenti perception."

90 Ibid., fol. bbb ii^{va}, v. Quare furiosi et amentes et alij similibus infirmitatibus laborantes prohibentur a perceptione huius sacramenti: "nisi habeant lucida interuallis / et tunc in illo tempore quo interuallum habeat dari possunt eis hec sacramenta."

91 Ibid., fol. bbb iii^{vb}–bbb iiii^{ra}, v. An in sacramento extreme vnctionis sit aliquid quod est sacramentum tantum: "et aliquid quod est sacramentum et res: et aliquid quod est res tantum: et an imprimat characterem." See also *Alberti Magni de sacramentis*, 132.

92 Albertus Magnus, *Scriptum quartum super quartum sententiarum*, fol. bbb iiii^{rb}, v. An extrema vnctio possit iterari: "Responsio dicendum quod hoc sacramentum sicut vt cetera quedam iteratur si causa eorum iteratur."

93 Ibid.: "dicendum est quod extrema vnctio dicit a presumptione et signo extreme vite: et non ab extremo secundum actum et rem: sufficit enim quod presumatur extrema vite imminere ad hoc quod inungatur infirmus."

94 *Alberti Magni de sacramentis*, 133.

95 Albertus Magnus, *Scriptum quartum super quartum sententiarum*, bbb iiii^{va}, v. An in morbis cronicis debeat et possit semper iterari extrema vnctio: "puto quod si vltra annum remanet morbus post acceptam vnctionem iterari potest vnctio."

96 Ibid.: "magis in hac parte credendum est inspirationi ecclesie quam rationi coniecturanti ex incertis."

97 Thomas Aquinas, *Super quarto libro sententiarum preclarum opus*, q. 4: "effectus autem intentus in administratione sacramentorum est curatio moribi peccatorum."

98 Ibid., q. 23va, d. 23: "Sed extrema unctio est quaedam spiritualis medicina: quia valet ad remissionem peccatorum, ut habetur Iaco. v."

99 Ibid., q. 4va, d. 23: "Praeterea, omne sacramentum novae legis gratiam confert. sed per gratiam sit remissio peccatorum. ergo extrema unctio, cum sit sacramentum novae legis, operatur ad remissionem peccati."

spiritual debilities, the remnants of sins (*reliquiae peccatorum*).[100] In a disputed question, Thomas asked whether extreme unction removed venial sins. He replied that the sacrament might remit them, but it was established to remove the remains of sins.[101] What Thomas did not accept, in his commentary, was any idea that the primary purpose of anointing was physical healing on account of natural causes. What it effected was done by divine virtue. Moreover, any bodily cure was an effect secondary to the principal effect of spiritual healing. Nor did such a secondary effect of the sacrament always occur.[102]

Treating an argument that extreme unction was not mentioned in the Gospels (*in evangelio*) and thus was not established by Christ, Thomas, commenting on the *Sentences*, replied that he founded each sacrament of the New Law.[103] Matthew's Gospel mentions anointing by the apostles; but they only divulged the sacrament in the Epistle of James.[104] Aquinas added that the successors of the apostles could not abolish extreme unction, as Christ had founded the sacrament.[105]

Aquinas described olive oil as the material of the sacrament. The bodily healing it might cause signified spiritual healing.[106] Olive oil had a natural curative property, but consecration of it was required for spiritual healing.[107] It was consecrated by a bishop, who held the highest order in

100 Ibid., q. 4vb–q. 5ra, d. 23: "et ideo etiam Iacobus de remissione peccati conditionaliter loquitur dicens: Si in peccatis sit, dimittentur eis quo ad culpam: non enim semper delet peccatum quia non semper invenit: sed semper remittit quo ad debilitatem praedictam: quam quidem reliquias peccati dicunt."

101 *Quaestiones disputatae S. Thomas Aquinitatis doctoris angelici* (Paris: Franciscus de Honoratis, 1557), 119A; *Quaestio de peccato veniali*, a. 5: "Nec aliquid sacramentum novae legis est principaliter institutum contra peccata venialia, licet per ea peccata venialia remittantur; sed est instituta extrema unctio ad reliquias peccatourm tollendas."

102 Thomas Aquinas, *Super quarto libro sententiarum*, q. 5ra: "sed extrema vnctio non facit corporale sanationem ex proprietate naturali materie: sed ex virtute divina que operatur rationabiliter. Et quia ratio operans nunquam inducit secundarium effectum nisi Secundum quod expedit ad principalem: ideo ex hoc sacramento non sequitur corporalis sanatio semper: sed quando expedit ad spiritualem sanationem: et tunc semper eam inducit: dummodo ex naturali proprietate."

103 Ibid., q. 4ra: "ergo multo fortius omnia sacramenta nove legis habent institutionem ab ipso Christo."

104 Ibid., q. 4va: "tamen etiam de olei vnctione fit mentio in euangelio, Matth. vi, ubi dicitur quod apostoli oleo ungebant infirmos. Ad ii^{m} dicendum, quod magister dicit ab apostolis institutum: quia per doctrinam apostolorum nobis promulgata est eius institutio." Aquinas added that Christ did not experience extreme unction because he was sinless.

105 Thomas Aquinas, *Super quarto libro sententiarum*, q. 4ra: "sed ecclesia que est in successoribus apostolum habet eamden auctoritatem quam apostoli habuerunt, non posset auferre sacramentum extreme unctionis. ergo apostoli non instituerunt, sed ipse Christus."

106 Ibid., q. 4vb: "ergo et extrema unctio per sanationem corporale, quam exterius efficit significat et causat spiritualem." Thomas, in a sermon, treated oil as a means of healing, but also for light and cooking, and as a sign of mercy; see Thomas Aquinas, *The Academic* Sermons, trans. Mark-Robin Hoogland (Washington, DC: The Catholic University of America Press, 2010), 238–40.

107 Thomas Aquinas, *Super quarto libro sententiarum*, q. 5rb: "Sed contra est: quia in omnibus alijs unctionibus est materia consecrata prius. ergo, cum hoc sacramentum sit quedam unctio requirit materiam consecratam."

the body of Christ.[108] Extreme unction also required a proper form, and the whole Church used the same same words in conferring it.[109] The form was in the deprecative, as in the Latin text of James.[110] The words of administration, *vngo hos*, expressed the intent of the sacrament, but its effect was achieved through divine mercy.[111]

Although James said that anointing "pertains only to the sick" (*solis infirmis competit*), Thomas said that it mainly pertained to the seriously ill. This was especially true of those in danger of death.[112] Children and the mentally ill were not to be given the sacrament except if they were capable of recognizing it.[113] Thomas also said that the sacrament did not imprint a character on the souls of those leaving the "present" Church in death.[114] As extreme unction did not imprint a character, the sacrament could be repeated, including in successive illnesses of survivors.[115]

Aquinas drew a connection between remission of sin and the priestly power to anoint, saying that the laity could not absolve, and thus they could not remove the remains of sin by anointing.[116] A priest prayed on behalf of the Church, which none of the laity could do.[117] According to James, "presbyters" (priests), and not even deacons, could anoint. A bishop could anoint; but he could not go to all the sick in his diocese, delegating that role to his priests.[118]

Thomas taught that the body was to be anointed where the illness of sin was strongest, at the sense organs, the feet, and especially the loins of a man or the navel of a woman.[119] He drew a connection of the senses with sin, because "all our cognition has its origin in the senses." Anointing was

108 Ibid., q. 5[va].

109 Ibid., q. 5[vb]: "Praeterea, ad hoc est ritus vniuersalis ecclesie que quibusdam verbis vtitur in collatione huius sacramenti."

110 Ibid.

111 Ibid., q. 5[vb]–[q. 6][rb].

112 Ibid., [q. 6][va].

113 Ibid.: "hoc sacramentum non est dandum nisi recognoscetibus ipsum. sed tales non sunt furiosi et amentes. ergo eis dari non debet."

114 Ibid., [q. 6][vb].

115 Ibid., [q. 7][rb–va].

116 Ibid., [q. 6][rb]: "Sed contra est quia in hoc sacramento fit remissio peccatorum. sed laici non habent potestatem dimittendi peccata. ergo etc."

117 Ibid.: "sed fit in persona ecclesie in cuius persona orare potest quasi persona publica; non autem laicus, qui est persona privata."

118 Ibid.

119 Ibid., [q. 7][ra]: "Praeterea ibi debet adhiberi remedium ubi est maior vis morbi sed spiritualis morbus praecipue viget in renibus viris, et mulieribus in umbilico." See also ibid.: "in illis partibus tantum in quibus est radix spiritualis infirmitatis." However, the sex organs were not to be anointed because of their impurity; see [q. 7][rb] [*membra genitilia*].

to be done where all thoughts, including temptations, originated.[120] Even where a sense organ was defective or lacking, anointing was to be done nearby.[121] All this was to be done to purify the minds of those who faced death.

Dominican thought about extreme unction differed little after Albertus and Thomas. Peter of Tarentaise said that the act of anointing, not the oil used, was the sacrament.[122] It was instituted by Christ, and the apostles promulgated it. Extreme unction effected spiritual healing, making it a sacrament, not a sacramental.[123] Anointing removed spiritual infirmity contracted through venial sins. Sensuality caused the spiritual sickness of venial sin, whereas mortal sin originated in the mind. Thus the sense organs were anointed with spiritual medicine, just as afflicted organs were treated in a physical illness.[124] A secondary effect was curing the body, a sign of inner healing.[125]

Oil was the material, because it signified healing.[126] A bishop consecrated it, but priests anointed.[127] Because the sacrament was related to penance, it could not be administered by lay persons, even a saint like Geneviève.[128] Petrus attributed the form of words used in anointing to Gregory the Great. They were in the deprecative, concerned with the causality (*causalitas*) of the sacrament.[129] Anointing was a single sacrament, "a whole made up of particular acts" (*imo vnctio vniueralis ex particularibus conflata*).[130]

120 Ibid., [q. 7]rb: "omnia autem nostra cognitio a sensu ortum habet."

121 Ibid., [q. 7]rb.

122 Peter of Tarentaise, *In IV Libros Sententiarum commentaria* (Toulouse: Apud Arnoldum Colomerium, 1652; Ridgewood, N.J.: Gregg, 1964), 4:250B: "Ampliùs videtur quòd ipsa, vnctio, non oleum sit sacramentum. Nam nominatur hoc sacramentum extremae vnctionis, ergo est vnctio."

123 Ibid.: "extrema verò vnctio per se ordinatur ad aliquem effectum spiritualis sanationis, non per aliud: vnde sacramentum est, non sacramentale."

124 Ibid., 4:254A: "causa verò morbi peccatorum spiritualium, venialium maximè, viget in sensualitate: causa mortalium in mente: ideò organa sensuum debent oleo spiritualis medicinae inungi, non alia membra: datur enim haec medicina spiritualis per quondam similitudinem corporalis medicinae."

125 Ibid., 4:253A: "sanitas duplex, vna principalis ab infirmitate spirituali, quae contrahitur per venialia, per quam anima infirma reddebatur ad exeundum in actum gratiae vel gloriae: altera secundaria quasi effectus & signum illius, scilicet sanitas corporialis."

126 Ibid., 4:252A: "Effectus principalis huius sacrament est sanitas quaedam spiritualis, ideò ad eam significandam conuenienter ponitur oleum."

127 Ibid., 4:250B.

128 Ibid., 4:254A: "Inunctio illa non erat sacramentalis, sed miraculosa."

129 Ibid., 4:252B.

130 Ibid., 4:251A.

Children could not contract spiritual illness through venial sin and did not need anointing.[131] The mad (*prehenetici*) could be anointed while of sound mind, but otherwise they were incapable of the devotion needed for the effect of the rite (*res sacramenti*).[132] Because extreme unction did not imprint a character on the soul, it could be repeated as needed, even during a long illness.[133]

Thomas's student Hannibaldus de Hannibaldis argued that extreme unction was based on Christ's usage (*ex vsu Christi*). Oil was used to confer grace.[134] A bishop consecrated the holy oils on account of his superiority in the mystical body of Christ.[135] The words employed by a priest at the sickbed reflected three conditions: the sickness of the recipient, the imminence of death, and contrition.[136] The words expressed the healing intent of the sacrament.[137] The senses were anointed as causes of sin, just as an ailing body part was anointed.[138] The rite might heal venial sins or remove the remains of sin toward admission to glory.[139] Physical healing was secondary.[140] Because sin could recur, extreme unction could be repeated.[141]

131 Ibid., 4:255A: "Paruuli quamuis habeant infirmitatem corporalem: non tamen infirmitatem spiritualem contractatam ex peccatis venialibus, contra quam principaliter datur hoc sacramentum."

132 Ibid., 4:254B: "Aut petierunt in sana mente constituti aut non: in primo casu debet dari eis: in secundo non, quia ad hoc quod prosit, requiritur quaedam deuotio exterior, quae est res sacraenti, & sacramentum cuius non sunt capaces furiosi."

133 Ibid., 4:256A.

134 Hannibaldus de Hannibaldis, *Diui Thomae Aquinatis Ordinis Praedicatorum, doctoris angelici, secundum scriptum appellatum super quatuor libros sententiarum ad Hannibaldum Hannibaldensem* (Paris: Apud Gulielmum Chaudiere, 1574), fol. 536v: "ideo oleum sanctificari debuit, vt ex sanctificatione efficaciam habere, quia secundum Hugo. Sacramentum ex sanctificatione est causans gratiam."

135 Ibid., fol. 537r: "Sed quantum ad corpus Christi mysticum episcopalis ordo est supra sacerdotalem, & ideo in sacramento extremae vnctionis Episcopus materiam consecrat."

136 Ibid., fol. 537v. A priest was tasked with administering the sacraments conferring grace; see fol. 538v–539r.

137 Ibid., fol. 537v.

138 Ibid., fol. 539v: "Ad curationem autem morbi corporalis non oportet quod totum corpus inungatur, sed tantum partes in quibus est causa morbi. Sed quia origo morbi spritualis est in nobis ex quinque sensibus, ideo quando de essentia sacramenti est quinque sensus inungi scilict manus propter tactum, quoniam in pulpis digitorum praecipue tactus viget."

139 Ibid., fol. 538r: "Dicendum quod sicut illud effectus baptismi est interior ablutio a peccatis, quia sacramentum illud per modum ablutionis confertur, ita effectus huius sacramenti, quod confertur per modum medicationis, est sanatio per quae sit diuina virtute principaliter quidem spiritualia, quia consistit, secundum quosdam, in remissione peccatorum venialium, quia mortalia dicunt ante esse purgata per penitentiam, secundum alios vero in amotione reliquiarum peccati, vt homo plenarie purgatus ad gloriam admittatur."

140 Ibid.

141 Ibid., fol. 540r: "Dicendum quod morbus contra quem datur hoc sacramentum est iterabilis, quia contingit per diuersa peccata diuersam debilitatem spiritualem incurrere, & similiter infirmitatem corporalem iterari contingit, & ideo sine iniuria sacramenti potest sacramentum hoc iterari."

Durandus de Sancto Porciano said that extreme unction was for those leaving the world.[142] The sacrament was preparatory to eternal glory.[143] James had documented the origin of the rite with the apostles.[144] Durandus also cited James in a syllogism saying that the sacrament was a remedy for sin.[145] The rite, dealing with those leaving the world, "left [them] in the hand of God alone" (*in manu solius dei relinquuntur*).[146]

Olive oil was used because it alleviated pain (*mitagatiuum dolorum*).[147] The words of the rite conveyed divine mercy, removing the *sequelae* of sin[148] and any sins still present at the time of anointing.[149] Durandus said the sacrament could be repeated if an illness recurred, just as prayers could be said several times for a sick person.[150] A good lay person might offer more effective prayers for physical healing than did a bad priest. However, the priest offered public prayers for the Church, making them more effective spiritually.[151] Healing the body might occur with no bad effect on the soul;

142 *DDSP*, fol. 308vb: "Hic vero determinatur de extrema vnctione, quod est sacramentum exeuntium."

143 *DDSP*, fol. 254rb: "Ad tertium dicendum quòd in ve. le. non praecesit figura extremae vnctionis, quia extrema vnctio est praeparatoria ad gloriam quam tunc statim post mortem consequi non poterant sicut modo, similiter in confirmatione non datur plenitudo spi. san. ad robur & ideo non debuit praefigurari ante tempus plenitudinis gratiae."

144 *DDSP*, fol. 308vb: "Tertia vnctio est, qua vnguntur infirmi, et de hac ad praesens agitur, & hae duo sunt oleo simplici benedicto. Postea dicit hoc sacramentum institutum fuisse ab apostolis, vt habetur in canonica Iacobi."

145 *DDSP*, fol. 309ra: "Minor patet per beatum Iacobum in canonica sua, Quinto capitulo, vbi loquens de extrema vnctione dicit quòd si infirmus in peccatis fit, dimmitentur ei"; fol. 309rb: "Etiam beatus Iacobus non intendit loqui de sanitate corporis, quando dicit, *Et oratio fidei saluabut infirmum*. Sed de salute mentis subiungens modum praedictum, & alleuiabut eum dominus, &c."

146 *DDSP*, fol. 310ra.

147 *DDSP*, fol. 309rb.

148 *DDSP*, fol. 309ra: "Qvantum ad secundum, scilicet quis sit effectus eius, oportet dicere quòd dimissio culpae non solum propter auctoritatem beati Iacobi iam allegatam, Sed propter rationem quae talis est, sacramenta illud efficiunt quod significant, sed per formam huius sacramenti si rectè significatur remissio peccatsi. Est enim talis forma, 'Per istam vnctionem & piissimam misericordiam suam indulgeat quisti tibi dominus quicquid deliquisti per visum,' & sic de caeteris, ergo per hoc sacramentum fit dimissio peccatorum quantum ad culpam, vel quoad poenam culpae debitam, seu quamcunque aliam sequelam. Et quamuis istud fit clarissimum tam ex auctoritate sacrae scripturae iam allegata, quàm ex communi doctrina de formis sactamentorum, quod ipsae efficiuunt quod significant." Durandus notes at fol. 309va that anointing could relieve "depressio quam communiter tunc homines patiuntur."

149 *DDSP*, fol. 309rb.

150 *DDSP*, fol. 308vb: "Si enim morbus iteratur & vnctio, quae est medicina morbi iterari potest. Secunda causa est hęc, quia quum vnctio cum oratione operatur (vtrumque enim simul beatus Iacobus commemorat in canonica sua) si oratio iterari potest, quare & vnctio."

151 *DDSP*, fol. 310ra: "Dicendum quòd oratio priuata innitur meritis personae, & melior est si fiat à bono laico, quàm si fiat à malo sacerdote, sed oratio publica quae fit à ministro ecclesiae, & innititur communibus meritis ecclesiae melior est quàm oratio priuata cuiuslibet personae, dato quòd minister sit malus in se."

but those who received the sacrament devoutly still might not be cured.[152] Durandus said that the laity could administer the sacrament of necessity, baptism. The others required a grade of superiority in the Church, which the laity lacked.[153] Bishops could administer any sacrament, but they delegated extreme unction to priests.[154]

Petrus de Palude said that, because extreme unction effected spiritual healing, it only was to be given to those in need of such medicine.[155] It was especially intended for those who might die.[156] They could benefit from the sacrament as a "supplement to penance."[157] It prepared the soul for glory and infused the Spirit for support in the last battle with the devil.[158] Petrus thought that the sacrament removed spiritual obstacles to glory rather than primarily forgiving venial sins.[159]

Olive oil was the necessary material, and any change would vitiate the sacrament.[160] The oil was consecrated by a bishop, but priests were the usual ministers.[161] Petrus argued that anointing required absolving, and only a priest could do that.[162] Petrus considered the Ambrosian formula in the indicative, but the text of James in the Roman rite made the deprecative correct.[163] He dealt with the usual instructions for anointing the senses. Whoever lost a sense was to be anointed near that location. Whoever was born without a sense, like one born blind, was unable to sin in act but might want to use it sinfully, as sin lay in the soul, not the body.[164] Petrus

152 Ibid.: "Postea dicit quòd hoc sacramentum institutum est ad duplicem effectum, scilicet ad sanitatem animae & corporis, quia tamen non expedit homini semper quòd corporaliter alieuetur, ideo non semper in hoc sacramento sanitatem acquirit qui hoc sacramentum deuotè & fideliter recipit spiritualiter, scilicet quoad animam." See also fol. 310ra–b.

153 *DDSP*, fol. 309vb: "De laico patet sic, quia nullum sacramentum nisi sit mere necessitatis potest dispensari nisi ab illo qui habet aliquam gradum superioritatis in ecclesia, sed laicus non habet aliquem talem gradum."

154 *DDSP*, fol. 309vb–310ra.

155 Petrus de Palude, *Scriptum super quartum sententiarum* (Venice: Bonetus Locatellus, 1493), fol. 121vb: "sed curationis non est susceptiuus nisi infirmus."

156 Ibid.: "vnde solum grauibus infirmis de quorum vita probabiliter timetur imo magis creditur."

157 Ibid.: "quia extrema vnctio est quedam supplementum penitentie."

158 Ibid., fol. 122vb: "Quia ergo morte instante imminent grauissima temptatio inimici."

159 Ibid.: "Unde per hoc sacramentum imprimatur ornatus disponens ad augmentum glorie et feruorem charitatis vt sit homo fortior contra tentationem in morte et accipit spiritum sanctum ad robur in pugna hac." On venial sins, see fol. 122va–b.

160 Ibid., fol. 119va: "Et si mutaretur species est irritatio sacramenti . . . sed tale est oleum oliuarum respectu extreme vnctionis."

161 Ibid., fol. 119vb–120ra.

162 Ibid., fol. 121rb: "sed extrema vnctio virtitutem requirit in ministro sicut absoluere: et conficere et ordinare; propter quod in nulla necessitate potest non sacerdos iniungere."

163 Ibid., fol. 120ra–b.

164 Ibid., fol. 122rb: "Uel potest dici cum peccatum essentialiter sit in voluntate: non in sensu: dicitur peccare per visum cecus natus non per operationem imparatum sed elicitam: quia forte concupiuit videre

added that anointing did not imprint a character on the soul, allowing repetition.[165]

Petrus considered the question regarding whether children or the mad could be anointed. Young children and the perpetually mad could not use reason either to sin or understand the sacrament, but some mad persons had lucid intervals during which they could be anointed.[166] Those who had expressed a desire for extreme unction before falling into a frenzy could be anointed when in danger of death, but those who had not thought of it or refused it could not be anointed.[167]

To make the form for extreme unction available to priests, Antoninus of Florence included a copy in his *Confessionale "Defecerunt."* He added that secular priests thought the loins should be anointed but Dominicans advocated anointing over the kidneys.[168] Antoninus claimed in his vernacular *Confessionale "Omnis mortalium cura"* that extreme unction was a remedy against the devil's temptation of a dying person to fall into doubt.[169] He also treated the sacrament as removing venial sins.[170] The rite of extreme unction asked forgiveness for sins committed by each sense.[171] Antoninus reflected on the sins to which the senses could lead. For example, sight could lead someone to desire "vile things" (*cose vile*) instead of seeing the Eucharist (*negligente andar a veder el corpo di Christo*).[172]

Antoninus summarized anointing in his *Summa*, adding a draft sermon on the topic.[173] He said that the sacrament was instituted by Christ but promulgated by James. Extreme unction involved anointing "by a priest on the sense organs of a sick person" (*per sacerdotem in organis sensuum infirmi*). This was done for "spiritual cleansing" (*sanationem spiritualem*).[174] Olive oil was fitting for the rite because it signified lightheartedness and clarity of

---

inordinate vel habere visum vel huiusmodi. Et sic per visum peccauit materialiter et obiectiue: licet non instrumentaliter et subiectiue."

165 Ibid., fol. 122vb–123ra.

166 Ibid., fol. 122ra: "Prima quod propter hoc quod pueri et perpetuo furiosi non sunt iniugendi: qui esset mendacium in forma Quicquid deliquisti per visum etc."

167 Ibid.

168 Antoninus of Florence, *Summa confessionalis*, fol. xcviiirb.

169 Antoninus of Florence, *Confessionale "Omnis mortalium cura"* & *Libretto della dottrina christiana*; *Libretto della dottrina christiana* v. Extrema Unctione, "Cosí vngeno linfirmi perche in sul puncto de la morte il diauolo ilquale tempta le persone in fine de lopera de la fede sel potesse farli dubitare."

170 Ibid.

171 Antoninus de Florentia, *Tractatus de censuris ecclesiasticis*, University of Pennsylvania Ms. Codex 72, fol. 101va–102vb.

172 Antoninus, *Libretto della dottrina christiana* v. De li cinque sentimenti del corpo humano.

173 *Sancti Antonini de Florentia ordinis Praedicatorum summa theologica summa theologica*, 4 vols. (Verona: Ex Typographia Seminarii, 1740–41; Graz: Akamademische Druck- und Verlagsanstalt, 1957), 3:731–36.

174 Ibid., 3:731–32.

mind. According to custom, the oil was blessed by a bishop.[175] Antoninus cited the form of anointing, attributed to Gregory the Great, beginning, "By this holy anointing" (*Per istam sanctam unctionem*).[176] Anointing was to be done on the sense organs, "the beginnings of sin" (*principia peccati*), as well as the feet, loins, shoulder blades (*scapula*), and kidneys. Oil was to be applied near a mutilated organ, as a person lacking it might still desire to sin with it.[177]

Antoninus followed Thomas Aquinas in crediting the sacrament with "spiritual cleansing" (*sanatio spiritualis*) and with a secondary effect of corporeal healing.[178] Only sick persons "in danger of death" could receive the sacrament.[179] However, even those without reason, although unable to sin or repent, might retain effects of sin, keeping them from attaining glory. They might owe a penalty for sin, needing extreme unction for its release.[180] Antoninus required one's own priest to anoint "unless danger of death was imminent" (*nisi periculum mortis immineret*) and that priest was not available.[181] A priest who failed to go to a sick person was "guilty of his soul."[182] These same teachings were repeated in a sermon on extreme unction.[183]

The Franciscan Theology of Anointing

Bonaventure argued that extreme unction forgave venial sins.[184] Baptism forgave original sin, and penance forgave mortal sin, leaving only venial

175 Ibid., 3:732: "Habet oleum olivarum maximum convenientiam ad significandum ejus effectum, qui est hilaritas & claritas mentis . . . quod illud oleum oportet, quod sit ab episcopo benedictionem . . . qualis a tota ecclesia vel Romana consuevit."

176 Ibid., 3:732–33.

177 Ibid., 3:736.

178 Ibid., 3:733.

179 Ibid., 3:735.

180 Ibid., 3:733–34: "Aliquando autem infirmis jam perdidit usum rationis lapsus in phrenesim, ita quod peccare non potest, nec poenitere. Sed restat in eo infirmitas retardans ab actu gloriae, & poena debita peccato actuali." Antoninus added that receipt of anointing required less devotion than did reception of the Eucharist. However, children below the age of reason and the perpetually mad did not need the rite, although a mad person could receive it in a lucid interval. It could, however, be denied to those who were impenitent before losing the use of reason; see 3:735–36.

181 Ibid., 3:734.

182 Ibid.: "Si omittit ire, reus est animae illius." Four priests at Castellarquato could not explain why this happened frequently; see Bornstein, "Administering the Sacraments," 136.

183 Antoninus, *Summa theologica*, 3:674–76.

184 *Doctoris seraphici S. Bonaventurae opera omnia*, 4:589A; *In quattuor libros Sententiarum* IV, d. 23: "Et cum non sit contra originale nec contra mortale, reliquitur, quod sit contra peccatum *veniale*. Et hoc communis opinio tenet."

sin as the object of the sacrament.[185] Venial sin was a spiritual illness.[186] Bonaventure admitted that the sacrament might cure the body, because the soul's health affected it. However, this was a secondary effect, happening only *per accidens*.[187] A physical cure could result when the soul is "tranquilized, invigorated and made joyful."[188] The soul's passions might have bodily effects.[189] However, bodily cures could not affect an illness of the soul.[190] Bonaventure said that the cures the apostles performed by anointing (see Mk 6) happened before the institution of the sacrament of extreme unction, healing bodies, not souls.[191] Venial sins could recur; but their remission in one leaving the world was unlikely to require future cures. The sacrament cleansed the soul in this last trial and remitted part of the punishment of sins.[192]

Bonaventure had a strong impact on subsequent Franciscans. Richard of Middleton treated the sacrament as "a cause of internal spiritual anointing" (*causa spiritualis vnctionis interioris*).[193] Anointing remitted venial sin.[194] It pertained to those in danger of death;[195] but it could not be given to children below the age of reason, who were incapable of venial sin.[196]

Richard cited the decretal *Cum venisset* to demonstrate that oil designated "purity of conscience" and, therefore, had to be consecrated "by

185 *Doctoris seraphici S. Bonaventurae opera omnia*, 4:588B–589A: "Sed contra hoc est quod dicitur Iacobi quinto in institutione Sacramenti: Si in peccatis fuerit, remittentur ei: ergo istud Sacramentum est ordinatum contra aliquem *morbum peccati*; et hoc ipsum tangitur in Glossa."

186 Ibid., 4:589A: "et sic, cum anima possit trahere talia cremabilia, quae retrahunt a Gloria, instituit divina misericordia remedium, quo anima curare posset quantum ad remissionem culpae; et hoc est Sacramentum unctionis extremae."

187 Ibid., 4:589B: "Concedendae igitur sunt rationes probantes, istud Sacramentum valere ad corporales probantes, quod non valet principaliter contra illas, quoniam solum per accidens et ex consequenti valet."

188 Ibid.: "ideo non est mirum, si tranquillatur anima et vigoratur et laetificactur, si etiam hoc redundant ad corpus."

189 Ibid.: "Unde passiones animales multum redundat in carnalem, unde Sapiens dicit: *Spiritus tristis exsiccat ossa* [Ps. 18:22]."

190 Ibid.: "quia corporalis medicina non sanat spiritualem morbum."

191 Ibid., 4:592B: "quia unctio illa principaliter fiebat ad sanitatem *corporalem*, non ad *curationem spiritualem principaliter*."

192 Ibid., 4:589A: "Si autem loquamur, prout anima est in *statu egrediendi*; sic potest curari sine *iteratione*; et sic, cum anima possit trahere talia cremabilia, quae retraherent a gloria, instituit divina misericordia remedium, quo anima curari posset quantum ad remissionem *culpae* et etiam partis *poenae*; et hoc est Sacramentum Unctionis extremae."

193 *Clarissimi theologi magistri Richardi de Mediavilla super quatuor libros sententiarum Petri Lombardi* (Brescia: De Consensu Superiorum, 1591), 4:355B.

194 Ibid., 4:357B: "est sacramentum principaliter fremissionis venialium peccatorum, quia si digne sumatur per eam remissio venialium non tamen signicifatur, sed etiam causatur."

195 Ibid., 4:359B.

196 Ibid., 4:360A: "in paruulis non est veniale peccatum, ideo hoc sacramentum conferri non debet impęnitentibus." Richard extended this to the mad (*furiosis*).

a priest of the highest dignity" (*per sacerdotem supereminentis dignitatis*).[197] Priests were the ordinary ministers because bishops were too preoccupied to visit the sick. If no priest was available, the rite, not being entirely necessary, could be omitted. No lay person could anoint, not even a saint like Geneviève.[198] The senses and generative organs were to be anointed because of their connection to sin, together with feet "progressing" toward occasions of sin. "According to the custom of the Roman Church" (*secundum morem Romanae Ecclesiae*), there were several anointings in one rite.[199] Extreme unction did not impose a spiritual character on the soul, and so it could be administered for multiple illnesses or multiple states of one illness.[200]

Duns Scotus thought that extreme unction was instituted by Christ but promulgated by James to remove venial sins.[201] God had established it to do this.[202] This remission removed obstacles to eternal glory, leaving no room for further venial sins.[203] Scotus added that the recipient had to be penitent to receive the sacrament's grace.[204] The exterior sign reflected interior anointing of the soul.[205] Scotus concluded that extreme unction signified "the final cure of venial sins."[206]

Children and the mentally afflicted were not capable of receiving this grace, because they lack reason and the ability to commit venial sins.[207]

197 Ibid., 4:356B (X 1.15.1).

198 Ibid., 4:358B–359B, at 359A: "Vnde illud quod legitur de sancta Genouefa, quod oleo vngebat infirmos, & sanabunt, miraculosum fuit, non sacramentale." Izbicki, "Saint Geneviève and the Anointing of the Sick."

199 Ibid., 4:360A.

200 Ibid., 4:360B–361A: "ideo cum infirmo nullum imprimat indelibile effectum potest, & debet eidem homini pluries conferri, vel pro diuresis infirmatibus, vel pro eiusdem infirmitatis diuresis statibus supradictis."

201 Duns Scotus, *Ordinatio, Liber Quartus* in *B. Ioannis Duns Scotus opera omnia*, vol. 13 (Vatican City: Typis Polyglottis Vaticanis, 2011), d. 14–42, 298, at d. 23.

202 Ibid., 294: "possibile est Deum finaliter remittere venialia, ergo possibile est sibi instituere signum efficax istius remissionis."

203 Ibid.: "Hoc etiam congruum est, scilicet 'recursurum ab hac vita' finaliter a venialibus absolvi, quia ista non remissa essent impedimentum gloriae consequendae, et possent esse non remissa usque ad exitum, quia peccator quasi continue peccat taliter peccatus."

204 Ibid., 295.

205 Ibid.: "Cuius congruentia est, quia istud sensibile signum congruit effectui, scilicet interiori unctioni in curatione hominis."

206 Ibid., 294: "Cuius potest talis assignari ratio: 'Extrema unctio est unctio hominis infirmi poenitentis, in determinatis partibus corporis, cum oleo consecrato ab episcopo, ministrata a sacerdote, simul verba certa cum intentione divine efficaciter significans curationem finale venialium.'" See also 298.

207 Ibid., 295: "Et ex hoc excluduntur non utens ratione (ut parvuli) et qui non habet materiam poenitentiae, saltem qui non habent poenitentiam de venialibus ut perfecte innocentes; quia_etiam qui non utantur ratione, non possunt esse poenitentes, excluduntur furiosi et amentes, et hoc nisi per voluntatem praecedentem expressum praestantur illud velle."

The sense organs, the feet, and the loins were sites of sin.[208] The words of the sacrament were to be adjusted to the body part being anointed.[209] The oil had to be consecrated by a bishop.[210] A priest was to perform the rite; a non-priest attempting it would accomplish nothing.[211]

Franciscus de Mayronis treated extreme unction, with baptism, confirmation, and holy orders, as one of four anointings the faithful received. Anyone negligent in receiving them sinned mortally (*peccat mortaliter*).[212] Anointing had two effects, remission of venial sins and alleviation of bodily illness.[213] Franciscus added six interrogations of the sick, derived from Anselm of Canterbury, involving belief and regret for sins. The sick person was urged, if surviving, "to abstain from mortal sins" (*abstinere a peccatis mortalibus*). Franciscus added a seventh, whether the sick person placed Christ's merits between "you and these sins" (*inter te . . . et his peccatis*).[214] He added that the sacrament could be repeated when a sick person in danger of death requested it, even in a prolonged illness.[215]

Petrus Aureoli listed the effects of the sacrament, beginning: "The first effect is removal of venial sins in whole or in part."[216] The other effects were diminution of the punishment for sin, augmentation of grace, interior enlightenment (*claritas*), and happiness (*iocunditas*), limiting the devil's power, and sixth, "healing of the body, when it is expedient for the health of the soul."[217] Aureoli's list concluded with the dying person's profession of

208 Ibid., 295–96: "istae partes sunt organa potentiarum per quarum actus pecatur frequenter venialiter, utpote organa quinque sensuum et potentiae motivae. . . . Propter organum motivae ad progressivam, quae est principalis motiva, fit duplex unctio in duobus pedibus tamquam organis ad illum motum ordinatis . . . ita quod septem principales, videlicet in organis quinque sensuum, sed in organo principali motivae progressivae septem in organo principali potentiae generativae."

209 Ibid., 297: "Forma autem haec sextuaflex ad septem unctiones principales et: 'Per istam sanctam unctionem et suam piissimam misericordiam, parcat tibi Dominus quidquid – narium, linguae, tactus, vel huiusmodi – vitio deliquisti.'"

210 Ibid., 296–97: "Consecratio autem episcopalis est necessaria ad hoc ut sit materia apta, quia communiter in sacramentis consistentibus in usu, solus baptismus non requirit materiam specialiter consecratam, quia Christus tactu mundissimae carnis suae, quando voluit a Ioanne baptizari, totam aquam consecravit, hoc est in usum istum dedicavit."

211 Ibid., 297: "sicut si non sacerdos attentaret conficere, nihil faceret. Determinatio autem huius ministri habetur per illud Iac. 5: *inducat presbyteros*."

212 Franciscus de Mayronis, *In quatuor libros sententiarum* (Venice: Bernardinus de Novaria, 1520), fol. 211rb.

213 Ibid., fol. 211va: "remissio pecatorum venialium et alleuiatio egritudinis corporalis."

214 Ibid., fol. 211vb.

215 Ibid., fol. 211va: "sed si in eadem egritudine diu manet: et sit pluries in periculo mortis et petit hoc sacramentum pluries potest dari."

216 *Petri Aureoli commentariorum in quartum librum sentenntiarum* (Rome: Zannetti, 1605), fol. 159rb: "Primus est deletio venialium, & hoc in toto, vel in parte." A detailed discussion of this effect followed at 159rb–va.

217 Ibid., fol. 159rb: "Sextus effectus est corporis sanatio, vbi expediat animae sanitati."

faith, so that he or she might remain in the faith of the Church and pass eventually to the Church Triumphant in Paradise.[218]

THE CANON LAW OF ANOINTING

Early canon law regulated anointing the sick. The seventh-century collection of Cresconius contained a letter of Pope Innocent I concerning praying for the sick, laying on hands, and applying oil.[219] The *Pseudo-Isidorean Decretals* also included Innocent's text.[220] It preserved the idea that oil consecrated by a bishop could be used by all Christians.[221] A text of Pope Alexander I in that collection used Mark's Gospel to enjoin laying hands on the sick.[222] Burchard of Worms built on this tradition, adding the Council of Melde's requirement that each priest take three containers to the chief church of the diocese to receive holy oils for use in the following year.[223]

The Gregorian Reform's *Collection in Seventy-Four Titles* required annual renewal of chrism, the old supply being burned.[224] The collection of Anselm of Lucca also required annual renewal of chrism, citing a text of "Pope Fabian" as proof.[225] These regulations were applied to oil of the sick.[226] Ivo of Chartres included in his *Decretum* a canon of Pope Calixtus I, requiring that any believer facing death should be anointed. This text was rooted in the Epistle of James, but it also referred to the text of Pope Innocent I. It also says that penance was to precede unction.[227] The text attributes the practice of anointing to Mark's Gospel and the Church's custom.[228]

218 Ibid.: "quod permansit in fide Ecclesiae, & ideo securus egreditur ad populum triumphantem."

219 Zechiel-Eckes, *Die Concordia canonum des Cresconius*, 1:710–11.

220 *Decretales Pseudo-Isidorianae et Capitula Angilrami* (ed. Hinschius), 528.

221 Ibid.: "Quod non est dubium de fidelibus aegrotantibus accipi vel intelligi debere, qui sancto oleo chrismatis perungi possunt, quo ab episcopo confecto non solum sacerdotibus, sed et ab omnibus christianis uti licet in sua aut in suorum necessitate ad ungendum."

222 Ibid., 99: "In nomine meo demonia eicite, infirmos curate, aegros sanite, leprosos mundate, et cetera. Super infirmos etiam manus imponite, et bene habebunt."

223 PL 140:741A (IV, c. 79): "Ut presbyter in coena Domini ampullas tres secum deferat, unam ad chrisma, alteram ad oleum ad catechumenos inungendos, tertiam ad infirmos, juxta sententiam apostolicam, ut quando quis infirmatur inducat presbyteros Ecclesiae, etc."

224 *The Collection in Seventy-Four Titles*, 192–93.

225 Anselm of Lucca, *Collectio canonum*, 467.

226 The Ambrosian rite allowed not just consecration of oil of the sick on Holy Thursday but its blessing before laying hands on an ailing person; see *Monumenta veteris liturgicae Ambrosianae*, ed. Marco Magistretti (Milan, 1897–1905), 1:109–10 and 2:79.

227 Ivo of Chartres, *Decretum*, PL 161:862D–863B, at 863B: "Si ergo infirmi in peccatis sint, et haec presbyteris Ecclesiae confessi fuerint, ac perfecto corde ea derelinquere atque emendare sategerint, dimittentur eis. Neque enim sine confessione emendationis queunt dimitti."

228 Ibid., PL 161:863A: "Hoc et apostoli in Evangelio fecisse leguntur (Marc. VI), et nunc Ecclesiae consuetudo tenet, ut infirmi oleo consecrato ungantur a presbyteris, et oratione comitante sanentur."

Anointing in the *Decretum* and Its Commentaries

The *Decretum* of Gratian mandates renewing chrism annually on Holy Thursday, a requirement extended to oil of the sick.[229] Gratian cites James to show that priests were to anoint the sick.[230] A section of the letter of Pope Innocent I followed, saying bishops too could anoint.[231] The *Decretum* included a text attributed to Theodore of Canterbury, giving instructions for comforting the sick.[232]

Rufinus of Bologna offered an early exegesis of d. 95, which distinguishes chrism from oil of the sick.[233] He quoted Burchard of Worms as saying that a priest was to take three vials (*ampullae*) to the cathedral once a year to receive chrism, oil of catechumens, and oil of the sick.[234] Stephen of Tournai cited the Epistle of James, interpreting its reference to *presbyteros* as possibly referring to bishops.[235] Drawing on Rufinus, Stephen said that the sick were to be anointed with oil "sanctified" by the bishop on Holy Thursday.[236]

Later, the *Summa Parisiensis* said that bishops and priests could anoint the sick; but no one could grant the sacraments to the impenitent.[237] The *Summa Lipsiensis* offered a similar sentiment about the impenitent.[238] That text followed Rufinus in distinguishing chrism from oil of the sick, which is made, according to the Church's custom, with olive oil consecrated by the bishop on Holy Thursday.[239] Simon of Bisignano similarly distin-

229 Friedberg 1:1357 (*De cons.*, D. 3, c. 18). The same thing is said in D. 95, c. 4; see ibid., 1:332.

230 Friedberg 1:332 (*De cons.*, D. 95, p.c. 2 [A *dictum* of Gratian after c. 2]): "Oleo uero sanctificato permittitur eis ungere infirmos. Unde Iacobus ait: 'Infirmatur quis ex vobis? inducat pręsbiteros ecclesiae, qui orent super eum, unguentes eum oleo, et oratio fidei saluabit infirmum.'"

231 Friedberg 1:322 (*De cons.*, D. 95, c. 3).

232 Friedberg 1:1041 (C. 26, q. 7, c. 1): "unctione olei inuncti."

233 Rufinus, *Summa decretorum*, 190: "Mirum dicit, cum consuetudo ecclesie habeat, ut non crismate, sed puro oleo perungatur infirmus."

234 Ibid., 191.

235 Stephen of Tournai, *Die Summa*, 116: "et hoc nomine episcopi possint designari." Stephen added a distinction of oil of catechuments from oil of the sick.

236 Ibid.: "non enim perunguntur infirmi crismate, sed oleo, quod etiam in coena domini sanctificatur ab episcopo."

237 *The Summa Parisiensis on the Decretum Gratiani*, ed. Therence P. McLaughlin (Toronto: PIMS, 1952), [73]: "Sacerdotes possunt ungere infirmos et, si sacerdotes, multomagis episcopi, sed impoenitentes quibus nulla sacramenta concedunt, non isto oleo inunguntur, quia sacramentum est."

238 *Summa 'Omnis qui iuste iudicat' sive Lipsiensis*, ed. Rudolf Weigand et al. (Vatican City: Biblioteca Apostolica Vaticana, 2007), 1:394: "Vnde si manifestum est aliquem esse in notorio crimine et in extremis petat eucharistiam, cum tamen penitere non velit, dicimus ei omnia sacramenta neganda."

239 Ibid.: "Mirum dicit cum ex consuetudine ecclesie non crismate, sed puro oleo inungatur infirmus, quod etiam ab episcopo in cena Domini sanctificatur." The text also distinguished oil of the sick from oil of catechumens.

guished chrism from oil of the sick, adding that the unbaptized could only be anointed with chrism *ut baptismus*.[240]

Huguccio of Pisa said that not even the pope could make something not a sacrament into one, including oils consecrated by anyone but a bishop. However, simple priests anointed with the Church's permission.[241] Extreme unction aided both body and soul.[242] The rite was penitential, forgiving venial sins.[243] Huguccio distinguished between chrism, oil of catechumens, and oil of the sick. A bishop consecrated these; for oil of the sick for relief of the ailing.[244] That sacrament could only be given to the sick.[245] Huguccio thought that extreme unction could be repeated, but administered only to penitent persons in desperate circumstances.[246]

The Ordinary Gloss on the *Decretum* states that not even the pope could permit ordinary priests to confect chrism and other oils.[247] The Gloss asks why the sick were anointed and replied with two reasons: removing venial sins and adding to virtues.[248] It added that the sick might be healed of physical infirmities.[249] The Gloss then states that priests were the ministers of extreme unction, applying oil of the sick.[250] Priests without oil of the sick could use chrism because it contained oil, but not unconsecrated oil.[251] Moreover, priests should receive chrism (and other oils) from their own bishops.[252]

Guido de Baysio composed his *Rosarium super decreto* (ca. 1300), citing earlier canonists. Glossing D. 95, Guido said that bishops were not to

240 *Summa in decretum Simonis Bisinianensis*, ed. Pier V. Aimone Braida (Vatican City: Biblioteca Apostolica Vaticana, 2014), 83–84.

241 Huguccio, *Summa decretorum*, Admont Ms. 7, at d. 95, c. 1: "Sed nunquid papa posset similiter presbiteris permittere ut confecerent crisma." On Huguccio's thought on the sacraments, see Wolfgang P. Müller, *Huguccio: The Life and Writings of a Twelfth-Century Jurist* (Washington, DC: The Catholic University of America Press, 1994), 145–50.

242 Huguccio, *Summa decretorum*, d. 95, c. 2: "in corpore et anima ille iuuat."

243 Ibid.: "ad peccatorum remissionem. scilicet. uenialium."

244 Ibid., c. 3: "et dicitur oleum infirmorum consecrare."

245 Ibid.: "Sed nunquid in oleo non consecrato potest conferri hoc sacramentum." This last statement was offered as one alternative, but Huguccio never contradicted it.

246 Ibid.: "non debet dari nisi in articulo mortis . . . sed tales inpenitentes non debet inungi nisi desperatur de salute illorum."

247 Glo. Ord. at D. 95, c. 1: "Sed nunquid Papa posset eis concedere, vt chrisma conficerent? H. dicit quod non."

248 Ibid., c. 2: "Et est duplex causa quare infirmi iniunguntur, scilicet quia venialia delentur, & praestat augmentum virtutibus.

249 Ibid.: "& quia infirmus citius liberatur ab infirmitate corporali."

250 Ibid., c. 3: "vt dicunt quidam, episcopus chrismate, presbyter oleo inungit. H."

251 Ibid., c. 2.

252 Ibid., c. 3.

delegate the acts of a superior authority to an inferior one. Presumably, this included not delegating consecration of holy oils to simple priests.[253] The *Rosarium* distinguished chrism from oil of catechumens and oil of the sick.[254] Exterior anointing brought about interior anointing of the heart.[255] There were several acts of anointing, but only one sacrament with its single purpose.[256] The rite was administered only to those seeming likely to die.[257]

Writers on Liturgy

Writers on liturgy occasionally treated the oils in the context of Holy Thursday. Pope Innocent III preached a sermon on the feast speaking of differing washings. One was with tears, making chrism from oil and balsam.[258] Sicard of Cremona, canonist and liturgist, also wrote about the oils consecrated on Holy Thursday. Pain followed illness, and consolation by the Holy Spirit, "the Consoler," followed pain.[259] Visible oil cured infirmities, restoring and illuminating the body. Invisible grace, signified by anointing with oil, drove out vices, strengthened virtues, and enlightened "with the rays of the true sun."[260] Prayer was offered over the oil to add a blessing "for penitxzents and those about to die" (*pro pęnitentibus et migraturis*). When conferred on the dying, it destroyed sins, the cause of death.[261]

The elder Guillelmus Durantis, another jurist liturgist, when treating Holy Thursday, tied the gifts of the Spirit (1 Cor 12:8–9) to the types of oils. He said that the ability to nourish the weak and infirm belonged to oil of the sick.[262] It could heal the body and the mind.[263] This oil was to be consecrated during the canon of the Mass, drawing strength from Christ's

253 Guido de Baysio, *Rosarium super decreto*, fol. 98va (d. 95, c. 1).

254 Ibid., c. 4: "ad infirmos vngendos vt e. li. in c. vt presbyter."

255 Ibid., c. 1: "vnctione exterior visibili que est signum interioris vnctionis in corde."

256 Ibid., c. 2: "licet in sacramento extreme vnctionis plures sint vnctionem. Tamen vnum est sacramentum propter vnitatem a parte finis."

257 Ibid.: "quia non debet dari nisi infirmis qui secundum humanam estimationem videntur morti appropinquare. Secundum tho."

258 PL 217:399A: "Et lotio lacrymarum, quae procedunt ex arboribus ad sacramentum, in chrismatis confectione, quod ex oleo et balsamo consecratur."

259 *Sicardi Cremonensis episcopi mitalis de officiis*, ed. Gábor Sarbak and Lorenz Weinrich (Turnhout: Brepols, 2008), 473: "Oleum infirmorum medelam truit sauciatis, ęgritudinem sequitur dolor, dolorem consolatio, Paraclitus 'consolator' interpretatur."

260 Ibid., 471: "Sicut oleum uisibile infirmitates curat, artus recreat et illuminat, sic inuisibilis gratia, quę per oleum figuratur et per unctionem infunditur, uitia fugat, uirtutes corroborat et radiis ueri solis illustrat."

261 Ibid., 472: "sic gratia, quę per unctionem morienti confertur, destruat peccata, quę sunt causa mortis."

262 *Gvillelmi Dvranti rationale divinorvm officiorvm V–VI*, ed. Anselm Davril and Timothy Thibodeau (Turnhout: Brepols, 1998), 351: "quod artus lassos et infirmos reficit, ad oleum infirmorum."

263 Ibid.: "Ad oleum infirmorum pertinent gratia sanitatum, id est sanitas corporis et mentis." Durantis said oil of the sick was to be consectated first, citing Mk and Jas in support; see 352.

death to destroy the sins of the dying.[264] Durantis thus connected oil of the sick to the Lord's sacrifice.[265] Elsewhere, Durantis distinguished between external and internal anointing, where the one is the sign of the other.[266] Durantis said the sacrament was a sign of faith, driving out sins to give health and light to the soul.[267] "Concerning oil of the sick, we received authority received from the apostles" (*De oleo infirmorum auctoritatem accepimus ab apostolis*).[268]

Later Canon Law

Later canon law said little about anointing. The *Gregorian Decretals* contain only two texts on the subject, Pope Alexander III's *Quaesivit* and Pope Innocent III's *Cum venisset.*[269] In *Quaesivit,* Alexander addressed extreme unction, saying that a priest was able to administer the sacrament with only one cleric present or even when he was alone with a sick person.[270] The Ordinary Gloss on the *Extra* dealt briefly with *Quaesivit,* asking whether a priest could anoint without at least one cleric. To support its answer, the Gloss cited the Epistle of James, which mentioned priests in the plural, from *Cum venisset.* The presence of at least one cleric with the priest was normative. However, a priest could administer extreme unction alone in a case of necessity, as necessity knows no law.[271]

Cum venisset was issued by Pope Innocent III, dealing with differences between Greek and Roman practices in Bulgaria, requiring Greeks to follow the Latin practice when anointing. He said, "We wish you to know there are two species of anointing, external, which is material and visible, and internal, which is spiritual and invisible." The latter treated

264 Ibid., 353: "Primo, ibi rationabiliter oleum morientium conficitur ubi mors Domini consummatur, ut sicut mors Christi destruxit mortis auctorem, si gratia, que per unctionem morienti confertur, destruat peccata que sun causa mortis."

265 Ibid., 354.

266 *Gvillelmi Dvranti rationale divinorvm officiorvm I–IV,* ed. Anselm Davril and Timothy Thibodeau (Turnhout: Brepols, 1995), 97: "Vnctio exterior signum est interioris, interior uero non solum est signum, Id est signatum, sed etiam sacramentum."

267 Ibid., 98: "sic credendum est quod unctio olei consecrati, quod est signum fidei, peccata fugando, sanitatem anime confert et lumen ei prestart."

268 Ibid.

269 *Quinque compilationes antiquae* (ed. Friedberg), 1 5.26.9, X 5.40.14, X 1.15.un.

270 Ibid., 65. See also Friedberg 2:915: "Nos itaque tibi taliter duximus respondendum, quod sacerdos uno praesente clerico et etiam solus potest infirmum ungere."

271 Glo. Ord. at X 5.40.14: "Etiam solus.] Arg. contra in Apostolo, vbi dicitur: infirmatur quis in vobis? Inducat presbyteros ecclesiae: qui orent super eum. supra. de sacr. vnc. c. vnico. & sic videtur quod debeant esse plures: quia pluralia locutio quorum numero adminus contenta est. 4. q. 3. ca. si testes. ver. vbi numerus. Hoc intellige in necessitate, quae legem non habet. de conse. dist. i. sicut. & supra. de consue. Quanto."

the heart, the seat of the soul.[272] Among the practices mentioned was using oil of catechumens and oil of the sick, made from olives and blessed for use in "external and visible anointing" (*Ad exhibendam autem exteriorem et visibilem unctionem*).[273] The letter mentioned confirmation and consecration of altars by bishops, but it seemed to leave anointing the sick to local control.[274] Another letter told the primate of Bulgaria to consecrate chrism, oil of catechumens, and oil of the sick once a year, following the rite of the Roman curia.[275]

In a 1208 letter to the archbishop of Tarragona and his bishops about the conversion of Waldensians, Innocent said that they were to affirm anointing of the sick.[276] Likewise, Innocent sent a general letter about Waldensians converted to orthodoxy, saying that they were to affirm all the sacraments. Both letters required converted heretics to say: "We are to venerate anointing of the sick with consecrated oil."[277]

Commenting on *Cum venisset*, the Ordinary Gloss on the *Extra* repeated Innocent's statement about exterior and interior anointing.[278] Extreme unction was a rite of the New Law, not the Old; and, consequently, the Church did not "Judaize" in administering it.[279] Where *Cum venisset* mentioned the sick and quoted James, the Gloss referred to d. 95 of the *Decretum*.[280]

Pope Innocent IV, as a private doctor, composed an influential commentary on the *Gregorian Decretals*. Among the reasons for blessing oil, he said, was administering extreme unction.[281] The heart being the seat of the soul, Innocent said that the effect of anointing derived from the heart

272 Friedberg 2:131–34 (X 1.15.un.), at 131: "Scire te uolumas, duas esse species unctionis: exterioris, quae materialis est et visibilis, et interiorem, quae spiritualis est et invisibilis." Pope Innocent III referenced the Epistle of James to illustrate external anointing. Innocent IV, in a letter sent to Cyprus, said extreme unction was to be given to the sick according to the Epistle of James; see *The Synodicum Nicosiense* (ed. Schabel), 308–9.

273 Friedberg 2:131–34. Innocent's passage about ordination of priests using consecrated oil was deleted by Raymond of Peñafort when editing the *Extra*.

274 Canon law gave greater attention to reservation of the Eucharist and viaticum than to extreme unction; see Izbicki, *Eucharist in Medieval Canon Law*, chap. 4.

275 PL 215:281C–D: "Chrisma vero et oleum catechumenorum et infirmorum singulis annis in coena Domini, tam in ecclesia tua quam in qualibet Ecclesia Blaciae, fieri secundum consuetudinem Ecclesiae Romanae concedimus."

276 PL 216:1512A: "Unctionem infirmorum cum oleo consecrato veneramur."

277 PL 216:290C: "Unctionem infirmorum cum oleo consecrato veneramur."

278 Glo. Ord. at X 1.15.un., Casus.

279 Ibid.: "Dicit etiam quod sacramentum vnctionis, aliud figurat in nouo testamento, quam in veteri. vnde non iudaizat ecclesia vnctionis celebrans sacramentum."

280 Ibid., v. Infirmatur.

281 *Innocentii qvarti pont. maximi svper libros qvinque decretalivm* (Frankfurt, 1570; Frankfurt: Minerva, 1968), fol. 105rb: "(Et conficitur) supple ad exhibendam extremam vnctionem."

and the will.[282] The invisible grace of the Holy Spirit came with external anointing.[283] Unction might diminish physical affliction or even remove it, as well as promote eternal health.[284] Geoffrey of Trani repeated the idea of external and internal anointing. The exterior act represented the interior influx of grace, aiding worthy recipients.[285] Geoffrey said that oil of the sick could not be consecrated twice.[286]

Henricus de Segusio (Hostiensis) addressed anointing in his *Summa de titulis decretalium*.[287] He repeated the idea of exterior and interior unction. One anointed the body; the other bestowed grace.[288] The latter was not effective without the heart and the will.[289] Hostiensis mentioned extreme unction as one type of anointing,[290] while elsewhere he listed five sacraments every Christian was to receive: baptism, confirmation, the Eucharist, penance, and extreme unction.[291] All of these rites were necessary, but only baptism was crucial.[292] Extreme unction was medicine for the soul, to be received when death was near.[293] However, because it did not imprint a character on the soul, anointing could be repeated.[294]

Hostiensis also wrote a commentary on the *Extra*, including an exposition of *Cum venisset*. This too discussed internal and external anointing. Its spiritual effect was not seen by human eyes any more than the soul itself was visible. Only the Holy Spirit could discern it.[295] This sacrament had

282 Ibid.: "(Cor) . . . nisi de corde & voluntate procedat."

283 Ibid.: "(Vnctionem) id est, vnctio, id est, gratia spiritussancti inuisibilia, quae fiet in in anima corpore exterius vncto."

284 Ibid.: "(Infirmum) idest, infirmo proderit contra infirmitatem corporis, vt vel eam minuat, vel vt patientius toleret, & etiam proficiat ad salutem aeternam."

285 *Summa perutilis et valde necessaria do. Goffredi de Trano super titulis decretalium*, fol. 32vb: "Exterior signat interiorem. Interior autem est significatum exterioris et signum inuisibilis gratie quam vnctio visibilis agit et auget si digne sumatur."

286 Ibid., fol. 34ra.

287 X 1.15, *De sacra unctione*.

288 Hostiensis, *Summa aurea*, 209–10: "Duae exterior. scilicet. & interior. Per exteriorem visibiliter corpus iniungitur. per interiorem inuisibiliter cor. idest. anima."

289 Ibid., 210: "quia non fructificat vnctio, nisi ex corde & voluntate."

290 Ibid., 214: "quarto etiam iniunguntur in extremis, quae vocatur extrema vnctio."

291 Ibid., 216 (X 1.16): "Quintum. scilicet. extrema vnctio, est exeuntium de hac vita." Hostiensis cited James from his discussion of X 1.15. Similarly, the 1294 Council of Utrecht distinguished the five sacraments every Christian was to receive from the other two; see *Concilia Germaniae* 4:22–23.

292 Hostiensis, *Summa aurea*, 217.

293 Ibid., 219: "Idem de extrema vnctione: cùm enim sit medicina animae corporis, videtur quod adueniente morte apponi possit & debeat medicina, vt innuitur in authoritate Iacobi."

294 Ibid., 220.

295 Henricus de Segusio (Hostiensis), *Commentaria in I–II librum decretalium* (Venice: Apud Iuntas, 1581; Frankfurt: Vico Verlag, 2009), fol. 110vb–113rb, at 111rb: "[*Inuisibiliter*] Quia.scilicet. oculis corporeis non patet anima. nec sua vnctio, sed tantum spiritui sancto, qui intus operatur."

effect only from the heart and the will.[296] Hostiensis addressed the effect of extreme unction on the sick, affirming the exterior effect on the body and the interior effect on the soul. The rite removed venial sins and promoted virtues in the soul. Healing of the body occurred only when that was expedient for the soul.[297] Elsewhere, Hostiensis wrote down a verse about which sacraments could be repeated: "Baptism, orders, chrism [confirmation] are not repeated; the others are" (*Fons, ordo, chrisma non, caetera sunt iteranda*). Baptism, orders, and confirmation could not be repeated, because each imposed a character on the soul. The others, including extreme unction, could be repeated as needed.[298]

Johannes Andreae wrote at length on unction in his *Novella* on the *Gregorian Decretals*, distinguishing chrism from oil of catechumens and oil of the sick.[299] Extreme unction was administered to heal body and soul. The sacrament removed venial sins.[300] This exterior act, according to Pope Innocent IV, affected the soul internally.[301] Andreae made the unusual argument that the rite of extreme unction imposed a character on the soul, but he did not pursue the practical implications of this contention.[302] Elsewhere he said (as had Hostiensis) that only baptism, confirmation, and ordination imposed such a character.[303] Andreae added that the other sacraments could be repeated.[304]

The *Sacramentale* of Guillelmus de Monte Lauduno devoted a chapter to extreme unction. He summarized the sacrament, saying that it involved anointing with blessed oil together with prayer against resistance to spiritual healing. The rite might cure physical affliction if that was spiritually expedient.[305] Guillelmus said that the sacrament was called extreme unction because it was for those "laboring *in extremis*," unable to bear

296 Ibid.: "non operatur vnctio in anima, nisi ex corde & voluntate procedat."

297 Ibid.: "[*Infirmum*] Hic loquitur de sacramento extremae vnctionis, quod duplici de causa est ab ecclesia insitutum. Quo ad corpus, vnde sanat infirmum, & sic corpus alleuiat, si tamen expedat ei . . . Item quo ad animam, quia purgat peccata venialia, & quo ad prudentiam, securitatem, & maiorem constantiam."

298 Ibid., fol. 113va.

299 Johannes Andreae, *In primum librum decretalium novella commentaria* (Venice: Apud Iuntas, 1581; Turin: Bottega d'Erasmo, 1963), 171A.

300 Ibid., 171B: "[*Infirmum*] loquitur ergo hic de sacramento vnctionis extremae, quod institutum fuit ex duplici causa quo ad corpus sanandum, & animam sanandam, quia purgat venialia."

301 Ibid.: "[*Inuisibilis*] quae fit in anima corpore exterius vncto. Inno."

302 Ibid.: "[*Est signum*] . . . hic enim character impressus est animae est sacramentum, quia facit id quod significat."

303 Ibid., 172B.

304 Ibid.: "Fons, ordo chrisma non, sed cętera sunt iteranda."

305 Guillelmus de Monte Lauduno, *Sacramentale*, University of Pennsylvania Ms. Codex 72, fol. 48vb: "dic quod olei benedictio cum uerbali oratione materialis delunctio qua spiritualis infirmitas resistendi uiciis necnon corporalis infirmitas si expediat emininter xcv di. §. Sed quare [d. 95 p. c. 2 §. 1]." Friedberg 1:332 gives this this text as "Si quaeritur."

the severity of penance.[306] The purpose of the rite was fortifying human weakness against the illness of sin (*contra istam debilitatem*). Guillelmus sided with the Dominicans, saying that it removed the remains of original sin (*ex reliquiis peccati originalis*). The sacrament might also alleviate physical weakness "if it is expedient for the soul" (*si expediat anime*). It also increased devotion and augmented grace. The canonist added a verse by (supposedly) Pope Innocent III: "I anoint the dying so that there might be greater grace for me / And, the lighter the illness, the less my penalty" (*Ungor in extremis ut sit mihi gratia maior / Et leuior morbus et mea pena minor*).[307]

Guillelmus briefly stated that a priest or bishop was the minister of the sacrament and that olive oil was the material to be employed.[308] The form included making a cross over the eyes while saying: "Through this anointing and His most gracious mercy, may the Lord be lenient to you for whatever sins you have committed through sight" (*per istam vnctionem et per suam piissimam misericordiam indulgeat tibi dominus quicquid per uisum*). The priest was to anoint the other senses and the feet, applying oil near the site of any lost organ of sense.[309] The sacrament did not impose an indelible character and so could be repeated, but not during the same illness, avoiding the patient's thinking repetition would help toward a physical cure.[310]

INSTRUCTIONS FOR ANOINTING

Instructions for anointing abound. In England, for example, the initial emphasis was on chrism. By 1000 Aelfric said in a letter that chrism was best consecrated on Holy Thursday; and he denounced those who dared to sell it, setting a "vile price" on oil.[311] The laws of Edward and Guthrun threatened priests who did not "fetch chrism at the appointed day" with a fine.[312] After the Norman Conquest, local canon law developed further. Thus, the 1125 legatine council of Westminster forbade charging for "visiting

306 Guillelmus de Monte Lauduno, *Sacramentale*, fol. 48vb: "dic quia datur in extremis laborantibus quibus non est aliud remedium cum asperitates penitentiales sustinere non possint xxvi. q. vii. ab infirmis [C. 26 q. 7 c.]1."

307 Ibid., fol. 49ra.

308 Ibid., fol. 49ra–b.

309 Ibid., fol. 49rb.

310 Ibid.

311 *Councils & Synods* I, pt. 1, 250: "in qua die videtur tibi rectius debere consecrari crisma quam in illa die in qua Christus cetera charismata novi testamenti inchoavit"; ibid., 254: "et nimium mirror quomodo aussi sunt vendere sanctam crisma; emunt oleum vili pretio."

312 *Councils & Synods* I, pt. 1, 306. Similarly, see the Northumbrian Priests Law at 454.

the sick or unction"; and other councils repeated this prohibition.[313] The 1143 legatine Council of London forbade giving chrism or oil to "the contemptuous or the excommunicated."[314] A 1200 Council of Westminster quoted the Third Lateran Council, forbidding exaction of payment for the sacraments.[315] The 1221 Council of Oxford, pointed to the Fourth Lateran Council when condemning exactions for chrism and oil.[316] In an episcopal vacancy, oils still had to be consecrated. During a vacancy of the see of Canterbury, a bishop of Rochester wanted to consecrate chrism as a chaplain of the archbishop.[317]

More detailed consideration of the practice of extreme unction began in the thirteenth century under the influence of the Fourth Lateran Council and local canons of Paris. The Paris statutes had a wide-ranging influence, especially via students educated at the university, who carried these texts to their home sees. The crucial texts for ministry to the sick appeared in the episcopal constitions of Odo of Sully, bishop of Paris (1197–1208), under the title *De sacramento extremae unctionis*.[318] Odo's statutes did not discuss the theology of extreme unction. However, they gave instructions for carrying the sacrament to the sick and doing anointing properly. No money was to be exacted for the rite, although freewill offerings could be accepted. Priests were to teach those of their flocks fourteen years of age or older, rich or poor, about the availability of the sacrament. This

313 *Councils & Synods* I, pt. 2, 738: "Interdicimus etiam ut pro chrismate, pro oleo, pro baptismate, pro penitentia, pro visitatione infirmorum seu unctione, pro communione corporis Christi, pro sepultura, nullum omnino pretium exigatur." Similarly, see the 1138 council in ibid., 774, and those of the Council of Westminster (1173) in ibid., 979. An 1175 council quoted a canon from Tribur on this topic; see ibid., 986.

314 *Councils & Synods* I, pt. 2, 800. The *Constitutiones Cardinalis Ottoboni*, in *Provinciale (seu Constitvtiones Angliae)*, 81A–83A, mentions "Oleum Sanctificatum & Chrisma."

315 *Councils & Synods* I, pt. 2, 1065; Mansi 20:330. For the Lateran canon, see *Conciliorum oecumenicorum generaliumque decreta* II, pt. 1, 132–33 (c. 7). Only a small portion appeared in the *Liber extra*, see Friedberg 2:623 (X 3.39.7). Similarly see *Councils & Synods* II, pt. 1, 645 (Second Statutes of London) and pt. 2, 995 (Second Statutes of Exeter); *Lyndwood's "Provinciale,"* 12–13.

316 *Provinciale (seu Constitvtiones Angliae)*, 278A–279A: "De simonia. Jus Sepultura & Sacramenta Ecclesiastica nulli denegentur ob defectu pecuniae, nec pro Crismate quicquam petendum: petens autem Anathema sit. Stephanus in Concilio Oxon. primo. Firmiter Inhibemus, nè cuiquam pro aliqua pecunia denegetur, Sepultura, vel Baptismus, vel aliquod Sacramentum Ecclesiaticum, vel etiam Matrimonium contrahendum impediatur. Quoniam si quid pia devotione fidelium consuetum fuerit erogari, super hoc postmodum Volumus per Ordinarium loci Ecclesiis justitiam fieri, sicut in Generali Concilio expressus est Statutum. Absonum [*rectius* absurdum] etiam judicamus, quòd de caetero pro Chrismate & Oleo aliquid exigatur, vel erogetur, cùm toties hoc prohibitum reperiatur. Si quis verò contra hoc facere praesumpserit, Anathemate sit innodatus." William Lyndwood identified *Ad apostolicam* as the text cited by the Oxford council; see 279A. For "chrism money" sometimes exacted from clergy fetching the oils, see Cheney, *From Becket to Langton*, 153.

317 *Councils & Synods* I, pt. 2, 1033.

318 Mansi 22:680. The Paris statutes had influence as far away as Bordeaux and Narbonne; see Joseph Avril, "Mort et sepulture dans les status synodaux du Midi de la France," *Cahiers de Fanjeux* 33 (1998): 343–64, at 347.

teaching included the availability of repeated sacramental acts as needed. The laity were to be reminded that, if they recovered from all illness requiring unction, they could resume conjugal relations with a spouse. The order for extreme unction was to be made available to each priest in a manual.[319]

English councils, under Continental influence,[320] affirmed extreme unction as one of the seven sacraments. The influential first statutes of Salisbury affirmed: "The fifth, extreme unction, that is the sacrament of those going out [from this world], which prepares us for God's call."[321] These statutes told pastors to inform their congregations that anointing was available to anyone, young or old, rich or poor, from fourteen years of age upward able to understand its significance. The sacrament was to be given free of charge to penitents who requested it.[322] The rite could be repeated as needed, and a sick person who recovered could resume conjugal relations with his or her spouse.[323] The 1240 Statutes of Worcester told priests to warn their flocks that they were not to give up marital sex (*opus conjugale*) or eating meat, nor go about with bare feet, after recovery.[324]

Carrying oil to the sick received attention from English bishops. Statutes annexed to the canons of Oxford said that oil of the sick was to be

319 Mansi 22:680: "1. Cum reverentia deferatur oleum ſanctum ad infirmos, & eos ungant facerdotes cum magn honore & orationum celebritate, quæ ad hoc sunt ordinatæ, & nihil inde penitus exigatur, sive paupere, sive a divite: sed ſi quid gratis datum fuerit, gratis accipiant. 2. Ad sacramentum extremæ unctionis moneant populum sacerdotes, non tantum divites & senes, sed pauperes & juvenes omnes a tempore discretionis, maxime a quatuordecim annis & supra, & ad omnes communiter, ut se paratos exhibeant, cum necesse fuerit. 3. Doceant frequenter populum hujuſmodi sacramentum licite iterari, & sæpe recipi, scilicet in qualibet magna infirmitate unde metus est mortis: & post susceptum licite reverti ad opus conjugale eum qui convaluerit de infirmitate. 4. Librum qui dicitur Manualis habeant singuli ſacerdotes parochiales, ubi continetur ordo servitii extremæ unctioni, catechismi, baptismi, & hujusmodi."

320 Cheney, *English Synodalia*.

321 *Councils & Synods* II, pt. 1, 65: "Quintum extrema unctio, sacramentum scilicet exeuntium, quod vocationi dei nos preparat." See also the Statutes of Exeter (ca. 1225–37 and 1287) in ibid., pt. 1, 223, and pt. 2, 986; the Second Salisbury Statutes in pt. 1, 367; *Constitutiones Domini Othonis*, in *Provinciale (seu Constitvtiones Angliae)*, 9A–B.

322 *Councils & Synods* II, pt. 1, 90: "Et propter hoc precipimus quod ad sacramentum extremae unctionis moneant frequenter populum sacerdotes, in necessitate videlicet, et non tantum divites set pauperes, senes et minores, omnes maxime a quattuordecim annis et supra; et omnibus petentibus et penitentibus gratis exhibeant hoc sacramentum in necessitate, cum fecint humiliter requisiti." Short versions of this Salisbury canon appear in the Statutes for an English Diocese (ca. 1222–25) in ibid., pt. 1, 146, and the second Salisbury Statutes in pt. 1, 372–73. The statutes were repeated in full when Richard Poore transferred from Salisbury to Durham; see pt. 1, 444.

323 *Councils & Synods* II, pt. 1, 90–91. For a statement that extreme unction could be repeated, see the First Statutes of Chichester in pt. 1, 457.

324 *Councils & Synods* II, pt. 1, 305: "Sunt autem quidem ut audivimus qui post perceptionem huius sacramenti sanitati pristine restituti nephas reputant vel uxores suas cognoscere vel carnes comedere vel etiam aliqua ratione nudis pedibus ambulare." The same statutes warned against putting off the sacrament out of aversion or fear; see ibid., 306. This was also mentioned by the Statutes of Wells in ibid., pt. 2, 596. The see of Winchester repeated the Salisbury warnings to those who recovered at pt. 2, 707. The Second Statutes of Exeter treated these superstitions as heresies against which priests were to preach in pt. 2, 996.

carried with reverence and administered with devotion, having been kept securely against anyone attempting to do horrible things (*horribilia*) with it.[325] A Salisbury canon too said oil should be carried reverently to the sick.[326] According to the statutes of Wells, the priest was to be ready night and day to perform this ministry.[327] The statutes of Lincoln (ca. 1239) warn priests not to allow the sick to die without confession, communion, and extreme unction.[328] The third statutes of Worcester say that a priest who lets the sick die without these rites shows himself to be useless, pernicious, and worthy of removal.[329] The 1281 Provincial Council of Lambeth states that extreme unction is to be administered when there were signs of approaching death.[330] The council added that the insane could receive extreme unction during a lucid interval (*lucidum intervallum*) or if they requested it before slipping into frenzy or "alienation of mind."[331]

Many statutes of the archdiocese of Canterbury were included in William Lyndwood's *Provinciale*. The seven sacraments were reaffirmed in John Peckham's canon "Ignorance of Priests" (*Ignorantia sacerdotum*), which said that souls received an increase of grace from it.[332] Walter Reynolds's canon "When great" (*Cum magna*) required carrying oil of the sick reverently. Persons fourteen or older were to be admonished to receive the sacrament devoutly. Peckham's canon "When of holy chrism" (*Cum sacri*

325 *Councils & Synods* II, pt. 1, 146: "Cum magna reverentia deferatur oleum infimatorum ad infirmos, et ipsos ungant sacerdotes cum magna devotione et orationum celebritate que ad hoc sunt ordinate." This and other earlier statutes about anointing were reenacted by Walter Reynolds in 1322; see the archepiscopal statutes at the end of *Provinciale (seu Constitvtiones Angliae)*, 39B.

326 *Councils & Synods* II, pt. 1, 91: "Cum reverentia deferatur oleum sanctum ad infirmos, et eos ungant sacerdotes cum magno honore et orationum celebritate, que ad hoc sunt ordinate; et nichil inde sicut nec pro aliis sacramentis exigatur sive a paupere sive a divite." The Salisbury canons appear in a different order in the *Constitutiones cuiusdam episcopi* (ca, 1225–30) in ibid., 190. Similarly see Mansi 22:734, another set of canons from an uncertain place. The Scottish council of 1225 (Mansi 22:1240) says: "post hoc sacramentum licet converti ad opus conjugale, & ad alia, ut prius licita."

327 *Councils & Synods* II, pt. 1, 596.

328 Ibid., 268: "ne eorum negligentia, quod absit, moriatur infirmus sine confessione aut dominici corporis communione aut unctione extrema."

329 Ibid., 305: "Sacerdos autem qui se pigrum exhibit in visitandis infirmis, ex quo quandoque forsitan accidit quod egrotus absque confessione vel dominici corporis et sanguinis perceptione decedat, expers unctionis extremae, perniciosum se non solum inutilem subditis exhibit et tantam eis per incuriam per nos noverit condigna pro viribus animadversione plectandam."

330 Ibid., 905: "et extrema unctio, que tantum illis dari debet qui gravis infirmitatis indiciis videntur mortis appropinquare periculo . . ." This source is quoted in pastoral manuals; e.g., *Oculus sacerdotis*, University of Pennsylvania MS 721, fol. 18va; John of Burough, *Pupilla oculi*, fol. 105ra.

331 *Councils & Synods* II, pt. 2, 905.

332 *Lyndwood's "Provinciale,"* 14–15. See also *Councils & Synods* II, pt. 2, 901–5. Lyndwood divided *Ignorantia sacerdotum* between the titles *De summa Trinitate* (Lib. 1, t. 1), *De sacramentis iterandis vel non* (Lib. 1, t. 7), and *De officio archiprebyteri* (Lib. 1, t. 11). For the reference to extreme unction, see *Provinciale (seu Constitutiones Angliae)*, 43B.

crismatis) required priests to secure a new supply from the bishop annually and burn last year's supply.[333] Another canon of Archbishop Reynolds, "Sacrament of extreme [unction]" (*Sacramentum extremae*), states that no one was to receive extreme unction more than once in a year.[334] In addition, a canon of Edmund of Abingdon, *Fontes*, required keeping the Eucharist, chrism, and oil under lock and key.[335] A canon of Robert Winchelsea, "As parishioners" (*Ut parochiani*), required parishes to have a manual with the appropriate texts, as well as a pyx, lantern, and bell for taking viaticum to the sick.[336]

Lyndwood glossed *Ignorantia sacerdotum*, reiterating that extreme unction was for those going out from this world.[337] Nor was it to be given to those with hope of recovery.[338] It was medicine for the souls of the dying.[339] Lyndwood said that the rite was the remedy for venial sins.[340] Writing about simony, he warned against using custom to legitimize exactions before administration of the sacrament.[341] These glosses supported anointing those losing use of reason,[342] where extreme unction could be conferred to them during a lucid interval.[343]

Oil of the sick was distinguished from oil of catechumens in the commentary on *Cum magna*, because of their different blessings by a bishop.[344] Because the sacrament pertained to those leaving the world, balsam,

333 *Lyndwood's "Provinciale,"* 12–13. See also the so-called Statutes of John Peckham in *Councils & Synods* II, pt. 2, 1120–21.

334 *Lyndwood's Provinciale,"* 13–14. For a previous synodal provision to this effect, see the Second Statutes of Worcester in *Councils & Synods* II, pt. 1, 171: "et semel in anno unctione infirmorum inungi."

335 *Lyndwood's "Provinciale,"* 103. See an earlier English canon on reservation of oils in Mansi 22:1159 (canons for the 1222 Council of Oxford). These texts and others are derived from Odo of Sully's statutes; see Mansi 22:677.

336 *Lyndwood's "Provinciale,"* 105.

337 *Provinciale*, in *Provinciale (seu Constitvtiones Angliae)*, 43B, v. *Extrema Unctio*: "Et Istud Sacramentum dicitur exeuntium, quia tantùm exeuntibus de hac vita confertur, ut *infrà dicam*."

338 *Provinciale*, 44A, v. *Appropinquare*: "Sit apparet, quòd si sit verisimilis spes de convalescentia, non debere ministrari hoc Sacramentum: ubi tamen timetur de morte, non debet collatio ejus nimiùm differi; *ut infra* patet ex textu."

339 *Provinciale*, v. *Gravis infirmatio.*

340 *Provinciale*, v. *Salute.*

341 Ibid.: "*Detur*. Sc. gratis; non vendantur, nec etiam praetextu Consuetudinis, juxta quam forsitan ministranti hoc sacramentum aliquid solebat dari, ministratione Sacramenti differatur. Sed postquam Sacramentum ministraverit, licitè potest exigi id quod consuevit solvi à parte Consuetudinis in eâ parte laudabilis."

342 Ibid., vv. *Compotes, Phrensi & Alienatione mentis.*

343 *Provinciale*, 44B, v. *Dilucidum intervallum*: "Unde *dilucidum intervallum* dicitur, illud spatium temporis quo furiosus amens & insaniens, sive mente captus, seu alias phreneticus, de quo hic loquitur, clarum sensum habet ad rationabiliter loquendi & intelligendi . . ."

344 *Provinciale*, 36A, v. *Oleum infirmorum*: "veritas tamen est, quòd diversa sunt, & diversam habent Benedictionem, sicut in Pontificali pleniùs cominetur."

focused on good deeds in life, was not the appropriate material. Olive oil was used because it represented purity of conscience.[345] Lyndwood said that the sick had to request anointing, including its being requested by a mad person in a lucid interval.[346] The sacrament was to be taken to the sick, rather than the sick carried to the priest.[347] Lyndwood said that a priest who went to the sick without the Eucharist but with holy oil was to wear gown and stole but not to have light and bell precede him.[348] Lyndwood believed that a cleric, or at least "a literate layman" (*unum laicum literatum*), should accompany the priest.[349] They were to show reverence by using the correct acts and words.[350] The words were prayerful, using a form attributed to Gregory the Great.[351] The sacrament forgave the venial sins of adults.[352] Although it pertained more to the spirit, spiritual healing could bring about a corporeal cure.[353]

Lyndwood's treatment of *Cum sacri* focused on the consecration of oils.[354] A priest could not receive these from his bishop except in an emergency, when one bishop could aid another by providing them.[355] New oils were to be gotten each year, and the old ones burned, just as worn out ecclesiastical cloths were burned.[356] Lyndwood also considered the possibility of a parish being far from the cathedral. If the priest's messenger had not delivered the new supply before a pastoral act had to be performed, the curate could use older materials.[357]

345 *Provinciale*, 36B, v. *Ungentes cum Oleo*.

346 Ibid.: "*Inducat*. Hic includitur postulatio vel desiderium infirmi; ubi innuitur, quòd non debet dari nisi petentibus verbo, vel signo manifesto, & habentibus usum liberi arbitrii, qui soli petere possunt: unde consuevit dici, non est ungendus Furiosus, Morio, Parvus . . . nisi furiosus haberet dilucida intervalla, in quibus Sacramenta recognosceret."

347 *Provinciale*, 36A, v. *Ad infirmos*.

348 Ibid.: "*Reverentia*. scilicet cum superpellicio & stola; tamen sine lumine, & sine Campanae pulsatione, quae duo debent dumtaxat haberi in deportatione sacramenti eucharistiae ad infirmum, vel alium extra Ecclesiam communicandum."

349 Ibid., v. *Sacerdotes*.

350 Ibid.: "*Magnà devotione*. Sc. sub timore Dei, & observatione diligenti eorum quae pertinent ad istud Sacramentum: ut viz. diligenter intendant his, quae facere, & verbis proferre habent circa ministrationem Sacramenti."

351 Ibid., v. *Orationem*.

352 *Provinciale*, 36A–B, v. *Annorum*.

353 *Provinciale*, 36B, v. *Salvabit infirmum*.

354 *Provinciale*, 36B–37A: "*Episcopos*. Ad quos solos pertinet Chrismatis confectio, *9 di. illud. 26. q. 6. si jubet*."

355 *Provinciale*, 37B, v. *Locorum Episcopis*: "Sed nunquid Episcopus alterius Dioecesios tenetur Chrisma tradere Presbiteris alterius Episcopi? Dic quòd, si cessante causà rationabili non dederit, peccat: quia Episcopi tenentur ad invicem sibi auxilium praebere."

356 *Provinciale*, 37A, v. *Concremandum*. Izbicki, "*Linteamenta altaria*."

357 *Provinciale*, 37B, v. *Vel quanto citiùs*.

Glossing *Sacramentum extremae*, Lyndwood concentrated on the repetition of sacraments. Baptism, confirmation, and ordination could not be repeated; penance, the Eucharist, matrimony, and extreme unction could.[358] Lyndwood said that anointing should be done once during an illness unless suffering extended into a second year.[359] He treated a relapse (*recidivum*) as a second illness, which could occasion anointing.[360] The gloss on *Fontes* said that the baptismal font, chrism, and holy oils were to be kept locked up on account of magic (*sortilegia*).[361]

On the Continent, the 1310 constitutions of Fiesole said that extreme unction could be repeated as necessary "in fitting ways, places, and times."[362] The statutes of Autun said that anointing was to be administered only "when there is fear of death" (*cum metus est mortis*), but it could be repeated as needed.[363] The see of Maurienne forbade multiple priests from doing a single anointing, on pain of suspension. Priests were to keep holy oils properly and avoid simony in their administration.[364]

Within the Empire, following the Fourth Lateran Council, councils focused on the sacraments, including extreme unction. A provincial Council of Trier (1227) required priests to warn their flocks that anointing was medicine of body and soul, repeatable as needed. They were to know which vessel held oil of the sick and devoutly administer the sacrament, saying the right words.[365] The 1298 synod of Würzburg required that the manual for priests include the order for extreme unction.[366] Those statutes also commanded teaching the faithful about the sacrament and being ready to administer it. They also repeated Lateran IV's requirement that physicians urge the sick to send for a confessor, with care for the soul preceding care of the body.[367]

358 *Provinciale*, 41A–B, v. *Iterari*.

359 *Provinciale*, 41B, v. *Quolibet anno semel*: "Sed in una infirmitate non debet bis inungi, nisi eadem infirmitas ultra annum protrahatur, ita quòd in uno anno propter unam infirmitatem nequaquam bis inungatur." Lyndwood cited John of Freiburg on this topic.

360 *Provinciale*, 41B, v. *Gravi infirmitate*.

361 *Provinciale*, 247B–248A: "*Propter sortilegia*. Quae honestius est tacere quàm dicere."

362 Trexler, *Synodal Law*, 235: "modis, locis, et temporibus aptis."

363 *Thesaurus novus anecdotorum* (ed. Martene and Durand), 4:470.

364 Ibid., 4:530, 534, 543–44.

365 *Concilia Germaniae* 3:527A and 529B: "Item ad Sacramentum extremae unctionis moneant Sacerdotes populum sibi subditum, quia est medicina corporis & animae & pluries potest iterari, quando contingit pluries lethaliter id est mortaliter egrotare . . . & Sacerdotes exhibentes devote exhibeant, & ipsa verba extremae unctionis proprio ore proferantur, nihil inde exigentes ab infirmis . . . & diligenter discernant Sacerdotes, in quo vase sit oleum sanctum, in quo vase sit oleum infirmorum."

366 Ibid., 4:26B.

367 Ibid., 4:30B–31A: "Ad Sacramentum extremae Unctionis populum saepe moneant Sacerdotes non tantum divites, sed & pauperes, & maxime a XIIII annis & supra, ut ad id omnes pariter, cum fuerit

The diocese of Worms threatened a priest who willingly used old chrism with deposition.[368] A council in Strasbourg (1435) forbade one priest saying the words, while another applied the oil.[369] The 1481 synod of Tournai issued instructions about taking viaticum or oil to the sick, including that the priest was to dress decently.[370] A 1446 Würzburg synod told priests not to wear clogs when delivering the sacraments even in bad weather and on muddy roads.[371] A 1483 statute from Constance was severe about priests processing wearing clogs or scandalously bare-headed, and it threatened violators of these instructions with the bishop's vengeance. The statute also mentioned indulgences gained by those accompanying the priest.[372] The see of Olomouc condemned exaction of payments "for holy liquids, chrism, and oil" (*pro sacris liquoribus vel crismate et oleo*).[373]

Instructions for Greek priests on Cyprus, issued by the Latins, required them to teach their flocks that there were seven sacraments, including extreme unction, ignoring Greek sacramental theology.[374] The Council of

necesse, exhibeant se paratos, sacrum Oleum cum magna reverentia portantes. Doceant saepe sacerdotes populum, hoc Sacramentum posse iterari, & recipi in qualibet magna necessitate, unde mortis metus poterit formidari. Statutum est in Concilio Generali, & districte injunctum medicis corporum, ut cum eos ad infirmos vocari contigerit, ipsos ante omnia moneant & inducant, ut medicos advocent animarum, ut postquam infirmis fuerit de spirituali provisum, salute; ad corporalis medicinae remedium salubrius procedatur: si quis autem medicorum hujusmodi satisfecerit conpetenter: ceterum cum anima multo pretiosior sit corpore; sub interminatione anathematis prohibetur, ne quis medicorum pro corporali salute adquirenda aegro suadeat, quod in periculum animae convertatur."

368 Ibid., 6:664B: "*De Crismate, & aliis Sacramentis.* Item ne quis chrismet, de veteri Chrismate, sub poena depositionis."

369 Ibid., 5:236A–B: "Damnamus quorundam errorem conferentium Ecclesiastica Sacramenta, maxime in extrema unctione, videlicet, quod unus inungit, alter profert verba Sacramenti. Sub poena igitur suspensionis prohibemus talia de cetero attentari; sed in omni Sacramento unus idemque actum faciat, & verba proferat, quae desiderant Sacramenta."

370 Ibid., 5:526B: "Item statuentes ordinamus, ob reverentiam Ss. Sacramenti, ut Sacerdos accedens visitare infirmos cum Sacramento Eucharistiae, aut extremae Unctionis, faciat lumen ante se deferre, ac nolam sonare, & in habitu decenti publice incedat."

371 Ibid., 5:341B: "Statuimus preterea, ut secundum statuta Canonum Sacerdotes tantum, non alii in extremis laborantes infirmos in viatico, & confessione procurent, campanam semper secum deferentes, ex cujus sono devotio fidelium excitetur ad tanti reverentiam Sacramenti. Insuper nullus de cetero Sacerdotes in deportatione saluberrimi Corporis Domini nostri Sacramenti, quantumcunque aura mala, via lubrica, vel lutuosa existat, in calopediis ire presumat."

372 Ibid., 5:560A–B: "Sacerdotes eum Divinissima Eucharistiae, & extremae Unctionis Sacramenta ad infirmos deportant, incaute deportant, incaute cum calopedibus, &c. scandalose, et turpiter, capite nudo, aut vix bireto superposito, ornatis capillis in mundi conspectum procedant; districte praesenti statuto inviolabiliter duraturo sancimus, ut constitutio proximae praeinserta firmiter observetur, ac quilibet Presbyter sic infirmos Eucharistiae, & extremae Unctionis Sacramentis accidens abque [!] calopedibus, & capite almutio, si saltem tali in loco almutia solita sint portari, alioquin caputio Clericali per collum tracto, ut sola facies nuda appareat, devotionis religionis praecedente lumine, & campanella juxta ejusdem constitutionis tenorem incedat: indulgentias inibi expressas Christi Fidelibus in Domino elargientes. Si qui vero hanc constitutionem nostrum servare contempserint, & se ultionem nostram gravem non evasuros agnoscant."

373 *Synody a statuta Olomoucké* (ed. Krafl), 126, 191–92, 207, 222.

374 *Synodicum Nicosiense*, 122–23. Kappes, "A New Narrative."

Limassol (1298) issued regulations for extreme unction, requiring priests to teach the faithful aged fourteen or older about the sacrament, including that it was for those in danger of death. Although anointing could be repeated, it was not to be performed more than once in the same illness.[375] By 1320, Archbishop John of Nicosia forbade priests requiring payment for anointing but permitted accepting voluntary offerings.[376]

Visitation Records

Occasionally, visitation records touch on the housing and carrying of oils for ministry to the sick. The visitations by Henri de Vézelay, archdeacon of Hiémois (1267–68) note occasional defects of a chrismatory, including its lacking keys for locking.[377] The same was true occasionally in the 1342 visitation of the archdeaconry of Totnes.[378] A visitation of the diocese of Hereford in 1397 found a "vessel of holy oil" (*vas olei sancti*) without a lock.[379] The 1427 visitations of the archdeaconry of Madrid occasionally mentioned the presence in pairs of small vessels for holy oils, called "chrismers" (*crismeras*) or "ampules" (*ampulas*).[380]

Some churches of the archdeaconry of Josas near Paris, including Mareil-Marly and Mesnil-Saint-Denis, admitted to visitors that they violated diocesan statutes by not renewing oils or having little available. Some supplies had not been renewed for two, three, or four years. Clergy were ordered to obtain fresh oils.[381] Other churches in that archdeaconry were ordered to secure vessels for oils on pain of a fine, even if they only acquired containers of wood or tin.[382] One church in Vitry was ordered to clean the vessel in which oils were kept.[383] The chaplains of two churches were told to label the oils, distinguishing them.[384] A parish in Bretigny was ordered to secure a tin oil stock to use when visiting the sick.[385] The church

375 *Synodicum Nicosiense*, 198–99.

376 Ibid., 230–31: "In extrema unctione nil petatur, sed si sponte offeratur, licite possit percipere."

377 Delisle, "Visites pastorales," 463, 465, 467.

378 Colton, "A Visitation of the Archdeaconry of Totnes in 1342," 112, 114, 116. One parish had a wooden chrismatory; see 115.

379 Bannister, "Visitation Returns of the Diocese of Hereford in 1397," *The English Historical Review* 45 (1930): 92–101 and 444–63, at 97.

380 De Andrés, "Actas de la visita," 173, 175, 185, 203, 208–9, 214, 232.

381 *Visites archidiaconales de Josas*, 7, 9, 31–32, 53, 68, 75, 77, 79, 88, 101, 275, 278, 316, 357, 362–63, 364, 386, 389.

382 Ibid., 7, 18, 33, 54, 69, 244, 346, 404.

383 Ibid., 81.

384 Ibid., 65 and 91.

385 Ibid., 240.

of Les Molières had tin ampules for the oils but kept them behind a small window by the altar.[386]

Pastoral Literature

In addition to local canons and visitations, priests were often guided by pastoral texts. These, derived from law and theology, were often composed by friars. Thus, the Dominican John of Freiburg summarized extreme unction as he expanded the *Summa* of Raymond of Peñafort. John repeated the Dominican opinion that the sacrament removed the debility left by both original and actual sin.[387] The sacrament was to be administered with blessed oil by a priest accompanied by a cleric or a "literate layman."[388] The rite was for those in danger of natural death, not for those going to war or voyaging.[389] The priest was to anoint the senses, the first roots of sin (*principia peccandi*).[390] John said a priest taking up anointing where another stopped was not to repeat what aready had been done.[391] He noted that there was disagreement over when extreme unction could be repeated, leaving the decision to the pope.[392]

John noted that agitated (*frenetici*) or mindless (*amentes*) persons who requested it while of sound mind might be anointed. The sacrament required internal devotion the mad lacked; and an afflicted person might be irreverent toward the sacrament.[393] Extreme unction could, however, be performed in a lucid interval of a mad person.[394]

John of Freiburg's *Summa* was made widely available in the alphabetical *Summa Pisanella* by the Dominican Bartholomacus de Sancto Concordio. In the fifteenth century, it was updated by the Franciscan Observant Nicholas of Osimo.[395] It also appeared in an Italian version by Giovanni

386 Ibid., 308.

387 Johannes de Friburgo, *Summa confessorum* III, t. 24, q. 142: "effectus eius principalis est quedam spiritualis sanatio quia datur contra quemdan debilitatem vel ineptitudinem que in nobis relinquitur ex peccato actualis (!) vel originali."

388 Ibid., q. 143. On the oil, see q. 141.

389 Ibid., q. 141.

390 Ibid., q. 146: "Cum ergo omnis nostra cognitio incipiat a sensu: ideo sensus in nobis propria rincipia peccandi: ideo in hoc sacramento instrumenta quinque sensuum: tanquam proprie radices peccandi inunguntur."

391 Ibid., q. 140.

392 Ibid., q. 147.

393 Ibid., q. 145: "Dicendum quod aut tales petiuerunt in sana mente constituta: aut non. In primo casu debet eis dari; in secundo non: quia ad hoc quod possit requiritur quedam deuotio interior quam furiosus habere non potest."

394 Ibid.: "nisi haberent lucida interualla in quibus sacramentum recognoscerent: quia tunc est in aliquo statu conferri posset."

395 Nicholas of Osimo, *Supplementum Summae Pisanellae.*

delle Celle, the *Summa Magistrutia*.[396] A German alphabetization circulated as the *Summa Bruder Bertholds*.[397]

The *Pisanella* treated extreme unction as a cure for the illness of sin, a single sacrament perfected through multiple actions.[398] It was not fully effective until all anointings had been done.[399] Olive oil consecrated by a bishop was the material of the sacrament.[400] Its words were in the deprecative. Two forms of words, *Per istam* and *Ungo hos*, were provided.[401] The senses, were anointed, together with feet and loins, because these were the "first roots" of sin. Even those who lacked an organ, like an eye, or had lost use of it, were to be anointed there or nearby.[402] Concerning the minister, Bartholomaeus referred readers to the writings of Aquinas; but Nicholas said that a priest had to anoint, assisted by a cleric or even a layman.[403]

Young children were unable to comprehend extreme unction, which was intended for ailing adults. The rite was denied, moreover, to those going to war or voyaging. The sick suffered a defect of nature, but these others might suffer a defect of fortune.[404] Similarly, those suffering mental

396 Giovanni delle Celle, *Summa Magistrutia*, Yale University Ms. 759; available at brbl-dl.library.yale.edu/vufind/Record/3817069.

397 Helmut Weck, *Die "Rechtssumme" Bruder Bertholds: Eine deutsche abscedarische Bearbeitung der "Summa confessorum" des Johannes von Freiburg: Die handschriftliche Überlieferung* (Tübingen: Niemeyer, 1982).

398 Nicholas of Osimo, *Supplementum Summae Pisanellae*, v. Unctio extrema: "Extrema unctio sacramentum est. quia pertingit ad effectum qui est curatio morbi peccati. vt ex verbis Jacobi vlti. c. patet . . . Et est vnum sacramentum licet plures actiones sunt de eius perfectione que tamen conueniunt ad vnum significandum et causandum. Hec est sententia Tho, in iiij. dist. xxiij."

399 Ibid.: "Respondeo secundum Tho. in iiij. dist. xxiij. Si iam alique partes iniuncte sunt. quid factum est. iterari non debet. sed vnctiones que restant per alium sacerdotem compleantur."

400 Ibid.: "Materia est oleum oliue ab episcopo consecratum. et tale oleum et eius consecratio sunt de necessitate huius sacramenti." See also v. Oleum sanctum siue chrisma.

401 Ibid., v. Unctio extrema: "Forma est oratio deprecatiuus dicendo. Per istam sanctam vnctionem et suam pijssimam misericordiam indulgeat tibi dominus quisquid deliquisti per visum. etc. Verba etiam indicatiui modi que secundum morem quarumdam ecclesiarum premittuntur orationi. non sunt de substantia sacramenti vt premittendo sic. Vngo hos oculos oleo sanctificato in nomine patris et filij et spiritussancti."

402 Ibid.: "Que partes corporis inungi debent. Respondeo secundum Al. Pe. et Tho. inunguntur instrumenta quinque sensuum tanquam *prime radices peccandi*. Oculi propter visum. Aures propter auditum. Nares propter oderatum. Labia propter gustum. Manus propter tactum. Qui maxime viget in pulpis digitorum. Pedes vero propter vim motiuum Renes vero propter vim appetitiuam a quibusdam inunguntur. Idem in mutilatis aut cecis debent inungi loca magis propinqua"

403 Ibid.: "Respondeo secundum Tho. vbi supra. A. solus sacerdotibus [!] nec alius potest inungere etiam in articulo necessitatis Sacerdos autem conferre potest presente vno cleric. Et etiam solus in necessitate secundum Bon. et Host. A. hoc vltimum clare habetur in .c. quesiuit ex. de ver. sig. Et idem quod in hoc .§. notatur in su. eo. tit. q. xliij. vbi etiam dicitur quod laicus quoque posset in necessitate auxiliari in hoc sacerdoti ei respondendo. B."

404 Ibid.: "Respondeo secundum Pe. [de Trantasio] et non nisi adultis infirmis. in articulo mortis constitutis ex ipsa infirmitate. Vnde nec datur euntibus ad bellum aut nauigantibus seu hijs qui mox occidendi sunt. quia talis mors non imminent ex defectu nature. Sed ex euentu fortune . . . Pueris non. quia non habent infirmitatem specialem contractum ex peccato actuali. nec dispositionem deuotionis habere possunt ad hoc sacramentum. Con. Tho. vbi. supra."

afflictions were unable to comprehend extreme unction except during a lucid interval.[405] Because sicknesses are not perpetual, anointing could be repeated, a relapse being treated as another illness. Those suffering from a repetitive illness like epilepsy (*idropsis*) could be anointed if threatened with death.[406] The *Pisanella* raises the question regarding a person presumed dead who returned to life. The reply distinguished baptism, confirmation, and orders, which could not be repeated, from penance, the Eucharist, extreme unction, and matrimony, which could be provided even for someone returned to life.[407]

The last major Dominican text on pastoral care before the Reformation was the *Summa Sylvestrina* of Silvestro Mazzolini, Prierias. His treatment of anointing (*unctio ecclesiae*) was founded on the writings of Thomas Aquinas and Petrus de Palude. Extreme unction was the only sacramental anointing.[408] The *Summa* treated oil consecrated by a bishop as essential to the rite. Not even the pope could permit substitution of unconsecrated oil.[409] The form was given in the deprecative mode.[410] Prierias summarized the teaching of Aquinas concerning the remains of sin: "The principal effect is the cleansing and strengthening of the spirit against the debility left over from actual or original sin: or the remission of sin as far as its remains."[411] A secondary effect was healing of the body (*sanatio corporis*) when it fit with the primary, spiritual effect.[412]

405 Ibid.: "Respondeo secundum Pe. Si sana mente constituti non pecierunt non debet dari. Si vero pecierunt dari debet. Tamen hic addendum secundum Tho. et Al. quod illis furiosis et amentibus precipue dari non debet qui verisimiliter sacramento possunt facere irreueretiam per aliquam immundiciam nisi ipsi haberent lucida interualla in quibus saceramentum recognoscerent."

406 Ibid.: "Respondeo secundum Tho. in iiij. Iterari potest sine aliqua iniuris sacramenti quia non habet effectum perpetuum quod sanitas corporis et mentis qui sunt effectus eius amitti possunt. In eadem quoque egritudine iterari potest si primo quidem sit in periculo mortis et euadat ac etiam postea recidiuum paciatur quia erit quasi alia infirmitas. Et similiter si sit egritudo diuturna vel ydropsis quia tunc debet fieri quando videtur perducere ad periculum mortis. Et si illum articulum euadat eadem infirmitate durante et postea ad similem statum reducatur iterum potest inungi. quia iam est aliud infirmitatis status. Quamuis sit eadem infirmitas." Nicholas added that anointing could be repeated if the illness lasted beyond a year.

407 Ibid., v. Sacramentum, "Vnde etiam si quis resuscitaretur non esset rebaptisandus. aut reconfirmandus. aut reordinandus. Secus in alijs iiij. sacramentis xxxij. q. licite. et j. q. j. quod quidam . . . et sic iterari potest matrimonium eucharistia. penitentia et extrema vnctio."

408 Sylvester Prierias, *Summa summarum que Sylvestrina nuncupatur* (Lyon: Platea, 1520), fol. cccxlviii[ra–b]. In this context, Prierias cited c. *Cum venisset.*

409 Ibid., fol. cccxlviii[rb]: "Non posset etiam papa statuere quod fuerit hec inunctio oleo non consecrato." The pope could make other changes in the rite, but no inferior prelate could.

410 Ibid.: "quod est forma deprecatiua dicendo per istam sanctam vnctionem." Prierias referred to Aquinas's accepting the indicative, as in the Ambrosian rite; see ibid.

411 Ibid., fol. cccxlviii[va]: "et dicit s. Tho. in iiij. quod effectus eius principalis est sanatio et roboratio spiritus contra debilitatem relictam ex peccato actuali vel originali: siue remissio peccati quo ad reliquias."

412 Ibid.

Prierias said that a priest, especially a pastor, was the proper minister of the rite, even "in a case of necessity" (*in articulo necessitatis*). A cleric or layman might assist, giving liturgical responses.[413] Another priest might be licensed by the pastor to act in a case of necessity. A religious, however, could not administer extreme unction.[414] Only adults in danger of death "from infirmity or old age" (*ex infirmitate vel senectute*) were proper recipients of anointing.[415] The sacrament was not to be administered to those "who cannot recognize it and receive it with devotion."[416] This omitted the mindless or the mad, who might be irreverent toward the sacrament, except during a lucid interval (*lucida interualla*).[417] The perpetually insane (*furiosi perpetuo*) were not ordinarily to receive anointing, especially if they had been impenitent before going mad. However, anyone who had led a good life, mindful of salvation in death more than in life, could be regarded as wanting the sacrament.[418] The patient was to be anointed on the "instruments" of the five senses, as well as the feet and loins, the last "on account of the power of appetite" (*propter vim appetetiuam*).[419] The rite could be repeated as needed. This was not essential, but its omission out of contempt was not acceptable.[420] Sylvester added that the priest should cease anointing if he realized the person had died.[421]

The Franciscan Astesanus de Ast, in the fourteenth century, gave a brief summary of extreme unction. The rite was a single sacrament with several acts. It was "inspired by the Holy Spirit" (*a spiritusancto inspiratum*) and promulgated by James, commanded by the other apostles to do so.[422] The rite was to be administered with olive oil with deprecative words. It was not to be granted unless the recipient was truly ill. Venial sins were remitted if the sacrament was "worthily received" (*digne suscipiatur*).[423] A priest was to administer the sacrament, preferably "with a one cleric present" (*presente*

413 Ibid.: "etiam auxiliante laico in necessitate et respondent."

414 Ibid.

415 Ibid.

416 Ibid.: "hoc sacramentum exhiberi non debet his qui non possunt illud recognoscere et cum devotione."

417 Ibid., fol. cccxlviii$^{va–b}$.

418 Ibid., fol. cccxlviii^{vb}: "sed si erat bone vite non presumitur immemor sue salutis in morte plusquam in vita" vnde presumitur quod petiuit licet non probetur." Prierias added a warning against anointing those who might show irreverence to the sacrament, but he disagreed with manuals which said the sacrament could be given only to those who requested it during a lucid interval.

419 Ibid., fol. cccxlviii^{vb}–ccxlix^{ra}.

420 Ibid., fol. cccxlix^{ra}.

421 Ibid., fol. cccxlviii^{vb}: "Et si inter vnctiones apparenter deficiat que sequuntur omittende sunt."

422 Astesanus de Ast, *Summa de casibus conscientiae* V, t. 41.

423 Ibid.

vno clerico).[424] The "five places of the senses" (*quinque loca sensuum*) with the feet, the means of motion, and the loins "on account of the generative power" (*propter generatiuam*), were to be anointed. Anointing was done near the location of a mutilated sense organ, as the soul still could desire sinning there.[425] Because illnesses could recur and others were occasional, like epilepsy (*idropsis*), anointing could be repeated. A long-term illness might require repeated anointings, especially if the person relapsed.[426]

Another fourteenth-century Minorite, John of Erfurt, said that extreme unction, the fifth sacrament, prepared the soul for the celestial fatherland.[427] Thus, the rite was only for the dangerously ill.[428] John described the sacrament as curing venial sins, which obstruct the path to glory for those *in articulo mortis*. Only secondarily might extreme unction cure bodies.[429] Although anointing by lay persons had ceased, John still distinguished cures effected with blessed oil from the sacramental acts of priests. Saints, male or female, might heal bodies through their merits; but only priests, acting for the Church, provided sacramental grace.[430]

The oil was to be consecrated by a bishop for sick persons. The form was deprecative, according to the Roman rite.[431] The priest was to anoint the organs of sensation, generation, and motion, a list once made by Bonaventure. These organs were the means of sin, through which guilt was contracted.[432] John said that those who could not understand the sacrament, such as children and the mad, were not to be anointed, unless the latter "asked for it when of a sound mind" or during a lucid interval.[433] Otherwise, the rite was for dangerously ill adults.[434]

The Franciscan teaching on extreme unction was summarized by Angelus Carlettus in the *Summa Angelica*.[435] The use of olive oil consecrated

424 Ibid.

425 Ibid.

426 Ibid.: "iterum potest inungi."

427 Johannes de Erfordia, *Die Summa confessorum*, 2:900: "extrema unctio datur gratia ad evolandum in patriam."

428 Ibid., 2:902.

429 Ibid., 2:901: "principalis est sanitas corporalis, scilice curatio venialium quae impediunt animam a perceptione gloriae. secundarius est sanitas corporalis."

430 Ibid. The *Penitential of Cummean* conflated the intercession of saints with the ministry to the sick described by James; see *Medieval Handbooks of Penance*, 100.

431 Johannes de Erfordia, *Die Summa confessorum*, 2:900–901.

432 Ibid., 2:902: "est autem triplex potentia animae, per quas maxime anima contrahit culpam ex coniunctione carnis, scilicet, sensitiva, generativa, progressiva: ideo debent iniungi." The feet too were anointed because they went to places of sin (*progressio*).

433 Ibid.: "nisi in sane mentis constituti petierunt."

434 Ibid.

435 See, e.g., Angelus Carlettus, *Summa angelica de casibus conscientie* (Lyon: Mollin, 1511), fol. cccl[rb].

by a bishop, the form of words, and administration by a priest to those in danger of death were all affirmed.[436] Those lacking reason, children or the mindless, were anointed only when an adult expressed a desire for the sacrament before being afflicted.[437] The priest was to anoint the senses, the feet, and the loins of a man. He was not to touch the loins of a woman; but an alternative site, the navel, was not listed in his text.[438] Angelus, added to Petrus Aureoli's seven effects of extreme unction an eighth, removing mortal and venial sins when the sick person did not obstruct the rite's effects.[439] Angelus said that extreme unction was not essential for the sick, but it was not to be omitted out of contempt. It could be repeated in the same illness if the situation changed during a long convalescence.[440]

One of the most popular guidebooks for priests, the *Manipulus curatorum*, said that anointing was intended to relieve both spiritual and physical pain.[441] It identified the foundation of the sacrament with Christ's sending the apostles to preach and cure (Mk 6).[442] The form of the sacrament in the *Manipulus* was liturgical. At the anointing of the senses, the priest was to say: "Through this anointing and his most tender mercy, may God forgive you whatever faults you have committed through seeing, hearing, etc."[443]

The sacrament was to be given to those in danger of death "because they are already passing away," thus easing them toward salvation.[444] Because the sacrament was tied to penance, it could heal the weaknesses of sinners, even adding physical healing. Anointing the senses, as well as the feet and loins, dealt with human weakness.[445] The author cited James as proof that a priest was the minister of extreme unction. If one priest died

436 Ibid., fol. cccl[ra–b].

437 Ibid., fol. cccl[ra]: "Quibus potest conferri. R'. infirmis existentibus in periculo mortis. De quibus probabiliter dubitatur de morte pueris autem vel euntibus ad bellum aut alio modo in periculo casuali mortis non datur secundum communiter doc. nec etiam amentibus: nisi ante amentiam ipsa petissent et dando nullam [ir]reuerentiam facerent et secundum sanctum Bo. [Bonaventure] in. iiij. di. xxiij. tantum debet dari infirmis qui in mortali non sunt et ratione vtentibus et in articulo mortis existentibus et veniale peccatum habentibus. alij. non."

438 Ibid., fol. cccl[ra–b]: "Que partes corporis debent iungi. R' quod instrumenta quinque sensuum. scilicet. oculi: aures: manus nares: labia: pedes. et renes. mulieribus tamen non vnguntur renes propter honestatem." Angelus followed with advice to anoint near the site of a mutilation.

439 Ibid., fol. cccl[rb]: "Octauus secundum S. Tho. in. iiij. dist. xxiij. tollit peccatum veniale et mortale etiam quantum ad culpam; dummodo non opponatur obex ex parte recipientis."

440 Ibid.

441 Guido of Monte Rochen, *Handbook for Curates*, 119.

442 Ibid., 118.

443 Ibid., 119. The text also provides a form from the Ambrosian Rite.

444 Ibid., 119–20.

445 Ibid., 120–22.

while conferring the sacrament, another was to complete the rite.[446] The sacrament was to be given to anyone who requested it, even the insane, if they had expressed the desire while of sound mind.[447] Priests could anoint a person not just once but in any crisis or relapse. If the patient recovered, he or she could return to normal life.[448]

England had its own writings on the cure of souls, William of Pagula's *Oculus sacerdotis* (*Priest's Eye*) and John of Borough's *Pupilla oculi* (*Pupil of the Eye*).[449] The *Oculus* said little about the theology of extreme unction in its *Pars dextera*, just that it was designed, primarily, to alleviate sin and, secondarily, to cure illness.[450] A patient was anointed on the verge of death. Failure of a priest to minister to one so ill was a serious offense.[451] If the ailing person relapsed or survived and became gravely ill again, the sacrament could be repeated.[452] A mad person could receive anointing during a lucid interval.[453] William cribbed from Anselm's interrogation of the dying, adding an exhortation falsely attributed to Augustine of Hippo.[454]

The *Pars dextera* warned against anointing those already dead.[455] Those who received unction were told they were receiving the Holy Spirit's anointing (*sancti spiritus tipicalis unctio*).[456] William also included an excerpt from the *Speculum penitentis* of Guillelmus de Montibus, promising forgiveness of venial sins not only for receiving extreme unction but for reciting the *Ave Maria*, the penitential psalms, and a litany.[457]

446 Ibid., 120.

447 Ibid., 121.

448 Ibid., 122–23.

449 Leonard E. Boyle, "*Oculus sacerdotis* and Some Other Works of William of Pagula," *Transactions of the Royal Historical Society* 5, no. 5 (1955): 81–110.

450 William of Pagula, *Oculus sacerdotis*, fol. 18va: "Duplex est causa quare iunguntur infirmi. Una est causa quia per huius unctionem delentur uenialia peccata. Et huius unctio prestat augmentum uirtutibus. Alia est causa quia infirmus per huius unctionem citius liberatur ab infirmitate corporali, xcv di. §. Sed istud [d. 95, p. c. 2] in glossa."

451 Ibid.: "Et si ex contemptu uel ex negligentia hoc sacramentum (pretermittatur) periculosum est et dampnabile."

452 Ibid.: "Istud sacramentum extreme unctionis debet tamen illis dari quibus grauis infirmitas indiciis mortis appropinquare uidetur."

453 Ibid.: "Et si contingat eos frenesi uel quacumque alienacione mentis laborare, si ante alienacionem errant de sua salute solliciti, (consulitur) nicholominus quod hoc sacramentum illis fiducialiter ministretur, in constitutione de lambeth. pecham c. ignorantia §. ult." See *Councils & Synods* II, pt. 1, 905.

454 William of Pagula, *Oculus sacerdotis*, fol. 18va–19vb. *Sancti Anselmi admonitio morienti*, PL 158, 685B–688B; Pseudo-Augustinus, *De visitatione infirmorum*, c. 6 (PL 40:1151).

455 William of Pagula, *Oculus sacerdotis*, fol. 20rb: "Et hoc est prohibitum."

456 Ibid., fol. 19vb–20ra.

457 Ibid., fol. 20va. Guillelmus de Montibus, *Speculum penitentis*, in Joseph Goering, *William de Montibus (c. 1140–1213): The Schools and the Literature of Pastoral Care* (Toronto: PIMS, 1992), 209–10.

The catechetical *Pars sinistra oculi* dealt briefly with extreme unction.[458] It repeated the purposes of anointing, spiritual and physical healing, adding the verse of (supposedly) Pope Innocent III: *Ungor in extremis, ut michi gratia maior. Et morbus leuior, et mea culpa minor.*[459] William of Pagula quoted (supposedly) Augustine on how a Christian should face death positively, expressing the need for divine mercy.[460]

John of Borough's *Pupilla oculi*, grounded in Scholastic theology, treated topics ranging from the establishment of extreme unction by Christ[461] to the role of anointing in forgiving venial sins. John of Burough said that the primary effect was spiritual; but it might lead to healing, or at least to temporary remission of bodily suffering.[462] The text included the interrogation of the dying attributed to Anselm, emphasizing trust in Christ's death for forgiveness and entry into Paradise.[463] An exhortation followed, urging humble acceptance of infirmity while preparing for death and judgment.[464] A large portion of the exhortation derived from the Sarum order for visiting the sick, added for the instruction of simple priests (*ad instructionem sacerdotum simplicium*).[465] A detailed order for anointing the sick was also added.[466] In addition, the *Pupilla* specified that extreme unction was to be given to the mad only in their lucid intervals; and it denied the sacrament to children too young to understand it.[467] The text also allowed repetition of the sacrament following a relapse.[468]

There were also pastoral instructions in the vernacular, including a work by the Austin canon John Mirk.[469] His *Instructions for Parish Priests* listed the sacraments, including, "And the last elynge wyth-owte fayle."

458 William's thinking about this section is revealed by his comment that holy orders pertains only to the "perfect," the clergy, not to the laity; see *Oculus sacerdotis*, fol. 73rb.

459 Ibid. See Hans Walther, *Initia carminum ac versuum medii aevi* (Göttingen: Vandenhoeck und Ruprecht, 1959), no. 32183. Another verse about the sacrament is found in Lewis Burton Hessler, *The Latin Epigram of the Middle English Period: With Special Reference to Ms. Reg. 17C xvii, fol. 17b–18* (Menasha, Wis.: Collegiate Press, 1916), 8: "Non est ungendus furiosus, iniquus, parvus. Est tum ungendus, si petit ipse furens."

460 William of Pagula, *Oculus sacerdotis*, fol. 20va.

461 John of Burough, *Pupilla oculi*, University of Pennsylvania, MS Codex 75, fol. 104rb: "Institutum fuit sacramentum extreme uncionis immediate a Christo."

462 Ibid., fol. 104rb–107ra.

463 Ibid., fol. 105vb–106ra. This interrogatory is an incomplete version of the *Admonitio morienti et de peccatis suis nimium formidanti*; see PL 158:685C–688B.

464 Ibid., fol. 106ra.

465 Ibid., fol. 106rb–vb.

466 Ibid., fol. 106vb–107ra.

467 Ibid., fol. 105ra.

468 Ibid., fol. 105ra–b.

469 John Mirk, *Instructions for Parish Priests*, ed. Edward Peacock, 2nd ed. (London: Trübner, 1902; Woodbridge: Boydell, 1996).

The priest was to teach this, backed by his own clean living.[470] Mirk offered instructions for dealing with the dying, "But he that schale be an-oynt, Aske hym thus euery point, 'art thow fayn, my brother,' say, That thow dyest in crysten fay?'" There followed an interrogation about belief in Christ's passion, based on Anselm's text, followed by an injunction to trust Christ.[471] These injunctions ended, *Tunc vngatur infirmus* ("Then the sick person is anointed").[472] Mirk also allowed the priest to say on behalf of a dying person, "Into your hands [, oh Lord]."[473]

Extreme unction also was addressed in John Thoresby's *The Lay Folks' Catechism*: "The fyft sacrament is the last enoynting. With oyle thus is halowed and handeled of prest to them that he wate ere of skillwise elde. And that he seis silkerly in peril of dede: In lightenese and alegeaunce of their sekenesse. If god wil that thai turne ogayne to hele, And als in forgynesse of venyale synnes, And in lessyne of peyne, if thai passe hethn." Like the Franciscans, Thoresby said that the sacrament offered forgiveness of venial sins and possible remission of pain, even if the sufferer was not restored to health.[474]

We come closest to pastoral practice in the manuals for priests composed for each diocese. The order for anointing the sick in the *Rituale Romanum* is a good example. The priest, having been to the house to give communion, was to take the oil and return there while saying a psalm. After wishing the household peace, he is to say a series of prayers before sprinkling the sick person with holy water. The priest was to say a brief litany, invoking Zenobius, Bernard, and Francis. In Florence he could add Reparata.[475] Next the *Rituale* allowed for confession and absolution.[476] After absolution, the assisting priests were to say the penitential psalms. While they said these or just after, the minister was to put oil on his thumb.[477] Then the priest was to anoint eyes, ears, nostrils, lips, hands, feet, and loins (*lumbos*), saying the words for each sense, beginning *Per istam sanctam unctionem*. At that last location, the priest was to pray for forgiveness of what had been done by the sick person with the loins "as

470 Ibid., 16–17.

471 Ibid., 56–57. For the seven questions the priest was to ask a dying person, derived from Anselm of Canterbury, see *Pastors and the Care of Souls* (ed. Shinners and Dohar), 195–96.

472 Mirk, *Instructions for Parish Priests*, 57. An exposition of the celebration of Mass followed this rubric.

473 Ibid., 137.

474 *The Lay Folks' Catechism or the English and Latin Versions of Archbishop Thoresby's Instructions for the People* (London: K. Paul, Trench, Trübner, 1901), 68–69.

475 *Rituale Romanum* (Florence: Buonaccorsi, 1485), fol. a ii^{v}–b i^{v}.

476 *Rituale Romanum* (Florence: Per Antonium Francisci, ca. 1484), fol. [a 8]v–b i^{r}.

477 *Rituale Romanum*, fol. b i^{r-v}: "Dum autem psalmi dicuntur uel cum dicti fuerint: sacerdos inuncto pollice in oleo sancto dicat . . ."

a vice of the flesh" (*carnis vitio*). After each anointing, the priest was to dry that spot with a cloth to be burned later.[478] He could leave a cross before the sick person (*crux remaneat coram infirmo*) before returning to the church. However, if the sick person was dying, the priest was to shift to the commendation of the soul.[479]

North of the Alps, the Rouen order for visiting the sick proceeded from the penitential psalms to a litany, invoking Martial of Limogres, Denis, Geneviève, Quentin of Amiens, Ouen of Rouen, and Louis IX. Petitions were offered against sudden and eternal death and for aid in the hour of death. The litany concluded with a series of prayers, one invoking the healing of Hezekiah: "O God, Who to King Hezekiah" *(Deus qui ezechie regi)*.[480] After these prayers, the sick person could confess "if necessary" (*Hic infirmis confiteatur si necesse fuerit*). The priest then was to use a form of absolution, especially if the patient had a papal privilege.[481] The priest was to make a sign of the cross on the sick person's breast, saying the formula for Ash Wednesday: "Remember, man, that you are dust."[482] Then the priest was to anoint eyes, ears, lips, nostrils, hands, feet, and breast, using the formula, "By this anointing and its most pious mercy" (*Per istam unctionem et suam piisimam misericordiam*). Having anointed the sick person, the priest could give communion "if it will be necessary" (*si necesse fuerit*). Whether communion was given or not, the priest was to say prayers and blessings, ending with the prologue of John's Gospel.[483]

The Coutance manual too moved from the penitential psalms to a litany mentioning Denis, Louis, and Geneviève. It also invoked help against sudden and eternal death, asking help: "In the hour of death succor him. On the day of judgment."[484] There followed prayers, beginning with *Deus qui ezechie regi*.[485] Provision also was made for confession and absolution.[486] The instructions included anointing a man's loins but a woman's

478 Ibid., fol. b i^{v}–b ii^{v}, at b i^{v}–b ii^{r}: "Minister uero tergat locum inunctum cum stuppa: reponens eam in uase mundo: et sic sacrat post quamlibet unctionem."

479 Ibid., fol. b iii^{r}–b iiii^{r}.

480 *Manuale secundum usum insignis ecclesiae Rothomagensis* (Rouen: Morin, ca. 1500), fol. 34v–38r.

481 Ibid., fol. 38r: "Et nota. Si penitens petatur et uelit absolui auctoritate apostolica virtute litterarum de perpetuum seu alias."

482 Ibid., fol. 38v. "Deinde sacerdos faciat crucem cineris in pectore infirmi dicendo. Memento homo quia cinis es et in cinere reuerteris."

483 Ibid., fol. 38v–40r.

484 *Manuale secundum usum ecclesie Constanciensis*, fol. 25v–28v: "In hora mortis: succurre et domine. In die iudicii." A marginal note provided the feminine *ea* to substitute for the masculine *ei*.

485 Ibid., fol. 28v–29r.

486 Ibid., fol. 29r–v.

navel.[487] Prayers asked forgiveness of sins committed "on account of the ardor of the libido" (*per ardorem libidinis*) and purification of mind and body (*ad purificationem mentis et corporis*).[488] The rite ended with the prologue of John's Gospel.[489]

The Angers manual allowed the use of a feminine form (*dicitur audiuua eam*) in the litany, which invoked Louis and Geneviève.[490] A series of prayers preceded anointing the senses, the loins of a man or the navel of a woman, and finally the feet. The priest washed and dried his hands before throwing the water into the fire (*et proiiciat lauaturam in igne*).[491]

In the Paris use, the litany preceding anointing was to be said "in the presence of the sick person" (*in presencia infirmi*). The list of saints invoked concluded with *Sancta Genouefa*.[492] One prayer referred to the patient as "laboring in infirmity of body" (*in infirmitate corporis laborante*). Immediately before anointing, the priest was to pronounce absolution of sins.[493] The anointing of the senses, loins (man) or navel (woman), and feet was to follow. Then the priest was to wash his hands with salt water and discard the liquid.[494] There followed prayers, blessings, and absolution.[495] The priest was to show the sufferer a cross and evoke a profession of faith in French (*vulgari idiomate*) from those without Latin. The priest could conclude with an exhortation, and friends too might exhort the sick person. The priest also could give communion, but only after the sick person had confessed.[496]

The Reims manual provided for problems that the priest might face. If the sick person was not *in extremis*, an exhortation in French began, "Receive the holy sacraments of the Church devoutly" (*Les sains sacraments de leglise receuz deuotement*). If death was imminent, the priest was

487 Ibid., fol. 29v: "Ista unctio fiat viris in lumbis: et feminis in umbiculo."

488 Ibid., fol. 30r.

489 Ibid., fol. 30r–31r.

490 *Manuale ad usum precelebris ecclesie Andegauensis*, fol. xxxvi^{v}–xxxviii^{v}.

491 Ibid., fol. xxxix^{r}–xliii^{v}.

492 *Manuale secundum usum ecclesiae Parisiensis* (Paris: Mourand, 1497), fol. e^{i}va–e^{ii}vb. See also the Paris pontifical in Paris BN Lat. 961, fol. ccxxxviii^{v}.

493 Ibid., fol. e^{ii}vb–e^{iii}rb.

494 Ibid., fol. e^{iii}vb–e^{iiii}ra. The Paris pontifical included a form for anointing a priest's hands and one for a woman's navel; see Paris BN Lat. 961, fol. ccxxxiiii^{r}. The latter refers to sins committed *per ardorem libidinis*.

495 *Manuale secundum usum ecclesiae Parisiensis*, fol. e^{iiii}ra–e$^{[v]}$rb.

496 Ibid., fol. e$^{[v]}$rb–va, "Et alia hortamenta secundum discretionem dicat sacerdos. et amici infirmi: De sacramento etiam eukaristie petenti infirmo sicut et cetera sacramenta minisretur . . . Si enim infirmis prius petat sacramentum eukaristie sibi (prius confessione facta de peccatis) ministretur."

to anoint quickly, avoiding death without unction.[497] A sick person could be anointed once in a year if fourteen years of age or older. The text added a verse from Hostiensis: "A mad person, a fool, a child is not to be anointed."[498] The manual provided the penitential psalms for a case which was not urgent (*Si uero infirmis non urgeatur*).[499] A litany was followed by prayers, including *Deus qui famulo tuo Ezechie*.[500] The priest was to wash his hands and reverently open the repository of oil. Then he was to put oil on the left palm so that he could anoint with his right thumb, starting with the right eye and then the left, making the sign of the cross.[501] The rite was to conclude with the sign of the cross made over the sick person and showing him or her a crucifix, saying an exhortation in French (*in gallico*) over a lay person but in Latin over a priest. Then the crucifix was to be presented to him or her to kiss (*ad osculanda*). The priest was to sprinkle the person with holy water and say in French, "God remain with you. Amen" (*Dieu demerire auec vous. Amen*).[502]

In England, the York manual began its instructions for the rite with the rubric *De extrema unctione*. After hearing confession, the priest was to apply oil with his right thumb to the eyes, right and then left, using this form of prayer: "By this holy unction and His pious mercy and through the intercession of the Blessed Virgin Mary and all the saints, may the Lord pardon you whatever sins you have committed by sight." Thereafter he was to use similar prayers when applying oil to the ears, lips, nose, and hands. Priests were to be anointed on the outside of the hand, having been anointed on the inside at ordination. Other persons were to be anointed on the inside of the hand. In York, the feet, heart, and navel were treated with oil.[503] The manual also maintained that only a priest could administer the sacrament, and he was to advise the faithful that it could only be

497 *Manuale seu agenda ad usum Remensem* (ca. 1500), [173]–[74]: "Si infirmis habeat sanum intellectum et ultima hora non urgeat eidem insinuetur verbis gallicis administratio sacramenti in hunc modum . . . Et si de morte proximorum dubitetur et vltima hora urgeat non dicat septem psalmi infra scripti neque orationes. Sed ungatur infirmis prout in his continetur prout in his continetur versibis. Versus. Si trahat ungendum dolor extremus sie psalmis Hunc ungas citis ut non moriatur inunctus."

498 Ibid., [174]: "Non est ungendus furiosus morio paruus."

499 Ibid., [174]–[81].

500 Ibid., [181]–[85].

501 Ibid., [185]: "Et primo presbiter lotis minibus et exterus locellum seu uasi in quo sacrum recoditur oleum reuerenter aperies inde per instrumentulum uasculi guttulas olei sacri distillans in palma sua sinistra dispositus ad ungendum pollice suo dextro tegumen ungat olei dexteri signum crucis imprimendo postea sinistri."

502 Ibid., [190].

503 *Manuale et processionale ad usum insignis ecclesiae Eboracensis*, 50–51, with a cross in the middle of the word *unctionem* to indicate when the priest was to apply the oil. If a person had lost a sense organ, the priest was to anoint near its location; see ibid., 54. On the anointing of priests' hands, see *The Rationale divinorum officiorum of William Durand*, 93–94.

received by those fourteen years of age or older, those able to discern its significance.[504]

The Sarum Use also states that extreme unction followed confession.[505] When the priest prepared to anoint, he was to start his attendants reciting psalms. Each of these was to be said while one of the sense organs was anointed, plus the feet and either the loins of a man or the navel of a woman. The priest was to finish by washing his hands with salted water and drying them on a cloth, which was to be burned with its ashes buried in the cemetery.[506]

The manuals from lands neighboring France differed somewhat in instructions for extreme unction. The Tournai manual told the priest to start anew from the church and enter the home of the sick person with a greeting.[507] He was to say prayers and "a few consoling words" (*paucis verbis consoletur*) before inquiring whether confession was necessary.[508] Either way, the priest was to say the penitential psalms and a litany invoking Eligius and Medard.[509] The bystanders were asked to pray for the sick person, so that he or she would receive the sacrament for the soul's welfare.[510] The priest was to begin the rite by washing the places for anointing out of reverence.[511] Next, oil was administered using a finger, a rod, or a stick (*spatula*) before drying those places with a cloth.[512] The usual formula, *Per istam sacram unctionem*, was to be used at each sense. A nearby place was used for any lost organs. Finally, the priest was to show the patient a crucifix, admonishing him or her to keep in mind Christ's passion and have patience.[513] Additional instructions told the priest to adjust the prayers to the condition of the patient and to add local patron saints to the litany. Nor was a sick person to be neglected in an epidemic (*morbus contagiosus*).[514]

504 *Manuale et processionale*, 54.

505 Aimé Georges Mortimort, "Prayer for the Sick and Sacramental Anointing," 133.

506 *Manuale et processionale*, 49*–50*.

507 *Manuale pastorum ad uniformem administrationem sacramentorum aliorum officiorum ecclesiasticum per civitatem et dioecesim Tornacensem* (Louvain: Masius, 1591?), 44.

508 Ibid., 45.

509 Ibid., 45–58.

510 Ibid., 58: "Moneat Sacerdos circumstantes vt pro infirmo orent, vt ad salutem animae suae suscipiat hoc Sacramentum Extremae Vnctionis."

511 Ibid., 44: "Pro administrando Sacramento extremae Vnctionis reuerentiae causa lauantur partes quae inungi debent."

512 Ibid., 60: "Hic linum vel stuppam habeat Sacerdos paratam ad detegendum oleum membris inunctis: & pollicem vel virgulam intingat in oleum sacrum."

513 Ibid., 60–64.

514 Ibid., 64.

The manual for Toul invoked Leodegar and Gangolf.[515] It differed most significantly in the formula for anointing, beginning "I anoint you with holy oil" (*Inungo te de oleo sancto*). The individual locations for unction extended beyond the senses to the head, neck, throat, between the shoulder blades and the chest, but not the loins or navel.[516] Provision also was made for anointing the place where pain was worst.[517]

The Lausanne manual began extreme unction with the material, olive oil blessed by a bishop, and the form for anointing the sense organs.[518] The form was the usual *Per istam sanctam unctionem*, and the oil was to be made ready on a small dish (*scutella*) for application with pieces of flax (*stupis*). The loins were not to be anointed, but the blind and amputees were to be anointed near lost senses.[519] Lausanne placed the penitential psalms at the end of extreme unction with communion following. Before leaving, the priest was to sprinkle the sick person with holy water and give him or her a crucifix on which to gaze.[520]

The diocese of Chur invoked local saints like Florian and Odile of Alsace.[521] Although many manuals provided slightly different wording for men and women, that for Chur told the priest to adjust the terms he used by gender.[522] After saying prayers, the priest was to urge the need to confess.[523] Following confession, the priest was to pray, "God who send blessed Peter to Tabitha" (*Deus qui beatum Petrum misisti ad Thabitam*) and *Deus qui famulo tuo Ezechie*. He also was to inquire whether the sick person had been confirmed by a bishop, before anointing the senses with the usual form of words and oil on a thumb (*tincto pollice*).[524] At the conclusion of the rite, the priest was to wash the oil vessel and the thumb

515 *Manuale seu rituale ad usum ecclesie Tullensis* (Bamburg: Sensenschmidt, ca. 1482), fol. [19]r–[21]v.

516 *Manuale ad usum ecclesie Tullensis*, fol. [24]r–[25]v.

517 Ibid., fol. [25]v: "Ad locum vbi dolor plus imminent. In nomine patris et filij et spiritussancti sit tibi hoc punctio olei sanctificati."

518 *Manuale seu officiarium saceerdotum secundum usum ecclesie et diocesis Laudunensis* (Paris: Ad Signum Rose Rubie, 1538), fol. xxii^{v}: "Postea ungatur infirmus. Materia huius sacramenti est oleum oliuarum ab episcopo benedictum. Forma autem est verba que dicit quando ungit infirmum in membris que sunt organa sensuum."

519 Ibid., fol. xxii^{v}–xxiii^{r}: "Secundum consuetudinem diocesis Laudunensi. Renes non ungantur . . . In mutilatis et cecis debent inungi loca magis propinqua."

520 Ibid., fol. xxiii^{r}–xxvi^{r}.

521 *Agenda sive exeqviale divinorum sacramentorvm pro ecclesiis parrochialibus dioecesis Curiensis* (Rosach: Straub, 1590), fol. Z [4]^{v}–Aa 2^{v}.

522 *Agenda dioecesis Curiensis*, fol. Aa 2^{v}: "Sacerdos semper notat an sit vir vel mulier et secundum hoc ponat genus terminorum."

523 Ibid., fol. Aa 3^{r}: "Admoneat sacerdos infirmum si habeat aliqua confiteri."

524 Ibid., fol. A 3^{r}–[4]^{v}.

used in anointing before administering viaticum.[525] The priest was to say a post-communion prayer and urge the sick person mildly (*blandè*) to bear God's scourge patiently for the purgation of sins.[526]

The Basel manual added Pantaleon, Oswald, Leonard, Gall, and Othmar, as well as Ursula with her companions (*cum sodalibus*), to the litany.[527] The priest was to warn the patient to confess, if it had not yet been done (*si prius non erat confessus*); absolution was to follow.[528] The sick person was anointed in the form of a cross on the senses and the feet. Then the priest was to wash the places anointed and clean his hands with salt water.[529] The sick person was to say the Creed, unless the priest had to say it in the vernacular with the patient following along if possible.[530] The priest was to conclude by giving the sick person a crucifix to kiss (*ad osculandum*) and sprinkle holy water before departing.[531]

The manual for Constance had the litany begin with the priest inviting the sick person and the bystanders to join in prayer.[532] Among the saints invoked were Gall, Udalrich, Ursula, and Hildegard.[533] The manual had the priest lay a hand "on the head of the sick person" (*super caput infirmi*) while invoking the Trinity.[534] After anointing senses and feet, the priest was to say a psalm and prayers, one of which invoked the Apostle James.[535] The priest was to urge patience on the sick person, before hearing confession and granting absolution. The Constance book urged use of the vernacular version of the *Confiteor* with lay persons.[536] The manual added viaticum after the instructions for unction and confession, and a last exhortation to patience.[537]

525 Ibid., fol. A [4]^{v}–Bb 2^{r}.

526 Ibid., fol. Bb 2^{r}.

527 *Informatorium sacerdotum* (Basel: Wennsler, 1488), fol. e [i]$^{r-v}$.

528 Ibid., fol. e [4]^{r}.

529 Ibid., fol. e [4]^{v}–e [5]^{v}.

530 Ibid., fol. e [5]^{v}: "Deinde infirmis dicat. Credo in deum patrem useque ad finem si possit. Vel sacerdos dicat in vulgari ante infirmum ut similiter dicat et si non possit bene ore dicere."

531 Ibid., fol. e [6]^{v}.

532 *Obsequiale sive benedictionale secundum ecclesiam Constantinensem* (Augsburg: Ratdolt, 1510), fol. xvi^{r}: "Dicat sacerdos ad infirmum et astantes. Inuocemus deum et sacerdos suos pro salute huius infirmi."

533 Ibid., fol. xvi$^{r-v.}$

534 Ibid., fol. xvii^{v}–xviii^{r}.

535 Ibid., fol. xviii^{v}–xix^{r}, at xix^{r}: "Omnipotens sempiterne deus: qui per os beati Jacobi apostoli tui hoc mysterium infirmis omnibus facere precepisti."

536 Ibid., fol. xx^{r}: "Utile videtur fieri materna lingua propter astantes laycos. Ich armer füdiger mensch."

537 Ibid., fol. xx^{r-v}.

The manual for Worms had the priest use a litany with a sick man or woman answering, "Pray for me."[538] The Trier pontifical gave a short form for extreme unction, omitting the initial litany. It did require anointing the body, probably the loins, on account of sins committed "on account of the ardor of the libido" (*per ardorem libidinis*).[539] The pontifical allowed administration of viaticum afterward (*Post hęc tradat ei eucharistiam*). Only then did the text add a litany, invoking, among others, Gereon of Cologne (written *Gregon*).[540] The prayers at the end of the rite sometimes had feminine forms written above the male forms.[541] The 1574 manual for Trier had the priest address the patient in German while showing a crucifix.[542]

The Cologne pontifical differed substantially from that of Trier. It had the priest lay hands on the sick person, saying an antiphon and a prayer: "Look, Lord, on Your servant laboring in the infirmity of his body" (*Respice domine famulum tuum infirmitate sui corporis laborantem*). Then the sick person was anointed on the head, neck, eyes, ears, nostrils, lips, throat, shoulders, breast, hands, heart, and feet. Each act's words began, *Ungo te*. A special anointing was reserved for the place with greatest pain (*vbi maior dolor est*).[543] The priest was to offer communion, followed by prayers. "When death is approaching" (*Appropinquante obitu*), a litany was to be employed with more prayers. After the person expired, the corpse was to be carried to the church where a responsory, the *Pater noster*, and a prayer were to be said in conclusion.[544]

The 1562 Cologne manual added instructions to the priest, saying that he needed to know to whom to give the sacraments, how to deal with excommunicates in front of witnesses (*testibus*) so that they would not be deprived of viaticum (*ne viatico priuentur*) and how to dress for visitation of the sick with holy oil (*cum sacro Oleo*), before proceeding with light, cross, and holy water.[545] The text added the interrogation attributed to St. Anselm.[546]

538 *Agenda secundum ritum et ordinem ecclesie wormaciensis*, fol. c ii^{v}: "Ora pro eo vel ea. et dicat infirmus Ora pro me."

539 *Pontificale Trevirense*, Paris BN 13315, fol. 197r. Mention of the loins was omitted from a later diocesan manual; see *Agenda ecclesiae Trevirensis*, cxxxvi and cl–cli.

540 *Pontificale Trevirense*, fol. 200vb.

541 Ibid., fol. 204v–210v.

542 *Agenda ecclesiae Trevirensis*, cxli–cxliii.

543 *Pontificale Coloniense*, Cologne Cathedral Chapter Codex 139, fol. 96r–99v.

544 *Pontificale Coloniense*, fol. 100r–112r. An *Ordo in agenda mortuorum* followed at ibid., fol. 112r–120v.

545 *Agenda ecclesiastica Coloniensis*, fol. c ii^{v}. Instructions regarding how lay persons were to respond to the litany appeared at ibid., fol. d [1]^{v}.

546 Ibid., fol. [d 4]^{r}.

Farther afield, the diocese of Augsburg had the priest invoke the nine choirs of angels in the litany.[547] The bystanders were to respond *Amen* to each formula for anointing the senses, as well as the neck, breast, and feet. Lepers were to be anointed with a rod or stick (*spatula*), which was burned afterward (*sed spatula postea faciat comburi*).[548] Once extreme unction had been performed, the priest could administer viaticum "in the way in which the sick are accustomed to communicate" (*more quo infirmi communicari solent*).[549] The manual added provisions for difficult situations. Priests were not to anoint those expecting a violent death. They could grant it to persons mentally afflicted who had a lucid interval and requested the sacrament devoutly. The frenzied who requested extreme unction could receive it if there was no fear of irreverence for the sacrament. Otherwise they were to be denied it.[550] The Augsburg instructions noted that the sacrament was usually given to those aged at least eighteen, making allowance for a younger person who could tell good from evil and devoutly requested the rite.[551]

The Minden book began extreme unction at the head, but not on the forehead, where he or she was anointed at confirmation (*et non ad frontem ubi in confirmatione a Christo inunctus est*).[552] The sick person was also to be anointed on the breast (*pectus*).[553] The text included an interrogation of the sick attributed to Jean Gerson.[554] The Regensburg manual invoked in its litany Wolfgang, Cunegunde, and Walburga.[555] The Brixen book invoked Corbinian, Rupert, and Wolfgang, as well as Ursula and her companions.[556] The diocese of Passau called upon Volgang and Ursula.[557] The Eichstätt manual invoked Willibald and Wunnibald, together with

547 *Obsequiale Augustense Augustense im Auftrag von Friedrich II, Graf von Zollern, Bischof von Augsburg* (Augsburg: Ratdolt, 1487), fol. lxiii^{r-v}.

548 Ibid., fol. lxvi^{v}–lxvii^{v}. The priest also was to anoint a woman about to give birth (*puerpera*); see fol. lxvii^{v}.

549 Ibid., fol. lxviii^{v}.

550 Ibid., fol. lxix^{r}: "Non detur sanis violentiam mortem expectantibus. Freneticis vero et stolidis habentibus lucida intervalla: si tunc ex deuotione petunt: et possunt recipere absque periculo: tunc detur eis: etiam si iam frenesi laborarent: ita tamen quod diligenter precaueatur ne irreuerentia sacramento exhibeatur aliqualiter: quod tamen non conceditur: si prius lucido interuallo durante deuote non petierunt."

551 Ibid.: "Communiter tenetur: quod inungendus debet habere etatis sue. xviij. annos. Si tamen minoris esset etatis: et discernere posset bonum a malo: posset in minori etate (si haberet deuotionem et desiderium specificum recipiensi) inungi."

552 *Agenda Mindenensis dioecesis*, fol. xxix^{r}.

553 Ibid., fol. xxix^{v}.

554 Ibid., fol. xxxii^{v}–xxxv^{r}.

555 *Obsequiale Ratisponense*, fol. xxii^{r-v}.

556 *Obsequiale Brixinense* (Augsburg: Ratdolt, 1493), fol. lvi^{va-b}.

557 *Agenda seu benedictionale secundum vsum sancte ecclesie Patauiensis*, fol. xvi^{vb}.

Cunnigunde and Walburga.[558] Naumburg invoked Gothard, Gall, and Walburga.[559] Merseberg invoked a list of female saints, including Birgitta, Walburga, and Hedwig.[560] That manual also included formulas for anointing breast and shoulder blades.[561]

On the borders of the Empire, the see of Prague had a litany calling upon the nine choirs of angels, as well as Vitus, Wenceslaus, Adalbert, Ludmilla, and Ursula.[562] After laying hands on the sick person, the priest was to pray for the Lord's servant, male or female as required.[563] The formula for each anointing began differently from the usual *Per istam sanctam unctionem*, beginning *Ungo* instead. For example in the case of the eyes, "I anoint your eyes with sanctified oil" (*Ungo oculos tuos oleo sanctificato*) was to be used.[564]

The Olomuc manual began the litany with an admonition to the sick person (and possibly the bystanders) to invoke those saints who were named.[565] Among these were Wenceslaus, Wolfgang, Adalbret, Bernardinus, and Ludmilla.[566] The Bratislava manual listed Adalbert, Wenceslaus, Stanislas, and Hedwig, as well as Mary of Egypt, in its litany.[567] The Esztergom *Obsequiale* is notable only for distinguishing the prayers for the sick which must be said from those which were optional.[568]

In Scandinavia, the Danish church of Roskilde gave instructions for visiting the sick. Among these was an injunction that anointing was for a sick person whose life was in doubt. Anointing was to be done once in a year, even for one who fell ill more often. The manual limited the sacrament to three times in a lifetime, however often illness occurred.[569] The litany

558 *Obsequiale Eystetense* (Eichstätt: Reyser, 1488), fol. xxi[r–v].

559 *Agenda Numburgensis* (Naumburg: Saale, 1502), fol. xix[r].

560 *Agenda Merseburgensis* (Merseburg: Brandis, 1480), fol. 15r.

561 Ibid., fol. 18v–19r.

562 *Obsequiale Pragense*, fol. xxiiii[r], xxv[r], xxvi[r].

563 Ibid., fol. xxix[v]: "Hic imponat manum super infirmum. Vel [infirm]am. Respice domine famulum. vel [famul]am. tuum. vel [tu]am."

564 Ibid., fol. xxx[v]–xxxi[v].

565 *Agenda Olomucensis* (Nürnberg: Stuchs, 1498), fol. c iii[r]: "Postea admonendus infirmis vt inuocet hos sanctos qui nominadi sunt."

566 Ibid., fol. c [6][r–v].

567 *Liber agendarum rubricae dioecesis Wratislaviensis emendatus* (Wroclaw: J. P., 1510), fol. x[vb]–xi[rb].

568 *Obsequiale Strigoniense* (Nürnberg: Stuchs, ca. 1490), fol. c [i][v]: "Collecte sequentes de necessitate non sunt. sed si qui eas vult legere ex deuotione potest."

569 *Manuale curatorum secundum usum ecclesie Rosckildensis*, 26: "De sacra unctione est notandum quod infirmo amministrati non debet, nisi de vita desperatur, quia cura maxima debetur sacro oleo . . . item nota quod non debet infirmo sacri Olei unctio amministrari: nisi semel in anno. Licet sepius ille idem infirmatur. Nec etiam in tota uita. Licet inungi plus quam tribus uicibus. Licet sepissime ipsum contingat infirmari."

asked delivery of the patient from his or her illness (*ab egritudine sua*).[570] The prayers after the litany included "Lord God, Who spoke through the Apostle James" (*Domine deus qui per apostolum iacobum locutus est*). An accompanying antiphon said, "May God bring help to this sick person on his [her] bed of pain" (*Opem ferat huic infirmo deus super lectum doloris eius*).[571] Another antiphon begged God to "medicate him with spiritual medicine" (*medica eum spirituali medicamine*).[572] The rite of unction used the less common form, *Ungo te oleo sancto*.[573] The manual mentioned the possibility of confession and communion inserted between these prayers and anointing.[574]

In Sweden, the Linköping manual permitted hearing confession before saying the penitential psalms.[575] The litany mentioned Olaf, Canute, Eskil, Botvid, and Birgitta.[576] Anointing was available to the sick person who desired it (*Si desiderat inungi*).[577] The *Ungo te* form of words was to be used in the administration of extreme unction.[578] On the Iberian peninsula, a priest of Coimbra could celebrate Mass to aid the suffering person before going to the sickbed.[579] The Coimbra rite for anointing included vernacular instructions for placing oil on the loins of a man or the navel of a woman to relieve sins of lust.[580]

In Castile, the Toledo manual provided in Spanish for extreme unction following confession and communion, or a complete Mass (possibly at the bedside). In the latter case, the priest might conduct a procession to the sick person accompanied by other clerics with cross, holy water, and consecrated oil. His arrival was to follow the usual practice of greeting the household.[581] After saying a psalm, the priest was to proceed to anointing. Each repetition of the formula *Per istam sanctam vnctionem* was to be followed

570 Ibid., 28.

571 Ibid., 28 and 30: "Opem ferat huic infirmo deus super lectum doloris eius."

572 Ibid., 33.

573 Ibid., 33–35.

574 Ibid., 32.

575 *Manuale Lincopense* (Söderköping: In Edibus Olaui Vlrici, 1525): "Hic audiat confessionem, si sit necessaria. Deinde secuntur VII psalmi poenitentiales."

576 *Manuale Lincopense*, 73–74. Olaf, Eskil, Botvid, and Birgitta also appear in the *Manuale Aboense* (Halberstadt: Stuchs, 1522), fol. xviii^{r} and xix^{r}.

577 *Manuale Lincopense*, 78. The text inserted communion between prayers and anointing; see 79–80.

578 Ibid., 81–83.

579 *Manuale secundum consuetudinem almae Coimbricensis ecclesiae*, fol. xli^{r}: "Celebrata missa pro infirmo: veniat sacerdos cum clericis."

580 Ibid., fol. xvi^{r}: "Nos lombos aos omes et as femeas no vmbliguo. Per istam vnctionem et suam pijssimam misericordiam indulgeat tibi dominus quicquid peccasti per libidinem."

581 *Manuale seu baptisterium secundum vsum ecclesie Toletane*, fol. [e 7]$^{rb–va}$ and [e 8]^{rb}: "Celebrata missa pro infirmo veniat sacerdos cum clericis ceteris et ipse indutus alba et stola et precedunt ministi cruce et aqua

by a prayer and a psalm.[582] Unlike some instructions, Toledo expected the priest to anoint the loins.[583] After anointing, the priest was to say a litany invoking, among others, the Holy Innocents (*Omnes sancti innocentes*).[584]

The manual of Palencia was unusual in opening with a discussion of the sacraments. The largest part of the exposition of extreme unction was usual, including the emphasis on consecrated oil and the anointing of the senses. The text included the loins as a site of anointing on account of carnal delight.[585] The form of the sacrament was the familiar *Per istam sanctam vnictionem*.[586] The manual described the effect of the sacrament, "The effect is the cleansing of the mind; [and], insofar as is expedient, of his [or her] body too" (*Effectus vero est mentis sanatio: in quantum autem expedit ipsius etiam corporis*).[587] An important instruction was that the priest was to hasten to the sickbed so that the sick person would not die without the sacrament.[588] To that end he was to make himself aware of how sick parishioners were faring and move them to receive the sacrament.[589] The priest was to take holy water and his manual. If possible, other priests were to accompany him. However, their presence was not essential. Only the sick person's own priest, "the true minister of the sacrament" (*qui est verus minister huius sacramenti*) was essential for the rite.[590]

The priest was advised to anoint quickly if death was imminent, adding later what he had omitted.[591] If the new supply of holy oils had yet to arrive, he could use old oil of the sick without punishment for violating the canons.[592] The manual did prohibit anointing those condemned to death, extending the prohibition to those going to sea or to war, even if they requested it (*etiam si petierint*).[593] If group of sick persons were in a hospital

benedicta et oleo sacrato: ingressu autem domum: primum dicat sacerdos. Antiphona. Pax huic domui et omnibus habitantibus in ea."

582 *Manuale secundum vsum ecclesie Toletane*, fol. f [i]^{ra}–[f 6]^{va}.

583 Ibid., fol. [f 5]$^{ra–b}$: "Unctio ad lumbos . . . Oratio. Domine sancta pater omnipotens sempiterne deus qui fragilitatem conditione confirmas."

584 Ibid., fol. [f 7]^{va}–[f 8]^{rb}.

585 *Manuale secundum vsum sanctę Ecclesię Pallantinę*, fol. A ii^{v}: "in renibus propter delectationem ibidem vigentem."

586 Ibid., fol. ii^{v}–iii^{r}.

587 Ibid., fol. iii^{r}. A reference to the Epistle of James followed.

588 Ibid., fol. lxxvii^{v}: "cito pergat ne discedat infirmus sine hoc sacramento."

589 Ibid.: "Sit diligens sacerdos in suis infirmis visitandis, vt possit videre in qua dispositione existunt."

590 Ibid.

591 Ibid., fol. lxxviii^{r}: "antequam infirmus moriatur, vngat cito infirmum, et postea prosequatur totum quod ex officio desuerit."

592 Ibid.

593 Ibid., fol. lxxviii^{v}. Extreme unction also was not to be administered in a time of interdict because it was not essential, as was baptism.

room or in one home, the priest could anoint them in one rite (*cum vno officio tantum*).[594] The text was accompanied by instructions in Spanish.[595] One of these instructions required using a feather (*pluma*) to apply oil.[596]

The Astorga manual treated anointing as requiring preparation of vestments, cross, book, and holy water, as well as oil of the sick, a small rod, and a bit of linen to use in unction.[597] The priest was to attempt interrogation of the sick person about any sins just remembered (*meminit*). Warnings against the devil's temptations were to be accompanied by reminders of divine mercy. If death was imminent, the priest was to omit psalms and prayers, proceeding to anointing, using the common form of the words.[598] The priest was to use the penitential psalms and a litany, invoking Leander, Isidore, and Ildefonso.[599] The instructions referred to anointing a woman on the navel and a man on the loins. Each actual anointing was to be followed by a long prayer.[600] The priest could do extra anointing where the sick person hurt most (*donde mas se agrauiare*) before concluding the rite with the sprinkling of holy water.[601]

The Salamanca manual gave instructions for extreme unction similar to those from Astorga. An exception is a passage bridging viaticum and anointing, which states that it was better, if the sick person was able to understand instructions, that he or she be admonished to raise the mind to the creator devoutly to receive extreme unction.[602] The instructions indicated who was or was not to receive the sacrament, including its omission in a time of interdict.[603] The ritual was similar to that in other Spanish manuals, including psalms and prayers after the anointing of each sense or body location.[604] Among these acts was anointing on or near men's loins

594 Ibid., fol. lxxix^v^.

595 See, e.g., ibid., fol. lxxx^r^.

596 Ibid., fol. lxxxix^v^.

597 *Manuale secundum consuetudenem Astoricensis ecclesie* (León, 1526), fol. lxi^r^: "Pro administratione isto sancto sacramento preparentur superpelitium / stola / crux / liber et aqua benedicta."

598 Ibid., fol. lxi^r–v^: "Si infirmus agonizauerit intantum quod dubitetur de eius vitae pretermisiis psalmis omnibus et orationibus: vngatur cum illis orationibus videlicet Per istam sanctam vnctionem."

599 Ibid., fol. lxiii^vb^.

600 Ibid., fol. lxv^v^: "Et mulieres in vmbilico. Et viri in lumbis." For the prayers, see ibid., fol. lxv^v^–lvii^r^, with a rubric at fol. lxvii^r^: "Hic ponatur oleum hominibus in lumbis et mulieribus in vmbilico" with the following prayer referring to sins committed "per ardorem libidinis."

601 Ibid., fol. lxvii^r^.

602 *Manuale secundum consuetudinem alme ecclesie Salamanticense*, fol. xxxix^v^: "immo Melius est. quod infirmus intelligat: et moneatur a saccerdote: vt mentem eleuet ad suum creatorem: et quod attinet et deuote recipiat sacramentum vnctionis."

603 Ibid., including an instruction to procede directly to anointing if death appeared to be imminent.

604 Ibid., fol. xxxix^v^–xlviii^r^. The Calahorra manual only gave the forms of the basic rite without the additional prayers and psalms; see *Manuale secundum consuetudinem Calagurritanensis et Calceatensis ecclesiarum*, fol. lxv^v^–lxvi^r^, where a formula for anointing the breast (*in pectore*) was included.

and a women's navels on account of lust, or above it out of respect.[605] The litany invoked Sts. Leander, Isidore, Ildefonso, Leocadia of Toledo, and Eulalia of Barcelona.[606]

In the lands of the crown of Aragon the Urgell manual opened with prayers and the possibility of confession. Then it moved to anointing, done with the thumb *(police)* or a rod in the form of a cross, where each spot is cleansed with cloth.[607] The priest anointed the senses as well as the breast, "on account of the ardor of the libido" (*per ardorem libidinis*), and the feet.[608] The rite included full absolution granted by divine and ecclesiastical authority.[609] The text concluded with instructions to abridge the rite on account of the nearness of death.[610] A prayer to be said when a person was in agony and nearing death followed.[611]

The Barcelona *Ordinarium* provided an exhortation of the sick person in the vernacular, before confession.[612] The litany invoked Eulalia, a local saint.[613] The text permitted a priest to go directly to anointing if death appeared to be imminent, adding omitted prayers later, if possible.[614] The instructions also said anointing the breast (*pectus*) was to mention pardon for lust and carnal thoughts of the heart.[615]

The Majorca *Ordinarium* emphasized Marian devotion. On the way to the sick, the priest and his associates were to say (*sotto voce*) the *Canticum graduum beatae Mariae*.[616] If time permitted, they could say the office of the Virgin or some other office.[617] The litany included the Spanish martyr

605 *Manuale secundum consuetudinem alme ecclesie Salamanticense*, fol. xlvi^{v}: "Septima vnctio in lumbis: vel Paulo inferius vel in latere si aliter commode non potest fieri: vel in umbilico si fuerit femina; vel paulo superius propter honestatem."

606 Ibid., fol. xliv^{v}–l^{r}.

607 *Ordinarium sacramentorum benedictionum et aliarum rerum*, fol. cxxi^{v}: "et statim in qualibet vnctione terga team cum bombice siue coto: vel stupa."

608 Ibid., fol. cxxi^{v}–cxxii^{r}.

609 Ibid., fol. cxxiiii^{v}: "Et absoluetur plenaria a pena et a culpa. Auctoritate omnipotentis dei: et eius apostolorum Petri et Pauli: et sancta romane ecclesie: ac summi pontificis domini nostri pape."

610 Ibid., fol. cxxiiii^{v}–cxxv^{r}.

611 Ibid., fol. cxxv^{r-v}: "Sequens oratio debet dici quando infirmus est in agonia: et desperatur de eius vita. Proficiscere anima de hoc mundo."

612 *Ordinarium Barcinonense*, fol. u ii^{r}–[u 3]^{r}. An exhortation to adore the cross and a profession of belief also were provided in Catalan; see fol. v ii^{r-v}.

613 Ibid., fol. [u 4]^{ra}: "Sancta Eulalia. Ora."

614 Ibid., fol. v i^{v}: "Nota quod si infirmus fuerit in tali dispositione quod timeatur ipsum mori antequam peruenires ad vnctionem: tunc omnibus dimissis vngas illum primo. Et postea procede. et dic omnia alia: si tempus ille datum fuerit."

615 Ibid., fol. [v 3]^{v}: "Per ardorem libidinis siue etiam per preuas cogitationes cordis."

616 In this case, the *Maginificat.*

617 *Ordinarium de administratione sacramentorum cum pluribus additionibus adeo necessariis secundum ritum alme sedis maioriensis*, fol. lv^{r}: "et eundo ad domum egrotantis exeundo ab ecclesia submissa voce

Cucufas.[618] These instructions included anointing the breast against sexual sins.[619] The rite concluded with words of comfort in Catalan and a grant of thirty days' indulgence for those who accompanied the priest.[620]

The Cartagena manual, following Franciscan theology, states that extreme unction is "the final cure" of venial sins.[621] The sacrament was administered to a penitent sick person with oil "consecrated by a bishop" (*ab Episcopo consecrato*), anointing body parts while saying the appropriate words, a teaching summarized at the beginning of the rite as "the way of anointing" (*Modus vngendi*).[622] A priest was to carry oil of the sick "covered" (*copertum*) and "reverently in the right hand" (*in dextra reuerenter*). Holy water and a lantern were to precede, especially at night (*de nocte*). On the way to the sick person, the priest was to recite psalms.[623] The breast was anointed on account of lustful thoughts of the heart (*per prauas cordis cogitationes*).[624] The litany mentioned the holy physicians Cosmas and Damian, as well as Leander, Isidore, Ildefonso, and Eulalia.[625] It also asked for deliverance on the day of judgment.[626] The rite concluded with absolution, applying any indulgences, and a reading from the Gospel of Mark (16:14–20).[627] Further instructions said that a sick person *in tali agone* was to confess and be absolved, with any indulgences added, before anointing.[628] If the patient died between acts of anointing, the rite was to cease, followed by prayers for the dead.[629]

---

cum suis socijs decant. Canticum gradum beate marie et si opus fuerit dicatur officium beate marie eundo et redeundo vel de alio officio vti apparebit sacerdotis ministranti dictum sacramentum."

618 Ibid., fol. lvi^{rb}.

619 Ibid., fol. lix^{v}–lx^{r}: "Per cogitatum ac etiam ardorem libidinis in pectore."

620 Ibid., fol. lxii^{r}.

621 *Ordinarium manuale de ministratione sacramentorum secundum consuetudinem ecclesię Carthaginensis* (Granada, 1545), fol. iv^{v}: "ex institutione diuina efficaciter significans curationem finale venialium." See also fol. v^{r}.

622 Ibid., fol. lxxxix^{v}: "Sequitur sacramentum extreme vnctionis: quod est vnctio hominis inf[i]rmi pęnitentis in determinatis partibus corporis cum oleo ab episcopo consecrato: ministrata a sacerdote cum intentione debita certa verba proferente: que ex institutione diuina efficaciter signant finale curationem venialium." See also fol. iv^{v} and v^{r}.

623 Ibid., fol. lxxxix^{v}.

624 Ibid., fol. lxxxxvii$^{r–v}$.

625 Ibid., fol. lxxxxviii^{r}–lxxxix^{r}.

626 Ibid., fol. lxxxxix^{v}: "In die iudicij. Libera eum domine."

627 Ibid., fol. ci^{r}–cii^{v}.

628 Ibid., fol. cii^{v}.

629 Ibid.: "si infirmus post primam et secundam vnctionem decesserit / tunc cesset ab vnctione / et dicattur vnum responsorium pro defunctis cum versu et oratione." Instructions in case the priest died mid-rite followed.

5

THE HOUR OF DEATH

he last line of an antiphon sometimes sung at Compline reads: *amarae morti ne tradas nos.*[1] This can be translated as "Do not deliver us to bitter death." The text begins with the familiar sentiment, "In the midst of life we are in death" (*media vita in morte sumus*). Vincent of Beauvais tied the inevitability of death to birth from a woman's womb. Knowledge of such an origin and the inevitability of death was supposed to inspire preparation through devout meditation and patience in times of affliction. Vincent tied the origins of this practice not just to scripture and to a Christian saint, Basil of Caesarea, but also to Plato and Pythagoras.[2] He also offered thoughts on the misery of human life and the condition of the body after death.[3]

Both devout clergy and pious laity were known to contemplate the coming of death, "the king of terrors." However, recently scholarship

1 *Breviarium ad usum insignis Ecclesie Eboracensis* (London: Surtees Society, 1880), 1:328.

2 *Speculum historiale Vincentii* (Venice: Liechtenstein, 1494), fol. 397ra: "Tria quippe in humano corpore consideranda sunt: origo sordida vita misera: mors necessaria. i. ex necessitate contingens. Homo enim noster interior de immundo semine conceptus est. ad laborem natus. Velit nolit moriturus . . . Mortem semper ad omnium pendere oculos: et ideo semper habendam ab omnibus pre oculis semperque meditandam. sicut scriptum est in ecclesiastico. Memorare nouissima tua. etc. In huius autem meditatione plato et Pythagoras et basilius noster christianorum philosophus sapientiam posuerunt."

3 Ibid., fol. 397ra–b.

has argued that vigilant preparedness rather than outright fear governed contemplation of life's last scene.[4] This preparation included prayers for the dying and measures to help the departed gain release from Purgatory, which often was presented as a world of temporary pain, a middle estate between Heaven and Hell. In Purgatory those who were not damnably wicked but needed to have imperfections removed were cleansed.[5] Belief in that middle state and the desire to help friends and family escape from it governed practices as diverse as deathbed penance, restoration of ill-gotten gains, and the gaining of indulgences, whether for oneself or the beloved deceased.[6] In addition, there was a long-standing belief that angels and demons contested over the soul of a dying person, hoping to claim the individual for Heaven or Hell.[7]

PREPARATION FOR DEATH

A priest called to give extreme unction at a sickbed often found the patient near death, and he was expected to comfort that person in the final hour. The dying person was expected to respond to these rites by making a last affirmation of faith.[8] However, the priest, finding the patient near death, could use a short form of each sacrament, especially extreme unction. Likewise, the sufferer might not be lucid, or at least might be deprived of the power of speech. In such cases, the priest was expected to rely on the testimony of those attending at the sickbed to testify to the sick person's penitence. They were asked to aid his or her passage to the afterlife by prayers, alms, and fasting.[9]

More was expected of the dying than just an affirmation of faith. Any person dying without a will already prepared was expected to make one

4 Robert W. Shaffern, "Death and the Afterlife in the Middle Ages," in *The Routledge History of Medieval Christianity 1050–1500*, ed. R. N. Swanson (London: Routledge, 2015), 173–84, at 173.

5 For an image of souls in Purgatory, see Roger S. Weick, *Time Sanctified: The Book of Hours in Medieval Art and Life* (New York: Braziller, 1988), 127, fig. 113b.

6 Shaffern, "Death and the Afterlife in the Middle Ages," 173–80. On the origins of Purgatory, see Jacques Le Goff, *The Birth of Purgatory* (Chicago: University of Chicago Press, 1986), and James B. Gould, *Understanding Prayer for the Dead: Its Foundation in History and Logic* (Eugene, OR: Wipf and Stock, 2016).

7 Means, *Penance in Medieval Europe*, 83 and 85.

8 Swanson, *Religion and Devotion in Europe*, 32.

9 This practice was encouraged by Hostiensis; see *Summa aurea*, 1830–31. See also Shaffern, "Death and the Afterlife in the Middle Ages," 181.

at the last, remembering the poor in the disposition of property.[10] These benefactions could extend beyond alms to the support of charitable institutions. For example, Nicholas of Cusa's visitation of the cathedral chapter in Brixen involved asking about the care of the sick in the local hospital they supported.[11] His hospital in Bernkastel-Kues hosted elderly men.[12] Medieval hospitals provided care of souls, at least by setting religious pictures in chapels and refectories.[13]

Apart from benefactions, a dying person was expected to make restitution of ill-gotten gains toward salvation and release from Purgatory. Thus, a manifest usurer had to provide for restoration of illicit profit.[14] Those whose gains came from robbery and extortion also could offer restitution to those they harmed, possibly under clerical pressure.[15] The Regensburg manual permitted the confessor of a sick person to ask about making restitution.[16] (The obligation of restitution was extended eventually to the New World. Bartolomé de Las Casas used the doctrine of restitution to pressure conquistadors to give back to indigenous populations any ill-gotten gains.)[17] Both restitution and testamentary benefactions were expected the help a soul avoid Hell and shorten the time spent in Purgatory. Antoninus of Florence treated the souls in Purgatory as still belonging to the Church Militant and thus able to be helped by others' prayers, although unable to

10 Duffy, *The Stripping of the Altars*, 322–23; *Concilia Germaniae* 5:193 (Salzburg, 1420). Andreas Escobar, *Lumen confessorum*, fol. 9rb, expected the priest to urge making a will, including leaving alms for the good of the soul.

11 *Acta Cusana* 2/2, ed. Johannes Helmrath and Thomas Woelki (Hamburg: Meiner, 2016), 646–47 (no. 3861), "De hospitali Brixiensi." Cusanus added mention of his hospital at Kues at 647.

12 Meike Hensel-Grobe, "Funktion und Funktionalisierung: Das St. Nikolaus-Hospital in Kues und die Erzbischöfe von Trier im 15. Jahrhundert," in *Funktions- und Strukturwandel spätmittelalterlicher Hospitäler im europäischen Vergleich*, ed. Michael Matheus (Stuttgart: Steiner, 2005), 195–212.

13 For the Eastbridge Hospital of St. Thomas the Martyr, Canterbury, see *A History of the County of Kent*, ed. William Page (London: Victoria County History, 1926), 2:209–16. For the Hôtel-Dieu, Beaunne, with its altarpiece depicting the Last Judgment, see Barbara Lane, "*Requiem aeternam dona eis*: The Beaune *Last Judgment* and the Mass of the Dead," *Simiolus: Netherlands Quarterly for the History of Art* 19 (1989): 166–80.

14 Trexler, *Synodal Law*, 279–83.

15 See, e.g., the will of Francesco di Giovanni Romani Bonaventurae in James A. Palmer, *The Virtues of Economy: Governance, Power and Piety in Late Medieval Rome* (Ithaca, NY: Cornell University Press, 2019), 41–68.

16 *Obsequiale Ratisponense*, fol. xxx^r^. The absolution of excommunicates was included in the Regensburg instructions; see fol. xxxi^v^–xxxiii^v^.

17 *To Heaven or to Hell: Bartolomé de Las Casas's "Confessionario,"* ed. David Thomas Orique (University Park: Pennsylvania State University Press, 2018); *The Directory for Confessors 1585: Implementing the Catholic Reformation in New Spain*, ed. Stafford Poole (Norman: University of Oklahoma Press, 2015), 13–14 and 131.

help themselves. The prayers of living members of Christ were to help such persons more swiftly join the Church Triumphant.[18]

The provision of prayers for the dead became institutionalized. Aside from benefactions to churches and religious houses, a dying person with sufficient means might endow a chapel or, as in England, a chantry to guarantee the celebration of masses benefitting the founders, their kin, and their friends. Even those who could not fund such a foundation could have Mass celebrated on the anniversaries of their deaths.[19] These arrangements reflected not just efforts at commemoration and relief from purgatorial pains but participation in a spiritual economy that treated grace almost as a quantity that could be computed toward both spiritual and temporal ends.[20]

This was only one of the ways in which preparation of the soul for death was promoted. Later medieval art included images of corpses on *transi* tombs, sometimes with the living person being depicted above and the decaying corpse below.[21] Other tombs only showed the cadaver.[22] Image cycles of the dance of death or *danse macabre* showed King Death leading away men and women of all life's estates, greatest to least.[23] At least one of these works was composed by Jean Gerson. Each person was addressed by Death, beginning with the pope and the emperor, and including an infant. Included among these was a physician, who admitted that there was no remedy for death.[24] Gerson concluded that many lived as though "no death would follow" (*mors nulla sequitur*). However, the wise lived as if "Hell's dread swamp" was not to be feared.[25] Images of the three living

18 *Sancti Antonini de Florentia ordinis Praedicatorum summa theologica*, 3:1619: "Nam tales quum decedentes ub gratia sint membra ecclesiae, & viva ex gratia capacia nostrorum suffragiorum, quia non sunt in gloria, sed poena, nec per opera sua valeant satisfacere, subsidium habere possunt a nobis . . . Quam ergo sint illi de purgatorio viva membra, militantis ecclesiae, ex bonis, quae fiunt fidelibus, qui sunt corpus mysticum Christi, inde recipiunt suffragium sublevationis poena, vel liberationis citioris."

19 Palmer, *Virtues of Economy*, 81 and 103–32; K. L. Wood-Leigh, *Perpetual Chantries in Britain* (Cambridge: Cambridge University Press, 1965).

20 Jacques Chiffoleau, *La comptabilité de la au-delà: les hommes, la mort et la religion dans la region d'Avignon à la fin du Moyen Âge vers 1320–vers 1480* (Paris: Albin Michel, 2011).

21 Paul Binski, *Medieval Death: Ritual and Representation* (Ithaca, NY: Cornell University Press, 1996), 139–52; Philippe Ariès, *The Hour of Our Death: The Classic History of Western Attitude Toward Death over the Last One Thousand Years*, trans. Helen Weaver (New York: Vintage Books, 2000), 113–14.

22 Rubin, *Corpus Christi*, 307–8.

23 Some of these texts focused entirely on men or women; see *Danse Macabre of Women: Ms. Fr. 995 of the Bibliothèque Nationale*, ed. Ann Tukey Harrison (Kent, OH: Kent State University Press, 1994); William M. Ivins, Jr., *The Dance of Death Printed at Paris in 1490: A Reproduction Made from the Copy in the Lessing J. Rosenwald Collection* (Washington, DC: Library of Congress, 1945).

24 Gerson, *Oeuvres completes*, 7:286–301, at 295: "Contra la mort n'a medicine."

25 Ibid., 7:301: "Sic igitur cuncti sapientes vivere certent Ut nihil inferni sit metuenda palus."

and the three dead had the three live persons confronted by three corpses, showing them their fate.[26] However, the most elaborate of these pictures seem to undermine this message by providing rich images of the living in contrast with corpses and skeletons, an ostentatious form of humility.[27]

Among preparations for death, one was devout meditation, a genre known at least from the time of Bonaventure and carried over by Martin Luther into Protestantism.[28] Some images in books of hours present a devil and an angel contesting the fate of a dying person, usually depicted as male, at the deathbed.[29] An exception, found in the Coëtivy Hours shows a woman on her deathbed (fig. 19) and the Virgin receiving her soul (fig. 20).[30] Altarpieces depicting the sacraments also show a dying man receiving extreme unction.[31]

A good death required accepting angelic aid in the last hour, while rejecting the devil's temptation to despair. Texts for such meditations might be anonymous or composed by a known person like Henry Suso or Thomas Hoccleve. Among the topics on which meditation might be done were the signs of imminent death. Individuals might also look at an image of St. Christopher in the nearest church in hope of avoiding sudden death on that day.[32]

Devout persons might also read a version of the *Ars moriendi* or *Art of Dying Well*. These texts were supposed to help with avoiding *mors improvisa*, unforeseen death, through spiritual preparation.[33] Some are anonymous; but a brief *Ars moriendi*, called the *Medecine de l'ame*, was composed in French by Jean Gerson in the early fifteenth century. It provided an exhortation to remember mortality, bearing the pain of illness and the

26 Binski, *Medieval Death*, 134–38, plate VIII.

27 Ashby Kinch, *Imago Mortis: Mediating Images of Death in Late Medieval Culture* (Leiden: Brill, 2013), 208.

28 Mark Chinca, *Meditating Death in Medieval and Early Modern Devotional Writing* (Oxford: Oxford University Press, 2020).

29 For a picture of a man receiving viaticum, see Weick, *Time Sanctified*, 125, fig. 109. The most common exception was the dormition of the Virgin.

30 Richard Gameson and Catherine Nicholson with Andrew Beeby, "The Admiral, the Virgin, and the Spectrometer: Observations on the Coëtivy Hours (Dublin, Chester Beatty Library MS W082)," *Gesta* 59 (2020): 202–31, at 214 and 216.

31 *L'héritage de Rogier van der Weyden*, ed. Véronique Bücken and Griet Steyaert (Brussels: Uitgeverij Lannoo, 2013), 82 and 151.

32 Kinch, *Imago Mortis*, 7–9, 19, 35–68.

33 Roger Chartier, "Les arts de mourir (1450–1600)," *Annales: Economies, Sociétés, Civilisations* 31 (1976): 51–75; Mary Catherine O'Connor, *The Art of Dying Well: The Development of the Ars moriendi* (New York: Columbia University Press, 1942); Duffy, *Stripping of the Altars*, 310–15. Images of St. Michael and Satan contesting for possession of a dying person's soul also appeared in art; see Ariès, *Hour of Our Death*, 115.

sorrow of death with patience toward purification of the soul. The exhortation was followed by interrogations, with the priest inquiring and the sick person responding. He or she was to affirm the true faith and seek pardon for sins. The latter part of the text suggests prayers to God, the Virgin, angels, and saints, especially a holy person, male or female, to whom the sick person had particular devotion. The last part was concerned with the sacraments, especially his or her "last sacrament" (*son derrain sacrement*), extreme unction, and the "holy sacrament of the altar" (*le saint sacrement de l'autel*). Practical advice to priests included instructions on dealing with a person who had lost the use of speech, presenting a crucifix to contemplate and mentioning the priority of confession over medicine for the body, a tacit reference to *Cum infirmitas*.[34]

A shorter form of *Ars moriendi* addressed the four last things: death, burial, Hell, and Heaven, both feared torments and hoped for joys. An English translation by Anthony Woodville, from a French version of a Latin tract by Denys the Carthusian, reads: "What thing is more horrible than dethe." The text recommended despising worldly goods and "retorne vnto his creator." The text offered lessons in humility and meekness, reminding readers how great men of the past, including Julius Caesar and "the mighty Sampson," died.[35]

Books of hours often included the Office of the Dead with associated images of the deathbed, requiem services, and burial. The devout were to pray these texts with an eye toward the welfare of past persons and their own future fate.[36] A commendation of souls could be added to the Office, especially "on the day of the commemoration of souls" (*in die commemorationis animarum*).[37] Parish churches, like All Saints, Bristol, contained the tombs of prominent parishioners with provisions in their wills for commemorative masses and prayers to help deliver their souls from Purgatory.

34 *Manuale ad usum Parisiensem* (Paris: Mauraud, 1497), fol. o ii^{rb}–[o 5]^{va}; Gerson, *Oeuvres completes*, 7:301–407, at 407: "le pape commande par expresse decretalle a ung chascun medecin qu'il ne ordonne point medicine au malade lequel il visite, se non que par avant il ait exhorté le malade d'appeller le medecin de l'ame, c'est assavoir son confesseur." Gerson added advice that hospitals should see to the welfare of the souls of their patients. A *De scientia bonae mortis* attributed to Jean Gerson appears in University of Pennsylvania Ms. Codex 750, fol. 31r–37v.

35 *The Devil's Mortal Weapons: An Anthology of Late Medieval and Protestant Vernacular Theology and Popular Culture*, ed. Joanna Miles (Toronto: PIMS, 2018), 167–76. See Duffy, *Stripping of the Altars*, 308–09; Franco Mormando, "What Happens to Us When We Die? Bernardino of Siena on 'The Four Last Things,'" in *Death and Dying in the Middle Ages*, ed. Edelgard E. DuBruck and Barbara I. Gusick (New York: Lang, 1999), 109–42.

36 Wieck, *Time Sanctified*, 124–48; Wieck, "The Death Desired: Books of Hours and the Medieval Funeral," in *Death and Dying in the Middle Ages*, 431–76.

37 *Manuale seu agenda ad usum Remensem* (Reims, ca. 1500), fol. F[iv]^{r}–+[x]^{v}.

The prayers might be offered for them by the parish clergy or by chantry priests. (It is less clear what prayers were offered for the poor after their burials. However, they may have been included on a parish's bede-roll toward common prayers.)[38]

Many of the dead in crowded urban cemeteries—those buried and then dug up to make room for fresh internments—ended up as bones in charnel houses. Found within cities, these might be visited by processions through cemeteries or have chapels serving as sites of devout prayer and reflection, in all cases serving as an evident *memento mori*.[39] Not everyone was pious, even in the face of death. Some persons might use charms or even sacred things to extend life. Likewise, pregnant women might use prayer girdles and other means to ease childbirth and avoid dying while delivering a child.[40] However, no one could avoid their mortality.

Some objects survive from the Middle Ages, the sixteenth century, and later centuries designed to serve as examples of *memento mori*, physical reminders of mortality visible to those unable to read an *ars moriendi* or disinclined to do so. Among these objects are *Pater noster* beads in shapes such as skulls. There also are pendants with *memento mori* themes. These served both as luxury objects and reminders of mortality.[41] Even books of conduct literature could include reminders of mortality and the uncertainty of the hour of death, as well as the need to focus on higher things.[42]

Beguines sometimes played a role in comforting the dying.[43] Medieval confraternities often had chaplains whose duties included praying for deceased members. The members of such societies made preparations to support ailing brothers and guarantee them a proper burial.[44] Similarly,

38 Burgess, *The Right Ordering of Souls*, 83–162. See Michael M. Sheehan, "English Wills and the Records of the Ecclesiastical and Civil Jurisdictions," *Journal of Medieval History* 14 (1988): 3–12. On chantries, see Wood-Leigh, *Perpetual Chantries*. The Paris statutes wanted a priest present when a will was made; see Mansi 22:680. On bede-rolls, see Shaffern, "Death and the Afterlife in the Middle Ages," 183.

39 Katherine M. Boivin, "Two-story Charnel House and the Space of Death in the Medieval City," in *Picturing Death 1200–1600*, ed. Stephen Perkinson and Noa Turel (Leiden: Brill, 2021), 79–103.

40 E. Bozoky, *Charmes et prières apotropaïques* (Turnhout: Brepols, 2003); Don C. Skemer, *Binding Words. Textual Amulets in the Middle Ages* (University Park: Pennsylvania State University Press, 2006).

41 *Museum Schnütgen: A Survey of the Collection* (ed. Woelk and Beer), 362–65 and 392–93. Stephen Perkinson, "Death Commodified: Macabre Imagery on Luxury Objects, c. 1500," in *Picturing Death 1200–1600*, 278–307, at 291–93 and 295–96.

42 *The Babees' Book: Medieval Manners for the Young*, trans. Edith Rickert and L. J. Naylor (Cambridge: Middle English Series, 2000), 25 and 66.

43 Christine Guideta, "The Role of the Beguines in Caring for the Ill, the Dying and the Dead," in *Death and Dying in the Middle Ages*, 51–72.

44 Richard C. Trexler, *Public Life in Renaissance Florence* (Ithaca, NY: Cornell University Press, 1980), 33, 252–56, 406; Burgess, *Right Ordering of Souls*, 72; Louisa Foroughi, "'To sey or thinke otherwise':

the four nations of the University of Paris had regular liturgical services for deceased benefactors and colleagues.[45]

THE DEATHBED

As early as Carolingian times, hospitals existed for "the poor and the sick," who might die in their assigned beds.[46] The burgeoning economy of the twelfth and thirteenth centuries supported many more such hospitals for the sick or elderly, founded as acts of charity or penance.[47] Confraternities often sponsored hospitals, which had to bury deceased inmates and occasionally pilgrims who died in their care.[48] Moreover, a confraternity in Bologna both comforted those condemned to death and ran a hospital for the dying.[49] Confraternities also staged plays to comfort those faced with thoughts of death.[50] However, sick persons usually died in their own beds at home. Medieval art usually depicted a man, probably one with wealth and social standing, in that role, receiving extreme unction. Often acolytes, wives, and friends appeared in these scenes as witnesses. Family and friends might indeed gather for the last scene of a life; but it was the priest who was expected to provide the comforts and consolation of prayers, including the "Commendation of the soul" (*Commendatio animae*) to be said at the deathbed.[51] The 836 Council of Aachen expected the priest to combine commendation of the soul with last communion and Christian burial.[52] Even where a priest was not able to be present at a deathbed, he

Ordinary Theology and Facing Death in Late Medieval Norwich," *Religions* 2 (2018); available at doi.org/10.3390/rel9030067.

45 William J. Courtenay, *Rituals for the Dead: Religion and Community in the Medieval University of Paris* (Notre Dame, IN: University of Notre Dame Press, 2019).

46 MGH *Capitula regum Francorum, nova series* 1, 1:552–53.

47 Adam J. Davis, *The Medieval Economy of Salvation: Charity, Commerce and the Rise of the Hospital* (Ithaca, NY: Cornell University Press, 2019).

48 David M. D'Andrea, *Civic Christianity in Renaissance Italy: The Hospital of Treviso, 1400–1530* (Rochester, NY: University of Rochester Press, 2007), 81.

49 Gioia Filocamo, "Sin, Emotions and Sounds: Dealing with Death in the *Laudario* of the Confraternity of Santa Maria della Morte," in *Renaissance Religions: Modes and Meanings in History*, ed. Peter Howard, Nicholas Terpstra, and Riccardo Saccenti (Turnhout: Brepols, 2021), 231–47.

50 Kathleen Falvey, "Scaffold and Stage: Comforting Rituals and Dramatic Traditions in Late Medieval and Renaissance Italy," in *The Art of Executing Well* (ed. Terpstra), 13–30.

51 The Commendation occasionally followed the Office of the Dead in books of hours; see Wieck, *Time Sanctified*, 131 and 173.

52 MGH *Concilia* II, pt. 2, 712: "Denique si finem urgentem perspexerit, commendet animam Christianum domino Deo suo more sacerdotali cum acceptatione sacrae communionis, corpus sepulturae, non ut mos gentilium, sed sicut Christianorum."

was expected, according to the Paris statutes, to "absolve" a parishioner with psalms and prayers appropriate to the deceased.[53]

The faithful were expected to be prepared for death even before the priest came. One text provided six things the dying might find "very necessary and useful at the end of life" (*multum necessaria et utilia in fine vite*). They were to turn their thoughts away from the world, be neither presumptuous nor despairing, offer themselves as a living sacrifice, bewail past sins, approach death as a share in Christ's passion, and avoid the temptations offered by the devil.[54] John of Freiburg warned those surrounding a deathbed not to hasten the person's death. Such actions required absolution by the bishop.[55] The Apostolic Penitentiary said that a person who died before the priest could visit and administer the sacraments was to receive a Christian burial.[56]

We have some accounts of deathbed administration of the sacraments. Most of these are edifying anecdotes, like those from the necrology of Corpus Domini, Venice. Some of these death notices simply referred to a sister having received "the sacraments." Other sisters, however, were reported to have been "almost rapt" after receiving viaticum. Sister Felicitas Buono saw "a lovely child," the Christ child, in the opened tabernacle shortly before falling terminally ill.[57] Likewise, the beguine Marie d'Oigny was reported to have kept a cheerful and exalted face (*hilaritatem et exaltantis faciem*) despite death's pain. Only when the corpse was washed was it discovered how she had been affected by fasting and bodily ailments. A Cistercian monk was mentioned as a witness to the sister's passing.[58] A narrative of the death of Hathumoda, first abbess of Gandersheim, recounts her reception of anointing and viaticum, as well as "final reconciliation" and her kissing the cross. This edifying scene was accompanied by suitable

53 Mansi 22:681: "Sacerdotes audito parochiarorum suorum obitu, statim absolvent eos cum psalmis pro defunctis, & collecta." Jean Gerson called this absolution "by way of supplication" (*per modum deprecationis*); see *Oeuvres completes*, ed. Palémon Glorieux, 10 vols. (Paris: Desclée, 1960–73), 9:643–44.

54 University of Pennsylvania Ms. Codex 750, fol. 39v–41v. A similar text follows at fol. 41v–43r.

55 See, e.g., Johannes de Friburgo, *Summa confessorum* (Augsburg: Zainer, 1471) II, t. 1, q. 10: "Pone aliqui custodientes laborantem in extremis de consilio alicuius transtulerunt vel verterunt ipsum super aliud latus vt citius moreretur."

56 *Repertorium poenitentiariae Germanicum* (ed. Schmugge), vol. 6, no. 3562.

57 Bartolomea Riccoboni, *Life and Death in a Venetian Convent: The Chronicle and Necrology of Corpus Domini, 1395–1436*, trans. Daniel Bornstein (Chicago: University of Chicago Press, 2000), 19, 64–82, 93, 97.

58 *Speculum historiale Vincentii*, fol. 406rb.

psalms, litanies, and prayers.[59] Priests were not supposed to enter nuns' cloisters, but Birgittine priests were permitted to enter the nuns' house to administer last rites.[60]

The passing of Reginald of Orléans, a leading figure in the early Dominican order, according to the friars' hagiography, was a good death; but it involved an unusual approach to the rite of anointing. According to Rodrigo de Cerratto, when Reginald was offered extreme unction, he replied that he did not need it. The Virgin Mary had anointed him on his sickbed in Rome some years before while St. Dominic prayed for him. This anointing removed any stirring of lustful desire. However, Fra Reginald agreed to receive last anointing to set a good example for others.[61]

There are occasional human dramas on record. When the Florentine Giovanni Morelli lost his son Alberto at age nine without his receiving sacramental comfort, the bereaved father felt guilty. Later, when his younger son, Antoniotto, died, Giovanni could take a little comfort from the fact that this son died "confessed, communed, and oiled."[62] The Florentine merchant Gregorio Dati was more edified by the death of Ginevra, his third wife, who was comforted by the reception of the sacraments and a papal letter absolving her sins. She expired at the hour of Christ's death on the cross, probably the liturgical hour of Nones.[63] In 1497, John Dalton, a merchant of Hull, expressed on his deathbed a wish to die repentant in the unity of the Church.[64] So did the Norwich widow Avelyne Carter in 1508.[65]

Less edifying was the death of Alice Gysbye of London. The priest delayed in an ale house and arrived when she no longer was coherent. He showed her the host, and her neighbors called for her to speak. None of this availed.[66] The neighbors, who expected an edifying scene, with Alice displaying her orthodoxy and trust in Christ, were disappointed.[67]

59 Frederick S. Paxton, "Agnes of Corvey's Account of the Death of Hathumoda, First Abbess of Gandersheim," in *Medieval Christianity in Practice*, ed. Miri Rubin (Princeton, NJ: Princeton University Press, 2009), 53–63.

60 Birgitta Fritz, "The History and Spiritual Life of Vadstena Abbey," in *A Companion to Birgitta of Sweden and Her Legacy in the Later Middle Ages*, ed. Maria H. Oen (Leiden: Brill, 2019), 132–58, at 140. Sisters also were permitted to tend ailing brothers in their house.

61 Thomas M. Izbicki, "The Vision of Reginald of Orléans and the Shaping of Dominican Identity," *Memorie Domenicane* 87 (2017): 339–59, at 347.

62 Trexler, *Public Life in Renaissance Florence*, 172–74 and 186.

63 Bornstein, "Administering the Sacraments," 135–36.

64 Robert W. Shaffern, "Death and the Afterlife in the Middle Ages," 172–84, at 182; Duffy, *Stripping of the Altars*, 324.

65 Duffy, *Stripping of the Altars*, 321.

66 Ibid., 322.

67 Ibid., 323–27.

Something worse, deathbed refusal of the sacraments, was depicted in the Taymouth Hours. One image shows a demon turning an ailing merchant away from a priest who is holding a ciborium and host.[68] This illustrated the belief that the devil had a last chance at the deathbed.[69]

As Agostino Patrizzi wrote in his book of ceremonies, both pope and cardinals were subject to mortality. Ceremonies surrounded a dying pope. Looking at the deaths of two contemporary popes, Nicholas V and Pius II, he detailed these rites; but what was essential, he said, were the sacraments, especially confession and viaticum. The pope's confession was to include begging forgiveness from those around him and asking his confessor for indulgences. If time permitted, the pope could receive "other sacraments," presumably extreme unction.[70]

Antoninus of Florence gave unusual attention to the "state of the dying" (*De statu morientium*) in his *Summa*. This discussion began with a distinction between the three homes of the faithful: the inward home (the conscience), the residence of the family, and the tomb. The dying person had to provide for each of these.[71] Considering the "labors" involved in dying, Antoninus said one could not enter glory and attain spiritual prizes except through them. The labors would end, but the reward would not.[72] Antoninus, following Petrus de Palude, warned that those who did not bewail their sins would not avoid death. Those who died suddenly, mindless, or mad might be damned.[73] According to Antoninus, prayers could be said secretly (*occulte*) for suicides in case they repented "at the last minute" (*in ultimo momento*).[74] Anyone truly penitent "is not damned" (*non damnetur*). If his or her penance was not perfect, he or she still faced time in Purgatory.[75]

The archbishop of Florence advised on the disposition of worldly goods, including by restitution of ill-gotten gains. Restitution to persons

68 Kathryn A. Smith, *The Taymouth Hours: Stories and the Construction of the Self in Late Medieval England* (London: British Library, 2012), 245, fig. 147.

69 Shaffern, "Death and the Afterlife in the Middle Ages," 182.

70 *Caeremoniale Romanum of Agostino Patrizzi, Piccolomini* (Ridgewood, NJ: Gregg, 1965), fol. lxii^{v} and lxvi^{r-v}.

71 Antoninus, *Summa theologica* 3:443–44: "De triplici domo, scilicet conscientiae, familiae, sepulturae, quibus providendum est in morte."

72 Ibid., 3:444. "ad magna praemia non potest perveniri, nisi per magnos labores; & labor quidem cum fine, sed merces sine fine erit."

73 Ibid., 3:450: "Et secundum Petrum de Palude, si talis, qui adhuc non doluit de peccatis, subito non advertat mori, vel quia subito spirat, vel sit amens aut phreneticus, damnatus est."

74 Ibid., 3:451. Antoninus denied suicides burial in church (*in ecclesia sepeliendi*).

75 Ibid.

offended and bequests to the poor were superior to giving things for "buildings," apparently including churches.[76] A warning was included in Antoninus's *Summa* against putting off will-making late in an illness and doing other things which might harm the heirs and cause disputes.[77] The dying had a right to choose a site for burial. Antoninus advised choosing a site where there would be prayers and masses offered by very devout ministers.[78] Pomp and vanity displayed in burials did not benefit the soul (*nihil prosunt animae defuncti*).[79] Sale of burial sites was dismissed as simony, because those places were holy (*sacer*).[80]

COMMENDATION OF THE SOUL

The priest was to pray over a person in his or her last hour. Especially he was to use a version of the text called the *Commendation of the Soul.* Prayers in a *Commendation* invoked God's mercy on the individual's soul with formulaic expressions and biblical examples of the blessed deceased. Otherwise, the text of the *Commendatio animae* was not fixed throughout Western Christendom. Priests used the local version, while the dying always were supposed to beg Jesus to save their souls. These formulae were so widespread that they even found their way into works of Romance literature, including the *Chanson de Roland* and the *Cantar de mio Cid.*[81]

A detailed example of the commendation can be found in the *Rituale Romanum*. The *ordo* began with a litany, including petitions asking for liberation "from divine wrath" (*ab ira tua*), "a bad death" (*a mala morte libera eum domine*), and "the pains of Hell" (*a penis inferni*).[82] The litany was to be followed by a set of prayers, "The Christian soul departing from this world" (*Proficere anima christiana de hoc mundo*), "Merciful God, through Christ our Lord" (*Per christum dominum nostrum deus misericors*), "I commend

76 Ibid., 3:445–46: "Sed, si vult salubriter providere saluti animae suae, dimittat restituenda certa certis personis, & incerta pauperibus, non aedificiis." Antoninus gave a great deal of attention to the wills made by the dying and any gifts they might offer; see 3:451–72.

77 Ibid., 3:449–50.

78 Ibid., 3:447: "Puto autem unicuique melius & utilius esse sepeliri, ubi fiunt plura suffragia missarum & orationum & a devotioribus ministris." Antoninus also dealt with the canonical portion due to a parish if a parishioner chose burial elsewhere; see 3:474–79. Izbicki, "The Problem of Canonical Portion," 459–73.

79 Antoninus, *Summa theologica*, 3:447.

80 Ibid.

81 Gianluca Valenti, "La *commendatio animae* dans les littératures romanes des origins," in *La formule au Moyen Âge II: Actes du colloque international de Nancy et Metz, 7–9 juin 2012* (Turnhout: Brepols, 2015), 237–55.

82 *Rituale Romanum*, fol. b iiii^{r}–[b 5]^{v}.

you, dear brother, to omnipotent God" (*Commendo te omnipotenti deo charissime frater*), "Receive, Lord, the soul of your servant" (*Suscipe domine animam famuli tui*), and "We commend to you, Lord, the soul of your servant" (*Commendamus tibi domine animam famuli tui*). These asked God to receive the soul mercifully. For an anxious person (*si anxiatur*), the priest could also say the psalm "Give thanks to the Lord, as [he is] good" (*Confitemini domino quoniam bonus*; Ps 117). Once the soul had departed, the priest was to say, "We commend to You, Lord, the soul of Your servant" (*Tibi domine commendamus animam famuli tui*). The body was to be taken to the church, where the priests would surround the bier and pray.[83]

Some local manuals for priests provided a script for the *Commendatio animae*. That used in Florence, following the Roman use, provided several prayers with space, marked N. (*nomen*), to be said "at the onset of death" (*prouicino mortis*).[84] The ritual was to end once the person died, with the body being carried to the church. Standing round the bier, the clergy present were to say prayers beginning with "Deliver me, Lord, from eternal death" (*Libera me domine de morte eterna*).[85]

Another example can be found in the manual for Naples.[86] The initial litany matched that in the *Rituale Romanum*. For those near death, the priest was to say the prayer, *Proficere anima christiana de hoc mundo*, followed by four more prayers and the psalm *Confitemini domino*.[87] A responsory to follow the departure of the soul (*egressa autem anima*), "Give aid, saints of God, come hither angels of the Lord" (*Subuenite sancti dei, occurrite angeli domini*), had musical notation.[88] After that responsory, the clergy were to say a prayer and then wash the body. The body was to be clothed "in fitting clothes" (*conguis vestibus*) and placed on a bier. The priests were to sing responses while carrying the body to the church.[89]

The Rouen manual allows a transition from either extreme unction or communion of the sick to the *Commendatio animae* with the text *Subvenite sancti dei, occurrite angeli domini*, also provided with musical notation.[90] It

83 Ibid., fol. [b 5]^{v}–c iiii^{v}.

84 *Ordo ad baptizandum secundum curiam Romanum* (Florence: Bonaccorsi, 1495), fol. b i^{v}–b [vi]^{v}.

85 Ibid., fol. b [vi]^{v}: "Quando mortuus perductus fuerit in ecclesia omnes clerici stat circa feretrum et incipient. R'., Libera me domine . . .

86 *Manuale Romano-Neapolitanum*, fol. xxi^{v}–xxii^{r}.

87 Ibid., fol. xxii^{v}–xxv^{r}.

88 Ibid., fol. xxv^{r-v}.

89 Ibid., fol. xxv^{v}–xxvi^{v}, followed by an *invitatorium* and the priests vesting for a requiem Mass. An office for dead children appears at fol. xxxviii^{r-v}.

90 *Manuale secundum usum ecclesiae Rothomagensis* (Paris: Morin, ca. 1500), fol. 40v.

provides slightly different texts for men (*pro viris*) and woman (*pro muliere*). The version for men is more detailed, beginning with the brief prayer *Tibi domine commendamus animam famuli tui* or a longer one, *Misericordiam tuam, domine, sancte pater, omnipotents eterne deus* ("Your mercy, Lord, holy father, omnipotent, eternal God"). The latter asks that the angels carry the soul to the bosoms of the patriarchs Abraham, Isaac, and Jacob (*in sinibus abrahe ysaas et iacob patriarche*).[91] Next we have psalms, beginning with "On the departure of Israel from Egypt" (*In exitu Israel de Aegypto*; Ps 113:1), each accompanied by sung antiphons and several prayers, ending with "God, the creator of all the faithful" (*Fidelium deus omnium conditor*), asking pardon for the dying person's sins.[92] The commendation for women changes the words *famuli tui* to *famule tue* but differs little otherwise.[93]

The Coutance *Commenatio anime pro viris* too begins with the antiphon *Subvenite* before providing a similar combination of psalms, prayers, and sung antiphons. In that manual, the commendation was to be used "when the soul will depart from the body" (*dum egressa fuerit anima a corpore*).[94] The *Commendatio pro mulieribus* is mostly a summary for women of the longer text for men.[95]

One version of the Paris manual contains a similar commendation of souls (*Recommendatio animarum*).[96] That manual includes musical notation for *Subvenite sancti* with the antiphons "May Christ, who called you, receive you" (*Suscipiat te christus qui uocauit te*) and "May a chorus of angels receive you" (*Chorus angelorum [te]suscipiat*).[97] There are not separate texts for men and women. Instead the opening prayers provide alternative wording, *animam famuli tui uel famule tue*, in the prayers *Tibi domine commedamus* and *Misericordiam tuam sancte pater*.[98] The selection of psalms, as elsewhere, begins with *In exitu Israel*, followed by the prayer, "Omnipotent, eternal God, who [put into] the human body the soul in your likeness" (*Omnipotens sepiterne deus qui humano corpori animam ad similitudinem tuam*).[99] The commendation concludes with prayers, includ-

91 Ibid., fol. 41r–v.

92 Ibid., fol. 41v–51v.

93 Ibid., fol. 51v–54r.

94 *Manuale secundum usum ecclesie Constanciensis*, fol. 31v–40v.

95 Ibid., fol. 41r–v.

96 *Manuale ad usum Parisiensem* (Paris: Mauraud, 1497), fol. i ii^{vb}–k iii^{rb}. The book also contains a *Confessio generalis* in French attributed to Jean Gerson; see ibid., fol. m [7]^{vb}–n [6]^{vb}.

97 *Manuale ad usum Parisiensem*, fol. i ii^{v}–i iii^{r}, i iiii^{rb}, k ii^{va}.

98 Ibid., fol. i iii$^{rb–va}$.

99 Ibid., fol. i iiii$^{rb–vb}$.

ing one for the anniversary of a death (*Pro anniuersario*). "Lord God, grant remission to the soul of your servant" (or "maid servant"; *Deus indulgentiarum domine da anime famuli tui vel famule tue*). The book adds a prayer to be said if the *Recommenatio* was used on what is now called All Souls Day (*in crastino omnium sanctorum*), "God, the creator and redeemer of all the faithful" *(Fidelium deus omnium conditor et redemptor*).[100] That feast, according to the *Legenda aurea*, was founded to commemorate the soul being snatched away from demons but not receiving suffrages for their delivery from Purgatory.[101]

The Chartres pontifical gave a more elaborate instruction for beginning the commendation, permitting more than one ecclesiastic, and even the lay faithful, to say the deathbed prayers together with the priest.[102] The text alternated antiphons like *Chorus angelorum te suscipiat* with a series of prayers, ending with the death of the sufferer and the prayer "Incline Your ear, Lord" (*Inclina domine aurem tuam*). Then the body was to be carried from the house to the church with a prayer, "Receive, Lord, the soul of Your servant N." (*Oratio quando effertur de domo. Suscipe domine animam serui tui N*).[103]

In England, if the sick person was dying, the York manual provides the priest with prayers for commendation of the soul (*Commendatio animae*). This rite was composed of psalms with antiphons and prayers. The very term "commendation" appears in the prayer: "We commend to You, Lord, the soul of your servant N., that, deceased, he (or she) may live with you forever, and wipe away whatever sins he or she may have committed on account of the fragility of worldly behavior via the pardon of your pious mercy." The texts chosen were intended to soothe the mind of the dying person. Thus, the antiphon for certain of the psalms employed says, "May a chorus of angels receive you and place you in the bosom of Abraham. May you have eternal rest with Lazarus who once was a pauper." Jesus was

100 Ibid., fol. k iii$^{ra–b}$.

101 Jacobus de Voragine, *The Golden Legend: Readings on the Saints*, trans. William Granger Ryan (Princeton, NJ: Princeton University Press, 1993), 2:280–90. All Souls Day had a Cluniac origin; see Edward McNamara, "All Souls' Day and the Vigil Mass," *ZENIT: The World Seen from Rome*, available at zenit.org/2014/10/29/all-souls-day-and-the-vigil-mass/. This feast was added on November 2, following the Feast of All Saints, which had been settled on November 1; see H. A. P. Schmidt, "The Meaning of All the Saints," *Mediaeval Studies* 10 (1948): 147–61.

102 *Pontificale Carnotensis*, Paris BN Lat. 945, fol. 195r–v: "Incipit commendatio animę. Cum igitur anima in agone sui exitus dissolutio corporis uisa fuerit laborare conuenire student fratres uel clerici quisque fideles. & agatur hoc modo commendatio."

103 Ibid., fol. 195v–199.

asked to grant the dying person's soul a share in his resurrection.[104] Priests often showed the sufferer a crucifix and said (or had the patient say) a version of the prayer which begins: "Lord Jesus Christ, son of the living God, we pray you to set Your Passion, cross and death between Your judgment and our souls, now and at the hour of our death . . ."[105]

After death, the corpse was to be sprinkled with holy water and carried to the parish church. The Psalm "Out of the depths I have cried to you" (*De profundis clamavi ad te*; Ps 129 [130]) and the responsory "Deliver me, Lord, from eternal death" were among the texts employed for this procession. The *Libera me* was to be said, together with the *Pater noster*, when the body reached the church from which it would be buried following the requiem Mass.[106]

On the borders of France, the see of Tournai had a commendation of the soul which began with a litany, including a petition against "a bad death" (*a mala morte*). If the person was "in the agony of [the soul's] departure and had become anxious" (*cum in agone sui exitus anima anxiatur*), the manual offered a series of prayers. One asked delivery of the person's soul just as various holy persons had been delivered from peril. Among those mentioned were Enoch and Elijah, delivered "from the common death of the world" (*de communi morte mundi*).[107] Another remedy for anxiety was the saying of psalms and further prayers.[108] The departure of the soul was to be accompanied by a responsory, *Subvenite sancti dei*, with further prayers and psalms.[109]

The diocese of Toul begins the commendation with a litany invoking Sts. Aprus of Toul and Menna of Lorraine. Each invocation asks intercession for the dying person's soul.[110] The litany was followed by prayers, an exhortation to the soul, and petitions for the dying, beginning "Accept,

104 *Manuale et processionale ad usum insignis ecclesiae Eboracensis*, 55–58. The death of a priest required certain variants from the process for a lay person, including the washing of the body by other priests.

105 A version of this prayer appears in both Latin and the vernacular in the York Hours of the Cross; see *The Lay Folk Mass Book or the Manner of Hearing Mass*, ed. Thomas Frederick Simmons (London: Trübner, 1879), 84–85 and 350. It can be found among the *Septem Precationes Sancti Gregorii de Passione Christi*; available at www.preces-latinae.org/thesaurus/Filius/SeptemSG.html: "Domine Iesu *Christe*, Fili Dei vivi, pone passionem, crucem, et mortem tuam inter *iudicium tuum* et animam meam."

106 *Manuale et processionale ad usum Eboracensis*, 58–59.

107 *Manuale pastorum ad uniformem administrationem sacramentorum aliorum officiorum ecclesiasticum per civitatem et dioecesim Tornacensem* (Louvain: Masius, 1591?), 125–32.

108 *Manuale Tornacensis*, 132–35.

109 Ibid., 135–40.

110 *Manuale seu rituale ad usum ecclesie Tullensis* (Bamburg: Sensenschmidt, ca. 1482), fol. [29]v–[33]r: "Parce domine parce famulo tuo . . . Intercede pro anima eius."

oh Lord, Your servant or Your handmaid" (*Suscipe domine seruum tuum vel ancillam tuam*).[111]

The Lausanne manual began a commendation, partially sung, with *Subvenite*, followed by prayers, psalms, and antiphons like *Suscipiat vos Christus* and *Chorus angelorum*, ending with absolution of the dying person. The manual provided a shorter version in case of imminent death, but it also considered the possibility of adding matins from the Office of the Dead with nine lessons (*cum nouem lectionibus*) if the agony was prolonged.[112] The Tarentaise manual offered prayers to be said while the corpse was still in the house. Among them, the priest was to say a prayer, "God, the giver of life" (*Deus dator vite*) before the corpse was carried to the church.[113]

Farther afield, the Prague manual had a rubric for ushering a dying person out of this world (*de morientis conductu ab hoc seculo*).[114] Its prayers included the *Pater noster*.[115] The script for the departure of the soul (*In egressione anime*) had a litany with the response: "Deliver the soul of your servant" or "maid servant" (*Libera domine animam famuli. vel [famu]le. tui. vel tue*).[116] After death, the corpse was to be washed and laid out (*Tunc corpus lauetur et lazarizetur* [from *laxare*]). Then, before it was dressed (*antequam vestimentis induatur*), more prayers were said.[117] Yet more prayers accompanied placing the body on a bier to be carried to the church.[118]

The Olomuc commendation of the soul, like many others, began with the antiphon *Subvenite* and prayers begging mercy on the departing soul.[119] The rite shifted "at the departure of soul from body" (*In egressu anime de corpore*) to the psalm *In exitu Israel.* As the body was placed on the bier, the priest was to say the prayer *Suscipe domine animam serui tui N.* before the corpse was carried to the church.[120]

111 Ibid., fol. [33]r–[38]v.

112 *Manuale seu officiarium sacerdotum secundum usum ecclesie et diocesis Laudunensis* (Paris: ad signum Rose Rubre, 1538), fol. lvi^{v}.

113 *Manuale ad usum Tharentasiensis* (Geneva: Belot, 1508), fol. d ii^{r-v}.

114 *Obsequiale Pragense* (Nürnberg: Stucks, 1496), fol. xxxiv^{v}.

115 Ibid., fol. xxxiv^{v}–xxxvi^{v}.

116 Ibid., fol. xxxvi^{v}–xxxviii^{r}.

117 Ibid., fol. xxxviii^{r}–xli^{r}.

118 Ibid., fol. xli^{r}–xlii^{r}.

119 *Agenda Olomucensis* (Nürnberg: Stuchs, 1498), fol. S ii^{v}–[S 5]^{v}.

120 Ibid., fol. [S 5]^{v}–t [i]^{r}.

The Bratislava manual included an interrogation of the sick person.[121] Specific prayers were assigned for death's agony, when it was perceived (*Et iam videtur agonizare*). These included *Proficiscere anima christiana* and *Libera domine anima serui tui vel serue tue.*[122] After the patient's death, the priest was to urge the bystanders to pray, beginning: "Let us pray devoutly for the soul" (*Oremus deuote pro anima*). The prayers to be offered differed between priest, layman, and laywoman.[123]

The Esztergom manual began with the same litany used in visitation of the sick and then began its prayers for the dying with the antiphon *Proficiscere.*[124] If the soul lingered in the body, a deacon or priest could read the passion narratives. Then a crucifix was placed before the sick person as a reminder of the Christian faith.[125] Further prayers were to be offered until the soul departed, then the body was to be washed, sprinkled with holy water, and blessed with incense before being carried to the church accompanied by the antiphon "May the angels lead you into paradise" (*In paradisum deducant te angeli*) and the psalm *In exitu Israel.*[126]

In Denmark, the Roskilde manual placed the *Commendatio animae* after the soul's departure from the body.[127] It began with the familiar antiphon *Subvenite.* Among the prayers was one mentioning the creation of humanity "in Your image" (*ad similitudinem tuam*).[128] The concluding prayer asked that the deceased enjoy eternal beatitude and be raised with the saints at the final resurrection.[129]

In Sweden, the Linköping text began the commendation with the antiphon *Subvenite.*[130] Among the prayers to be employed, as at Roskilde, was *Omnipotens sempiterne deus, qui humano corpore animam ad similitudinem [tuam].*[131] Among the concluding prayers were a generic one *Pro defuncto,*

121 *Liber agendarum dioecesis Wratislaviensis emendatus* (Wroclaw: J. P., 1510), fol. xv^{r}–xvi^{r}.

122 Ibid., fol. xviii^{r}–xxii^{r}.

123 Ibid., fol. xxii^{v}–xxiii^{v}.

124 *Obsequiale Strigonensis* (Nürnberg: Stuchs, 1496), fol. c iii^{v}–[c 5]^{v}.

125 Ibid., fol. [c 5]^{v}: "Si adhuc in corpore tardauerit anima infirmi legat aliquis diaconus vel presbyter passiones dominicas. et ponatur crux Christi ante conspectum eius. et de fide catholica mentionem faciat."

126 Ibid., fol. [c 5]^{v}–[c 8]^{v}.

127 *Manuale curatorum secundum usum ecclesie Rosckildensis*, 36: "Post egressum anime infirmi Commendatio anime eius." Similarly see *Manuale Upsalense* (Stockholm: Ghoban, ca. 1486), fol. 49v.

128 *Manuale curatorum secundum usum ecclesie Rosckildensis*, 36–37.

129 Ibid., 38.

130 *Manuale secundum titulum ecclesie Lincopensis* (Söderköping: In Edibus Olaui Vlrici, 1525), 91.

131 Ibid., 93.

one *Pro femina,* and one *Pro sacerdote*, as well as additional prayers *Pro patre et matre* and *Pro benefactoribus.*[132]

The manual from Palencia included the interrogations of the dying attributed to St. Anselm.[133] The text also provided an exhortation of those in danger of death (*en el articulo dela muerte*), warning against scrupulosity and despair.[134] That manual contained a commendation of the soul for a person "in agony" (*en el agonia*). The text included special prayers for the anxious soul (*Et si anxiatur adhuc anima*). The dying person also was to kiss the cross (*Et osculetur crucem*).[135] The manual provided additional prayers for those whose death agony was prolonged. Likewise, the Athanasian Creed and the passion narrative from John's Gospel could be employed.[136] At last, the priest would say the *Recommendatio defunctorum* over the corpse before it was carried to the church.[137] The Salamanca manual also provided the text of the passion according to John and the Athanasian Creed.[138] The Salamanca text included a warning against temptations inspired by the devil, providing remedies for them.[139] A series of prayers at the sickbed invoked the Virgin Mary, asking her aid for the dying person.[140] Among the concluding prayers was one asking the archangel Michael, understood as a psychopomp, to aid the soul before the divine judge.[141]

The Majorca manual gives a shorter form for the commendation of the soul. It begins with a litany invoking, among other things, the cross and passion for deliverance of the sick person.[142] A series of prayers, beginning with *Proficiscere anima Christiana,* was provided to be said when death was near, especially when the person was in pain or anxious.[143] Psalms were added to these prayers for comforting the anxious, as was the Apostles'

132 Ibid., 94–95.

133 *Manuale secundum vsum sanctę Ecclesię Pallantinę*, fol. xci^{v}–xcii^{r}. See *Sancti Anselmi admonitio morienti*, PL 158:685B–688B.

134 *Manuale secundum vsum sanctę Ecclesię Pallantinę*, fol. xcii^{v}–xciii^{v}. This exhortation refers to the Anselm text.

135 Ibid., fol. xciiii^{v}–xcix^{v}.

136 Ibid., fol. xcix^{v}–cviii^{r}. The manual also provides Gospel texts to accompany prayers for the sick; see fol. lxxi^{r}–lxxv^{r}.

137 Ibid., fol. cviij.

138 *Manuale secundum consuetudinem alme ecclesie Salamanticense*, fol. liiii^{r}–lv^{v} and lvi$^{r–v}$.

139 Ibid., fol. lix^{v}–lx^{r}.

140 Ibid., fol. lv^{r}–lxvii^{v}.

141 Ibid., fol. lxvii^{v}: "Sancte michael archangel succurre huic anime: apud altissimum iudicem."

142 *Ordinarium de administratione sacramentorum cum pluribus additionibus adeo necessariis secundum ritum alme sedis maioriensis*, fol. lxiii^{rb}: "Per crucem et passionem tuum. libera eum domine."

143 *Ordinarium sedis maioriensis*, fol. lxiii^{r}: "Deinde pro vicino morti cum agone in sui exitus. Anima visa fuerit anziri fiant hec sequentia."

Creed.[144] The commendation ends with the prayer *Tibi domine commendamus animam famuli tui* and an absolution.[145]

All liturgical orders for death and burial originated in the ordinary course of mortality. However, the coming of the Black Death (1346–53) disrupted these expectations. Many persons of all ages and both sexes died in large numbers. Epidemic mortality led to informal internments in "plague pits."[146] This great epidemic and subsequent outbreaks have been credited variously with greater concern for commemoration of the dead, increased offerings to charities, foundation of confraternities, macabre depictions of death, greater love for worldly comfort, and more zealous cultivation of the interior life of the soul.[147]

There are indications that the Black Death affected burials in two contrary ways: occasional abandonment of traditional rites, including because local priests died or fled their congregations, and "codification" of the same rites, telling priests how they should comfort the dying and bury the dead. Houses of religious orders, especially enclosed monasteries, suffered high mortality. However, unlike surviving diocesan priests, who lost respect among the faithful, surviving friars, Dominicans and Franciscans, who went about ministering to afflicted populations and burying their dead received greater respect.[148] An example of reaction to the burials of plague victims is a complaint at King's Lynn that only one candle was carried before their corpses.[149] Another witness was Boccaccio, who complained that no more respect was paid the victims than would have been given to "dead goats."[150] One religious phenomenon of this epidemic is the development of cults of plague saints, including Roch and Sebastian.

144 Ibid., fol. lxiv^{v}–lxvi^{r}.

145 Ibid., fol. lxvi$^{r–v}$.

146 Maryanne Kowaleski and Sharon N. DeWitte, "Black Death Bodies," *Fragments: Interdisciplinary Approaches to the Study of Ancient and Medieval Pasts* 6 (2017): 1–37.

147 Binski, *Medieval Death*, 121–22 and 126–34; Samuel K. Cohn, Jr., *The Cult of Remembrance and the Black Death: Six Renaissance Cities in Central Italy* (Baltimore: Johns Hopkins University Press, 1992). Flagellant processions and increased attacks on Jews have been attributed to the Black Death; see Philip Ziegler, *Black Death* (Stroud: Alan Sutton, 1991), 62–80.

148 Elina Gertsman, "Visualizing Death: Medieval Plagues and the Macabre," in *Piety and Plague*, 64–89, at 65 and 67; Ziegler, *Black Death*, 211–15. At least one fifteenth-century tract told priests not to flee during an outbreak; see Thomas M. Izbicki, "A Tract on the Plague Falsely Attributed to Juan de Mella," in *Homenaje a Pedro Sainz Rodriguez* (Madrid: Fundacion Universitaria Española, 1986), 3:367–72.

149 John Aberth, *Doctoring the Black Death: Medieval Europe's Medical Response to Plague* (Lanham, MD: Rowman & Littlefield, 2021), 107.

150 Gertsman, "Visualizing Death," 65.

This was part of a larger resort to prayer in hope of placating God's righteous anger.[151] Prayers against infection could be solicited by the clergy in sermons and letters, and processions invoking divine aid against disease became common. Masses were developed to be said in time of epidemic, and the Virgin Mary was petitioned to provide aid.[152] One of the remedies proposed for the plague was cleansing the soul of sin, which shared common ground with the Lateran decree *Cum infirmitas*.[153]

ARTES MORIENDI IN PASTORAL MANUALS

The Urgell manual contains an *Ars moriendi*, something not ordinarily found in a manual for priests. The entire text is didactic and built on the works of Gregory the Great. It begins with a prologue connecting the death of the individual to that of Christ, following his example, "because every action of Christ is an instruction" (*Cum omnis Christi actio sit instruction*). The savior foresaw, it says, at the time of his passion, the deaths of his disciples.[154] The opening section of the text deals with practicalities and preparations for death. The first of these "documents" focuses on leading the sick person to penance, "confessing with sorrow of heart" (*cum dolore cordis confitendo*). The next deals with the making of wills. Another section focused on securing prayers and requiem masses for the dead, including anniversary masses, preserving the memory of the departed.[155] An instruction treats preparing the sickroom, equipping it with a crucifix and images of Mary or a saint the person had venerated while well.[156] Priests were not to offer false hope of recovery (*spe salutis*) to the sick. Instructions are included for exhorting the sick to true penance, including remembering any sins which might have been forgotten. That section concludes with

151 Sheila Barker, "The Making of a Plague Saint: Saint Sebastian's Imagery and Cult Before the Counter-Reformation," in *Piety and Plague from Byzantium to the Baroque*, ed. Franco Mormando and Thomas Worcester (Kirksville, Mo.: Truman State University Press, 2007), 90–131; Aberth, *Doctoring the Black Death*, 129–36.

152 *The Black Death* (ed. Horrox), 111–57.

153 Aberth, *Doctoring the Black Death*, 275.

154 *Ordinarium sacramentorum benedictionum et aliarum rerum*, fol. cxxvi^{r},

155 That section cited Duns Scotus in a discussion of prayers; see *Ordinarium secundum sacrosancte Urgellensis ecclesie ritum*, fol. cxxvii^{r}. Shaffern, "Death and the Afterlife in the Middle Ages," 181, notes the availability of trentals of masses and the efficacy of other practices, including the rosary.

156 *Ordinarium secundum sacrosancte Urgellensis ecclesie ritum*, fol. cxxviii^{r}: "aut alterius sancti quem pridem sanus venerabatur." Holy water and a "blessed light" (*Lux etiam benedicta*) were to be provided, the latter to drive out demons.

the dying person's need to be helped by others with their prayers and alms. Sick persons were to be told to imitate Christ while the use of reason remained.[157]

The brief second part is an exhortation to a good death given in the vernacular. It includes a reminder that through death one could come to "the glory of paradise."[158] The sick person was to think on the mercies of Jesus, offering his or her life as a sacrifice. The pain was to be accepted toward the remission of sins.[159] The third and longest part recommended measures to be taken in death's agony.[160] This too was in the form of exhortations, some to be said while the patient was contemplating a cross. Once more the sick person was urged to accept the situation with firm faith. Recourse was urged to the Virgin Mary, as well as to the archangels Michael (psychopomp) and Raphael (healer). In addition, the patient was to think about Christ's passion, relying on the crucified savior for mercy. The text ends with a blessing and a recommendation of the soul.[161] The same *Ars moriendi* also appears in the manual of Cartagena.[162]

Another *Ars moriendi*, found in some early printed books, begins: *Quamvis secundum philosophum tertio Ethicorum*. The pastoral practicalities found in the first part of the Urgell and Cartagena texts gave way to a moralizing approach. The preface warns against the temptations that the devil offered "in an extreme illness" (*in extrema infirmitate*). The text also warns about those who were slow to face their mortality, especially those not believing the possibility of death coming quickly (*nequequam credens se tam cito mortiturum*). The largest part of the book contrasts the devil's temptation (*temptatio dyaboli*) with the "good inspiration of an angel" (*bona inspiratio angeli*). Each temptation, including spiritual pride, despair, false hope of survival, and avarice, was expounded, followed by its remedy. Each portion of text was illustrated with woodcuts showing demons or angels close to the sick man lying in bed, offering either temptations or good counsel. The book ends with an injunction to pray while still able to talk and having the use of reason (*agonisans loqui et vsu rationis*). The last two pictures show the soul being taken up by an angel in the

157 Ibid., fol. cxxvi^{r}–cxxix^{r}.

158 Ibid., fol. cxxix^{v}: "per auisar / e mostrar vos lo cami general dela mort corporal: per lo qual se munta ala gloria de paradis."

159 Ibid.

160 Ibid., fol. cxxx^{r}: "Tertia pars de exercicio seruando in agonia mortis."

161 Ibid., fol. cxxx^{r}–ccxxxvii^{r}.

162 *Ordinarium manuale de ministratione sacramentorum secundum consuetudinem ecclesię Carthaginensis* (Granada, 1545), fol. ciii^{r}–cxviii^{v}.

form of a baby and that soul being weighed by the archangel Michael, the baby soul outweighing worldly goods.[163]

Burial

Each of these texts, the commendations of the soul and *artes moriendi*, whatever their differences of detail, was designed to comfort the dying and bring them to salvation. The commendation texts were often lengthy; but the priest was permitted to use his judgment of the situation, abridging long rituals to focus on the essentials: confession, absolution, and anointing. It was best that death not occur before the last blessings had been given. Death was to be followed by carrying to the church for burial rites, rituals offering the prospect of salvation of the deceased and including the possibility of an early release from Purgatory. (The extension of spiritual benefits to the dead was controversial, but such benefits were popular.)[164] Indulgences too might be provided for use at the deathbed. These practices also were intended to provide comfort not just for the dying but for living family and friends, while reminding them of their own mortality. In the last moments, the priority of spiritual welfare, established in texts like the canon *Cum infirmitas*, prevailed over any last hopes of physical survival.

Burial completed a Christian's pilgrimage on Earth. On the day of the funeral, the priest might begin with the Office of the Dead. Then a requiem Mass (*missa pro defunctis*) would follow. The propers allowed for thoughts of eternal rest and Paradise, as well as relief from fear of death, thoughts intended to comfort the bereaved. However, a requiem Mass excluded Alleluias and other celebratory material. It also came to include the sequence *Dies irae*, invoking the terrors of the day of judgment.[165] This rite was developed over centuries of prayers for the dead, including those held at the tombs of martyrs and confessors. The requiem Mass was sung with plain chant until more complex compositions were added, beginning in the fifteenth century.[166] Parents of dead children might be in special need of comfort. If the child died unbaptized, there was hope that the infant soul went to Limbo, an intermediate state, rather than to Hell. For

163 *Ars moriendi ex variis scripturarum sententiis* (Leipzig: Kachelofen, 1495?).

164 Robert W. Shaffern, "The Medieval Theology of Indulgences," in *Promissory Notes on the Treasury of Merits: Indulgences in Late Medieval Europe*, ed. R. N. Swanson (Leiden: Brill, 2006), 11–36.

165 There is no room here to examine the depictions of the Last Judgment often set above the doors of churches to remind parishioners of the just judgment of both saved and damned.

166 Thierry Maertens and Louis Heuschen, *Doctrine et pastorale de la liturgie de la mort* (Bruges: Apostolat Liturgique Abbaye de Saint-André, 1957).

the parents of baptized infants, there would be a full requiem Mass, with comforting texts, and burial in consecrated ground.[167] After the requiem was concluded, the body was carried to the gravesite. There the priest said further prayers, sometimes using a different form for a man than for a woman.[168]

Pictures of requiem masses and burials in books of hours tend to show rites for clergy or the well-to-do laity. Such images might show a priest celebrating Mass or singers chanting the Office of the Dead near a coffin covered with a rich cloth and set on a bier.[169] The procession to the grave might also show a cloth-covered coffin being carried by clergy.[170] The burials of the poor might only have involved a corpse wrapped in a shroud.[171] Recent archaeology shows burials of a wide swath of population, even of the tombs of the poor. Internments especially were rushed during an epidemic or famine, as well as after a battle.[172] Only the prominent and prosperous could afford commemoration with carved tombs, brass grave slabs, bequests, and chantry chapels.[173]

Further attention should be given to the deaths and burials of medieval children. The incidence of infant mortality, although hard to establish for the Middle Ages, is believed to have been high.[174] One historian hypothesized that as many as half of children died before age two.[175] Even

167 Donald Mowbray, "A Community of Sufferers and the Authority of Masters: The Development of the Idea of Limbo by Masters of Theology at the University of Paris (c. 1230–c. 1300)," in *Authority and Community in the Middle Ages*, ed. Mowbray, Rhiannon Purdie, and Ian P. Wei (Stroud: Sutton, 1999), 43–68; Sally Crawford, "Baptism and Infant Burial in Anglo-Saxon England," in *Medieval Life Cycles: Continuity and Change*, ed. Isabelle Cochelin and Karen Smyth (Turnhout: Brepols, 2013), 55–80.

168 The instructions for the requiem and burial appear together in *Manuale secundum usum ecclesiae Parisiensis* (Paris: Mourand, 1497), fol. k iii[rb]–[L vi][va]. The Rouen manual has separate graveside prayers for each sex; see *Manuale secundum usum insignis ecclesiae Rothomagensis*, fol. 97v–109r.

169 See, e.g., Weick, *Time Sanctified*, 126, fig. 112; 127, fig. 113a. See also Binski, *Medieval Death*, plate III.

170 See, e.g., Weick, *Time Sanctified*, 128, fig. 115.

171 Ibid., 130, fig. 119; Binski, *Medieval Death*, plate V. Side pictures show a corpse being sewn into the shroud and the body being enclosed in a plain box and then carried in it.

172 For the insights provided by investigating large-scale burial sites, see, e.g., Brian Connell, Amy Gray Jones, Rebecca Redfern, and Don Walker, *A Bioarchaeological Study of Medieval Burials on the Site of St Mary Spital: Excavations at Spitalfields Market, London E1, 1991–2007*, MOLA Monograph 60 (London: Museum of London, 2012). For a mass burial after a battle, see Binski, *Medieval Death*, 49.

173 Binski, *Medieval Death*, 70–122.

174 Nicholas Orme, *Medieval Children* (New Haven, Conn.: Yale University Press, 2001), 113; Ann G. Carmichael, "Health, Disease and the Medieval Body," in *A Cultural History of the Human Body in the Medieval Age*, ed. Linda Kalof (London: Berg, 2014), 39–57, at 56–57; Zvi Razi, *Life, Marriage and Death in a Medieval Parish: Economy, Society and Demography in Halesowen, 1270–1400* (Cambridge: Cambridge University Press, 1980), 87–88 and 144.

175 Dale Kent, "Women in Renaissance Florence," in *Virtue and Beauty: Leonardo's "Ginevra de'Benci" and Renaissance Portraits of Women*, ed. David Alan Brown (Washington, DC: National Gallery of Art, 2001),

those who survived infancy might die before age twelve.[176] The clergy were especially concerned with newborns who might die unbaptized. In the Ordinary Gloss to the *Decretals of Gregory IX* (1234), Bernard of Parma followed the Augustinian theology of original sin, treating exclusion of unbaptized infants from the beatific vision as the lightest punishment for the Fall. He described the deaths of infants as occurring daily, requiring emergency baptism in cases of imminent death.[177] (A late development was the idea that unbaptized infants were sent to Limbo.)[178] The Gloss also cited the fact that infants inherited original sin from their parents as proof that they did not need to consent to baptism, as adults had to do. This opened the way to baptism of endangered neonates by anyone with water, the right words, and the proper intention.[179]

Those infants who died unbaptized were to be buried outside consecrated ground, possibly just outside the parish cemetery. A thirteenth-century statute of Cambrai may have meant this when it stated that a baby born dead was *extra cymiterium tumuletur*.[180] The burial site of unbaptized infants might even be absorbed later into a growing city, as Florence came to contain the Piazza del Limbo.[181] A baptized infant, however, seems to have received decent burial with other members of the parish.[182]

All of the buried, adults and children both, were expected to be raised to face the Last Judgment. A reminder of this was included in a requiem Mass as the sequence *Dies irae*. Only the last words, "Pious Lord Jesus, give them rest" (*Pie Jesu Domine, Dona eis requiem*), diminished the terrifying impact of this invocation of the last trumpet calling all souls, reunited with their bodies, to rise from their graves.[183] Those whose bodies and souls had been reunited were to face Christ, the just judge, on that last day.[184]

24–47, at 31–32.

176 Razi, *Life, Marriage and Death in a Medieval Parish*, 87–88 and 144.

177 Glo. Ord. at X 3.42.3, Casus: "Absit enim, vt diversi paruuli pereant, quorum quotidie tanta multitudo moritur, quin Deus aliquod remedium illis procurauerit ad salutem."

178 Mowbray, "A Community of Sufferers."

179 Glo. Ord. at X 3.42.3.

180 *Statuts synodaux*, 4:31.

181 Jacqueline Marie Musacchio, *Art, Marriage and Family in the Florentine Renaissance Palace* (New Haven, Conn.: Yale University Press, 2008), 39.

182 *Children, Death and Burial: Archaeological Discourses*, ed. Eileen Murphy and Mélie Le Roy (Oxford: Oxbow, 2017).

183 This use of the *Dies irae* continued in the Tridentine Latin Mass, see *Missale Romanum ex decreto ss. Concilii Tridentini restitutum summorum pontificum cura recognitum* (Vatican City: Typis Polyglottis Vaticanis, 1962), 706.

184 Albertus Magnus, *Scriptum quartum diui Alberti Magni super quartum sententiarum* (Basel: Jacobus de Pfortzen, 1506), fol. pp^{ra-b}.

Depictions of this scene could show the just and unjust being raised from the same graveyards to different ends, salvation or damnation.[185]

185 Binski, *Medieval Death*, 43, 161, 174, 178, 197, 203, 204–14; Johanna Scheel, "Feeding Worms: The Theological Paradox of the Decaying Body and Its Depictions in the Context of Prayer and Devotion," in *Picturing Death 1200–1600*, 164–87, at 185, fig. 8.8.

EPILOGUE

THE REFORMATION, TRIDENTINE REFORMS, AND MISSIONS ABROAD

The practice of administering sacraments at the sickbed endured throughout the Middle Ages. Priests went to the homes of the dangerously ill to administer penance, viaticum, and anointing. All local forms of ministry to the sick and dying shared common ground. Priests used biblical texts, antiphons, litanies, and prayers. Following the Epistle of James, they anointed the sick with consecrated oil. Although the order of the sacraments administered at the sickbed varied, confession opened the way for viaticum and extreme unction. Parishioners expected spiritual consolation; and they might hope for physical healing if it did not impede the soul's welfare. This was the pattern of instructions for ministry down to the Reformation, although it is difficult to discern whether these instructions were followed, or at least adapted, at the sickbed.

Although there were challenges to Eucharistic theology and penitential practice, extreme unction rarely was challenged. However, Thomas Netter accused John Wyclif and his followers of rejecting the sacrament and denying its good effects on the ailing. Netter responded that extreme unction was founded by Christ and the apostles. His polemic reemphasized the value of oil consecrated by a bishop for the rite. Netter concluded that Wyclif had a mind empty of the orthodox faith (*mens vacua fidei orthodoxae*) and cold charity.[1]

This final sacrament was "in play" in the sixteenth century, involving Catholics and Protestants of various stripes. The Reformers began by rejecting certain aspects of medieval Catholicism. However, they had to develop substitutes for the rites they rejected. Martin Luther accepted extreme unction in an early sermon;[2] but he soon rejected it, saying that anointing the sick with oil consecrated by a bishop rested on "a faulty exegesis of James 5:13–16." This line of argument first appeared in the *Babylonian Captivity of the Church* (1520).[3] Luther said that James referred to the healing power of the sick person's faith. Extreme unction itself was a human creation or, at most, a rite devised by the apostles alone. Luther dismissed the Epistle of James as not written by an apostle, and its plural reference to the elders (presbyters) meant that their prayers were more important than the oil. Luther also complained that very few were physically healed by that rite on their sickbeds. Miraculous healing had ceased in the Church long before. In a 1519 sermon on preparing for death, Luther shifted the emphasis away from deathbed drama to trust in God's mercy. The sacraments were signs of the victory God promised to the dying.[4]

Luther's *Confession of the Articles of Faith against the Enemy of the Gospel and All Kinds of Heresies* describes making extreme unction a sacrament as "nonsense."[5] The Reformer added that Rome had produced a rite which was nothing (*hoc nihil est*). Luther's reliance on faith also vitiated the idea of the deathbed triumph *in extremis* over the twin temptations of presumption and despair. Nor was suffering a part of penance in this life, let alone in Purgatory.[6] Lutheran ordinances still accepted prayers for healing, along with confession and communion of the sick, offering spiritual consolation in the face of mortality.[7] This was a step away from the

1 Thomas Netter, *De sacramentis* (Venice: Bassanesi, 1758; Farnborough: Gregg, 1967), 939–45. Friar William Woodford also accused Wyclif of rejecting extreme unction; see Ian Christopher Levy, *Holy Scripture and the Quest for Authority at the End of the Middle Ages* (Notre Dame, IN: University of Notre Dame Press, 2012), 96.

2 Donald F. Duclow, "'Dying Well' from the Fifteenth Century to Hospice," *Lutheran Quarterly* 38 (2014): 125–47, at 133.

3 *Reformation Writings of Martin Luther*, trans. Bertram Lee Woolf, 2 vols. (London: Lutterworth, 1952), 1:319–29.

4 *The Annotated Luther*, vol. 4: *Pastoral Writings* (Philadelphia: Augsburg Fortress, 2016), 283–305.

5 *The Annotated Luther*, vol. 2: *Word and Faith* (Philadelphia: Augsburg Fortress, 2005), 274–75.

6 Duclow, "Dying Well."

7 Ronald K. Rittgers, *Reformation of Suffering: Pastoral Theology and Lay Piety in Late Medieval and Early Modern Germany* (Oxford: Oxford University Press, 2012), 189 and 329n80.

interplay of spiritual and bodily healing evident in Catholic ministry to the sick and dying.

The Council of Trent reaffirmed confession and the real presence in the Eucharist. Focusing on the sick, the assembly discussed extreme unction in its first period, in 1547, resuming that discussion in the second period, 1551–52. The fathers focused on Protestant errors, including Philip Melanchthon's claim that James meant that the elders of the people, not priests, had done anointing of the sick. Trent, in reply, affirmed anointing as a sacrament providing spiritual and even physical healing.[8] The council drew on Mark's Gospel and the Epistle of James for proof that Jesus established the sacrament.[9] The Servite Hieronymus of Bologna argued that denying that extreme unction was a sacrament made Christ a liar.[10] These conclusions were not reached without controversy. Some of the fathers argued, unsuccessfully, that the sacrament be called anointing of the sick, not extreme unction. That change of name, the majority decided, would contradict the Council of Florence and favor the Protestants.[11]

Pre-Tridentine Catholicism was imported into the New World by Spanish clerics. This "spiritual conquest" involved founding institutions, catechizing, and baptizing. Later it was stabilized with diocesan structures and the full pomp of Spanish Catholicism.[12] Implanting the church included bringing rites for the sick to indigenous populations who had never heard of Christ.[13] The catechism of Pedro de Córdoba for the "Indians" included a summary of extreme unction as "administered to

8 *Concilium Tridentinum, diariorum, actorum, epistolarum, tractatuum nova collectio*, ed. Görres Gesellschaft, 13 vols. (Freiburg in Breisgau: Herder, 1901 / 2001), 6:96–97 and 99–123; 7.1:239–41 and 287. For condemned articles and related canons, see 7.2:292–325 and 330–40; and André Duval, *Des sacraments au Concile de Trente* (Paris: Cerf, 1985), 223–79.

9 Charles W. Gusmer, *'And you visited me': Sacramental Ministry to the Sick and Dying*, rev. ed. (New York: Pueblo, 1989), 6–11 and 33–34.

10 *Concilium Tridentinum*, 6:103.

11 The seven sacraments had been listed in the Decree of Union with the Armenians, promulgated in a session of the Council of Florence on November 22, 1439; see COGD II, pt. 2 (Turnhout: Brepols, 2013), 1237. André Duval, "L'extrême-onction au concile de Trente: Sacrement des mourantes ou sacrament des maladies," *La Maison-Dieu* 101 (1970): 127–72.

12 Robert Ricard, *The Spiritual Conquest of Mexico: An Essay on the Apostolate of the Mendicant Orders in New Spain: 1523–1572*, trans. Lesley Byard Simpson (Berkeley: University of California Press, 1966). One variation in the New World was the development of visionary communities under the tutelage of friars; see John Leddy Phelan, *The Millennial Kingdom of the Franciscans in the New World* (Berkeley: University of California Press, 1970). Another was dealing with large-scale Negro slavery; see C. R. Boxer, *The Church Militant and Iberian Expansion 1440–1770* (Baltimore: Johns Hopkins University Press, 1978), 30–38.

13 Las Casas wanted conquistadors confronted with their sins on their deathbeds to win penitence and restitution; see David Thomas Orique, *To Heaven or to Hell: Bartolomé de Las Casas "Confessionario"* (University Park: Pennsylvania State University Press, 2018), 62–67 and 76–77.

those who are dying, and it is sufficient for the pardon of sins."[14] These rites and practices were carried to the southwest of North America and the Philippines.[15] Tridentine reforms were imported by councils in Mexico City and Lima, which were more intent on practical measures than on debating dogma.[16] In Portuguese Brazil, Jorge Benci, relying on Tridentine decrees, said that slaves should be taught about anointing of the sick.[17]

The rite of extreme unction was contained in post-Tridentine manuals, like the Roman ritual of 1614. Its practice remained largely unchanged down to the twentieth century, reserving anointing for those in danger of death. Only in the time of Pope Pius XII would the Catholic Church move toward a more general rite of anointing the sick.[18] Tridentine decrees also entered into the manuals for confessors published in Latin or the vernacular, including the *Manuel de confessores* of Martín de Azpilcueta, used in Spanish America.[19] Through such texts, Trent influenced ministry to the sick.

Although Trent focused most on the Lutherans, another Protestant tradition emerged, now called Reformed. Whereas the Lutherans adapted received practices to a new theology, these Reformers broke with the past. In Basel, Oecolampadius provided an order the laity could use at home, phasing out Catholic practices. In Strasbourg, Martin Bucer abandoned anointing in favor of exhorting the sick and reading scripture to them.

14 Pedro de Córdoba, *Christian Doctrine for the Instruction of the Indians* (Coral Gables, Fla.: University of Miami Press, 1970), 114. This catechism included caring for the sick and wounded; see 116. In a catechetical text, Juan de Zumárraga, archbishop of Mexico, reaffirmed extreme unction as a sacrament of necessity; see José Luis Egío, "Pragmatic or Heretical? Editing Catechisms in Mexico in the Age of Discoveries and Reformation (1539–1547)," in *Knowledge of the "Pragmatici": Legal and Moral Theological Literature and the Formation of Early-Modern Ibero-America*, ed. Thomas Duve and Otto Danwerth (Leiden: Brill, 2020), 243–81, at 270.

15 As late as 1771 sick persons in the Philippines were carried to church in hammocks for last rites; see John N. Schumacher, "The Manila Synodal Tradition," *Philippine Studies* 27 (1979): 285–348.

16 Osvaldo R. Moutin, "Producing Pragmatic Literature in the Third Mexican Provincial Council," in *Knowledge of the "Pragmatici"* (ed. Duve and Danwerth), 282–95. The catechism of the council included instructions for administering extreme unction and absolving the dying; see *The Directory for Confessors 1585* (ed. Poole), 64–65, 76–77, 148, 151; on the conversion and instruction of indigenous peoples, see 20–21, 32, 37, 152.

17 Gustavo César Machado Cabral, "Jesuit Pragmatic Literature and Ecclesiastical Normativity in Portuguese America (16th–18th Centuries)," in *Knowledge of the "Pragmatici"* (ed. Duve and Danwerth), 151–86, at 164, 167, 170, 176, 179.

18 Gusmer, *"And you took me in,"* 34–35; Mortimort, "Prayer for the Sick and Sacramental Anointing," 132–37.

19 Manuel Bragagnolo, "Managing Legal Knowledge in Early Modern Times: Martín de Azpilcueta's *Manual for Confessors* and the Phenomenon of Epitomisation," in *Knowledge of the "Pragmatici"* (ed. Duve and Danwerth), 187–242.

The Lord's Supper, however, could be celebrated for those attending the sickbed.[20]

The Reformed tradition was most strongly represented across Europe by John Calvin's *Institutes*, which contained a brief but pungent critique of extreme unction. Calvin called the rite a "fictitious" sacrament. Catholic priests were engaged in a "hypocritical stage-play, by which, without reason or result, they would resemble the apostles."[21] Priests pretended they had the gift of healing; but their rite lacked "any promise" of cures.[22] Calvin interpreted James as describing the anointing of all the sick, not just those who were "half-dead carcasses." James and Mark referred to "common oil," not material consecrated by bishops. Calvin also said that the prayers of those who visited a sickbed "would not be in vain."[23] In Geneva, opportunities to seek miraculous cures were eliminated. Instead, the sick were to consult physicians, relying on the medical profession. Deacons were to watch over hospitals and the sick.[24] Ministers were to offer prayers and provide spiritual comfort.[25]

The *Ecclesiastical Ordinances* from Calvin's Geneva placed the burden of summoning a minister on the sick person or those in attendance. The Senate of Geneva acted against those ministers who failed to visit the sick, especially in a plague year. Forms of prayers for the sick were published, but Calvin favored celebrating the Lord's Supper at the sickbed. There was no room in Geneva for public carrying of consecrated elements to ailing parishioners. Moreover, the Reformed tradition expected the dying to display their faith, edifying those around them.[26]

Catholic orders for visiting the sick were used in England down to the reign of King Edward VI (1547–53). Eventually, those rites were challenged by Reformers, who did not accept extreme unction as a sacrament.[27] Change

20 Elsie Anne McKee, *The Pastoral Ministry and Worship in Calvin's Geneva* (Geneva: Droz, 2016), 595–98.

21 *Institutes of Christian Religion by John Calvin*, trans. Henry Beveridge, 2 vols. (London: Clarke, 1949), 2:636.

22 Ibid., 2:637. Calvin added the contention, "those murderers, who do more by slaying and butchering than by curing."

23 Ibid., 2:638. Calvin concluded with a reference to the letter of Pope Innocent I, found in the *Chronicles* of Sigebert, referring to all Christians using oil "in their own necessity, or that of their friends."

24 See "John Calvin Draft Theological Ordinances," in Calvin, *Theological Treatises* (Philadelphia: Westminster, 1954), 64–65.

25 Jeffrey R. Watt, "Calvin's Geneva Confronts Magic and Witchcraft: The Evidence from the Consistory," *Journal of Early Modern History* 17 (2013): 215–44, at 243.

26 McKee, *Pastoral Ministry and Worship*, 601–22.

27 See Martin Luther, *Confession of the Articles of Faith against the Enemy of the Gospel and All Kinds of Heresies*, in *The Annotated Luther*, vol. 2: *Word and Faith*, 274–75. Although Luther described making extreme unction a sacrament as "nonsense," he admitted that anointing was mentioned in the Bible and could be

came slowly, however; and practices were subject to political upheavals. A vernacular version of the Latin rite for visiting the sick appeared in the first prayer book issued on the young king's behalf. This Order for Visitation of the Sick permitted communion, as well as anointing of those who desired the rite.[28] A simplified version appeared in the second prayer book of Edward VI, reflecting a stricter application of Reformed norms. At home, communion was permitted for the sick and others present, but anointing was omitted. (Whether communion was from the reserved sacrament or a bedside Eucharist was not explained.) Examination of belief and exhortation of the sick person are prominent in the text.[29]

Versions of these offices reappeared under Elizabeth I, following the brief reinstatement of Catholicism under Queen Mary. The 1559 *Book of Common Prayer* included an exhortation of the sick, which could be cut short if necessary, followed by an examination of belief. Confession and communion were permitted, the latter administered according to a rite similar to that prepared under Edward VI.[30] What remained sure in Anglicanism was that the clergy were expected to comfort the sick and dying using an *ordo*, just as had their medieval predecessors, but without anointing.[31] Recusant Catholics, however, retained a belief in extreme unction as a sacrament, with priests and books imported from the Continent providing consolation.[32] Despite their differences, both groups, Catholics and Protestants, retained a common commitment to helping the faithful face illness and death when earthly remedies were exhausted.

The rites and beliefs of these competing churches were transported to Protestant Europe's colonies. Protestant churches had their own diasporas, preparing clergy and laity to take their beliefs and rites to North America and the West Indies. Anglicans migrated to colonies like Virginia with their doctrines and rites, but not a resident episcopate. In New England,

---

done at the sickbed with prayers and admonitions. Luther's criticism was not the first. The Hussites were accused of rejecting extreme unction as useless; see Mansi 30:238.

28 *The First Prayerbook of Edward VI* (Oxford: Parker, 1877), 350–71; *The Two Liturgies A.D. 1549, and A.D. 1552*, ed. Joseph Ketley (Cambridge: Cambridge University Press, 1844), 135–43.

29 *The Two Liturgies*, 311–17.

30 *The Book of Common Prayer of 1559: The Elizabethan Prayer Book*, ed. John E. Booty (Washington, DC: Folger Shakespeare Library, 2003), 300–308. Richard Hooker accepted communion of the sick for spiritual comfort; see Norman Doe, "Richard Hooker, Priest and Jurist," in *Great Christian Jurists in English History*, ed. Mark Hill and R. H. Helmholz (Cambridge: Cambridge University Press, 2017), 115–37, at 126.

31 See the annotations to *The First Prayerbook of Edward VI*, 350–71.

32 *Christian Doctrine Composed by R. Father Robert Bellarmine of the Society of Jesus, and Cardinal Translated into Better English Than Formerly* (n.p.: printed for A. L., 1676), 28.

the Puritans created their own Christian communities, planting a new Zion in the wilderness. The Puritans left room not just for God but for the devil, who was regarded as a cause of sickness. Little effort was made at first to convert indigenous peoples or imported slaves.[33] The Scandinavian Lutheran tradition took root where the Swedes founded colonies in Delaware and Pennsylvania. The Dutch Reformed survived the loss by the Netherlands of its North American colonies to the English.[34] Quakers and Moravians found homes in Pennsylvania, as some Roman Catholics did in Maryland.[35] (Only in later centuries were Protestant missions of various stripes founded in parts of Africa.)[36] The history of ministry to the sick and dying in the Protestant colonies in the first centuries requires further research.

33 Kenneth Scott Latourette, *A History of the Expansion of Christianity*. 7 vols. (New York: Harper & Brothers, 1937–45), 3:186–239; Bruce Kaye, *The Rise and Fall of English Christendom: Theocracy, Christology, Order and Prayer* (London: Routledge, 2018), 198. Emory Elliott, "The Legacy of Puritanism," in *Divining America*, available at nationalhumanitiescenter.org/tserve/eighteen/ekeyinfo/legacy.htm; Richard Godbeer, *The Salem Witch Hunt: A Brief History with Documents* (Boston: Bedford, 2011), 8 and 37–38.

34 With the end of Sweden's control of its American colonies, many Swedish Lutherans became Episcopalians: see John Albin Stabb, "Why Did the Colonial Swedish Lutheran Congregations become Episcopalian," *Anglican and Episcopal History* 61 (1992): 419–31. On the Dutch Reformed, see Latourette, *History of the Expansion of Christianity*, 3:194–99.

35 Latourette, *History of the Expansion of Christianity*, 3:197–205.

36 Ibid., 3:240–46.

SELECT BIBLIOGRAPHY

PRIMARY SOURCES: GENERAL

Acta conciliorum et epistolae decretales, ac constitutiones summorum pontificum, vol. 6. Paris: Ex Typographia Regia, 1714.

Acta Cusana, vol. 2. Edited by Johannes Helmrath and Thomas Woelki. Hamburg: Meiner, 2016.

Albertus Magnus. *De sacramentis*. Edited by Albertus Ohlmeyer. Opera omnia 26. Münster: Aschendorf, 1958.

———. *Scriptum quartum diui Alberti Magni super quartum sententiarum*. Basel: Jacobus de Pfortzen, 1506.

Alliot, J.-M., ed. *Visites archidiaconales de Josas*. Paris: Picard, 1902.

Amalar of Metz. *On the Liturgy*. Edited and translated by Eric Knibbs. 2 vols. Cambridge, MA: Harvard University Press, 2014.

Andreas Escobar. *Lumen confessorum*. University of Pennsylvania Ms. Codex 1215.

Angelus Carlettus. *Summa angelica de casibus conscientie*. Lyon: Mollin, 1511.

Anselm of Lucca. *Collectio canonum una cum collectione minore*. Edited by Friedrich Thaner. Innsbruck: Libraria Academica Wagneriana, 1906–15; Aalen: Scientia, 1965.

Antoninus of Florence. *Confessionale "Omnis mortalium cura" & Libretto della dottrina christiana*. Venice: Reynaldus de Novimagio, 1479.

———. *Confessionale "Defecerunt."* Speyer: Drach, 1487.

———. *Summa theologica*. 4 vols. Verona: Ex Typographia Seminarii, 1740–41; Graz: Akamademische Druck- und Verlagsanstalt, 1957.

———. *Tractatus de censuris ecclesiasticis*. University of Pennsylvania Ms. Codex 72, fol. 75r–149r.

Ars moriendi ex variis scripturarum sententiis. Leipzig: Kachelofen, 1495?

Astesanus de Ast. *Summa de casibus conscientiae*. Nürnberg: Koberger, 1482.

The Babees' Book: Medieval Manners for the Young. Translated by Edith Rickert and L. J. Naylor. Cambridge: Middle English Series, 2000.

Bannister, A. T. "Visitation Returns of the Diocese of Hereford in 1397." *The English Historical Review* 44 (1929): 279–89, 444–53; 45 (1930): 92–101, 444–63.

Bartholomaeus de S. Concordio. *Summa Pisanella*. Princeton University Ms. P21.

Biblia latina cum glossa ordinaria, facsimile reprint of the editio princeps of Adolph Rusch of Strassburg [1480]. Edited by Karlfried Froehlich and Margaret T. Gibson. 4 vols. Turnhout: Brepols, 1992.

Biblia sacra cum postillis Hugonis de Sancto Caro. 7 vols. Basel: Amberbach, 1498.

Biblie iampridem renouate pars quinta & pars sexta. Basel: Amerbach, 1502.

Bonaventura. *Doctoris Seraphici S. Boniventurae opera omnia*, vol. 4. Quaracchi: Collegio S. Bonaventurae, 1889.

———. *Sermones dominicales*. Edited by J. G. Bougerol. Grottaferrata: Collegio S. Bonaventurae, 1977.

The Book of Common Prayer of 1559: The Elizabethan Prayer Book. Edited by John E. Booty. Washington, DC: Folger Shakespeare Library, 2003.

Calvin, John. *Institutes of Christian Religion by John Calvin*. Translated by Henry Beveridge. 2 vols. London: Clarke, 1949.

———. "Draft Theological Ordinances." In his *Theological Treatises*, 64–65. Philadelphia: Westminster, 1954.

Cawley, Martinus, ed. and trans. *Send Me God: The Lives of Ida the Compassionate of Nivelles, Nun of La Ramés, Arnulf, Law Brother of Villers, and Abundus, Monk of Villers*. Turnhout: Brepols, 2003.

Christian Doctrine Composed by R. Father Robert Bellarmine of the Society of Jesus, and Cardinal Translated into Better English Than Formerly. n.p.: Printed for A. L., 1676.

Colton, G. G. "A Visitation of the Archdeaconry of Totnes in 1342." *English Historical Review* 26 (1911): 108–24.

Conciliorum Oecumenicorum Generaliumque Decreta. Edited by Giuseppe Alberigo and Alberto Melloni. 4 vols. Turnhout: Brepols, 2007–17.

Concilium Tridentinum, diariorum, actorum, epistolarum, tractatuum nova collection. Görres Gesellschaft, 13 vols. Freiburg in Breisgau: Herder, 1901–2001.

Constitutiones concilii quarti Lateranensis una cum commentariis glossatorum. Edited by Antonio García García. Vatican City: Biblioteca Apostolica Vaticana, 1981.

Corpus Iuris Canonici. Edited by Emil Friedberg. 2 vols. Leipzig: Tauschnitz, 1879; Graz: Akamademische Druck- und Verlagsanstalt, 1955.

Danse Macabre of Women: Ms. Fr. 995 of the Bibliothèque Nationale. Edited by Ann Tukey Harrison. Kent, OH: Kent State University Press, 1994.

Decrees of the Ecumenical Councils. Edited by Norman Tanner. 2 vols. Washington, DC: Georgetown University Press, 1990.

Decretales D. Gregorii papae IX svae integritati vna cvm glossis restitvtae. Venice, 1595.

Decretales Pseudo-Isidorianae et Capitula Angilramni. Edited by Paul Hinschius. Leipzig: Tauchnitz, 1863; Aalen: Scientia, 1963.

Decretum Divi Gratiani. Lyon: Ioannes Pidaieus, 1554.

Delisle, Léopold. "Visites pastorales de maître Henri de Vézelay, archdiacre d'Hiémois, en 1267 et 1268." *Bibliotheque de l'École des Chartes* 54 (1883): 457–67.

Deusdedit. *Die Kanonessamlung des Kardinals Deusdedit*. Edited by Victor Wolf von Glanvell, vol. 1. Paderborn: Schöningh, 1905; Aalen: Scientia, 1967.

Documents on the Papal Plenary Indulgences 1300–1517 Preached in the Regnum Teutonicum. Edited by Stuart Jenks. Leiden: Brill, 2018.

Duns Scotus. *Opera omnia*, vol. 13. Vatican City: Typis Polyglottis Vaticanis, 2011.

Durandus de Sancto Porciano. *Super sententias theologiae Petri Lombardi commentariorum libri quatuor*. Paris: Apud Carolam Guillard, 1550.

Eudes of Rouen. *The Register of Eudes of Rouen*. New York: Columbia University Press, 1964.

Felinus Sandeus. *Commentaria in V libros decretalium*. 3 vols. Basel: Froben, 1567.

The First and Second Prayer Books of Edward VI. London: Dutton, 1968.

Franciscus de Mayronis. *Sermones ab adventu cum quadragesimali*. Venice: Bernardinus de Novaria, 1491.

Friedberg, Emil, ed. *Quinque compilationes antiquae nec non Collectio canonum Lipsiensis*. Leipzig: Tauchnitz, 1882; Graz: Akamademische Druck- und Verlagsanstalt, 1956.

García García, Antonio, ed. *Synodicon Hispanum*. 13 vols. Madrid: Biblioteca de Autores Cristianos, 1981–2017.

Geoffrey of Trani. *Summa perutilis et valde necessaria super titulis decretalium*. Lyon: Morin, 1519; Aalen: Scientia, 1968.

Gerardi Cameracensis acta synodi Atrebatensis. Edited by Steven Vanderputten and Diane J. Reilly. Turnhout: Brepols, 2014.

Gregorio de Andrés. "Actas de la visita al arcedianazgo de Madrid en 1427." *Hispania sacra* 38 (1985): 153–245.

Guido de Baysio. *Rosarium super decreto*. Lyon: Siber, 1497.

Guido of Monte Rochen. *Handbook for Curates: A Late Medieval Manual on Pastoral Ministry*. Translated by Anne T. Thayer. Washington, DC: The Catholic University of America Press, 2011.

Guillelmus de Monte Lauduno. *Sacramentale*. University of Pennsylvania Ms. Codex 72.

Guillelmus Durantis the Elder. *Rationale divinorum officiorum*. Edited by Anselm Davril and Timothy M. Thibodeau. 3 vols. Turnhout: Brepols, 1995–2000.

———. *The "Rationale divinorum officiorum" of William Durant of Mende: A New Translation of the Prologue and Book One*. Translated by Timothy M. Thibodeau. New York: Columbia University Press, 2007.

Hannibaldus de Hannibaldis. *Diui Thomae Aquinatis Ordinis Praedicatorum, doctoris angelici, secundum scriptum appellatum super quatuor libros Sententiarum ad Hannibaldum Hannibaldensem*. Paris: Apud Gulielmum Chaudiere, 1574.

Hostiensis (Henricus de Segusio). *Commentaria et lectura in decretalibus*. 6 vols. Venice: Apud Iuntas, 1581; Frankfurt: Vico, 2009.

———. *Henrici de Segusio cardinalis Hostiensis in primum* [*-sextum*] *decretalium librum commentaria*. 6 vols. Venice: Apud Iuntas, 1581; Turin: Bottega d'Erasmo, 1965.

———. *Henrici de Segusio summa aurea*. Venice: Apud Iacobum Vitalem, 1574; Turin: Bottega d'Erasmo, 1963.

Hugh of St. Cher. *In epistolas omnes D. Pauli, Actus Apostolorum, epistolas septem canonicas, Apocalypsin B. Ioannis*. Lyon: Soc. Bibliopolarum, 1669.

Hugh of St. Victor on the Sacraments of the Christian Faith (De sacramentis). Translated by Roy J. Deferarri. Cambridge, MA: Medieval Academy of America, 1951.

Huguccio of Pisa. *Summa decretorum*. Admont Ms. 7.

Humbert of Romans. *Humberti sermones ad diuersos status cum epistola de tribus votis substantialibus*. Hagenau: [Gran], 1507–8.

Innocent IV, Pope. *Svper libros qvinque decretalivm*. Frankfurt: Lechler, 1570; Frankfurt: Minerva, 1968.

Jacobus de Marchia. *Sermones dominicales*. Edited by Renato Lioi. Ancona: Bibl. Francescana, 1978.

Johannes Andreae. *In primum* [*-sextum*] *librum decretalium novella commentaria*. Venice: Apud Iacobum Vitalem, 1581; Turin: Bottega d'Erasmo, 1963.

Johannes de Burough. *Pupilla oculi*. Cambridge, Corpus Christi College Manuscript 255. Available at *Parker Library on the Web*, parkerweb.stanford.edu/parker/.

———. *Pupilla oculi*. University of Pennsylvania Ms. Codex 75.

Johannes de Erfordia. *Die Summa confessorum des Johannes von Erfurt*. Edited by Norbert Brieskorn. 3 vols. Frankfurt: Lang, 1980.

Johannes de Friburgo. *Summa confessorum*. Augsburg: Zainer, 1476.

Ketley, Joseph, ed. *The Two Liturgies A.D. 1549 and A.D. 1552*. Cambridge: Cambridge University Press, 1844.

Larson, Atria, ed. *Gratian's "Tractatus de penitentia": A New Latin Edition with English Translation*. Washington, DC: The Catholic University of America Press, 2016.

Lay Folks' Catechism or the English and Latin Versions of Archbishop Thoresby's Instructions for the People. London: K. Paul, Trench, Trübner, 1901.

Lay Folks Mass Book or the Manner of Hearing Mass. Edited by Thomas Frederick Simmons. London: Trübner, 1879.

Leonardus de Utino. *Sermones aurei de sanctis*. Ulm: Zeiner, 1475.

The Life of Juliana of Mont-Cornillon. Translated by Barbara Newman. Toronto: Peregrina, 2002.

Luther, Martin. *The Annotated Luther.* Edited by Hans J. Hillerbrand, Kirsi I. Stjerna, and Timothy J. Wengert. 6 vols. Philadelphia: Augsburg Fortress, 2015–17.

Mansi, Giovan Domenico. *Sacrorum conciliorum nova, et amplissima collectio.* 53 vols. Paris: Welter, 1901–27; Graz: Akamademische Druck- und Verlagsanstalt, 1961.

Martène, Edmond, and Ursin Durand, eds. *Thesaurus novus anecdotorum.* 5 vols. Paris: Sumptibus Florentini Delaulne, 1717.

McNeill, John, and Helena Gamer, eds. *Medieval Handbooks of Penance: A Translation of the Principal "Libri poenitentiales": and Selections from Related Documents.* New York: Columbia University Press, 1938.

MGH *Capitularia regum Francorum.* Vol. 1, edited by Alfredus Boretius. Hanover, 1883; Hanover: Hahn, 1984. Vol. 2, edited by Alfredus Boretius and Victor Krause. Hanover: Hahn, 1890; Hanover: Hahn, 1980.

MGH *Concilia.* 5 vols. Hanover: Hahn, 1893–2012.

Miles, Joanna, ed. *The Devil's Mortal Weapons: An Anthology of Late Medieval and Protestant Vernacular Theology and Popular Culture.* Toronto: PIMS, 2018.

Mirk, John. *Instructions for Parish Priests.* Edited by Edward Peacock. 2nd ed. London: K. Paul, Trench, Trübner, 1902; Woodbridge: Boydell, 1996.

Netter, Thomas. *De sacramentis.* Venice: Bassanesi, 1758; Farnborough: Gregg, 1967.

Nicholas Eymeric. *Directorium inquisitorum.* Edited by Francisco Peña. Rome: Stamperia del Popolo Romano, 1587.

Nicholas of Osimo. *Supplementum Summae Pisanellae.* Reutlingen: Greyff, 1482.

Orique, David Thomas. *To Heaven or to Hell: Bartolomé de Las Casas "Confessionario."* University Park: Pennsylvania State University Press, 2018.

Panormia Project. Available at www.wtamu.edu/~bbrasington/panormia.html.

Patrizzi, Agostino. *Caeremoniale Romanum of Agostino Patrizzi, Piccolomini.* Ridgewood, NJ: Gregg, 1965.

Pedro de Córdoba. *Christian Doctrine for the Instruction of the Indians.* Translated by Sterling A. Stoudemire. Coral Gables, FL: University of Miami Press, 1970.

Peter Aureoli. *Commentariorum in quartum librum sentenntiarum.* Rome: Santa Maria in Aracoeli, 1605.

Peter Lombard. *The Sentences.* Translated by Giulio Silano. 4 vols. Toronto: PIMS, 2007–10.

Peter of Tarentaise. *In IV Libros Sententiarum commentaria.* 4 vols. Toulouse: Apud Arnoldum Colomerium, 1649–52; Ridgewood, NJ: Gregg, 1964.

Peter the Chanter. *Summa de sacramentis et animae consiliis.* Edited by Jean Albert Dugauquier. 5 vols. Louvain: Nauwelaerts, 1954–67.

———. *Petri Cantoris Parisiensis verbvm abbreviatvm, textus alter.* Edited by Monique Boutry. Turnhout: Brepols, 2012.

Peter the Venerable. *The Letters of Peter the Venerable*. Edited by Giles Constable. 2 vols. Cambridge, MA: Harvard University Press, 1967.

Petrus de Palude. *In quartum sententiarum*. Venice: Bonetus Locatellus, 1493.

———. *Sermones quadragesimales thesauri noui*. Strasbourg: Flach, 1494.

Pontal, Odette, and Joseph Avril, eds. *Les statuts synodaux français du XIIIe siècle*. 9 vols. Paris: Bibliothèque Nationale, 1971–2011.

Poole, Stafford, ed. *The Directory for Confessors 1585: Implementing the Catholic Reformation in New Spain*. Norman: University of Oklahoma Press, 2018.

Poos, L. R., ed. *Lower Ecclesiastical Jurisdiction in Late-Medieval England: The Courts of the Dean and Chapter of Lincoln, 1336–1349, and the Deanery of Wisbech, 1458–1484*. Oxford: British Academy, 2001.

Raymond of Peñafort. *Summa de poenitentia et matrimonio cum glossis Johannis de Friburgo*. Rome: Tallini, 1603; Farnborough: Gregg, 1967.

Riccoboni, Bartolomea. *Life and Death in a Venetian Convent: The Chronicle and Necrology of Corpus Domini, 1395–1436*. Translated by Daniel Bornstein. Chicago: University of Chicago Press, 2000.

Richardus de Mediavilla. *Super quatuor libros sentiarum Petri Lombardi*. Brescia: De Consensu Superiorum, 1591.

Robert Grosseteste. *The Letters of Robert Grosseteste Bishop of Lincoln*. Edited by Frank A. C. Mantello and Joseph Goering. Toronto: University of Toronto Press, 2010.

Rubin, Miri, ed. *Medieval Christianity in Practice*. Princeton, NJ: Princeton University Press, 2009.

Rufinus. *Summa decretorum*. Edited by Heinrich Singer. Paderborn: Schöningh, 1902; Aalen: Scientia, 1963.

Schmugge, Ludwig, ed. *Repertorium poenitentiariae Germanicum*. 10 vols. Tübingen / Berlin: Niemeyer / De Gruter, 1998–2016.

Shinners, John, and William Dohar, eds. *Pastors and the Care of Souls in Medieval England*. Notre Dame, IN: University of Notre Dame Press, 1998.

Sicard of Cremona. *Sicardi Cremonensis episcopi Mitralis de officiis*. Edited by Gábor Sarbak and Lorenz Weinrich. Turnhout: Brepols, 2008.

Simpson, W. Sparrow, ed. *Visitations of Churches Belonging to St. Paul's Cathedral in 1297 & in 1458*. London: Camden Society, 1895; New York: Johnson Reprint, 1966.

Stephen of Tournai. *Die Summa über das Decretum Gratiani*. Edited by Johann Friedrich von Schulte. Giessen: Roth, 1891; Aalen: Scientia, 1965.

Sylvester Prierias. *Summa summarum que Silvestrina nuncupatur*. Lyon: Platea, 1520.

Thomas Aquinas. *The Academic Sermons*. Translated by Mark-Robin Hoogland. Washington, DC: The Catholic University of America Press, 2010.

———. *Opera omnia,* vol. 12: *Tertia pars summae theologia & Supplementum*. Rome: Ex Typographia Polyglotta, 1906.

———. *Opera omnia,* vol. 15: *Summa contra gentiles liber quartus*. Rome: Commissio Leonina, 1930.

———. *Quaestiones S. Thomas Aquinitatis doctoris angelici.* Paris: Franciscus de Honoratis, 1557.

———. *Sancti Thomae Aquinatis doctoris angelici ordinis Praedicatorum opera omnia*, vol. 11: *Quaestiones de quolibet.* Parma: Fiaccadori, 1859.

———. *Super quarto libro sententiarum preclarum opus.* Venice: Herbort, 1481.

Thomas of Chobham. *Summa confessorum.* Edited by F. Bloomfield. Louvain: Analecta Mediaevalia Namurcensia, 1968.

Thomas of Strasbourg. *Commentaria in IIII. Libros sententiarum.* Venice: Ex Oficina Stellae, 1564; Ridgewood, NJ: Gregg, 1965.

Timmins, T. C. B., ed. *The Register of John Chandler Dean of Salisbury 1404–1417.* Devizes: Wiltshire Records Society, 1984.

Vincent Ferrer. *Sermones Sancti Vincentii ordinis predicatorum de temporiis estivalis.* Lyon, 1510?

Vincent of Beauvais. *Biblotheca mundi seu speculi Vincentii tomus tertius qui speculum morale inscribitur.* Douai: Typographica B. Bellerie, 1624; Graz: Akamademische Druck- und Verlagsanstalt, 1964.

Weigand, Rudolf, ed. *Summa "Omnis qui iuste iudicat" sive Lipsiensis*, vol. 1. Vatican City: Biblioteca Apostolica Vaticana, 2007.

William of Auxerre. *Summa aurea.* Edited by Jean Ribaillier. Paris: CNRS, 1985.

William of Pagula. *Oculus sacerdotis.* University of Pennsylvania Ms. Codex 721.

Zechiel-Eckes, Klaus. *Die Concordia canonum des Cresconius: Studien und Edition*, vol. 1. Frankfurt: Lang, 1992.

PRIMARY SOURCES: LOCAL COUNCILS AND SYNODS

Agenda ecclesiae Trevirensis. Trier: Rotaeus, 1574.

Agenda ecclesiastica Coloniensis. Cologne: Apud Theodorum Baxer, 1562.

Agenda Merseburgensis. Merseburg: Brandis, 1480.

Agenda Mindenensis dioecesis. Leipzig; Lotter, 1522.

Agenda Numbergensis. Naumburg: Saale, 150?

Agenda Olomucensis. Nürnberg: Stuchs, 1498.

Agenda secundum ritum et ordinem ecclesie wormaciensis. Speyer: Drach, ca. 1500.

Agenda seu benedictionale secundum usum sancte ecclesie Patauiensis. Passau: Hammen, 1498.

Agenda sive exeqviale divinorum sacramentorvm pro ecclesiis parrochialibus dioecesis Curiensis. Rosach: Straub, 1590.

Breviarium ad usum insignis Ecclesie Eboracensis, vol. 1. London: Surtees Society, 1880.

Concilia Germaniae. Edited by Johann Friedrich Schannat and Joseph Hartzheim. 11 vols. Cologne: Typo Viduae Ioann. n.p.: Wilhelmi Krakam et Haeredum Christiani Simonis, 1759–90.

Councils & Synods with Other Documents Relating to the English Church. Vol. 1, edited by Frederick M. Powicke and Christopher R. Cheney. Oxford: Clarendon Press, 1964. Vol. 2, edited by Dorothy Whitelock, Martin Brett, and Christopher N. L. Brooke. Oxford: Clarendon Press, 1981.

Informatorium sacerdotum. Basel: Wenssler, 1488.

Liber agendarum rubrice dioecesis Wratislaviensis emendatus. Wroclaw: J. P., 1510.

Liber pontificalis Chr. Archieiscopi Eboracensis. Edited by William George Henderson. Edinburgh: Surtees Society, 1873.

Lyndwood, William. *Lyndwood's "Provinciale": The Text of the Canons Therein Contained, Reprinted from the Translation Made in 1534*. Edited by J. V. Bullard and H. Chalmer Bell. London: Faith Press, 1929.

———. *Provinciale (seu Constitvtiones Angliae)*. Oxford: Hall, 1679; Farnborough: Gregg, 1968.

Manipulus siue manuale uel potius practica ministrandi sacramenta secundum consuetudinem sanctae matris ecclesie Conchensis. Cuenca: In Torculari Christofori Gallici et Francisci de Alpharo Impressorum, 1528.

The Manual from Notmark. Edited by Knut Ottosen. Copenhagen: Gad, 1970.

Manuale Aboense. Halberstadt: Stuchs, 1522.

Manuale ad usum precelebris ecclesie Andegauensis. Rouen: Le Roux, 1543.

Manuale ad usum Tharentasiensis. Geneva: Belot, 1508.

Manuale curatorum secundum usum ecclesie Roeskildensis. Edited by Joseph Freisen. Paderborn: Junfermann, 1898.

Manuale et processionale ad usum insignis ecclesiae Eboracensis. Durham: Surtees Society, 1875.

Manuale pastorum ad uniformem administrationem sacramentorum aliorum officiorum ecclesiasticum per civitatem et dioecesim Tornacensem. Louvain: Masius, 1591?

Manuale Romano-Neapolitanum. Rome, ca. 1478.

Manuale sacerdotum continens ecclesie sacramenta et administrandi ea. Paris, 1523.

M*anuale sacerdotum secundum ususm diocesis Carnotensis*. Paris: Yolande Bonhomme, 1544.

Manuale secundum consuetudinem almae Coimbricensis ecclesiae. Lisbon: Gazini, 1518.

Manuale secundum consuetudinem alme ecclesie Salamanticense. Madrid: In Edibus Joannis Junte, 1532.

Manuale secundum consuetudinem alme ecclesie Salamanticensis. Salamanca, 1532.

Manuale secundum consuetudinem Astoricensis ecclesie. Leon, 1526.

Manuale secundum consuetudinem Calagurritanensis et Calcianensis ecclesiarum. Logroño: In Edibus Michaelis de Eguia, 1532.

Manuale secundum titulum ecclesie Lincopensis. Söderköping: In Edibus Olaui Vlrici, 1525.

Manuale secundum usum ecclesie Constanciensis. Rouen: Le Bourgeois, 1494.

Manuale secundum usum ecclesiae Parisiensis. Paris: Mourand, 1497.

Manuale secundum usum insignis ecclesiae Rothomagensis. Rouen: Morin, ca. 1500.

Manuale secundum vsum sanctę Ecclesię Pallantinę. Medina del Campo: Canto Fratres, 1554.

Manuale seu agenda ad usum Remensem. Reims, ca. 1500.

Manuale seu baptisterium ad usum alme ecclesie Toletane. Toledo: Pegnitler, 1484.

Manuale seu officiarium saceerdotum secundum usum ecclesie et diocesis Laudunensis. Paris: Ad Signum Rose Rubre, 1538.

Manuale seu rituale ad usum ecclesie Tullensis. Bamburg: Sensenschmidt, ca. 1482.

Manuale Upsalense. Stockholm: Ghotan, ca. 1486.

Nicholas of Cusa. *Akten zur Reform des Bistums Brixen.* Edited by Heinz Hürten. Heidelberg: Winter, 1960.

Obsequiale Augustense. Augsburg: Zainer?, 1471.

Obsequiale Augustense im Auftrag von Friedrich II, Graf von Zollern, Bischof von Augsburg. Augsburg: Ratdolt, 1487.

Obsequiale Brixiense. Augsburg: Ratdolt, 1493.

Obsequiale Eystetense. Eichstätt: Reyser, 1488.

Obsequiale Pragense. Nürnberg: Stuchs, ca. 1500.

Obsequiale Ratisponense. Nürnberg: Stuchs, 1491.

Obsequiale seu baptismale secundum chorum almae ecclesiae Strigonensis. Nürnberg: Stuchs, ca. 1500.

Obsequiale sive benedictionale secundum ecclesiam Constantinensem. Augsburg: Ratdolt, 1510.

Obsequiale Strigonensis. Nürnberg: Stuchs, 1496.

Ordinarium de administratione sacramentorum cum pluribus additionibus adeo necessariis secundum ritum alme sedis maioriensis. Valencia: Joffre, 1516.

Ordinarium manuale de ministratione sacramentorum secundum consuetudinem ecclesię Carthaginensis. Granada, 1544.

Ordinarium sacramentorum Barcinonense. Barcelona: Posa, 1501; Barcelona: Institut d'Estudis Catalans, 1991.

Ordinarium sacramentorum benedictionum et aliarum rerum a sacerdote animarum curam regent agendarum secundum sacrosancte Urgellensis ecclesie ritum. Lyon: Cornelius de Septemgrangis, 1548.

Ordo ad baptizandum secundum curiam Romanum. Florence: Bonaccorsi, 1495.

Pontificale Carnotensis. Paris MS BN Lat. 945.

Pontificale Coloniense. Cologne Cathedral Chapter Codex 139.

Pontificale Parisiense. Paris MS BN Lat. 961.

Pontificale Rothomagense. Paris MS BN nouv. acq. lat. 306.

Pontificale Trevirense. Paris MS BN 13315.

Rituale Romanum. Florence, ca. 1484.

The Synodicum Nicosiense and Other Documents of the Latin Church of Cyprus, 1196–1373. Edited by Christopher Schabel. Nicosia: Cyprus Research Center, 2001.

Synody a statuta Olomoucké diecéze období středověku. Edited by Pavel Krafl. Prague: Historický ústav AV ČR, 2003.

Trexler, Richard C. *Synodal Law in Florence and Fiesole, 1306–1518*. Vatican City: Biblioteca Apostolica Vaticana, 1971.

SECONDARY SOURCES

Abraham, Erin V. *Anticipating Sin in Medieval Society: Childhood, Sexuality, and Violence in the Early Penitentials*. Amsterdam: Amsterdam University Press, 2017.

Alexandre-Bidon, Daniële. *La mort au Moyen Âge XIIIe–XVIe siècle*. Paris: Hachette, 1998.

Appleford, Amy. *Learning to Die in London, 1380–1540*. Philadelphia: University of Pennsylvania Press, 2015.

Ariès, Philippe. *The Hour of Our Death: The Classic History of Western Attitude Toward Death Over the Last One Thousand Years*. Translated by Helen Weaver. New York: Barnes and Noble, 2000.

Austin, Greta.*Shaping Church Law Around the Year 1000: The "Decretum" of Burchard of Worms*. Farnham: Ashgate, 2009.

Baldwin, John. *Masters, Princes and Merchants: The Social Views of Peter the Chanter and His Circle*. 2 vols. Princeton, NJ: Princeton University Press, 1970.

Bankhead, Ivan. "Thomas Aquinas on Mental Disorder and the Sacraments of Baptism and the Eucharist: *Summa Theologica* 3.68.12 and 3.80.9 Revisited." *Journal of Disability and Religion* 20 (2014): 239–64.

Binski, Paul. *Medieval Death: Ritual and Representation*. Ithaca, NY: Cornell University Press, 1996.

Bird, Jessalynn. "The Construction of Orthodoxy and the (De)construction of Heretical Attacks on the Eucharist in *pastoralia* from Peter the Chanter's Circle in Paris." In *Texts and the Repression of Medieval Heresy*. Edited by Caterina Bruschi and Peter Biller, 45–61. York: York Medieval Press, 2003.

Blum, Jacob M. *Reformation of the Senses: The Paradox of Religious Belief and Practice in Germany*. Urbana: University of Illinois Press, 2019.

Boase, T. S. R. *Death in the Middle Ages: Mortality, Judgment, Remembrance*. New York: McGraw-Hill, 1972.

Bowers, Barbara, and Linda Keyser, eds. *The Sacred and the Secular in Medieval Healing Sites, Objects and Texts*. London: Routledge, 2016.

Bowker, Margaret. *The Secular Clergy in the Diocese of Lincoln 1495–1520*. Cambridge: Cambridge University Press, 1968.

Boxer, C. R. *The Church Militant and Iberian Expansion 1440–1770*. Baltimore, MD: Johns Hopkins University Press, 1978.

Boyle, Leonard E. *Facing History: A Different Thomas Aquinas*. Louvain-La-Neuve: Fédération Internationale des Instituts d'Études Médiévales, 2000.

———. "The *Oculus sacerdotis* and Some Other Works of William of Pagula." *Transactions of the Royal Historical Society* 5, no. 5 (1955): 81–110.

Bozoky, E. *Charmes et prières apotropaïques*. Turnhout: Brepols, 2003.

Brown, Catherine. *Pastor and Laity in the Theology of Jean Gerson*. Cambridge: Cambridge University Press, 1987.

Burden, John. "Reading Burchard's *Corrector*: Canon Law and Penance in the High Middle Ages." *Journal of Medieval History* 46 (2020): 77–97.

Burgess, Clive. *The Right Ordering of Souls: The Parish of All Saints Bristol on the Eve of the Reformation*. Woodbridge: Boydell, 2018.

Campbell, William H. *Landscape of Pastoral Care in 13th Century England*. Cambridge: Cambridge University Press, 2017.

Chartier, Roger. "Les arts de mourir (1450–1600)." *Annales: Economies, Sociétés, Civilisations* 31 (1976): 51–75.

Chavasse, Antoine. *Études sur l'onctione des infirmes dans l'*église du IIIe *au XIe siècle*, vol. 1. PhD diss., Lyon, 1942.

Cheney, Christopher R. *English Synodalia of the Thirteenth Century*. Oxford: Oxford University Press, 1941.

———. *From Becket to Langton: English Church Government 1170–1213*. Manchester: Manchester University Press, 1956.

Chiffoleau, Jacques. *La comptabilité de la au-delà: les hommes, la mort et la religion dans la region d'Avignon à la fin du Moyen Âge vers 1320 – vers 1480*. Paris: Boccard, 2011.

Chinca, Mark. *Meditating Death in Medieval and Early Modern Devotional Writing*. Oxford: Oxford University Press, 2020.

Clarke, Peter, and Sarah James, eds. *Pastoral Care in Medieval England: Interdisciplinary Approaches*. London: Routledge, 2020.

Cohen-Hanegbi, Naama. *Caring for the Living Soul: Emotions, Medicine and Penance in the Late Medieval Mediterranean*. Leiden: Brill, 2017.

Cohn, Jr., Samuel K. *The Cult of Remembrance and the Black Death: Six Renaissance Cities in Central Italy*. Baltimore: Johns Hopkins University Press, 1992.

Colish, Marcia L. *Faith, Fiction & Force in Medieval Baptismal Debates*. Washington, DC: The Catholic University of America Press, 2014.

Collins, Ross William. "The Parish Priest and His Flock as Depicted by the Councils of the Twelfth and Thirteenth Centuries." *The Journal of Religion* 10 (1930): 313–32.

Coulet, Noël. *Les visites pastorales*. Turnhout: Brepols, 1977.

Courtenay, William J. *Rituals for the Dead: Religion and Community in the Medieval University of Paris*. Notre Dame, IN: University of Notre Dame Press, 2019.

Cuschieri, Andrew. *Anointing of the Sick: A Theological and Canonical Study*. Lanham, MD: University Press of America, 1993.

Davis, Adam J. *The Holy Bureaucrat: Eudes Rigaud and Religious Reform in Thirteenth Century Burgundy*. Ithaca, NY: Cornell University Press, 2006.

———. *The Medieval Economy of Salvation: Charity, Commerce and the Rise of the Hospital.* Ithaca, NY: Cornell University Press, 2019.

DuBruck, Edelgard, and Barbara Gusick, eds. *Death and Dying in the Middle Ages*. New York: Peter Lang, 1999.

Duclow, Donald F. "'Dying Well' from the Fifteenth Century to Hospice." *Lutheran Quarterly* 38 (2014): 125–47.

Dudley, Martin R. "Sacramental Liturgies in the Middle Ages." In *The Liturgy of the Medieval Church*. Edited by Thomas J. Heffernan and E. Ann Matter, 215–43. Kalamazoo, MI: Medieval Institute, 2001.

Duffy, Eamon. *The Stripping of the Altars: Traditional Religion in England 1400–1580*. New Haven, CT: Yale University Press, 1992.

———. *The Voices of Morebath: Reformation and Rebellion in an English Village*. New Haven, CT: Yale University Press, 2001.

Duval, André. "L'extrême-onction au concile de Trente: Sacrement des mourantes ou sacrament des maladies." *La Maison-Dieu* 101 (1970): 127–72.

———. *Des sacraments au Concile de Trente*. Paris: Cerf, 1985.

Duve, Thomas, and Otto Danwerth, eds. *Knowledge of the "Pragmatici": Legal and Moral Theological Literature and the Formation of Early-Modern Ibero-America*. Leiden: Brill, 2020.

Eisenbichler, Konrad, ed. *A Companion to Medieval and Early Modern Confraternities*. Leiden: Brill, 2019.

Filocamo, Gioia. "Sin, Emotions and Sounds: Dealing with Death in the *Laudario* of the Confraternity of Santa Maria della Morte." In *Renaissance Religions: Modes and Meanings in History*. Edited by Peter Howard, Nicholas Terpstra, and Riccardo Saccenti, 231–47. Turnhout: Brepols, 2021.

Flanagan, Sabina. "Heresy, Madness and Possession in the High Middle Ages." In *Heresy in Transition: Transforming Ideas of Heresy in Medieval and Early Modern Europe*. Edited by John Christian Laursen, Cary J. Nederman, and Ian Hunter, 29–41. Burlington, VT: Ashgate, 2005.

Florez, Gonzalo. *Penitencia y unción de los enfermos*. Madrid: Ediciones Universidad de Navarra, 1993.

Foroughi, Louis. "'To sey or thinke otherwise': Ordinary Theology and Facing Death in Late Medieval Norfolk." *Religions* 9 (2018). Available at doi.org/10.3390/rel9030067.

French, Katherine L. *The People of the Parish: Community Life in a Late Medieval English Diocese*. Philadelphia: University of Pennsylvania Press, 2001.

———. *The Good Women of the Parish: Gender and Religion after the Black Death*. Philadelphia: University of Pennsylvania Press, 2008.

French, Katherine L., Kathryn A. Smith, and Sarah Stanbury. "An Honest Bed: The Scene of Life and Death in Late Medieval England." *Fragments: Interdisciplinary Approaches to the Study of Ancient and Medieval Pasts* 5 (2016). Available at hdl.handle.net/2027/spo.9772151.0005.003.

Gameson, Richard, Catherine Nicholson, and Andrew Beeby. "The Admiral, the Virgin, and the Spectrometer: Observations on the Coëtivy Hours (Dublin, Chester Beatty Library MS W082)." *Gesta* 59 (2020): 202–31.

Godbeer, Richard. *The Salem Witch Hunt: A Brief History with Documents.* Boston: Bedford, 2011.

Goering, Joseph. "The Internal Forum and the Literature of Penance." *Traditio* 59 (2004): 175–227.

Gusmer, Charles W. *And You Visited Me: Sacramental Ministry to the Sick and Dying.* New York: Pueblo, 1989.

Harper, Stephen. *Insanity, Individual and Society in Late-Medieval England: The Subject of Madness.* Lewiston, NY: Mellen, 2003.

Horrox, Rosemary, ed. *The Black Death.* Manchester: Manchester University Press, 2013.

Ivins, William M., Jr. *The Dance of Death Printed at Paris in 1490: A Reproduction Made from the Copy in the Lessing J. Rosenwald Collection.* Washington, DC: Library of Congress, 1945.

Izbicki, Thomas M. "*Manus temeraria*: Custody of the Eucharist in Medieval Canon Law." In *Proceedings of the Thirteenth International Congress of Medieval Canon Law.* Edited by Peter Erdö and S. A. Szuromi, 535–52. Vatican City: Bibliotheca Apostolica Vaticana, 2010.

———. *The Eucharist in Medieval Canon Law.* Cambridge: Cambridge University Press, 2015.

———. "Saint Geneviève and the Anointing of the Sick." *Catholic Historical Review* 104 (2018): 393–414.

Kaeppeli, Thomas, and Emilio Panella. *Scriptores Ordinis Praedicatorum medii aevi.* 4 vols. Rome: Ad S. Sabinae, 1970–93.

Kinch, Ashby. *Imago Mortis: Mediating Images of Death in Late Medieval Culture.* Leiden: Brill, 2013.

King, Archdale. *Eucharistic Reservation in the Western Church.* London: Mowbray, 1965.

Klebanoff, Randi. "Passion, Compassion and the Sorrows of Women: Niccolò dell'Arca's Lamentation over the Dead Christ for the Bolognese Confraternity of Santa Maria della Vita." In *Confraternities and the Visual Arts in Renaissance Italy: Ritual, Spectacle, Image.* Edited by Barbara Wisch and Diane Cole Ahl, 146–72. Cambridge: Cambridge University Press, 2000.

Koenig, Anne M. "Magicking Madness: Secret Workings and Public Narratives of Disordered Minds in Late Medieval Germany." In *The Sacred and the Sinister: Studies in Medieval Religion and Magic.* Edited by David J. Collins, 201–30. University Park: Pennsylvania State University Press, 2019.

Korpiola, Mia, and Anu Lahtinen, eds. *Planning for Death: Wills and Death-Related Property Arrangements in Europe, 1200–1600.* Leiden: Brill, 2018.

Krötzl, Christian, and Katarina Mustakallio, eds. *Approaching Death in Antiquity and the Middle Ages*. Turnhout: Brepols, 2011.

Lahtinen, Ann, and Mia Korpiola, eds. *Dying Prepared in Medieval and Early Modern Northern Europe*. Leiden: Brill, 2017.

Larmon Peterson, Janine. *Suspect Saints and Holy Heretics: Disputed Sanctity and Communal Identity in Late Medieval Italy*. Ithaca, NY: Cornell University Press, 2019.

Larrabe, José Luis. *La iglesia y el sacramento de la unción de los enfermos*. Salamanca: Ediciones Sigueme, 1974.

Latourette, Kenneth Scott. *A History of the Expansion of Christianity*. 7 vols. New York: Harper and Brothers, 1937–45.

Lawler, Michael G. *Symbol Sacrament: A Contemporary Sacramental Theology.* Omaha, NE: Creighton University Press, 1995.

Levy, Ian Christopher. *Holy Scripture and the Quest for Authority at the End of the Middle Ages.* Notre Dame, IN: University of Notre Dame Press, 2012.

Martimort, Aimé Georges. *Les 'ordines', les ordinaires et les cérémoniaux*. Turnhout: Brepols, 1991.

Matheus, Michael, ed. *Funktions- und Strukturwandel spätmittelalterlicher Hospitäler im europäischen Vergleich*. Stuttgart: Steiner, 2005.

McDonash, Patrick, C. F. Goodey, and Timothy Stainton, eds. *Intellectual Disability: A Conceptual History, 1200–1900*. Manchester: Manchester University Press, 2018.

McKee, Elsie Anne. *The Pastoral Ministry and Worship in Calvin's Geneva.* Geneva: Droz, 2016.

Meens, Rob. "Confession, Penance and Extreme Unction." In *The Cambridge History of Medieval Canon Law*. Edited by Anders Winroth and John C. Wei, 421–36. Cambridge: Cambridge University Press, 2022.

———. *Penance in Medieval Europe 600–1200*. Cambridge: Cambridge University Press, 2014.

Metzger, Marcel. *Les sacramentaires*. Turnhout: Brepols, 1994.

Metzler, Irinam. *Fools and Idiots? Intellectual Disability in the Middle Ages*. Manchester: Manchester University Press, 2016.

———. "Then and Now: Canon Law on Disabilities." In *Disability in Antiquity*. Edited by Christian Laes, 455–67. London: Routledge, 2017.

Michaud-Quantin, Pierre. *Sommes de casuistique et manuels de confession au Moyen Age (XII–XVI siècles)*. Louvain: Nauwelaerts, 1962.

Midelfort, H. C. Erik. "Sin, Melancholy, Obsession, Insanity, and Culture in 16th-Century Germany." In *Understanding Popular Culture: Europe from the Middle Ages to the Nineteenth Century*. Edited by Steven L. Kaplan, 113–46. Berlin: De Gruyter, 1984.

Mordek, Hubert. *Kirchenrecht und Reform im Frankreich: Die Collectio vetus gallica, die älteste systematische Kanonssamlung des Fränkischen Gallen, Studien und Edition*. Berlin: De Gruyter, 1975.

Mormando, Franco, and Thomas Worcester, eds. *Piety and Plague from Byzantium to the Baroque.* Kirksville, MO: Truman State University Press, 2007.

Mortimort, Aimé Georges. "Prayer for the Sick and Sacramental Anointing." In *The Church at Prayer,* vol. 1: *Principles of the Liturgy.* Edited by Irénée Henri Dalmais, Pierre Marie Gy, Pierre Jounel, and Aimé Georges Martimort, 117–37. Collegeville, MN: Liturgical Press, 1998.

Murchison, Krista A. *Manuals for Penitents in Medieval England from Ancrene Wisse to the Parson's Tale.* Martlesham: D. S. Brewer, 2021.

Neugebauer, Richard. "Medieval and Early Modern Theories of Mental Illness." *Archives of General Psychiatry* 36 (1979): 447–83.

O'Connor, Mary Catherine. *The Art of Dying Well: The Development of the "Ars moriendi."* New York: Columbia University Press, 1942.

Orlandi, Stefano. *S. Antonino (arcivescovo di Firenze, dottore della Chiesa): Studi bibliografici.* 2 vols. Florence: Edizioni il Rosario, 1959.

Palmer, James A. *The Virtues of Economy: Governance, Power and Piety in Late Medieval Rome.* Ithaca, NY: Cornell University Press, 2019.

Palmer, Robert C. *Selling the Church: The English Parish in Law, Commerce and Religion, 1350–1550.* Chapel Hill: University of North Carolina Press, 2002.

Parmegiani, Riccardo. *Il vescovo e capitulo: Il cardinale Niccolò Albergati e I canonici di S. Pietro di Bologna (1417).* Bologna: Bononia University Press, 2009.

Paxton, Frederick S. *Christianizing Death: The Creation of a Ritual Process in Early Medieval Europe.* Ithaca, NY: Cornell University Press, 1990.

Pazos-López, Ángel. "Los siete sacramentos." In *Base de datos digital de Iconografía Medieval.* Universidad Complutense de Madrid. Available at www.ucm.es/bdiconografiamedieval/mitra-episcopal.

Perkinson, Stephen. *The Ivory Mirror: The Art of Mortality in Renaissance Europe.* Brunswick, Maine: Bowdoin College Museum of Art, 2017.

Pfaff, Richard. *The Liturgy in Medieval England: A History.* Cambridge: Cambridge University Press, 2009.

Phelan, John Leddy. *The Millennial Kingdom of the Franciscans in the New World.* Berkeley: University of California Press, 1970.

Pickett, R. Colin. *Mental Affliction and Church Law: An Historical Synopsis of Roman and Ecclesiastical Law and a Canonical Commentary.* Ottawa: University of Ottawa Press, 1952.

Pixton, Paul D. *The German Episcopacy and the Implementation of the Decrees of the Fourth Lateran Council 1216–1245: Watchmen on the Tower.* Leiden: Brill, 1995.

Pontal, Odette. *Les statuts synodaux.* Turnhout: Brepols, 1975.

Poschmann, Bernhard. *Penance and the Anointing of the Sick.* New York: Herder and Herder, 1964.

Prügl, Thomas. "Die Verhandlungen des Basler Konzils mit den Böhmen und die Prager Kompaktaten als Friedensvertrag." *Annuarium historiae conciliorum* 48 (2016–17): 249–308.

Rawcliffe, Carole. *Medicine and Society in Later Medieval England.* Stroud: Sutton, 1995.

Ricard, Robert. *The Spiritual Conquest of Mexico: An Essay on the Apostolate of the Mendicant Orders in New Spain: 1523–1572.* Translated by Lesley Byard Simpson. Berkeley: University of California Press, 1966.

Ritchey, Sarah. "Affective Medicine: Later Medieval Healing Communities and the Feminization of Health Care Practices in the Thirteenth-Century Low Countries." *The Journal of Medieval Religious Cultures* 40 (2014): 113–43.

Rittgers, Ronald K. *Reformation of Suffering: Pastoral Theology and Lay Piety in Late Medieval and Early Modern Germany.* Oxford: Oxford University Press, 2012.

Rondinini Soldi, Gigliola. *Il Tractatus de principibus di Martino Garati da Lodi.* Milan: Cisalpino-La Golardica, 1968.

Rouillard, Philippe. "The Anointing of the Sick in the West." In *Handbook for Liturgical Studies.* Edited by Anscar J. Chupungco, 4:171–90. Collegeville, MN: Liturgical Press, 1997.

Rubin, Miri. *Corpus Christi: The Eucharist in Late Medieval Culture.* Cambridge: Cambridge University Press, 1991.

Salisbury, Matthew Cheung. *The Use of York: Characteristics of the Medieval Liturgical Office in York.* York: Borthwick Institute of Historical Research, 2008.

———. "Rethinking the Uses of Sarum and York." In *Understanding Medieval Liturgy: Essays in Interpretation.* Edited by Helen Gittos and Sarah Hamilton, 202–22. Farnham: Ashgate, 2016.

Salonen, Kirsi, and Ludwig Schmugge, eds. *A Sip from the "Well of Grace": Medieval Texts from the Apostolic Penitentiary.* Washington, DC: The Catholic University of America Press, 2009.

Schmitz-Esser, Romedio. *The Corpse in the Middle Ages: Embalming, Cremating and the Cultural Construction of the Dead Body.* Turnhout: Brepols, 2019.

Schumacher, John N. "The Manila Synodal Tradition." *Philippine Studies* 27 (1979): 285–348.

Sharp, Tristan, ed. *From Learning to Love: Schools Law and Pastoral Care in the Middle Ages: Essays in Honour of Joseph W. Goering.* Toronto: PIMS, 2017.

Sheehan, Michael M. "English Wills and the Records of the Ecclesiastical and Civil Jurisdictions." *Journal of Medieval History* 14 (1988): 3–12.

Singer, Julie. *Representing Mental Illness in Late Medieval France: Machines, Madness, Metaphor.* Woodbridge: Boydell, 2018.

Skemer, Don C. *Binding Words: Textual Amulets in the Middle Ages.* University Park: Pennsylvania State University Press, 2006.

Smith, Lesley. "The End of a Single World: The Sacrament of Extreme Unction in Scholastic Thought." In *The End of the World in Medieval Thought and Spirituality.* Edited by Eric Knibbs, Jessica A. Boon, and Erica Gelser, 281–313. Basingstoke: Palgrave Macmillan, 2019.

Snoek, G. J. C. *Medieval Piety from Relics to the Eucharist: A Process of Mutual Interaction.* Leiden: Brill, 1995.

Stadolink, Joe. "Gower's Bedside Manner." *New Medieval Literatures* 17 (2017): 150–74.

Stansbury, Ronald, ed. *A Companion to Pastoral Care in the Late Middle Ages (1200–1500).* Leiden: Brill, 2010.

Swanson, R. N. *Religion and Devotion in Europe, c. 1215 – c. 1515.* Cambridge: Cambridge University Press, 2012.

———, ed. *The Routledge History of Medieval Christianity 1050–1500.* London: Routledge, 2015.

Talbot, Charles H. *Medicine in Medieval England.* London: Oldbourne, 1967.

Terpstra, Nicholas, ed. *The Art of Executing Well: Rituals of Execution in Renaissance Italy.* Kirksville, MO: Truman State University Press, 2008.

Tolan, John. "Ramon de Penyafort's *Responses to Questions Concerning Relations Between Christians and Saracens.*" In *Convivencia and Medieval Spain: Essays in Honor of Thomas F. Glick.* Edited by Mark T. Abate, 159–92. Cham: Palgrave Macmillan, 2019.

Trexler, Richard C. *Public Life in Renaissance Florence.* Ithaca, NY: Cornell University Press, 1980.

Turner, Wendy, ed. *Madness in Medieval Law and Custom.* Leiden: Brill, 2010.

———. *Care and Custody of the Mentally Ill: Incompetent and Disabled in Medieval England.* Turnhout: Brepols, 2013.

———. "Defining Mental Afflictions in Medieval English Administrative Records." In *Disability and Medieval Law: History, Literature, Society.* Edited by Cory J. Rushton, 134–56. Cambridge: Cambridge University Press, 2013.

Turner, Wendy, and Sara Butler. *Medicine and the Law.* Leiden: Brill, 2014.

Turner, Wendy, and Tory Vandeventer, eds. *The Treatment of Disabled Persons in Medieval Europe.* Lewiston, NY: Mellen, 2010.

Valenti, Gianluca. "La *commendatio animae* dans les littératures romanes des origins." In *La formule au Moyen Âge II: Actes du colloque international de Nancy et Metz, 7–9 juin 2012*, 237–55. Turnhout: Brepols, 2015.

Walters, Barbara, Vincent Corrigan, and Peter Ricketts, eds. *The Feast of Corpus Christi.* University Park: Pennsylvania State University Press, 2006.

Watt, Jeffrey R. "Calvin's Geneva Confronts Magic and Witchcraft: The Evidence from the Consistory." *Journal of Early Modern History* 17 (2013): 215–44.

Wei, John C. *Gratian the Theologian.* Washington, DC: The Catholic University of America Press, 2016.

Wieck, Roger S. *Time Sanctified: The Book of Hours in Medieval Art and Life.* New York: Braziller, 2001.

Woelk, Moritz, and Manuela Beer, eds. *Museum Schnütgen: A Survey of the Collection.* Munich: Hirmer, 2018.

Wood-Leigh, K. L. *Perpetual Chantries in Britain.* Cambridge: Cambridge University Press, 1965.

INDEX